2⁰⁰

Betty
Friedan

RANDOM HOUSE NEW YORK

Betty
Friedan
Her
Life

Judith Hennessee

Grateful acknowledgment is made to the following for permission to reprint previously published material:

The Boston Globe: Excerpt from "The Lioness of Feminism" by Maria Karagianis (June 2, 1983) and excerpt from "Betty Friedan Is Still Telling It Like It Is" by Marian Christy (January 14, 1990). Reprinted courtesy of *The Boston Globe.*

The Daily News: Excerpt from "Friedan's New Idea: Blaming Feminism" by Beverly Stephen (August 9, 1981). Copyright © New York Daily News, L.P. Reprinted by permission.

JOHN DANIEL & Co.: Excerpts from *Feminist Convert: A Portrait of Mary Ellen Chase* by Evelyn Hyman Chase (1988). Reprinted by permission of the publisher, John Daniel & Co.

The New Leader: Excerpt from "Mama in Search of Herself" by Diane Ravitch (April 15, 1963). Reprinted by permission of *The New Leader.*

The New Republic: Excerpt from "The Women at Houston, with Thanks to Phyllis Schlafly for Bringing Them All Together" from the December 10, 1977, issue of *The New Republic.* Reprinted by permission of *The New Republic.*

The New York Times: Excerpt from "Mother Superior to Women's Lib" by Paul Wilkes (November 29, 1970); excerpt from "Feminists Scorned by Betty Friedan" by Deirdre Carmody (July 19, 1972); excerpt from "Growing Old with a Can-Do Attitude" by Christopher Lehmann-Haupt (October 11, 1993). Copyright © 1970, 1972, 1993 by The New York Times Company. Reprinted by permission.

Newsday: Excerpt from "An Addendum to Radical Chic" by Carol Agus. Copyright © 1987 by Newsday, Inc. Reprinted by permission.

Newsweek: Excerpt from "The New Woman" from the August 16, 1971, issue of *Newsweek.* Copyright © 1971 by Newsweek, Inc. All rights reserved. Reprinted by permission.

W. W. NORTON & COMPANY: Excerpts from *The Feminine Mystique* by Betty Friedan. Copyright © 1983, 1974, 1973, 1963 by Betty Friedan. Reprinted by permission of W. W. Norton & Company, Inc.

The Washington Post: Excerpt from "Women and Politics" by Sally Quinn (August 25, 1972); excerpt from "The Pedestal Has Crashed" by Sally Quinn (November 23, 1977); excerpt from "Growing Old and Liking It" by Judy Mann (September 15, 1993). Copyright © 1972, 1977, 1993 by The Washington Post. Reprinted by permission.

UNIVERSITY PRESS OF NEW ENGLAND: Excerpt from *No More Nice Girls* by Ellen Willis (Wesleyan University Press). Copyright © 1992 by Ellen Willis. Reprinted by permission of University Press of New England.

Library of Congress Cataloging-in-Publication Data

Hennessee, Judith.
    Betty Friedan: her life/ Judith Hennessee.
        p. cm.
    Includes bibliographical references and index.
    ISBN 0-679-43203-5 (hardcover)
    1. Friedan, Betty. 2. Feminists—United States—Biography. 3. Feminism—United States. I. Title.
HQ1413.F455 1999
   305.42' 092—dc21   98-24876
[B]

Random House website address: www.atrandom.com

Printed in the United States of America on acid-free paper

98765432

First Edition

BOOK DESIGN BY BARBARA M. BACHMAN

For my daughter, Nancy

Acknowledgments

I wish most to thank my friends who encouraged and sustained me during the six years I spent writing this book. I particularly want to mention Marlene Sanders, who first suggested the idea to me. A friend to both Betty and me, Marlene walked that tricky ethical tightrope with grace, honoring her obligations of friendship to each side. I also want to thank Marcia Cohen, who generously gave me all the research material she had gathered for her book *The Sisterhood,* saving me many hours of work.

I owe a special debt to Bill Mason and Elizabeth Rich—to Liz for weaning me away from an old beloved typewriter and introducing me to the computer; to Bill for inventing and customizing a brilliant program for me, and for his endless patience in helping me bond with the new technology.

Jean Faust sent me her files on early New York–NOW; Patricia O'Toole mailed a crucial document; Dr. Joan Thorn lent me an important tape; Alida Brill, Benita Eisler, Carl Friedan, Margaret Hobler, Judith Hole, Susan McKeever, Sydney Ladensohn Stern, and Mary Thom gave and lent me books.

Barbara Seaman took the trouble to call me when she met someone who could be helpful. Lois Gould steered me to an invaluable source who later became a friend. Erica Abeel introduced me to several members of the Friedan commune. Roger Boxill and Liz Rich were always on call for discussion, advice, and interpretation. Jacqui Ceballos, Carl Friedan, and Mary Jean Tully spent countless hours—days, actually—being interviewed. Carolyn Heilbrun, who was in the midst of writing a biography of Gloria Steinem, and Susan Brownmiller, who was working on a history of the movement, generously exchanged information and ideas. Susan also gave me the subtitle for this book.

My gratitude also to Amanda Nash for offering me a place to stay in her house in Cambridge when I first started researching, and for the personal kindness of Daphne Abeel and Patricia Chute. Theresa Grimaldi Olsen helped me become acclimated to Peoria. Arthur Herzog sheltered me in a blizzard. Caryl Stern shored me up on numerous occasions and backed her unwavering faith in my ability to overcome all obstacles with her open-ended hospitality and delicious meals.

Thanks also to Betty Friedan, who overcame her initial misgivings about an unauthorized biography and agreed to be interviewed, and invited me into her home.

I am grateful also to my main reader, Robert W. Stock, whose dispassionate, insightful comments helped me rethink the rough patches.

At the Schlesinger Library, where I spent many months researching, Eva Moseley, Anne Engelhart, Wendy Thomas, Ruth Hill, and Jesse Piaia were particularly helpful. At the Smith College Archive, Margery N. Sly was a bottomless fund of knowledge; my gratitude also to her successor, Karen Eberhart. Joanne Grewell, the librarian at Peoria High School, found old copies of *Opinion*, the student newspaper, for me, and gathered other memorabilia of the class of 1938. Karen Deller, the librarian at the Peoria Historical Society, Bradley University, offered intelligent personal assistance. At New York University, the programs and dinners of the biography seminar provided a meeting place to talk out problems with other biographers.

Many thanks also to my editor, Robert Loomis, for his deft hand and perceptive eye; and to my agent, Ellen Levine, for her unfailing attention and good judgment.

Many other people contributed in different ways to this biography. Their names are listed below, with my thanks.

Sydney Abbott, Pat Aleskovsky, Dolores Alexander, Shana Alexander, David Alpern, Ted and Pat Apstein, Mildred Arens, Phyllis Avery, Margaret Ayers, Donald Barr, Rosalyn Baxandall, Margaret Comstock Bayldon, Nikki Beare, Robert Bedell, Warren Bennis, Elaine Benson, Betty

Berry, Ann Birstein, Barbara Belford, Murray Teigh Bloom, Barbara Bode, Janet Bode, Nancy Borman, Patricia Bosworth, Phyllis Bosworth, Ivy Bottini, Gene Boyer, Kathleen Brady, Lillian Braude, Susan Braudy, Priscilla Buckley, Dr. Robert Butler, Toni Carabillo, Patricia Carbine, Richard and Gladys Carter, Sey Chassler, Phyllis Chesler, Lucinda Cisler, Nola Claire, John Cody, Noreen Connell, Joan Marble Cook, Dr. Harvey Cox, Margaret Croyden, Michael Curtis, Rebecca Davison, Paul Deutschman, Art D'Lugoff, Claudia Dreyfus, Arthur Dubow, Karen Durbin, Lorraine Dusky, Catherine East, Dr. Robert Easton, Mary Eastwood, Judy and Harold Edelman, Joanne Edgar, Judith Ramsey Ehrlich, Bebe Eisenhauer, Richard Ekstract, Cynthia and Howard Epstein, Frances Farenthold, Warren Farrell, Richard Farson, Judy Feiffer, Ronnie Feit, Nina Finkelstein, James Fitch, Noel Riley Fitch, Anne Taylor Fleming, Muriel Fox, Judy Freed, Daniel Friedan, Emily Friedan, Jonathan Friedan, Diana Gartner, Sally Gavin, Rabbi Laura Geller, Ludwig Gelobter, Neal Gilkyson Stewart, Peter Gilmore, Natalie Gittelson, Gloria Goldsmith, Harry Goldstein, Laurie Goldstein, Jean Block Gollay, Naomi Goodman, Vivian Gornick, Grace Glueck, Dr. Harold Greenwald, Tania Grossinger, Judith Mara Gutman, Dorothy Haener, Carol Hanisch, Elizabeth Forsling Harris, Rosalind Harris, Betty Benjamin Heilbrun, Howard Heller, Jay Herman, Aileen Hernandez, Jean Newburger Hiersteiner, Mario Ingersoll Howell, Carole Hyatt, Elizabeth Janeway, Mildred Jeffrey, Joseph Kastner, Bel Kaufman, Cathrael Kazin, Barbara Keil, Mim Kelber, Carole Klein, Anne Koedt, Lucy Komisar, Sheryl Kort, Lillian Kozak, Jonathan Kwitny, Lawrence Lader, Barbara Lamont, Ann Reiss Lane, Jack Langguth, Janice LaRouche, Richard Laupot, Johanna Lawrenson, Nydia Leaf, Dorchin Leidholdt, George Leonard, John Leonard, James Lerner, Ellen Levine, Suzanne Braun Levine, Barbara Love, Harriet Lyons, Marlene Macaro, Joseph Machlis, Jennifer MacLeod, Leslie Mandel, Ann Matthews, Senator Eugene McCarthy, Robert McCord, Ann McGovern, Martha McKay, Don McKinney, Marion Meade, Judith Meuli, Jerry Monroe, Celia Morris, Richard and Katherine Nash, Arlynn Nellhaus, Ann Nelson, Mary Perot Nichols, Catherine O'Neill, Jane O'Reilly, Ann O'Shea, John Parkhurst, Jane Pierson, Letty Cottin Pogrebin, Arthur Prager, Terry Pristin, Richard Reeves, Barbara Reisman, Ray Robinson, Betty Rollin, A. M. Rosenthal, Kathie Sarachild, Sheila Savage, Selma Shapiro, Elizabeth Shaw, James Silberman, Alan and Estelle Silverman, Wendy Slight, David Sloan, Joan Smith, Sally Bedell Smith, Jane Sorenson, Nathan Spero, Marian Stein Sprenger, Gloria Steinem, Madeleine

Stoner, Helene Szold, Marian Sweney Szold, Sheila Tobias, Patricia Trainor, Richard Ullman, Barbara Van Auken, Mary Vasiliades, Ann Waldron, Gerald Walker, Greta Walker, Jill Ward, Joseph Wershba, Catherine White, Virginia B. Whitehill, Jake Wirtshafter, Linda Wolfe, Susan Wood Richardson, Dr. Jane Wright, Peter Wyden, John Wykert, Fred Zeserson.

Contents

Introduction

When I was growing up, most of the women celebrated in American history books were footnotes—Betsy Ross, who sewed a flag; Clara Barton, who was a nurse. They did women's work, defined by service to others, high moral purpose, and low pay. I was keenly aware of the disparity in treatment between men and women but never understood the reasons for it. It seemed to have something to do with having babies, but I wasn't sure. Whatever it was, I resented it but had no idea of what to do about it. In 1963, in *The Feminine Mystique*, Betty Friedan made sense of it. She said it was not written in stone, it could be changed—and women themselves could change it. In August 1970 I joined the Women's Strike for Equality, marched down Fifth Avenue with thousands of other women, and became a member of NOW the next day. It was her march, her organization. In the years that followed, when the women's movement was crashing through barriers at breakneck speed, sure of its purpose, never doubting that it would succeed, I had the most exhilarating time of my life.

I didn't know Betty Friedan then. She was a towering figure, honored and feared, loved and reviled, who had a reputation for outrageous behavior. In time, rivals challenged her—feminism was never monolithic—and the movement changed. A new generation of leaders emerged, and Betty began to fade. But none of them could replace her; no one had her charisma or her strength.

In 1992 a mutual friend suggested that I write Betty's biography. It was one of those brilliant ideas that are so obvious in hindsight—the woman who had changed our lives, the most controversial woman of the second wave of feminism.

Betty was not happy about the idea. If I didn't know much about her, she knew less about me. The thought of a stranger, perhaps an unsympathetic one, exploring your life, uncovering things you might rather forget, interpreting your actions in her own way, not yours, was enough to make anyone nervous. When I approached her, she told me that five other women were also interested. She chose one of them to be her biographer. I became the unauthorized one. At first I had no interviews with her. Many of her friends were reluctant to talk to me, but others, fearing that I would get a one-sided picture from her detractors (who were more than delighted to talk), agreed to be interviewed. In 1996, the authorized biographer decided not to continue, and Betty made it known through friends that she had changed her mind about talking to me. We met four times—in her new apartment in Washington, in two restaurants in New York, and at her house in Sag Harbor. True to everything I had heard, she was unpredictable.

She had an endearing way of just bursting out with her thoughts, unedited, that made me feel I had known her for a long time. Less endearing were her sudden eruptions of temper. She was suspicious, having gotten what she called "traces" of me from the interviews I had done with her friends. Of necessity, I had asked them some unpleasant questions, which they had loyally reported to her. I was hoping she would be willing to talk about her personal life, but it was too much to expect from a woman who had managed, after more than three decades in the public eye, to avoid all such discussions. She was concerned with straightening the record on her role in the women's movement, and she clarified many questions for me. (For the rest, I relied on Carl Friedan, her ex-husband, many other people who knew them, and her papers in the Schlesinger Library at Radcliffe College.) We got on well. The last time we met we talked about mystery books, which we both love, and how hard it is to find a good one.

Early in my research I discovered that my subject was a woman of profound contradictions. She was a woman who yearned for a happy marriage and family life, yet urged others to fulfill themselves outside the family. A conventional woman who shook male-female relationships to the core. A reformer who started a revolution. A revolutionary who wanted to be part of the Establishment. An elitist who fought for working women; a class snob who fought for equality; a humanitarian who treated individuals, particularly women, badly. She was a feminist who preferred men, became girlish and flirtatious in their company, and deferred to them—and did not even like most women. In the final analysis, the great overarching cause of her life was not feminism but social justice.

All her life she tried to create real choices for women, to resolve the either/or equation, but in her own life the art of compromise eluded her. She could not accept anything less than first place: either she was at the pinnacle or she was nothing; either things would be done her way or she would remove herself from the scene.

To paraphrase a description of Franklin Delano Roosevelt, she had a first-class mind and a second-class temperament. Founders of movements are not necessarily nice people. She was rude and nasty, self-serving and imperious. But power has to be taken and used, and she had the major ego and drive—the sheer nerve—to do it: she was outspoken, aggressive and demanding; she had electric energy and a catalytic presence. The very qualities that enabled her to launch her crusade, to found NOW and lead the movement through its crucial early years—the qualities that made her a leader—alienated women from her. Beyond that, as a woman she was expected to be pleasant, and as a feminist she was expected to support other women. She collaborated in her own decline by attacking everyone she disagreed with and everything that deviated from her original vision.

Her insecurities were as great as her achievements, and her flaws cost her her leadership. But the movement she ushered in is immense, world-wide; it has permeated our lives; it is intrinsic to the public debate, and its issues have to be addressed. What she did for women outweighs the rest.

JUDITH HENNESSEE
December 7, 1998
New York City

Betty
Friedan

I

Roots

BETTY'S SCHOOL FRIENDS remember the delights of growing up in Peoria: the parties in her big redbrick house on Farmington Road; the kissing games; dancing to records played on the Victrola, on the black-and-white-tiled floor of the sunroom. Betty remembers being eternally uneasy amid the fun. She was always the outsider, the girl who was not pretty, when looks were everything; who was brilliant, when female intelligence was not valued; a child of intense passions and ambitions, when frivolity was the order of the day. She was a Jew in a world of WASPs; an immigrant's daughter surrounded by old-line families that had always "belonged." Smug and comfortable, with the conservatism of inland places, Peoria sheltered and molded her; it also irritated and angered her, providing her with something to react against, the way the oyster creates the pearl.

The city owed its life to the Illinois River, which curved around it and connected it to the Mississippi, to Chicago and New Orleans and the world beyond. Visited by the French explorers Jacques Marquette and Louis Joliet in 1673, the site became a trading post named for the Peoria Indians, and then a colonial village, with carpenter, blacksmith, cobbler, and trading shops lining its narrow streets. It also had a windmill, a wine-press, and an underground wine vault. During the Civil War it had a strong pro-slavery contingent, but it fought on the side of the Union; the house of a wealthy merchant provided a station on the Underground Railroad. Its character was set in the 1850s, when a wave of German immigrants arrived, sober, industrious, respectable, and dull. They built Peoria into a manufacturing center and a rail and shipping terminal, processing grain and meat and manufacturing farm machinery. In the mid-twenties, Caterpillar became the main employer. But most of all, Peoria was known for its distilleries. It was a Sinclair Lewis city saved from drabness by whiskey and by the business of corruption that grew around it. Downtown Peoria was wide open and had a reputation for wildness—gambling in taverns, gang wars, prostitution, and cops on the take. People who wanted to have a good time went to Peoria.

The river also brought vaudeville, from which came the line "Will it play in Peoria?" Around the circuit of cities—Chicago, St. Louis, Kansas City—Peoria was a byword for provincialism. All the great performers came—Sophie Tucker, Al Jolson, Eddie Cantor—and late at night the men would play cards with a local poker group, the Knights of the Round Table, one of whose members was Harry M. Goldstein, Betty's father.

Harry Goldstein was a classic immigrant success story. Born in 1882 in Russia, he had come to St. Louis with his impoverished family when he was about six. At thirteen he went off, on his own, to Peoria and began peddling collar buttons from a street-corner stand. (Adolph Zukor, the future Hollywood movie mogul, peddled furs on another Peoria street corner.) Harry moved on to diamonds and became active in the Jewish community; he was one of three men who organized the Peoria chapter of the Young Men's Hebrew Association in 1904. By 1908 he was the owner of a store, the Goldstein Jewelry Company ("the Tiffany of Peoria," Betty would call it), at 211 South Adams, one of the main downtown shopping streets. He was prosperous enough to put Ben, his youngest brother, through college and law school. Harry was a widower. After a brief marriage, his first wife had died of leukemia. He lived at the Jefferson Hotel, a four-hundred-room Victorian palace with luxury apartments on the upper floors, where most of Peoria's important social events were held.

So he was a man of substance when he fell in love with Miriam Horwitz, the daughter of Dr. Sandor Horwitz, another self-made man. Horwitz was born in Hungary in 1867, into a family of rabbis. After his parents died in 1873, he was shuttled back and forth among various poor relations, none of whom could afford to keep him but all of whom reverenced learning; they saw to it that he went to school. He paid for his education by peddling and giving Hebrew lessons. In the 1880s, during the great migration of Eastern European Jews, he came to America, put himself through medical school, married (1897), and became a police surgeon and medical examiner in Peoria. He also had a private practice. Miriam, an only child, was born on February 13, 1898.

Miriam's parents objected to the match. The age gap was too large—she was almost eighteen years younger than Harry—and he was a widower. Although he was very well read, he had no formal education and spoke with an accent. Miriam had attended Bradley Polytechnic Institute in Peoria, a combination high school and junior college, and graduated with an associate's degree in Literature.* (She had badly wanted to go to Smith, but her parents had refused to send her.) Despite his drawbacks, Harry had a lot to recommend him. He was genial and sociable, a family man; he was also prominent and respected. "She married him because he was established," said Helene Szold, an old friend of Miriam's. It is likely that the Horwitzes would have wanted a professional man for their daughter, one who would carry her another step up the ladder. They sent her out of town to break up the romance, but Miriam was strong-willed and she prevailed. She and Harry were married on February 3, 1920.

Betty was born on February 4, 1921, the year after the Nineteenth Amendment was passed, giving women the vote. It was an auspicious time, the beginning of the postwar wave of optimism when all things seemed possible. Warren G. Harding was about to move into the White House, inaugurating the wild spree of the twenties that would spiral to dizzying heights of prosperity, and Harry would spiral with it. The Goldsteins named their child Bettye Naomi, the final "e" being a fancification of the day. When their second child was born a year and a half later, they named her Amye. Like so many fashionable things, the "e" did not wear well, and both girls later dropped it. Harry Junior arrived in 1926, completing the family.

Life was a struggle at first. Betty was a sickly child. She had bow legs and had to wear iron braces for three years. Bronchitis afflicted her every winter, as did various lung problems that later developed into asthma. She could hardly see out of one eye and had to wear glasses. Her teeth had to be straightened. She was well aware of her disabilities. "All in all," she wrote dryly, "I have not been well endowed physically, neither with health nor with beauty."

---

* Bradley later became a college and then a university.

When she was three the family moved to a large three-story redbrick house at 105 Farmington Road. Farmington Road was then just a country road on the western edge of Peoria, but it was on the West Bluff, the best part of town. The river, vital to Peoria's economic life, also carved its social geography. As the city grew (it took up nine square miles and had a population of almost 100,000 when Betty was born) and laborers crowded in, the wealthy merchants moved away from the downtown area near the river and up to the bluff, where their mansions overlooked the water, commanding a scenic view of the Illinois River Valley.

The house sat on top of a hill across from Bradley Park. It was designed for entertaining, spacious enough for Miriam's luncheons and elegant afternoon bridge parties and for twenty or so of Betty's friends to play records and dance. A Steinway baby grand sat in a corner of the formal living room, and there was a game table for cards and jigsaw puzzles, with poker chips and a backgammon set under the raised top—Harry and Miriam loved cards and gambling. Across the center hall, rich cream-colored drapes hung at the dining room windows and a dark carved-wood rectangular table seated twelve. Its chairs were upholstered in the kind of heavy blue plush that made bare legs itch in the summer. At Miriam's end of the table, under the blue-and-rose Oriental carpet, was a buzzer that summoned a maid from the kitchen. Betty and Amy shared one of the four bedrooms. Betty spent hours at the window, looking across the front lawn at the trees and the stars and dreaming of what her life would be when she grew up.

Every Eden has a serpent; for the Goldsteins, it was anti-Semitism. It was as pervasive as the air, some of it the kind that was not recognized as such. Harry and Miriam were strivers who had arrived at an impasse. Harry's business friends in the chamber of commerce never saw him socially; after sundown, he might as well not have existed. The symbol of success, the Peoria Country Club, was restricted. All over America such walls were an inalienable fact, preserving and protecting, maintained by such heroes of business and industry as Henry Ford and William Randolph Hearst. In Peoria, Jews kept to themselves. "It was like blacks," said Betty's friend Robert McCord. "There was no integration." The poison spread; the Goldsteins, assimilated but not accepted, had their own secret squirmings. Betty noticed that her mother seemed ashamed of her father's accent. She herself thought less of him for allowing that superior attitude. Amy, too, felt ashamed: "I grew up feeling a mixture—he was very warm and affectionate and sentimental—loving him and soaking up affection, but also having this secret embarrassment."

Betty had a privileged childhood, cherished by her parents and cushioned by servants. The Goldsteins employed a nursemaid, a cook, and a butler-chauffeur. (Years later, at parties in Betty's apartment in New York, radical feminists would look askance as a black maid, wearing a white apron, passed hors d'oeuvres.) The family rose at seven. Betty and Amy had a race to get dressed, and walked in Bradley Park with their father before breakfast. They had their own sandpile to play in and made up games and poems. After their afternoon nap, their nurse took them back to the park; after supper, their parents took them for a drive. The girls united against Harry Junior, whom Betty regarded as a pest. Remembering a photograph Miriam had taken of them, Amy said, "Betty was so cute. She had straight dark brown hair with bangs and sort of turning up in front of each ear...and she had her arms around my waist. Our mother always dressed us in identical clothes...we had high ivory-colored leather shoes and high socks and these little pink dresses." In another picture, taken a few years later, Betty is unsmiling, serious, with huge dark eyes and a petulant mouth. Even then, she seemed to have an unchildlike sense of herself and her dignity.

Harry and Miriam placed a high value on appearances. For Harry, who had all the insecurities of an immigrant, it was important to live well and dress well, to make a good impression. Miriam had social aspirations and a sense of herself as a personage. She was strikingly attractive, petite, with brown eyes and dark hair, poised and gracious. Proud of the figure she cut, she spent hours at her bath and dressing table, which was covered with powders and lipsticks and pots of rouge, before an afternoon bridge party. "Our mother always looked as if she had just stepped out of Bergdorf's window," Amy said. "People turned around in the streets. She felt she was a fashion leader. She prided herself that people were imitating her, and this was very important to her."

To the outside world, the Goldsteins seemed to be a lovely family, but behind the walls of 105 Farmington Road lay a tangle of jealousies and rivalries. Betty and her mother were a genetic match, two controlling personalities, but Miriam dominated Betty, and Betty resented it. They clashed constantly over Betty's careless grooming and the messiness of her room. Harry Junior said, "She's been sloppy since she was a little girl. She would say, 'Boy, when I grow up I'm going to be rich so I can hire somebody to clean my room and make my bed.' Mother was finicky; girls were supposed to keep their room neat. Betty wouldn't do it. She was so brilliant, she wasn't interested in the ordinary things we were interested in." Betty developed a very jaundiced view of Miriam and her discontents. She noticed the pleasure her mother took in running her numerous charity organizations, how she basked in praise, and how her attacks of colitis suddenly disappeared when she was managing the store.

It was not until she wrote *The Feminine Mystique* that Betty realized how hobbled her mother had been and how the family had borne the brunt of her frustrations, and not until long after that was she able to come to terms with the guilt and sorrow of their lifelong quarrel. As a child, she had the insight, not the understanding, but that was enough—she had no intention of following in her mother's footsteps. She would be more than a wife and mother. She wanted her life to mean something, and she also "want[ed] success and fame."

Miriam was, in fact, perfect. She was even good at sports and driving. She was the gold standard against which Betty measured herself, only to discover she was made of a lesser metal. Perfect grooming was never her priority, and she was not naturally inclined to ladyhood. As a young girl she was awkward and ill-coordinated, and her mother was critical of her. At heart, Betty didn't really care about appearances or the social imperatives that ruled Miriam's life, the silent pacts that kept things running smoothly. She was moralistic, like her father, who was always reading lessons into movies. In the intolerant purity of adolescence, she judged Miriam harshly, being particularly disdainful of "the hypocrisies and phoninesses about my mother. She was so unctuous on the telephone— 'my dear sweet darling'—when you knew that the next thing she would say is 'that bitch.' " As an adult, Betty traced her own abruptness on the telephone to her reaction to her mother. "As a result, I virtually say 'you bitch' on the phone. Everybody screams at me for my telephone manner because I'm so brusque."

Miriam's accomplishments left little room for her less polished daughter and only served to make Betty insecure in her femininity. Throughout her life she lacked the sexual confidence to compete with other women, especially those who were beautiful and socially at ease. The only way to win was to make her own rules, refuse to accept others' standards. And so she renounced all the qualities that made Miriam a paragon and took the opposite tack. If she was the sore thumb, she made certain to stick out. According to Harry Junior, Miriam thought Betty deliberately made herself look like a frump, knowing it would pain her mother. What would Miriam's friends think, seeing those awful newspaper photos of Betty, the ugly duckling who refused to become a swan? Where Miriam was diplomatic, Betty was blunt; where Miriam was gracious, Betty could barely accept a compliment. She became gratuitously rude and bullying, saying whatever awful thing came into her head. In her unhappy moments she regretted her reaction deeply, berating herself for rejecting her mother's values, for taking pride in her careless housekeeping, and for her clumsiness at sports and driving. On the other hand, Betty's behavior also got her what she wanted. Few people could cope with it.

As a child she was extremely intolerant of frustration and had a formidable temper, inherited from her father. "She was a fearsome person," Harry Junior said. "She could rattle the windows. She was strong-willed, had wide swings of emotions, and she could scream—she had a volatile personality." There were a few violent episodes. Once she threw a book at Amy, who had to have stitches in her head. When she was five she hit a little boy over the head with a hoe. She lost patience with her best friend, Betty Ottenheimer (Otty), for being dull-witted, and yanked out some of her hair.

Harry Senior adored her. She was the firstborn, and he treated her like a son, reveling in her brightness. She had the premier position, the sense of entitlement. (Harry Junior was his mother's favorite.) Betty's father kept the childhood poems she wrote in a safe. When she was about six years old, Miriam took her and Amy to Bradley College to have their IQs tested. Betty's score was 180. Afterward, Miriam told them that Betty was a genius and that Amy was very artistic.

Betty gloried in her extraordinary intelligence, but her natural superiority created rifts in the family. The lines were drawn at the dinner table. Like Joseph P. Kennedy, another ambitious father, Harry believed in challenging his children at meals and encouraging them to express themselves. He would pose math problems, which Betty solved in an instant, and discuss the political issues of the day. Betty always spoke up. Amy remembered, "If there was a serious discussion at dinnertime, they would always direct it toward Betty; the things that were directed toward me would be the frivolous things."

The dinner table also shaped Betty's social conscience. "Our parents believed strongly in education and had a sense of civic responsibility," Harry Junior said. "It was our environment. We grew up with that. You knew you had to take care of fellow Jews; no one else wanted them. When Hitler was rampant, there were strong discussions. Grandfather came almost every night. [Dr. Horwitz's wife, Bertha, had died of leukemia in 1928.] If there was a communicable disease or other medical problem, we discussed it. It was a lively dinner table."

But Betty's brains took her only so far. Beyond the dining room table, in the really important things—beauty, physical grace, and social flair—

Amy surpassed her. Betty complained sorrowfully that she was not allowed to have a bicycle, but when Amy was old enough, *she* got one. Something similar happened with the car. Illinois had no license requirements; most of Betty's friends started driving when they were fourteen, but Miriam was too nervous to allow Betty that privilege. Even when she was sixteen her parents refused permission; but Amy, who had carefully watched others shift the gears, just got in and drove off one day, and that was that. Betty was determined to learn. The summer before her senior year in high school, when her parents were away, she persuaded the daughter of one of Miriam's friends to take her out for two weeks and mastered the clutch. Her mother finally let her have the car.

All of these skirmishes might have remained minor had it not been for a more serious rivalry between the sisters. For a girl growing up nothing mattered more, nothing contributed more to her self-esteem, than being pretty. As with health, the less one has of it, the more important it becomes. Betty had the attention and delight of the most important man in her life, but her father encouraged her mind, not her femininity. The way the girls were treated at the dinner table reinforced the distinction. In the Goldstein family, Amy was the pretty one.

Both girls had Bette Davis eyes—"bedroom eyes," with drooping upper eyelids—but Amy, who had naturally curly hair, resembled her mother. Betty took after her father. She had the Goldstein nose, long and prominent. (So did Harry Junior, but what looked good on a boy did not necessarily suit a girl. He was handsome, with a slim, athletic build.) And Amy, like Miriam, was endowed with the graces Betty lacked. In dancing school, Amy shone; Betty, who felt stiff, awkward, and shy, hated it. Amy was a natural flirt; Betty had no feminine wiles and scorned Amy for using them. Amy instinctively understood and followed the social rules. Betty, the rebel, could not and would not. "She was so straight, she didn't know the meaning of the word 'politic,'" Harry Junior said. One part of her loved feminine things—when she was older she wore ruffles and dainty sandals—but the rest of her was at war with the whole concept of the feminine. Her mother urged her to bob her nose. Nose jobs were becoming fashionable then, as part of the assimilation process. (Everyone had the same cute little button nose, however inappropriate to the rest of the face; aesthetic rhinoplasty was in its infancy.) Betty refused. In an obscure way, she may have been rebelling against her mother, but the promptings of her own nature were paramount. She would never deign to hide her imperfections. Her attitude was and would forever remain: This is how I am. Take me as I am.

. . .

BETTY WAS EIGHT when the Depression began. Harry Senior, who owned a luxury business, was hard hit. People were no longer spending their money on silver punch bowls and Spode china. Some of the Goldsteins' friends took the easy way out: they declared bankruptcy and put everything in their wives' names. But Harry was an honorable man; he worried about his employees, the people who depended on him, and he kept the store going. He even helped the two elderly sisters of his first wife. On Sundays Amy drove him to visit them, much to Miriam's annoyance. Mortgages and debts began to pile up. The Goldsteins were never poor, but the old careless ways were over. Betty would awaken in the night and hear her parents arguing about money. She blamed her mother. Miriam's love of expensive things and Harry's inability to pay for them led her to the gambling rooms of downtown Peoria, where she suffered heavy losses. The dinner table became their battlefield. Amy said, "My father, provoked by my mother, would become very angry, his face would redden, he would bang his fist down on the table, rise and storm out of the room." (Betty would use the same tactic in her epic battles in the women's movement, nonplussing weaker souls.) Betty, who was as extravagant as Miriam, came to believe that her own attitude, her discomfort with money matters and her reluctance to discuss them with men, grew out of these confrontations. Her response, as it had been to Amy, to so many painful things, was contempt—contempt for her father, because he allowed Miriam to treat him as if it were all his fault.

To make matters worse, with this turn in their fortunes Harry Senior became ill with heart trouble and hypertension and had to go to Florida during the winter. Miriam bloomed, her discontent gone. Betty noticed the change. At night when she said her prayers ("Now I lay me down to sleep" and the Shma Yisrael), she prayed for "a boy to like me best" and "a work of my own to do" when she grew up. "I didn't want to be discounted like my mother was until she took over the business," she wrote.

. . .

WHEN BETTY WAS six she went to the Whittier School, across the street from Bradley College, about four blocks from her house. Miles ahead of everyone else, she was skipped half a grade. In the fourth grade her mother intervened to have her skipped the other half—Miriam didn't want her to be in a February graduating class. All the "dummies" ended up in the February class—the slow learners, the children who were left back.

In the new grade Betty met her crowd, the friends she would stay with for the eight years of grade school and junior high: Anne Strehlow, Marian Sweney, Marian Lackland, Nancy Phalen, Marian Stein (Steiny), Jimmy McBrian, and the Easton boys, Bobby and Billy. (Bobby was Betty's favorite; she thought of him as her first beau.) They were the children of Peoria's leading citizens—the merchants and bankers, the doctors and lawyers, the owners of clothing stores and heating oil companies. They went to dancing school together at Miss Coleman's (who was delicately referred to as "a maiden lady"), where they wore white gloves and learned ballroom dancing and comportment. In the fifth grade Miss Coleman held an assembly, and Betty wore her first long party dress, a green taffeta trimmed with rosebuds. Her date, Jimmy McBrian, sent her a corsage. When the children reached the eighth grade, many of the wealthier parents hired a small ballroom in the Jefferson Hotel and threw lavish birthday parties.

Betty was the undisputed leader, full of mischievous ideas. She had a flair for gathering people and inventing clubs, as later in her life she would create national organizations. One of her first successes was the Baddy Baddy Club, whose purpose was to stir up a little excitement and madden her teachers. (Another purpose, as with all clubs, was to keep people out. Whoever didn't belong was labeled a Goodie Goodie.) After getting permission for the members to meet in the hall, she waved her arms and said in her gravelly voice (even then it was gravelly), "There's nothing bad enough," and proceeded to remedy the situation. At her signal in class they created an uproar: they dropped books in the middle of recitations, erupted in coughing fits, and refused to be monitors. When the principal threatened to expel them, Betty formed a spin-off, the Gummy Gummy Club: its members merely chewed thick wads of gum. She got a C in conduct.

After school the group convened in Betty's attic for their favorite game, Dress-up, choosing their characters—movie stars, spies, princesses—from the collection of Miriam's discarded evening dresses. Books were her food and drink. She read *Little Women, The Secret Garden,* stories of English families having adventures, *The Little Colonel,* the Bobbsey Twins and Nancy Drew series. During the hour or so it took to gobble each one down, she was transported. Dress-up evolved into Mystery. The girls invented secret codes and dastardly plots and sneaked around spying on their neighbors.

Soon they graduated from dress-up to kissing games, and Betty started another club, the JFF—Just for Fun. This one included boys. Every Friday night they played post office and truth and consequences. Spin-the-bottle was considered tacky. The action was discreet: a hug and a kiss in the closet.

For eighth and ninth grades they went to Roosevelt Junior High School. At her mother's urging (Miriam steered her life), Betty started to write for the school paper, *The Reflector.* Miriam couldn't wait to get Betty into writing—to take up her own abandoned career, as it were. Before her marriage, Miriam had been society editor on a local paper, but she left when she became pregnant. It was unseemly for pregnant women of her class to work; besides, Harry had insisted. Betty became society editor and book reviewer, much to her mother's pleasure. She also persuaded Miriam to let her drop the despised dancing and take acting, which she loved, at Mrs. Morrill's Children's Theatre at Bradley. In her last year of junior high her life was a social whirl, filled with friends. At parties, they drank champagne and thought they were terribly sophisticated.

And then quite suddenly it ended, like a game of musical chairs. She, who had been the ringleader and chief instigator, the one who generated all the excitement, was suddenly alone, abandoned by her friends. The creator of clubs was not chosen for the most exclusive club of all—the high school sorority. She was desolate. She was at the age of sexual awakening, but unlike the other girls, she hadn't begun to date. The year of loneliness that followed was the lowest point of her life. She blamed it primarily on anti-Semitism.

High school sororities were illegal in Illinois, but they flourished anyway, dominating social life. Their members threw the big Christmas and spring dances and the smaller weekend parties; they had barbecues and movie dates. There were three sororities and three fraternities, varying in wealth and social and intellectual importance. Jews, who made up only two or three percent of the students, were not entirely excluded; a handful of them pledged for the lesser and least social of the groups.

Anti-Semitism had not touched Betty so directly until now. Among her immediate friends it hadn't existed. Marian Sweney, who later married into one of Peoria's Jewish families, said, "When Betty wrote her first book, we read about her ostracism and the prejudice. We were so surprised. There never was anything like that in high school, I thought." Yet anti-Semitism had always undermined Betty in a subtle way, eroding her sense of security. Truly to belong meant being like Harriet Vance, a classmate who came from old money and was a member of the Daughters of the American Revolution—but that was a fantasy.

Anti-Semitism was not Betty's only difficulty. Because of overcrowding, Central High had instituted a double-shift system. Until a new high school was completed during her sophomore year, Betty was in the "afternoon" shift, from 9:30 A.M. to 3:30 P.M., while her friends were in the "morning" shift, from 8:00 A.M. to 2:00 P.M. But the scheduling difference could have been overcome. The boy-girl problem—the sexual sorting out—could not.

Having skipped a grade, Betty was a year younger than her friends. She believed herself to be broad-minded and more mature mentally than they, but she lagged behind them in physical development. Howard Heller, her cousin and classmate, said, "Betty tried to be one of the girls and couldn't. When she tried to smoke she was laughed at. She couldn't quite be a joiner. Classmates could be very cruel; they didn't understand her." Indeed, she was above all that. Generally speaking, she didn't think much of the other girls, either. All they ever did was gossip and talk about boys and getting married, she wrote in a high school paper.

Harry Junior thought the problem was looks. "When Betty was in high school she was ugly and had no boyfriends. She was popular and well-liked—fellows *liked* her. But if a girl didn't get invited to a dance, she felt ostracized." Amy thought the problem was social know-how. "If you wanted to have a date," Amy said, "you hid your brains. You couldn't be smarter than the boys."

But the problem, really, was *everything*. Betty overwhelmed people. She had a bossy streak, and she talked so much no one could get a word in. The idea of hiding her brains, or at least not featuring them so prominently—of deferring to boys—did not occur to her. She was a girl who not only read newspaper editorials but had strong opinions about them. Her friend Robert McCord said, "She always made it clear how she felt about things and was not a shrinking violet. Betty was always a very intense and focused person. And wanting to take a position—she liked to talk about things and debate. She was always on the cutting edge of things."

To some extent, this year of exclusion was self-imposed. Certainly she dramatized it. Her loneliness was very real, but Betty seemed to be in the grip of some Romantic fantasy. It was all very Byronic—she was the outcast, lonely, isolated, and friendless, the misunderstood artist, too sensitive for the smug bourgeois society to which she belonged. She neglected to call two of her old stalwarts, Otty and Steiny, deciding that they probably didn't want to see her anyway. She went for long walks in the park and spent hours mooning around an old abandoned cemetery near her house, reading poetry and crying. At night she knelt at her window and gazed into the darkness of Bradley Park, at the clean snow, the bare branches, and communed with her sorrow.

One afternoon, as she was walking home from school, laden with books, a group of laughing teenagers drove by, piled carelessly into a jalopy. She would have given anything to be with them, going to Hunt's, the local hangout, two blocks down the hill from her house. "Hunt's was our life," Marian Sweney said. "Hamburgers, milkshakes. We knew the curbies; we got out of our cars and car-hopped." The sight of the carful of friends, a vision of all that she yearned for, triggered something in her, and she made a promise to herself: "They may not like me now, but they're going to look up to me." It was a serious vow, not an I'll-show-you fit of pique—a motto for her future. She had made a choice. The popularity contest was over; she had lost, but she had seen a way around defeat.

Betty's traumatic year on the sidelines was not entirely spent with an empty dance card. Mrs. Morrill's Children's Theatre offered pleasure, escape, and the solace of being someone else. The comfort wasn't in the roles so much—hers were always small parts—as in the ambience. She enjoyed the camaraderie, the casual intimacy of the theatre, and the wickedness, too; it wasn't as straight-arrow as the rest of society. Being in the theatre was like being in a club. "I adored being in plays," she later told an interviewer. "I guess I was always a ham. I think that if in those days there had been actresses like Barbra Streisand, you know... [but] the idea of beauty then was Betty Grable. If you weren't blond and pert, how could you think of yourself as an actress?... Once I got to college I didn't even continue doing plays, because it was so ingrained in me that you had to be pretty to be an actress." Betty's favorite movie stars were Myrna Loy, Norma Shearer, and Bette Davis, actresses of substance who played roles in which women were more than wives and mothers. Predictably, she loathed Shirley Temple.

During the summer, Betty went to camp. Although she was inept at any sport that required serious coordination, she loved hiking, canoe trips, and nature. Occasionally, Otty's mother took her and Amy and Otty to the North Shore Country Club, a drive of about seventeen miles from downtown on a little two-lane road. North Shore was considered the Jewish country club; anyone could join. It was smaller than the elegant Peoria Country Club, and its golf course had only nine holes. Jews were also members of Peoria's third club, the Mt. Hawley, where one's money and dedication to golf overcame the unfortunate circumstances of one's religion.

In her junior year Betty was back on the morning shift with her friends, and the crisis was over. Her social life still left a great deal to be desired, but she had come to some decisions about herself and the way the world worked. Rather than rely on a few intimate friends who might let her down, she would have many superficial friendships. And instead of pursuing popularity, she would make her mark in school activities. And perhaps, success might lead to popularity.

Central High exemplified the golden age of American public schools, with courses ranging from Latin and physics to driver safety. It offered a staggering number of extracurricular activities, and Betty plunged in. According to a partial listing in her yearbook, *Crest,* she was on the staff of *Opinion* (the school newspaper) and *Tide* (its magazine), and a member of Charvice (the honor society), the Junior National Honor Society, the French Club, the Cue Club, Quill and Scroll (the honor society for writers), the Social Science Club, and Jusendra (the drama club). She also participated in debates.

In all that she did she reaped honors. In Jusendra, she directed plays and also landed the part of Mrs. Rochester, the madwoman in the attic, in *Jane Eyre.* The highlight of her acting career, it was only a two-minute walk-on, but Betty made it memorable. She crossed the stage emitting a hideously insane laugh, scaring the audience so much that they applauded her as she exited. She won a drama award on the strength of her performance.

For *Opinion,* she and John (Parky) Parkhurst wrote a column, "Cabbages and Kings," about everything and nothing, and turned the paper's back page into a miscellany of utter silliness and serious editorializing on school issues. Betty also wrote book reviews and poetry, including limericks: "There was once a dumb girl called Doreen. / She hadn't a thought in her bean. / She was such a dunce / That she only smiled once. / And now she's a cinema queen."

Betty's greatest success was neither on the stage nor in the newspaper. The triumph of her senior year was the founding of *Tide,* Central High's first literary magazine.* *Tide* set the pattern for many of Betty's future endeavors. It had its own *raison,* as all her projects would, but it also filled a void in her life. *Tide* brought her respect, even from people who might not have liked her; it was important, and it made her important; it was a group effort; it required creativity and hard work; and it resulted in close friendships with boys.

Betty started *Tide* with two girls, Evelyn Shemas and Dorothy Stimpson, editors of the senior yearbook, after her book reviews in *Opinion* were replaced with a letters-to-the-editor column. *Opinion* was largely a glori-

---

* The name came from Robert Burns's poem "Tam O'Shanter": "Nae man can tether time nor tide."

fied gossip column and an endless stream of social notes; the same names, those belonging to the sorority-fraternity crowd, appeared again and again. Betty wanted to write a literary column, but the powers that be told her no one would be interested. Angry, she decided that if the school wouldn't provide a place for good writing and ideas, she would do it herself.

One of the girls' first decisions was to recruit two boys—Douglas Palmer, a new arrival at school, who had been the editor of his New Jersey school paper; and Paul Jordan, who had been Betty's partner in chemistry lab. As she characterized them, the girls were "outspoken," Paul was "conservative," and Doug was "radical." She labeled herself "unpredictable." Everyone told them it couldn't be done, but they knew better.

Tide was sixteen pages of stories and poems, *Reader's Digest*–size. They put it together from scratch, soliciting and editing manuscripts, negotiating with a printer, and, for publicity, writing and performing in a radio program that dramatized the story of the magazine's creation. Their main problem was raising fifty dollars to print each issue. Advertising was out of the question—it was too undignified for such a high literary endeavor. Harry Senior saved the day by suggesting that they ask local businessmen to be sponsors—and agreeing to be one of them. The magazine was an instant success. At ten cents a copy, the first printing sold out, and they had to reorder.

Betty was thrilled. *Tide* was "the biggest thing in my life, an idea in my head and Doug's and Paul's made concrete," she wrote. The presence of the two other girls had somehow slipped below the horizon of her consciousness. This penchant for consigning female co-workers to oblivion would persist throughout her life and cause her a great deal of trouble later. In this case, the girls who co-founded *Tide* were not there for the special rewards Betty received.

After meetings at Paul's house, she stayed to talk. The boys teased her, and she loved it. At other times, she and Doug talked for hours on all the great subjects—life and death, love and ambition, God and the universe. She had a crush on him, but he and Paul both had girlfriends. When they graduated, he sent her a letter of praise and friendship, intense in its sincerity, saying that he had never known a girl more brilliant, prophesying that she would never be happy, and paying her what for him must have been the highest compliment: he enjoyed her company so much he wished she were a boy.

They published four issues of *Tide*. There was a fifth issue in their heads, composed of pieces they had been forbidden to print, all questioning the status quo. Judging from them, it is clear that Betty's politics were already formed and that she had the makings of a muckraker. One piece was on "social diseases," another on fraternities and sororities, a third on labor relations. The fourth, "Education for the Masses," which Betty wrote, was a diatribe against the "pompous pretensions" of high school education and how the people it shapes are not taught to think, only to memorize, leaving them fit for nothing but "the numbing influence of advertising, radio and movies." They were afraid of being expelled if they published the issue.

. . .

BETTY WAS NOT entirely satisfied with her accomplishments. She had really wanted to play the lead in *Jane Eyre,* not the character part, and it was galling to have come in only second in a speech contest. It was hard for her to accept anything less than first place. She was aware, however, that hers was a driven personality, that she would always be discontented and nothing would ever be enough.

At graduation, on June 9, 1938, she was one of six valedictorians. In a spoof of the class, an anonymous author imagined where they would all be twenty years hence: Doug Palmer would be "the new international dictator. He just gave the people of America, Europe and Asia 24 hours to get out.... Bettye Goldstein got her wish, too. I guess that book she wrote is pretty popular—'How to Be Popular and Why Bother'—it's all in verse, too."

In the fall Betty and Harriet Vance, also a valedictorian, took the train to Springfield, Massachusetts, and from there to Northampton and Smith College. Betty had also been admitted to Radcliffe, Stanford, and the University of Chicago; she was leaning toward Radcliffe, but there was no question of where she would go. Smith was the school that Miriam had longed for and talked about for years. Amy would follow her sister there two years later. Betty was more than ready to leave. Once on the train, she turned her back on Peoria.

The Passion of the Mind

BETTY LOVED SMITH. She loved the intellectual challenge, the excitement of learning for its own sake, drinking it in like an elixir. She heard people use "Peoria words," words she had seen in books but never heard spoken and didn't know how to pronounce. She no longer felt like a freak. Her shyness and self-consciousness vanished; people looked up to her. She took courses in everything from philosophy and economics to the Russian novel to zoology, more for the pleasure of discovery than out of any particular interest in them. Effortlessly, she rose to the top. She had found a sanctuary.

The campus was peaceful and bucolic, filled with old leafy trees and flowering bushes. A lake, Paradise Pond, occupied one corner, and large nineteenth-century brick houses, with columns and ivy, lined the quad. The college was encrusted with ceremony and tradition; there was compulsory chapel once a week and signouts for weekends. The house system was based on Harvard's; residences were run like homes, each with its own housemother and kitchen. In the dining room, the rules of gracious living prevailed: tablecloths, silver, and napkin rings; no trousers in the evening and no bathrobes at breakfast. Maids made the beds and served the meals. Smoking was permitted only in the smoking room, drinking not at all. Curfew was at ten P.M. The honor system demanded that a student turn herself in for infractions. The atmosphere was chummy; students could invite faculty members for dinner or coffee and get to know them better. Most evenings everyone played bridge after dinner. Life was very pleasant.

Among the Seven Sisters, Smith had a reputation as something of a country club, but the school was academically rigorous and had high expectations of its graduates. They would be active, get jobs, and do good in the world—but they would not start revolutions. For most, the highest aspiration was marriage. Essentially, Smith girls were groomed to be corporate wives. One of the last poems in Betty's 1942 yearbook begins: "We want a diamond ring / A great big shiny thing / The kind that makes you blink..."

Within a short time, Betty became a campus personality. People noticed her short, chunky body striding around the campus. She had a full face and dark, thick, shoulder-length hair, worn curled around her face and high on top in the style of the day. She dressed in the uniform: baggy Shetland sweaters and tailored white blouses, pleated skirts, and dirty saddle shoes or moccasins. Some people called her Bett-yee, teasing her for the spelling affectation, and some Cussie—she'd fallen off a bicycle and gotten a concussion, but most people thought it was because she was profane. She played bridge with the best, she organized expeditions to the movies in Springfield, and she hung out at Rahar's,* the local beer joint— but everything about her was serious; all her activities were purposeful. People pointed her out: she was the one who got all As, unusual at Smith. (Vassar was considered the brainiest of the Seven Sisters.) As with all commanding figures, opinions about her ranged from antipathy to admiration.

"Her room was a mess. *She* was a mess. But she was so far ahead of us intellectually, it didn't matter," said Jean Newburger, who lived in Betty's house, Chapin, across the street from the quad. "She was teased because of her seriousness, but she was fun to be with. She was respected as well." Margaret Hildeburn, another classmate, said, "Betty was well known on campus because she was inordinately bright. She had a lot of stimulating ideas. She scorned such things as the Smiffenpoufs. They were a barber-

---

* Rahar's was immortalized in Helen Eustis's mystery *The Horizontal Man*, in which a Betty-like character, full of questions and self-importance, plays by the rules except when she needs to break them, never hesitates to say what she thinks, solves the murder, and elopes with a scruffy local reporter.

shop quartet, informal. These were lightweights from her standpoint. And Grass Cops—we weren't supposed to walk on the lawns; there were paths. Betty sought out people who were bright. It always seemed she was compensating for the fact that she had no dates and didn't run around. She took it out by scorning those kids, and people didn't like that."

Yet Betty's dismissive exterior may have masked an entirely different attitude. A year behind her was another Midwesterner, Nancy Davis, the future Mrs. Ronald Reagan, priming herself for her acting career. She was the star of a musical comedy group. Nancy was not intellectual and did not get very good grades, but she, too, had a purpose. Betty had noticed her because of her own love of acting. "She was one of the few people that came out of Smith in that period who did have a career," Betty said. "So I followed that. She was in a group of people who did things, so I knew of her." (Years later, during the fight for the Equal Rights Amendment, Betty was on the press bus, covering the Republican Convention in Kansas City. "I sat down next to Nancy and said, 'As one Smith girl to another...' She said, 'Oh, Betty, you know that Ronnie and I are for equality and for rights, but not for the Equal Rights Amendment.' ")

Betty took many writing courses, producing dozens of short stories and poems that were rooted in her life. She seemed to be using them to vent her anger at her family and at things she could not speak about. "And Grey with Her Pearls," a portrait of her mother, is the story of a monstrously vain, self-satisfied woman who is never wrong about anything. Her husband has run off to have an affair, and all her friends commiserate with her. Throughout it all she is gracious and forbearing; nothing can pierce her armor. Another story, apparently about her father, "Create My Child of Spleen" (from *King Lear*) is a devastating picture of a sick and dying man, bitter and fearful, with a beautiful wife twenty years younger than he, whom he envies.

Another story, "The Scapegoat," is about the anti-Semitism she perceived at Smith. Like all the exclusive East Coast schools, Smith had a quota for Jews—8 percent—with a subquota for those who came from New York. "The Scapegoat," published in the *Smith College Monthly*, was based on an incident from Betty's freshman year, when she lived in a house with four upper-class Jewish girls from Cincinnati. A petition to President Franklin Delano Roosevelt was being circulated, asking that he ignore immigration quotas so that European Jews trying to escape Hitler could come to America. At a house meeting, Betty spoke up for the petition. None of the other Jewish girls said a word. The petition languished on the hall table for four days. Betty looked at it every day. A few of the other girls signed it, but not the four from Cincinnati. "The Scapegoat" is the story of a Jewish girl in a house like Chapin who doesn't quite fit in, who is perhaps a little bit too Jewish. She is slowly and relentlessly isolated by two other Jewish girls in the house who are afraid that their friends will tar them with the same brush, and they will no longer belong.

Betty wrote reams of poetry, much of it ironic, filled with the rhythms of Auden, MacLeish, and Pound. Some of her subjects were political: the shadow between the ideal and the reality of democracy. Others were personal: explorations of social hypocrisies; portraits of herself and unnamed classmates. "Smith Portraits, #13, The Character," is about a woman sifting through her options and choosing deliberately not to be "an old maid...dull...uninteresting..." Or "A housewife / Bridge in the afternoon / Domestic canary and aquarium fish / Cabbage smell..." Instead, "She will be a character / She will walk high through the streets / Her lips thin with disdain / Her words will sting / Bitter lashings / Sweet epigrams / They will flock to her tea urn / ... She will be satisfied with this."

Rather than major in English, which would have been easy, Betty decided on psychology, a subject that fascinated her. Freud-worship was de rigueur, but psychology was still in its frontier days, a wilderness open to exploration. Behaviorism was all the rage, offering a new vocabulary and a Pavlovian interpretation of personality. Psychology gave Betty an opportunity to work seriously—and more, to understand herself. People gravitated to psychology because it promised to untangle the mysteries of the mind and solve their emotional problems. Betty had had her first attack of asthma, which was thought to be psychosomatic, at the end of her freshman year. During every crisis of her life, her lungs would fail her. "It was a tremendous hindrance," Harry Junior said. "God knows what Betty would have accomplished if she hadn't had asthma."

The psychology department virtually adopted her. She studied under Kurt Koffka, one of the great Gestalt psychologists, who had come from Germany before the war, and Kurt Lewin, who was beginning to work out the basic principles of encounter groups. In 1940, her sophomore summer, the department sent Betty to Lewin's Child Welfare Research Station at Iowa University to study group dynamics with children.

In the spring of 1941, Betty became editor in chief of *The Smith College Weekly*. During her apprenticeship as a reporter and managing editor, she and the then editor in chief, Joan Marble, who was constantly being called before the dean and told she was a disgrace, had doubled the staff and transformed the newspaper from a quiet weekly to a crusading semi-weekly. Smith was a little too exclusive for them. "There was a social element," Joan said. "The Grass Cops wore beautiful cashmere sweaters and real pearls and went to Princeton every weekend. We thought there was an emphasis on style, not scholarship, and the college was out of touch with the modern world. The president of our class was picked because of her looks and name and accent. It was like an aristocracy. These were the people Smith loved and rewarded." Traditionally, the job of editor in chief went to a junior, who was chosen by the editors from the senior class. Betty's predecessors were far from unanimous in their selection. Her temper, her shotgun approach, and her lack of finesse almost cost her the honor. "Betty made a lot of enemies because she was very irascible when she was crossed," said assistant editor Priscilla Buckley, a sister of William F. Buckley, Jr. (Another sister, Aloise, was a reporter.) "She was elected editor in chief because she was so much brighter than anyone else; they couldn't not give it to her." As Harry Junior had observed, she didn't know the meaning of the word "politic."

Modeled after *The New York Times*, the revitalized paper, now called the *Smith College Associated News* (*SCAN*), was wide-ranging and political, aware of the world beyond Paradise Pond. "Whatever came to her attention she became fascinated by," said Priscilla Buckley. "Betty just sopped up learning. She had a brain that could amass material and organize it. She was full of fun, very quick and bright. There were a lot of meetings and excitement. We became very good friends."

As editor in chief, Betty inspired respect for her leadership and dismay at her outspokenness. Sally Gavin, an assistant editor, said, "She was bossy, but I did like her. We were a good group and we had fun together. She did not foster intimacy. It was more of a push-and-push-back relationship with Betty. She was a very strong woman." Neal Gilkyson, who wrote for *SCAN* and was later instrumental in publishing an excerpt from *The Feminine Mystique* in the *Ladies' Home Journal*, said, "I admired what Betty was doing at *SCAN*. Betty had a lot of impact. She was a standout. She stood out because there were not that many Jews. She was strident, she made herself felt everywhere—her editorials and her thoughts every week. Which made a lot of people not like her."

Betty became a crusading newspaper editor, a Big Woman on Campus. She found a slew of causes to take up arms against, or at least bring to everyone's attention. It was her duty to state her opinion, take a stand. She *wanted* to disturb the decorum, and she was fearless about it. Betty was decades ahead of her time in running critiques of courses; she also protested against the closed meetings held by the student government, Smith's restrictions on social life, and censorship of student publications. Some people got a little tired of all the Sturm und Drang: in one school skit a *SCAN* editor was portrayed as "a strident voice haranguing from a perpetual soapbox."

The crusade that was perhaps dearest to her heart was also one that got her into trouble with the administration. Secret societies had been part of the Smith tradition since the 1890s, when clubbiness was in high vogue. Smith had two such groups, the Ancient Order of Hibernians (AOH) and the Orangemen, dedicated to hijinks and socializing.* The societies were not really secret; everyone knew about them and had friends in their ranks. A *SCAN* reporter was a Hibernian. But because membership was "inherited" from mothers and older sisters who had gone to Smith, and girls from certain prep schools were also invited to join, the clubs set a snobbish tone; their members were people who "belonged." To Betty, the secret societies were anathema. She believed that they dominated the school, as the sororities had done at Central High, but now she had the power to do something about it. For a month she and her staff planned a campaign to find out what went on at the secret meetings and expose them.

Betty was away at a conference of editors when an urgent call came through to get back immediately. "All hell was breaking loose," she said. "It was in the local paper." On Saturday night, November 15, four *SCAN* staff members†—Priscilla Buckley, Madelon Berns, Maggie Comstock, and Nancy Stix—had sneaked into the room of the Orangemen's head and removed a heavy, padlocked chest two feet long. They hauled it through the window and down the fire cord,‡ dragged it to a car that belonged to Nancy Stix's Amherst date, and drove off to a field, where they unscrewed

---

* According to the "Constitooshun" of the AOH, written in drunken stage-Irish dialect, the patron saint was St. Patrick, "the estoteric [*sic*] color of the Society is grane. The emblem is the shamrock.... The National Disease is gangerene." The object of the Society "is the maintenance of churlish wit and promotion of hellish spirit in the college." In their hey-day, the societies held mock duels, mock weddings, ceremonials, oyster swallowings, song fests, and so on.

† The actual number of participants in the secret-society caper is uncertain. Some women say four, some three. A story in *SCAN* mentions two women aided by two men. Likewise, memories of some details are in slight disagreement. This account is pieced together from five sources.

‡ In case of fire, students were expected to wrap themselves in a loop of rope and let themselves down with a pulley.

its back. The contents were a terrible disappointment: robes, chant texts, and grooming rituals, including instructions on how to use Odo-ro-no, a deodorant. Such intimacies were not openly discussed at that time, but deodorant application was not enough to make a story. Still, the *SCAN* four copied the material before returning it to the chest. At that point they realized they had a problem. The raid had been an impetuous act, and it had never occurred to them that they would not be able to pull the chest back up. They had to leave it on the porch.

Unfortunately, while wrestling the trunk to the window, Nancy Stix had dropped her notebook. The culprits were caught and summoned to account for themselves to the warden of the college, Laura Scales, Class of 1900, an early Hibernian. Scales took the view that breaking and entering was not a legitimate method of news gathering, and that those who stole chests now would steal diamond rings later. She was ready to expel them. Alarmed, Betty went to bat for her people. While she did not condone their methods, she told the authorities, if they were expelled she would feel obliged to print the records they had copied. The administration came to a decision: copies of the records would be returned, the students would be dropped from the paper's editorial board and their names deleted from the masthead, and *SCAN* would be forbidden to print anything about the secret societies for a year "since it would be impossible for the editors of *SCAN* to distinguish between facts acquired through a misdemeanor and those already in their possession." The secrets would remain secret. Implicit in the decision was a threat to suspend publication of *SCAN*.

Betty could not accept this sort of control. In her eyes the paper was being censored and its autonomy compromised. She didn't see why the administration was getting involved at all, since *SCAN* was a student publication and should therefore come under the jurisdiction of student government. She appealed the decision, and the administration decided she had a point: the students would be subject to personal disciplinary action, and a trio consisting of Betty, the head of the Orangemen, and the president of student government would confer on anything to be published about the secret societies. So they kissed and made up, but the raiders did not get off scot-free. "There were individual punishments," Sally Gavin said. "Betty did have to fold. Those people couldn't be on the paper for a year. But they continued to work ex officio." One of them lost part of her scholarship.

. . .

THE MOST PROFOUND thing that happened to Betty at Smith was her radicalization. She became committed to Marxist philosophy, although she was never an ideologue. "She was the campus radical," an old friend said, "passionate, with wild hair. A firebrand." She joined the staff of *Focus,* a smudgy-looking magazine published by the American Student Union, a left-wing campus group. Bob Easton, her first beau, whom she visited at Harvard, remembered, "I had lefty feelings, but not as much as she. She contributed to the *Daily Worker.* She told me not to subscribe to it; she said, 'You'll be a marked man if you do.' "

When the Smith maids went on strike, and the American Federation of Labor sent representatives to persuade them and the building and grounds employees to join the union, Betty filled *SCAN* with sympathetic stories and sent a reporter to the meeting in town where the vote would be taken. *SCAN* was the only press there. The story, entirely favorable, ran on page one: "The atmosphere of the meeting was one of friendliness and cooperation...a vote was taken on every issue no matter how small." Betty even betrayed her own beliefs on censorship, going so far as to support the suspension of *Tatler,* another student publication, after it ran an offensive article, "Maids We Have Known and Loved." She also wrote an impassioned editorial, "The Right to Organize":

> As the Nazis rose to power in Germany they attacked and destroyed labor unions.... For fascism to survive all free and democratic institutions must be prohibited.... Union ... members are ... as American as the funny papers they read, the movies they see, the beer they drink, the streets they live on; their aims are basic to the protection and expansion of democracy in America.

On the face of it, the idea of Betty Goldstein, elitist to the core, getting sentimental over factory workers, is somewhat bemusing. Her politics came from books, she said—Steinbeck, Dos Passos, Marx, Veblen—and the Smith course on comparative "isms." She wrote that she had not even been aware of the workers in the Caterpillar factory in Peoria, who lived outside the charmed circle of the Bluff, most of whose children attended other high schools. Betty may have been stretching the point a bit. Her new knowledge must have been more of a coalescence than a sudden awakening. In high school she was not so wrapped up in her angst that she didn't pay attention. The unpublished labor piece for *Tide* would have been quite upsetting to the businessmen who sponsored the magazine. *Middletown* and Marx connected with a feeling that was already there, a need that grew out of her immigrant family, her Jewishness, her bout with the sororities, her urge to rebel against Peoria. She was snob enough not to be able to identify fully with workers, and egotist enough not to want to, but her impulses were humanitarian. Betty was an idealist who had a profound faith in democracy. Injustice—a whole group of people being discounted—aroused her passion. Labor's fight for economic justice was her first cause. It would occupy her for the next decade.

During the summer of her junior year, 1941, guided by Dorothy W. Douglas, her economics professor, she spent a few weeks at the Highlander Folk School in Monteagle, Tennessee. Thirty-five miles from Chattanooga, in the Cumberland Mountains, the school was set amid rural poverty. Most families in the area were on relief. The school itself was a frame farmhouse on a dirt road, with oak and dogwood trees in the front yard and a cornfield in back. Highlander was based on farmer-labor populist ideals and its teachers worked with the AFL and the CIO to organize the South. It was also a cultural and educational center for the area. The old Baptist hymn "We Shall Overcome" was popularized at Highlander. People came from all over the country—Duke, Vassar, the University of Chicago—to teach economics, labor organizing, and collective bargaining. In certain circles, Highlander was considered chic, and wealthy families sent their children to soak up egalitarianism. Some of the school's money came from the League of American Writers, a Communist-led organization; this connection launched an FBI Red hunt at Highlander, but nothing alarming was found. Eleanor Roosevelt was among those who contributed money for scholarships.

Betty enrolled as an intern in the Writers Workshop and asked for a scholarship—she couldn't afford both the train fare and the $30 fee. Although she had won a partial scholarship at Smith, she may have felt that the financial pressures on Harry Senior were too great. In addition to his medical bills, he was paying Amy's full tuition—$1,100 a year. (Amy had come to Smith in 1940.) It is also possible that the Goldsteins did not regard this foray into the lower depths as essential to Betty's education. Her father had spent his life climbing out of them.

At Highlander she wrote "Learning the Score," the story of her economic education, beginning with Peoria. It was a scathing attack on capitalism, class, and the mass media. The people on the Bluff, she observed, were the one percent of Peoria that did not derive its income from wages. She had also noticed that in junior high the Bluff children were put in separate classes from the others:

In Peoria intelligence seems to depend on what part of town you live in.... You never came into contact with the others.... My father's friends own the distilleries and banks and office buildings of Peoria. To them the profit of the employer is a sacred right ... employees should be grateful. If they try to organize they are being greedy, they are trying to steal what does not belong to them. If they were any good to begin with, they wouldn't be workers.... (I've heard my father's friends say things like this often.)

Betty was convinced that the labor movement would prevent fascism.

When she returned to Smith she wrote a class paper about her experience, calling Highlander "an honest place. A not-for-profit place," comparing the spirit of labor unions to the symbols of America: the flag, the Declaration of Independence, the Gettysburg address, Walt Whitman and Carl Sandburg. The ideas she expressed were fairly commonplace. Since the Depression, the entire culture, from Roosevelt's New Deal to the Group Theatre, had moved leftward. Intellectuals romanticized the masses and became enamored of socialism (or Communism) as a panacea for their ills. Paraphrasing Marx on religion, the social and cultural critic George Seldes remarked that "Communism is the opium of the intellectuals." Not even the news of the murderous by-products of the Russian experiment interfered with the dream of social justice. Fascism was the evil empire to be defeated.

Although Betty's editorials in *SCAN* were drenched in antifascist fervor, before Pearl Harbor she was against American intervention in the war. The Quaker pacifist position, not uncommon at Smith, held that international mediation was the answer to war. Betty's stand brought down on her the wrath of a faculty member, Mary Ellen Chase. Chase was a best-selling writer who had turned down a $35,000 offer from *Redbook* for the first serial rights to her book *Mary Peters* because she thought magazines were "second rate" and *Redbook* would be "a step down" for her. She was also a passionate Anglophile.

In May 1941, while London was being reduced to rubble, Betty wrote an editorial chastising professors who used their classrooms as a pulpit for their war views, "twisting the substance of the lecture ... is it not a misuse of authority, a misuse of the place and the time?" she asked. "In the past year we have seen the practice of political exhortation in the classroom become more and more common here at Smith.... War breeds fanaticism, hatred, hysteria."

Chase, who taught English composition and literature, was a woman who embraced controversy. Betty had already had a run-in with her. As managing editor of *SCAN*, Betty and Joan Marble had assaulted the sensibilities of the Smith establishment with an investigation of the college bookstore's prices and its function as a conduit for faculty books. The head of the bookstore, a close friend of Mary Ellen Chase, complained to the administration. Betty knew Chase would be angry about the antiwar editorial, but not the form her anger would take. Early Sunday morning after the editorial appeared, a friend ran to Betty's room, dragged her out of bed, wrapped a coat around her pajamas, handed her a comb, and pushed her in the direction of the chapel. The word was out that Chase was going to "blast" Betty in her sermon. She slipped into the chapel in time to hear Chase say, "The writer of the editorial was right—war does breed hatred—small, selfish, self-righteous hatreds aroused by those arguments of which the editorial speaks, hatreds of which we are all ashamed. Yet it breeds fine and noble hatreds also. And this war breeds the finest hatreds of all wars.... These are the hatreds which give to us whatever the nobility and dignity and life we have. Without them we contribute nothing to the time in which our life is passed."

Although Chase did not mention Betty by name, they remained antagonists for months and did not patch things up until after America entered the war, when Chase, rising above the occasion, wrote a letter of recommendation for Betty. It was February 1942, and Betty was thinking of applying to the University of Minnesota for a teaching position after she graduated. Chase had a friend there, the wife of a psychology professor. "She has the *bad* taste to spell herself Bettye Goldstein, but she's really better than that!" Chase wrote.

She hated me so for a year that I respected her terribly for it—you know the way you do respect people for honest extremes! Very likely she hates me now. I don't know or care—but she has a swell mind and is plain tops in psychology. She's a Neilson scholar here—which means the best in the college. She's got a fine head, and a sound sense of values. She's Jewish and a bit aggressive, but always for decent things. She loathes wealth—no, she isn't really poor!—I mean the sort of frippery which we get here from a lot of young things—and I really admire her. She hated me because I gave a talk in chapel against one of her editorials last year ... and I really don't blame her much because, of course, she had little chance to hit back, though when she had cooled off a bit, she wrote a corking editorial against my point of view. I had tea with her the other day and really first-class talk, and I told her I

should write [the recipient's husband] about her. She's one of the most bril-
liant girls we've ever had here, and we think she's bound for big things.

In the spring of her senior year, Betty anointed Sally Gavin as the next editor in chief. They were not close, but Betty took Sally aside to give her some advice. Betty had a strong sense of the dignity of her position and what was appropriate to it. "I was a real slob in college," Sally said. "I wore my father's old World War I khaki army coat. I didn't care much the way I looked. Neither did Betty. She was probably better groomed. She said, 'I want you to get your hair cut so it looks good, more distinctive. You should look outstanding.' She felt it was important for the editor that people knew who the editor was. I'm sure she felt people knew who *she* was, and I don't think she felt she had to change. I was a mousy little kid. I got my hair cut in a wavy Dutch bob. She told me I should wear red lipstick. I never wore lipstick—why bother?"

All in all, Smith had never seen anything like Betty Goldstein. Her influence was felt everywhere. She was a leader in campus affairs and a moral force, setting the tone and shaping the debate, and she was an award-winning scholar as well. In her sophomore year, she and a classmate had co-founded the *Smith College Monthly,* a literary magazine. She had been managing editor and editor in chief of *SCAN,* and she had published dozens of articles, stories, poems, and editorials. She had won a college literary prize and another for one of her editorials, "Let the Laughter Cease," in 1940. She was on the Activities Board and a member of the Psychology Club and the Phoenix Club, among others. Her scholarship was peerless. As a freshman she won the A. E. Hamm scholarship prize, which was half the income from $5,000. She was a Sophia Smith Scholar in 1939–40. She was a Junior Phi Beta Kappa and was elected to Sigma Xi, the Phi Beta Kappa for the sciences. She was even a junior usher (ushers held the ivy chain that seniors marched through at graduation). In her senior thesis, "Operationism in Psychology," written with Professor Harold Israel, she made an original contribution to behaviorism. And to send her on her way, at graduation Smith awarded her the Alumnae Association Fellowship for Graduate Studies. The president of Smith told her parents, "Betty has the most outstanding record of any student ever matriculated at Smith."

It had been a triumph of the mind. Betty's Smith experience had not been one of rah-rah Harvard-Yale football games and drunken fraternity parties. The boy who would like her best had not materialized. Bob Easton had visited her, and she had gone to Harvard a few times to see him. "I took her to her hotel," he remembered of one occasion. "She had a late date, and then she went out with someone I had introduced her to. He joined the ambulance corps in North Africa and was killed fighting Rommel. He was impressed with her left-wing politics."

Betty had a slightly different view of her encounter. She assumed that Bob had invited her only out of a sense of obligation. She saw her date again, in New York, but when he made advances to her, she could not believe he even liked her.

Nevertheless, she had acquired a great deal of self-confidence and made a lot of friends. She was proud of her "specialness." From the Smith atmosphere she had acquired certain values, among them the importance of doing something meaningful in the world, of using her life well. She had made some decisions about her future, settling on Berkeley to do her graduate work, and had begun to notice, in a formless way, the position of women in society. On a Harvard Law School visit at the invitation of a housemate, Jean Newburger, and her boyfriend, Walter Hiersteiner, she had attended some classes. "While in class," Walter said, "she said to me, 'It's a shame and it's ridiculous that women are not allowed in Harvard Law.'" In a 1942 class paper she wrote that she expected to marry, but her husband would not be a man who thought that a woman belonged at home. She believed, she wrote, "rather strongly in equality of the sexes." At the end of her senior year she dropped the final "e" from Betty.

Betty's college career had another side that nobody knew about. An insidious panic had begun to overtake her, clouding the respect and admiration she basked in. Her Peoria plan, that achievement would compensate for everything else, seemed to be breaking down. The asthma attack she'd had in her freshman year was followed by others; in the spring of her sophomore year she had one so ferocious that she spent several weeks in the infirmary. Miriam came to be with her. She went blank on her senior honors exam, although she still graduated summa cum laude. Her anxiety was so strong that she even entertained the notion that she might be mentally ill: in a psychology class she interpreted her Rorschach test as that of a schizophrenic.

Later, she came to see her feeling of dread as an identity crisis. In *The Feminine Mystique*, she wrote:

> I remember the stillness of a spring afternoon on the Smith campus in 1942, when I came to a frightening dead end in my own vision of the future.... 'Is

this really what I want to be?' The question shut me off, cold and alone, from the girls talking and studying on the sunny hillside behind the college house. I thought I was going to be a psychologist. But if I wasn't sure, what did I want to be? I felt the future closing in—and I could not see myself in it at all. I had no image of myself, stretching beyond college.

3

Meltdown

THE YEAR AT Berkeley, 1942–43, started well. Smith had armed Betty with a $600 fellowship; Berkeley had awarded her the Hattie Heller Graduate Scholarship, worth $375; and she succeeded, through a vacancy, to a university fellowship of $750. She studied under Erik Erikson, who was exploring the mystery of identity, and took his seminar on the difference between neurotic episodes and neuroses, especially in children. She wrote a paper on the way fantasies and behavior express inner needs, and chose as the subject and title of her master's thesis, "Critical Review of the Psychoanalytical Theory of Personality Types." The panic that had begun at Smith still ate at her but, as always, she operated at the top of her form, regardless of what was churning inside. Again, she was the star of the psychology department.

She soon grew dissatisfied. Berkeley in 1943 was a shadow of itself. Most of the promising young men had gone off to war, the most challenging intellectual level creamed away. The school was not up to her standards. She found it lackluster; compared to Smith it was less rigorous, not as tough-minded. When she presented her Smith honors thesis (a critique of B. F. Skinner's behaviorist theories) to a graduate colloquium, she was shocked to be told that if she hadn't presented it, she could have used it later for her Ph.D.—it was that good.

That Christmas in Peoria, she had a long talk with her father. The family was in a fragile state, enervated by Harry's long illness and still recovering from an uproar over Amy. Commonsense families like the Goldsteins rarely know what to do with their artistic children—there is no real slot for them—and Amy, stuck in the middle between Betty and Harry Junior, had made some confused decisions. Against her mother's advice, she had chosen Smith. Miriam thought her younger daughter would be happier in a large co-ed school, but Amy wanted to go where Betty went. It was an unfortunate choice. Smith belonged to Betty; Amy, two years behind, was completely overshadowed by her. Betty barely acknowledged her; indeed, most of Betty's friends were unaware that she had a sister. At the end of her sophomore year Amy fell in love with Eugene Adams, a divinity student at Tufts, and planned to leave college and marry him. He was not Jewish. At home there were tremendous arguments; Harry was apoplectic and threatened to disown her. Miriam talked him out of it. Finally, they made a deal: Amy could marry Eugene if she promised to get her college degree. She finished her last two years at Simmons College in Boston.

Now Harry was making his will. He was worried about money, afraid that Miriam would squander it after he was gone and be left with nothing. He was considering leaving it to the children instead, with Betty in charge. Betty rebuffed him. She wasn't interested in his money, she said. She couldn't really believe he was serious; her mother would be humiliated by such a hostile act. They talked about her career: she was thinking about abandoning psychology and going to medical school instead. Harry thought it was a terrible idea, that her life would be wasted if she became just another doctor.

This extraordinary idea hardly makes sense in light of Harry's ambitions for Betty. He had wanted her to be a boy, had treated her like a son, and fully expected her to be a great success. Medicine was the most honored of the professions, whether the practice was general or specialized. Even considering his illness and agitation, it is difficult to believe that he thought so little of doctors. Perhaps the argument with her father was so painful that Betty garbled the remembrance of it. She wrote about this episode many years later, when she was in a state of anguish and uncertainty about her life, and his precise words may have eluded her. In any event, she and her father were at odds about her future course.

Betty spent part of her vacation in Chicago, visiting a friend and researching her master's thesis at the University of Chicago library. Paul Jordan, her friend from *Tide*, was in medical school there, and they spent some time together. He approached her sexually, but it was a repetition of her experience with her Harvard date—she could not believe he was really interested in her, and she rejected him.

On Betty's return to Peoria she had a last terrible fight with her father, who lashed out blindly and accused her of behaving like a slut. He had jangled all her nerve centers—money, sex, career, identity—and thrown into relief the elements of her discomfort. Betty blamed the fight on his illness—perhaps the hypertension had affected his brain—but she was still outraged at having been wrongly accused, and possibly angry at herself for not having been able to respond to Paul. She left Peoria without even saying goodbye to him. A few days later, on January 11, 1943, he was dead.

Betty remained stony at his funeral. She did not cry. For many years she would recall his face as she saw it at the end—"angry, cold, mean." In leaving Peoria so abruptly, she had cut him out of her life. In the same ruthless way, she would later cut off friends who, in her perception, had let her down or betrayed her.

Harry Senior had been Betty's champion, her fondest supporter, the rock upon which her confidence was built—but he had also pushed her to move beyond the limitations of her sex even before she had had a chance to sample its pleasures. She was twenty-two, and she needed to know she was desirable. His death set her free sexually. Back at Berkeley, she deliberately and coldly began to take lovers, men whose greatest asset was their availability, and from whom she received little or no pleasure. It was a brazen flouting of convention. Although the war had loosened standards, girls were still expected to save their virginity for their husbands. Betty was a passionate and sensual woman to whom sex would always be of major importance; the men with whom she now experimented were less significant in themselves than as expressions of her need. She was beginning to shape her life according to her own standards.

In Berkeley she also pursued her interest in politics. To her surprise, she felt right at home—the campus leaned distinctly to the left. "I took a room in a house [2634 Channing Way] that turned out to be a center for radicals," she recalled. "I was wearing stockings and pearls—I was the lady from Smith." One of her boyfriends, David Bohm, had joined the Communist Party in November 1942. He was a protégé of Robert Oppenheimer, who was developing the atomic bomb at Los Alamos. Bohm, a brilliant physics graduate student, worked at the Livermore Radiation Lab in the Berkeley hills, trying to isolate the Uranium-235 isotope. (He was unaware of the Manhattan Project, and there is no indication that he ever gave away secrets.) Betty joined a political study group with him, other members of which were also Communists and left-wingers.

The FBI was investigating all the bomb builders, looking for security risks. On the strength of Betty's contacts, the FBI, which already had at least one informant inside Party headquarters, began rummaging through her life. Its report on her activities is a model of its kind, filled with hearsay, misinformation, and bad grammar. (There were three reports: May, June, and September 1944, the last two updating the first.) The agents were interested in her Highlander sojourn and the fact that she had supported the maids' strike at Smith. They stated that she belonged to the Young Communist League and had been making efforts to join the Communist Party and work for *People's World,* one of the party's newspapers, which was published in San Francisco. The Party, however, viewed her unfavorably and rejected her. According to one FBI source inside Spruce Street (Party headquarters), the Party had a surfeit of "intellectuals" on the labor side, and it was thought that Betty would be more useful to their cause as a psychologist. After months of sniffing around, the FBI backed off. The agents had found no proof that Betty was a member of the Communist Party.

If indeed Betty was considering joining the Communist Party, it is doubtful that she fully understood what she would have been getting into. She was not an ideologue and would have balked at the rigidities and orthodoxies, which changed instantly at a signal from Moscow, and at the intolerance of questions and ideas. She was an activist who pushed and prodded at inequities, whatever they were, and the only party line she followed was her own. The CP would have thrown her out within a week, had she not quit first.

On March 27, she learned that she had been awarded the most coveted prize in her field, the Abraham Rosenberg Research Fellowship. It was the largest grant available at Berkeley, a stipend of $1,000, enough to take her through her Ph.D. No one had ever won it before. The news should have filled her with joy; instead, the panic that she had so resolutely ignored at Smith became acute.

Trying to explain what happened, Betty later told an interviewer, "I fell in love with a guy that...I was so much in the mood for love then...with all the brilliance, I saw myself becoming the old maid college teacher.... There were idyllic picnics with cucumber sandwiches and wine.... He said, 'You can take that fellowship, but you know I'll never get one like it. You know what it will do to us.' ... It was the kind of either/or situation that is my constant burden in life; either I pursue my career or I sublimate my wishes to a man's."

Betty presented the story as a milestone on her road to feminism, a classic conflict, a choice that was no choice. But her dilemma meant much more to her than this particular boy. Even before that fateful meeting, she had been panicked at the idea of being a psychologist. Betty was so much brighter than the men at Berkeley; she could see this story repeating itself over and over throughout her life, see herself withering away, a prune in the Groves of Academe. Not to marry was unthinkable. She remembered certain Peoria women, the old-maid librarians and teachers, the woman doctor—and even some of her college professors. "None of these women lived in the warm center of life as I had known it at home," she wrote. "Many had not married or had children. I dreaded being like them."

There was also some unfinished business with Miriam. Betty did not want to be like her mother, restless and dissatisfied. "I was determined that I would find that feminine fulfillment which had eluded my mother," she later explained to an interviewer. To Betty, fulfillment meant combining marriage and a career. If she kept the fellowship, she wouldn't find love. If she turned it down, she would be abandoning her dream of success.

There was something else too, something she did not articulate until after she became a feminist. In the early seventies, thinking about her college years, she realized that her vaunted Smith education had been hollow at the core, and that this was true of all the women's colleges. At Bryn Mawr, M. Carey Thomas could make her famous apocryphal statement, "Our failures only marry"; and Millicent McIntosh, dean of Barnard, could tell her disbelieving students that she had five children and a husband as well as her job, and so could they; but these assurances had no underpinnings. In Betty's senior year at Smith, when she was editor of *SCAN*, she had been invited to meetings with her male counterparts at Ivy League schools and noticed a difference in the way they were treated. Unlike her, they were regarded as future leaders, the next generation that would run the country. It was that expectation, that tacit support system, that had launched them and kept them afloat, she believed.

She had two weeks to decide whether to accept the fellowship. The future stretched before her, an abyss. Achievement, which she had counted on to bring her love, had driven it away. Her life had fallen apart. "Did I think I would be choosing, irrevocably, the cold loneliness of that afternoon if I went on? I gave up the fellowship in relief. But for years afterward, I could not read a word of the science that once I had thought of as my future life's work; the reminder of its loss was too painful. I never could explain, hardly knew myself, why I gave up this career."

Amid paroxysms of coughing and asthmatic wheezing, and suffering from what can best be described as a nervous breakdown, Betty retreated temporarily to Peoria. She got a summer job as a reporter on the *Peoria Evening Star*, at $25 a week. The family had scattered, Amy to Boston and Harry Junior to the army. Miriam had sold the house and was living at the Jefferson Hotel. In the fall, Betty moved to New York and found a job as assistant news editor at $30 a week for the *Federated Press*, a small left-wing newspaper agency that provided stories to labor newspapers around the country. She had already written some pieces for them at Smith.

Betty shared an apartment in Greenwich Village with college friends, first at 51 Seventh Avenue South, and then, after they had a fight with the superintendent, at 17 Grove Street. The group included, at various times, Maggie Comstock, Madelon Berns, and Aloise Buckley from *SCAN*, and Harriet Vance, Betty's old Peoria friend. Through all her future peregrinations, Betty maintained ties with these women, cherishing Harriet Vance in particular: Harriet, who belonged to one of the first families of Peoria, had been the only person to invite her to parties during that lonely year in high school, and Betty never forgot.

Writing about those youthful days, Betty made it all sound larky and insouciant, the fun-loving Bohemian life in the Village, where artists and intellectuals could breathe free and young unattached women could have flings with men they would never dream of marrying. She and her friends shopped at Bergdorf's and Bendel's for black cashmere sweaters and Gucci gloves—on sale—and read *Vogue* under the hair dryer. They "had affairs with married men—hiding our diaphragms under the garter belts and girdles in the dresser."* Some of them found jobs that had been vacated by men who went to war; others worked at the daddy-subsidized jobs available to young women—research and publicity, with low-level chic that paid psychic income—and marked time until they could get married.

In truth, Betty was miserable, deeply depressed and mourning her father. She explained away her flight from Berkeley by blaming it on an unhappy love affair with a professor. Her asthma was barely under control with drugs. She had writer's block. Her editor at the *Federated Press* had to pull her paper out of the typewriter in order to make the deadlines. And she was in psychoanalysis, where she spent most of each hour trying to

---

* Getting a diaphragm involved major strategy. Many doctors would not prescribe them even for married women. Unmarried women generally went to a clinic wearing a dime-store wedding ring and using a false name. No one asked questions.

exorcise her mother. Her mother was paying for the analysis, she told friends, because after all, she was the reason Betty needed it. The analysis was completely absorbing: at the office she told the news editor, Miriam Kolkin, that she couldn't warm up to her because Kolkin had the same first name as her mother.*

The *Federated Press* had been founded in 1919 during the nominating convention of the Farmer-Labor Party in Chicago. It viewed life as a class struggle, and its pages chronicled the tooth-and-claw relationship between business and labor. Betty covered stories with relish, doing her research and writing tough, sarcastic pieces. "She had a big personality, a rich contralto voice, and spoke very fast. She was extremely bright and conceptual," one of the editors said. She wrote about the postwar strikes against corporations that refused to bargain: "They clearly wanted to provoke the unions into striking...they counted on breaking at last the American labor movement." Another story lambasted a plan by General Motors chairman Alfred P. Sloan, Jr. (and other captains of industry), to strip labor of its power and keep the government out of business—except to "hand over its [entire] wartime industrial plant and equipment to big business." She lashed out at the "profit-greedy distributors" who were fighting the wartime Office of Price Administration to raise milk prices, and blasted General Electric for storing the refrigerators it had made before V-J Day and refusing to sell them without a price hike.

After a while her depression lifted and she began to enjoy herself. She liked the men in the office, the rough informality, the boundless cynicism, the three-martini lunches. She became the chief problem solver for her college friends, in one instance finding a minister to perform a proper ceremony for Maggie Comstock, an Episcopalian, who was marrying a divorced man. No self-respecting clergyman would do it. "She called the husband of a classmate at Yale," Maggie recalled. "He refused, but he gave us the name of a retired Presbyterian minister."

When desperate friends needed abortions, Betty was the one they asked for help. She was the worldly one, the most radical among them, the one who had delved into the mysteries of psychology and could be depended on to be sympathetic. She was also a reporter, and reporters knew how to find out things that ordinary people did not. Abortion, a word so fraught with emotional and religious connotations that it was unprintable—newspapers called it "an illegal operation"—was a criminal act, and to justify it Betty had to invent little melodramas. In one story, a

---

* As Mim Kelber (her married name), Miriam Kolkin later became one of Bella Abzug's mainstays.

desperate friend had been with a sailor who had sailed away, and how could she face her fiancé? Another distraught friend had been dallying with a union leader who, alas, was committed to his marriage, and she was sure her wealthy father would throw her out of the house if he ever found out. Betty went with her friends to hidden rooms in back alleys and waited fearfully, hoping they wouldn't die; when the operation was finished, she took them home in taxis.

The *FP* staff socialized together and spent a lot of time hanging out at the bar in the Newpaper Guild building. Betty's circle included Communists, socialists, and pacifists, blacks and working-class people who never would have made it to the Bluff. She was living a kind of cashmere Marxist life, with two groups of friends that didn't mesh. Gladys Carter, who handled foreign news for the *FP*, said, "Smith friends came to New York a lot. She had a love-hate thing with them. She wanted to remain attached, wanted the connection, but sneered at them because of their foolish values. They just wanted a rich marriage, nothing fulfilling. She had very strong social views. She thought she was working for a place that was the advance guard for rights. And she had more of a rapport with people in that context than with Smith people. But Betty was finding it too difficult to take orders to ever be involved."

Betty and Gladys Carter became close friends. Gladys was a younger, less worldly woman who had grown up without Betty's class comforts, but they had something in common: "We both had an outstandingly good-looking sister," Gladys said. "We shared it—there is a pretty one, and you are not it. She had no feeling that her mother loved and supported her. Her father respected and valued her. She never regarded herself as beautiful. It was her intellect. She was always aware that she could succeed in things of intellectual capacity. She was always looking for the way to become a success. She wanted to be someone who was recognized as having achieved. Not fame. She was a hard worker, dogged and very conscientious."

Soon her Smith friends began to get married—Harriet Vance went back to Peoria to marry John Parkhurst; Madelon Berns married Bob Bedell, an engineer, and went to live in the south of France for a few years—and Betty moved to her own place, a small one-bedroom basement apartment in a brownstone at 8 West Eighty-sixth Street. It had a terrace in back, but no kitchen. Cooking was not on her mind. According to a co-worker, "She was not lonely. She was insecure. She had to prove herself with men. It was very important for her." She told people she had been engaged to someone overseas and gotten a Dear Jane letter and then went out and got drunk for a couple of days. (The "engagement" may have been a dramatization of her relationship to the Harvard man who was so impressed with her left-wing politics.) She double-dated with Miriam Kolkin and Fred Zeserson, the picture editor, and vacationed with Gladys on Fire Island, a hunting ground for singles. It was cheap and informal and had a spectacularly wide beach. "She went out with married men a lot," Gladys said. "There wasn't much else around. She was more sexually active than most. She was not a hypocrite. She was very straightforward about it."

The affairs tended to be unhappy. None of her men truly appreciated her. They liked her companionship, her vitality, her body, but never *her*, never her real self. Betty was not one to confide her deepest sorrows, but, said Gladys, "a few times, when we were drunk, it would spill out. She felt she was used by men because she was not their idea of what they wanted. There was a lot of conflict and resentment, feelings not reciprocated."

Betty was particularly hurt by an affair with Mike Krich, a writer who became a psychologist and taught at Columbia. He looked like Humphrey Bogart, she thought, with a "sardonic glint in his eyes." He was impressed enough by her to make her a character in *Sweethearts,* a novel he later wrote about his sexual escapades.* They made love on the beach, and she told her friends how wonderful it was. "He was her boyfriend and she was very attracted to him, but he found someone else," Gladys said. "It was an in-depth relationship. She was all broken up about it." They ran into him after the breakup, stirring old embers, and Betty, with her instinct for drama, staged a maudlin mock-suicide. "We were sitting at a bar at Ocean Beach, drinking martinis," Gladys said. "She decided she was going to drown herself. She was drunk. I pulled her back from the water. She was not really suicidal. The rest of the vacation—five or six days—was very pleasant."

All this time Gladys had been engaged. Just before the war ended her fiancé, Dick Carter, came home on a furlough, and they decided to marry immediately. It was going to be a City Hall wedding with just a few close family members in attendance, and Gladys couldn't invite Betty. But Betty, who hated to be left out of anything, came anyway. "It's one of the warmest gestures I can remember about her," Gladys said. "It's something

* He described her as a brave and brilliant, highly sexed woman whose favorite word was "polarization," who spoke "in question marks and exclamation points," and who "already had one foot in the door to important places." In the novel, their idyll ends suddenly when he runs into his old love at a Newspaper Guild Christmas party and marries her a few months later.

I always cherished." "I had to be here," she told Gladys. "I had to give you guys a kiss."

The end of the war brought changes to the *Federated Press*. In June 1945 a man named James Peck, the heir to Peck & Peck, a chain of shops that sold tailored clothes for women, was released from Danbury Prison, where he had been jailed for the duration as a conscientious objector. He came back to claim his job. Betty had been his wartime replacement, and under Newspaper Guild rules, he had seniority. Betty put up a terrific fight, but she couldn't win. She freelanced for a while, but the *FP* decided she was too good to lose—her stories were widely used by subscribers— and she was rehired in January 1946 at $60 a week.

A month later, she ran into trouble. Marc Stone, the brother of I. F. Stone, returned from the army to manage the *FP*'s Eastern bureau. The chemistry between him and Betty was poisonous. Stone insisted on control; she couldn't take orders. He had a temper to match hers, and the office rang with their insults and venomous fights. During one fight, she handed him a story and he threw it on the floor. During another, he threw a telephone book at her. If Marc was arrogant, said a staff member, "Betty was impossible to deal with."

Marc decided to reorganize the bureau. He planned to downgrade the news editor (he didn't like Miriam Kolkin, either) to assistant (Betty's job), get "a topflight new news editor," and force Betty to resign. His plot was foiled by the staff. The *FP* was run democratically, by a majority vote, and the staff voted no. Stone tried other tactics. He stopped giving Betty assignments and sent Fred Zeserson to cover stories that should have been hers. In one case he hired a freelancer to cover a story she had suggested. "I wouldn't send you to cover a dog fight," he told her. "Personally, I have no use for you whatsoever." Betty complained to the Guild's grievance committee, but nothing was done. In the end, she left.

In July 1946, the United Electrical, Radio and Machine Workers of America hired her as a reporter for their official organ, the weekly *UE News*. The paper ran the same sorts of stories as the *FP*. That same year she met Carl Friedan, home from the war.

4

Love

"HE BROUGHT ME an apple and told me jokes which made me laugh, and he moved in," Betty wrote in a brief, unsatisfactory, and rather flip account of her introduction to Carl. Their courtship grew out of a confluence of time and necessity (she was twenty-six, he twenty-eight), of strong sexual attraction, and overpowering emotional needs, and if the elements that composed it were perverse, they were binding. Betty and Carl were an improbable liaison between a Smith Phi Bete and a University of Massachusetts dropout, a girl who was chauffeured and a boy who had to hitchhike, a woman whose concerns were universal and a man who hugged the fringes. Marriages have been built on shakier structures and endured. The Friedans' lasted for almost twenty-two years, until the dynamic between them changed.

Carl Friedman was born in Chelsea, outside Boston, on September 22, 1919, the second of three boys, Hillel (Henry), the oldest, and Mark. His parents named him Casper Judah. His mother's sister, Ida, considered the name so ugly and created such a ruckus that after two weeks it was changed to Carl. Both parents had emigrated from Latvia, his mother as an infant, his father at sixteen, but, unlike Betty's father, for Leo Friedman the streets were not paved with gold. "He never got on with America,"

Carl said. "He was a highly skilled jeweler who worked on $300,000 rings at Shreve's in Boston and ruined his eyes." During the Depression he earned only $15 a week. The Friedmans lived in slums and moved frequently, one step ahead of the landlord. During the worst times they moved in with his mother's parents.

Matilda Shapiro, Carl's mother, suffered like Betty's under the constraints governing females. "She graduated from the eighth grade at the top of her class, but her father, a Talmudic scholar, refused to send her on." In the Orthodox tradition, the men studied and the women worked, keeping things going against wrenching odds. Carl's grandmother ran a dry-goods store. His mother worked as a secretary to the owner of a supermarket chain. She thought of herself as an intellectual and felt she had married beneath her. Her husband read only newspapers. Carl worked on weekends; he earned $1.75 on Saturday delivering grocery store orders, and on Sunday he had a paper route.

It was a loveless house whose anger and bitterness warped his childhood. "My mother had no love to give," he said. "She approved of nothing I did." Carl considered his mother "a hysteric. She and my father screamed at each other continually. She would threaten to kill herself. I never saw my father and mother kiss."

Carl was wild and untended and might have been utterly lost had it not been for his mother's younger sister, Polly. She bought him toys and baseball gloves and took him to the movies on Sunday. He did well in grade school and went on to Boston Latin, considered one of the best high schools in the country. Carfare was a nickel; sometimes Carl bought an ice cream cone and walked. He spent six years at Boston Latin and learned French and German.

His real life, however, was lived in a world of his own invention. Carl spent all his free time at vaudeville shows, learning to perform magic tricks. He practiced for hours. His mother did not approve of the theatre and thought magic a waste of time, but Carl was encouraged by his father, who built him a bird cage that he could make disappear, along with the bird inside. Magic became the passion and consolation of his teen years, his escape route, his means of transcendence. He became someone else, transforming himself into a wondrous, omnipotent creature, Carlyn the Magician, who could break the laws of the universe. He drove around New England to engagements that he booked himself—at vaudeville shows and summer hotels and camps—in a battered old Ford. Wearing a tuxedo, he produced rabbits and doves; he did memory tricks, and sleight-of-hand with cards and lighted cigarettes. His audiences loved it. He was applauded and appreciated.

When Carl was sixteen he started using the name Friedan; he wanted to be distinctive, he said. "I was going into the theatre, and there were half a dozen Friedmans in the theatre." (After he went into analysis, his Freudian therapist told him that he had taken out the "man" and the "ma.") When he and Betty married, Friedman was still his legal name. Betty also liked Friedan better than either Friedman or Goldstein. It was unique, self-created. In the 1960s, when they needed a passport to go to Antigua, they changed their name legally.

After Boston Latin, Carl went to the University of Massachusetts, a low-tuition land-grant college. He lived on fifteen-cent bread-and-bean dinners. In his second year he got a job as a maintenance man in a fraternity house in Amherst in return for a free room, but the job didn't last long. He was fired after a furnace accident in which he almost burned down the house. "He was always a rebel and very unconventional," said Al Silverman, a friend who went through high school and college with Carl, and became first a historian and then a businessman. "He was a very ingenious, innovative young man, but he was never successful dating. He was sexually insecure." Carl's academic career was also stunted—he was aimless, unfocused. "I never studied and always came out at the top in physics and math, but I never carried it through to real expertise," he said. Instead of studying, he hitchhiked from Amherst to Springfield to the vaudeville shows. Like Betty, he was drawn to the theatre, another kind of magic, a deeper escape. After two years, he transferred to Emerson College in Boston, a school entirely devoted to the theatre; there he studied playwriting, acting, and directing for a year. The following summer he got a job as an electrician at Oak Bluffs Theatre in Martha's Vineyard, and did magic shows in the mountains. On September 10, 1942, he enlisted in the U.S. Army Signal Corps.

Carl chose the Signal Corps for its amenities. It offered a nine-month civilian course, and he thought the war would be over by then. After basic training at Fort Monmouth, New Jersey, he went into the Army Specialized Training Program (ASTP) at New York University and studied the German language and culture in preparation for the Allied occupation. He lived just off Washington Square and more or less lolled around New York. During this time he fell deeply in love with a young woman named Ruth. "She was voted the prettiest girl in high school," he said. Carl was very serious about her, but she was involved with a Navy man.

Suddenly, the European offensive was on, and infantrymen were needed. Carl was assigned to an antitank division, the 69th Regimental, and shipped to Camp Shelby, Mississippi, to brush up on basic training.

He arrived in Scotland on the *Ile de France* in October 1944, and fought his way across Europe in some of the bloodiest battles of the war. Carl could never speak of these experiences, not even to Betty. His company was decimated. They took Leipzig in April 1945 and stopped there, waiting for the Russians.

After V-E Day, Carl became technical director of the Mickey Rooney Soldiers Show Company in Paris and traveled all over Europe with portable stage sets that he designed. They did *Golden Boy*, and *Up in Arms* with Danny Kaye. Carl drove his own jeep and threw parties in the château outside Paris where the company lived. "It was the most carefree time of my life," he said. He left the Army in February 1946 with a Bronze Star, and came to New York to look for work in the theatre.

As luck had it, virtually the only person Carl knew in New York was Fred Zeserson, an Army buddy who had preceded Carl out of the Signal Corps and was working with Betty at the *Federated Press*. Carl had found a walkup on 105th Street and was trying to live on his $20-a-week discharge money. Fred "knew a nice girl with an apartment," and Carl went over one evening on a blind date.

They had a late supper at Barney Greengrass, the Sturgeon King, a famous appetizer store, where Betty ordered one of the most expensive sandwiches on the menu. Carl, who had never had money, was scandalized. Betty was fascinated. Carl was altogether eligible. He was attractive and intelligent, with brown eyes and wavy hair, a broad nose, and an overbite. At five feet eight inches and 150 pounds, he did not cut a swath—he was even a bit nondescript—but Betty had enough presence for both of them. He had a Boston accent, which he kept all his life, and a quirky, offbeat sense of humor.

Carl was different from all her other men, and Betty pursued him; a week after they met, she went to Fred's on a Sunday afternoon to find him. Quite simply, she fell in love with him. They did not go to bed the night they met, but they did soon after, and within two months Carl moved in. They were both earthy people; they loved detective stories and the beach, and they talked for hours about the theatre and politics. Carl was neither as radical nor as committed as Betty was. His father was a socialist and had taken him to hear Eugene Debs and Norman Thomas speak, but Carl had remained skeptical. FDR was his idol.

Whatever their attractions to each other, as a couple Betty and Carl were an enigma to their friends. "We were surprised," said one of Betty's friends. "Carl was certainly not up to her intellectually, or to her interests. He was not good enough for her. She married him because she wanted to get married." On the other hand, Carl's friend Al Silverman said, "Betty couldn't get a guy. She was homely, with very few feminine qualities. No softness, charm, or warmth. She was bright, but she was obnoxious—a know-it-all. She was lucky to get Carl."

It was certainly true that Betty wanted to get married. Marriage was the ultimate proof of her femininity, a public announcement that she could compete and be successful as a woman. It was doubly important now that her dream of success had been thwarted, and she had little else to show for her life. If she did not have a big career, she had a man. Betty had been fazed before by the men of her own class, and a marriage to one of them seemed unlikely. Further, Carl's very deficiencies were reasons to marry him. If he was not her equal in education, ambition, and social standing, then she had the upper hand. She could control the relationship.

For his part, Carl needed Betty as desperately as she needed him. Above all, he was attracted by her warmth. She was a woman who could create a home out of nothing. She gave him a life—friends, parties, a whole world. Carl was frightened and uncertain, looking for a lifeboat. He thought he could be saved. "I was lonely in the city, and I moved in," he said. "It was comfortable, but it wasn't real love. She had an underlying warmth. She was in analysis. I knew I had a need for it [analysis]. That was an attraction. And just being lonesome. And getting sex regularly. You just fall into it. She was never my fantasy."

Even after they decided to marry, the omens were not encouraging. There was always a fight going on, like a persistent, low-grade infection. Carl was the cooler of the two. During flareups, he would offer to leave before Betty could throw him out. "No one expected them to get married," Gladys Carter said. "They fought and he called her names. They fought about everything, the most insignificant things. He was leaving the house and she wasn't ready, or he was looking for something and she had moved it. Betty fought with most people. She expected to fight."

Betty and Carl had their own doubts, which they decided to ignore. Neither measured up to the other's ideal. Each was secretly ashamed of the other. It bothered Betty that Carl had dropped out of school, and she didn't think he was responsible about money. An irreparable wound opened, one that might have been fatal if Betty had been less determined, when she found a letter he had written to his parents, describing his bride-to-be: she wasn't much to look at, he said, but she was so bright that he would never have to worry about money. (In Carl's memory, the part about the money was a joke.) When they went to Boston to visit his parents, Betty had an asthma attack, and she wondered later if she should have heeded its warning. She didn't know Carl's biggest secret: he was still in love with Ruth, who had married her Navy man.

They had to get married twice. They set the date for Sunday, June 15, 1947, in Boston, but they couldn't get married in Boston without a license, and they didn't have time to go up there and get one. They solved the problem by having a civil ceremony first, in New York. On Thursday the twelfth, they went to City Hall, across from Betty's office, on her lunch hour. Fred Zeserson and Gladys and Dick Carter were their witnesses. They all wore street clothes. Carl had such a bad case of premarital jitters that he considered not showing up for the ceremony, but things had gone too far, and his needs were greater than his doubts. "It was as if I were controlled by outside forces," he said. "I was pushed along, and this was the way it was going." After the ceremony they went to a bar and drank stingers to celebrate.

Betty and Carl had originally wanted a big New York wedding, but Carl's mother had other ideas. Traditionally, the bride's family has the wedding on home territory and pays for it, but Carl's mother, whom Betty detested, managed to move it to Boston and finesse Betty's mother (who had remarried and was now Mrs. Elmore Katz) into footing the bill anyway. "She said she was sick and we had to come to Boston," Carl said. About sixty guests came. "It was all Carl's relatives," Betty said.

Betty wore a light blue silk Indian dress and a flowered wreath around her head. The wedding was held in a hall with a huppa and a kosher dinner. Miriam came, and so did Amy, with her minister. Harry was in the Army. Grandfather Horwitz, who was in his eighties, was the hit of the wedding. "He wore an American Legion hat. He was pleased about my medals. My family loved him. He was like a Gilbert and Sullivan character," Carl said. (Recalling her wedding many years later, Betty did not remember her grandfather being present.)

That summer Carl put together an acting company for the Lakeside Summer Theatre in New Jersey, so the Friedans delayed their honeymoon until the end of the season. Betty came up with the idea of a group house at Lake Hopatcong, an inexpensive colony of cabins around the lake, near the theatre. She enlisted the Carters, the Zesersons, and a third couple, the Aronsons (Jimmy Aronson worked for another labor paper). They rented two two-bedroom houses, only one of which had indoor plumbing. After intense negotiations, they decided that since Carl was going to be there all week, he and Betty would stay in the main house; and since Fred's wife, Ruth, was pregnant, the Zesersons would also stay in the main house. That having been settled, they took up the housekeeping agenda, making rules about sharing food, cooking and cleaning, and scheduling guests. Betty and Carl, who were not particularly interested in house-keeping, ignored most of the rules. "Somewhere along the line, the kitchen would be a mess when we arrived," Gladys Carter said. "Dirty stove, sink counters. You'd come in, and there would be all this greasy gook. It was Carl and Betty. [Betty, who was working full-time at the *UE News*, usually managed to get out early.] After a while, we just cleaned it up. Then they decided our tastes were too upscale, and we shouldn't bring so much food. They pointed out that they didn't eat as much, and Carl was eating at the theatre, so they should contribute less money. Others pointed out that Carl was there all week with the leftover food. Finally we com-promised—they had a shelf in the fridge."

In the matter of weekend guests, signals kept getting crossed. "Betty never paid attention to whose turn it was to have guests," Gladys said. "We would bring someone out, and she would too, and say, 'Oh, you have guests? But this is the only weekend my guests could come; you'll really like them.' " Through it all they managed to remain friends, although the Aronsons swore they would never share with anyone again, and the Carters decided never to share with the Friedans again.

The Friedans edged into their life together as if venturing into a mine field, presaging the long battle that it would become. Forty-seven years later, Carl remembered giving Betty a detective story to read on the train to Hopatcong. "For a sadistic gag, I ripped out the last chapter," he said, still smiling at the joke. Betty couldn't help but notice that he didn't want her around the theatre. One day, while they were rowing on the lake, she began to cry. "You don't love me," she said. "It was all a mistake." Carl tried to reassure her—he was working eighteen hours a day, and he couldn't be with her—but Betty knew.

However disappointing those early months were, the Friedans had a joyous, loving honeymoon. When the summer stock season was over, they drove to Maine. They stayed in Kennebunkport and went to Mount Wash-ington in New Hampshire. Then they canoed down Long Lake to the Songas River and camped on a sandy beach. Alone in a magnificent forest, in the outdoors, which Betty loved, they found each other for a while. She hadn't really made a mistake; the marriage would work out after all. Betty believed that Carl fell in love with her on their honeymoon.

That fall they went to Peoria for Harry's wedding to Inette Cohen, whose family owned the biggest furniture store in town. Harry had fallen in love with Inette when he was seventeen, before the Army shipped him overseas in 1943. On his return, he went to UCLA, and Inette transferred there from the University of Minnesota. He decided to be a lawyer and was very excited at being accepted to Harvard Law School, but his father-in-law persuaded him to try out the business, and he remained in Peoria, ultimately becoming one of its leading citizens.

At the wedding, a lavish affair, Betty and Carl got drunk, embarrassing Harry: they were unpleasant drunks, loud and belligerent. But something about this big family gathering, the energy and connectedness, all the little children running around, touched them and transformed them, and they decided to have a child. "It was just that," said Carl. "We never talked about the future. We just gravitated into it."

Daniel Friedan was born on October 3, 1948, at the Flower–Fifth Avenue Hospital. Betty had been looking forward to the birth, to participating in this most miraculous of experiences, but Danny was born by caesarean section, and she was deeply disappointed. (In less exalted moments she understood perfectly well that even cows have babies, but this was the time of her "feminine fulfillment.") In the larger scheme of things, her actual participation in the birth mattered hardly at all. When the doctor decided on a caesarean, he went to Carl, not Betty, for permission. Carl waited on the front porch of the hospital, across the street from Central Park at 105th Street, crying uncontrollably. He didn't know why. They designed the birth announcement in the form of a theatrical ad: "A Friedan Production," across the top, and underneath, "Carl & Betty present Daniel Harry Friedan / World Premiere Oct 3rd, 1948 / 'Sensational' / —Walter Winchell. / 'A Smash Hit!' / —Variety. / Friedan Playhouse 8 West 86th St., N.Y.C." Carl painted the steam pipes on the ceiling, enlarged the cooking area, and wrote "Welcome Danny" on the mirror. They gave the baby the little back bedroom for a nursery and moved their bed into the living room.

On maternity leave from the *UE News,* Betty breast-fed Danny, wheeled him in the park, and immersed herself in Dr. Spock. She bought *The Modern House,* by George Nelson, and the basic cookbook for beginners, *The Joy of Cooking,* by Irma S. Rombauer and Marion Rombauer Becker. The Friedans were becoming part of that most despised and sneered-at class, "the bourgeoisie." Betty changed her mind about accepting the sterling silver her mother had wanted to give her as a wedding present—it had seemed so middle class. Now they wanted "things." Even the language they were using changed: the word "bourgeois" dropped out of circulation. "We were like our parents after all," she wrote.

Faced with a family to support, Carl was becoming overwhelmed by the same panic that had gripped Betty in her last year at Smith. "It was *me,* the job, I didn't know what I wanted to do. I was paralyzed," he said. Carl was an entrepreneur. He created his entire stock company from scratch—hiring, negotiating, managing, producing—and cleared over $4000 for the season. It was good money, but it ended on Labor Day.

Summer stock could be a gateway to a career in the theatre. In the 1940s, Broadway was at the peak of its greatness and glamour. Tennessee Williams, Arthur Miller, and Eugene O'Neill were writing, and hit musicals followed each other in glittering procession. Dozens of new plays opened each season. Intellectuals considered the movies second-rate, merely pop; the theatre, being live, was the finer art. There were hundreds of little summer playhouses around the country, filled with actors hoping to be discovered. Established stars played the leading roles—they were the draw—and big Broadway producers came to the shows. A few lucky people were lifted from obscurity—but Carl was not one of them. "I was never able to get together enough money to become a Broadway producer," he said.

Carl began publishing an annual guide, the *Summer Theatre Handbook*. He hustled for ads and wrote articles for the guide, but its earning power was limited. Betty was supporting the family with her $100-a-week salary, and she was not too happy about it. She wanted Carl to find a job in television, which was just beginning; he had a definite talent for advertising and publicity, she thought. During the winter of 1948 Carl went out every day, pretending to hunt for a job, but he was frozen with fear, incapable of presenting himself anywhere. He finally confessed to Betty, who persuaded him to borrow money from his aunt Polly and go into analysis. "A great deal of my analysis was how to deal with Betty," he said. He worked with a Freudian from Vienna who told him, to his dismay, that Betty was his mother; he had married his mother. Nevertheless, he managed to start his advertising career, going into a small venture with Fred Zeserson. Although he became more confident, he continued to shy away from the big agencies, always remaining unpolished, an outsider. "I think I was afraid to compete," he said. "I was always unsure of myself."

The apartment at 8 West Eighty-sixth Street had been designed for one person and was too crowded for the Friedan family. They moved to a roach-infested five-room apartment at 660 Riverside Drive at 148th Street, on the edge of Harlem. Gladys and Dick Carter lived a few blocks away, at number 790. In the 1948 elections, Betty campaigned for Henry Wallace, and she and Gladys stumped on street corners for their congressman, Vito Marcantonio, the American Labor Party candidate, who was considered the most left-wing member of the House of Representatives. By the summer of 1949, less than a year after Danny's birth, Betty had found a nurse for him and was back at work: the *UE News* had cut short her maternity leave. Betty continued to work for the UE until 1952, when she was pregnant with her second child. She enjoyed her job enormously, for the stimulation and the people, but she always looked back in anger at the union. Many times she wrote and spoke with eloquence and indignation of how the UE fired her rather than grant her a second maternity leave, and the story became a landmark in the Friedan annals, the first glimmer of her feminism. She told the story at length in a 1974 *New York* magazine article but changed the date and telescoped events to conform to the issue's theme, that 1949 had been a turning point in American life. Betty wrote that 1949 was the year the feminine mystique began to close in on her.

After she was fired, Betty complained to the woman who headed the grievance committee, who told her that it was her own fault for getting pregnant. She tried to rally her coworkers, but no one, male or female, supported her. The concept of sex discrimination, she said, did not exist. She also wrote that the union had replaced her with a man.

The actual circumstances were somewhat more complicated. In the 1940s and 1950s, women were fired as a matter of course for being pregnant. It was a standard practice to which they were supposed to acquiesce, and some of them even quit in advance. Betty, however, was entitled to a year's maternity leave under her union contract. The union might have decided to ignore that clause, as she said, but she was already restless. For one thing, she resented being shut out of the all-male meetings; for another, she saw no way to get ahead in her job. In July 1951 she applied to *Fortune* magazine for a job as a researcher, work that was well below her capacities. For Betty to have considered such a job indicates that she was unhappy at the *UE News* a year before she left. At the same time, the union, which published the newspaper, was going through its own trial by fire. These events cast doubt on her statement that she was fired.

In 1952 the postwar Red hunt was in full cry. The United Electrical Workers union, whose ranks were filled with Communists, was in double jeopardy, under siege by both the left and the right. Within, a minority faction of Communists schemed to take control (and succeeded). Without, the main force of the government—the FBI, the House Un-American Activities Committee (HUAC), Senator Joseph R. McCarthy, Jr., chair of the Investigations Subcommittee—was engaged in rooting out "security risks." Blacklists and loyalty oaths were the order of the day, guilt by association a casual assumption.

The hysterical atmosphere gave corporations a perfect reason not to negotiate with unions. In order to stay alive, the CIO, of which the UE was a member, had kicked it out in 1949 and set up a rival union untainted by Communists. The UE lost two-thirds of its membership, some of them to jail. (The *Federated Press* was also affected. In 1956 it folded.) The *UE News* went from weekly to bi-weekly and lost half its 400,000 circulation. It no longer needed all four members of its staff. Two were enough. Who should be let go? Tom Wright, the managing editor, had been there the longest. He and his wife and co-worker, Katherine Beecher (a descendant of the nineteenth-century antisuffragist Catharine Beecher), decided that she would leave. That left Betty and Jim Lerner, with whom she shared an office. She and Lerner worked together; they took the paper to the printers, and they traveled to various cities to cover stories and conventions. "We were very close, we were friends," Lerner said. "The decision was left to us. I had been there two years longer than Betty, and she was pregnant for the second time. She thought I would have a more difficult time finding a job. She accepted it. No way was there an intention to use her pregnancy against her. She agreed that in view of the circumstances it would be more logical for her to leave."*

Two of Betty's friends from the *Federated Press*, Miriam Kolkin and Fred Zeserson, agree with Lerner. But Nathan Spero, the electrical union's research director, who worked with Betty on stories, champions her: "Beecher went first because she was married. There were no other professional women in the *UE News* or the national office. It was hypocritical to release only women, considering the ideals and principles of the union. Betty was a better writer than Jim. She was a wonderful writer with great ideas. But the officers of the union decided. The policies they professed for negotiations were more advanced than the actual feelings in the office."†

However it happened, Betty left the *UE News* in 1952. With the exception of the *New York* story, of the nine years she devoted to the cause of labor there is scarcely a word in her books or magazine pieces. In interviews she dismissed the entire period as having no importance, as if she had been just passing the time. In one sense, she believed she was. After her precipitous fall from the heights of Smith, there was no movement in her career, no dramatic achievement she could point to.

* In Betty's recollection, the paper was downsized *after* she left, and she left *before* Katherine Beecher.
† The records that would verify one story or the other no longer exist, and the man who would have fired Betty is dead.

There were other reasons to remain silent. The rout of the Old Left and the trauma of the Red hunt remained long after the furor died down. In 1963, when Betty wrote *The Feminine Mystique,* things had shifted, but they hadn't changed—the intellectual focus of America had moved from the political to the sociological, but HUAC was still operating, and the civil rights movement was being Red-baited just as the labor movement had been. Betty would have lost her credibility as the leader of the women's movement had she let her old allegiances be known. She also had her public image to protect: She had become BETTY FRIEDAN, the suburban housewife who had fought her way through the mystique.

During her years as a labor reporter Betty received a complete education in women's issues, but there was no "click," no moment of truth. The UE was the most progressive of the labor unions. Years ahead of its time, it championed equal pay and maternity leave for women (though not unanimously), and some of its members favored revamping the sacred seniority rules to compensate blacks for having been previously excluded. (In practice, however, these ideals tended to fall apart. During bargaining, equal pay and other such benefits were the most negotiable items on the agenda and the first to be dropped.) Betty wrote about women for both the *FP* and the *UE News.* In "Pretty Posters Won't Stop Turnover of Women in Industry," one of her earliest "Wartime Living" columns for the *FP,* she discussed women on the assembly line who went home to a second job—shopping, cooking, laundry, housekeeping—and the difficulties of finding child care. There were many other such stories, culminating in a 1952 pamphlet, "UE Fights for Women Workers," whose thirty-nine pages detailed discrimination against working women by corporations and the double bind of black women. In May 1953, she went to the first national women's conference on record in the labor movement, the UE's National Conference on the Problems of Working Women. A guest speaker there said, "Women must be treated as equal members of society, not as recipients of favors." The words did not resonate.

5

Suburban Housewife

IN THE FALL of 1951, a year before she left the *UE News*, Betty heard about Parkway Village, a garden apartment development in Jamaica, Queens. It had been built to house United Nations employees, many of whom were unable to find decent housing outside of Harlem. Residential segregation was almost total except around the edges of black neighborhoods, where poor whites lived. Ex-GIs were also welcome at Parkway Village. The Friedans moved into a four-and-a-half-room apartment, renting for $118.50 a month. It was a little expensive, but there was a co-op nursery for Danny and a lawn where children could play.

Parkway Village was a unique international community where people lived out the ideals of the U.N.—the brotherhood of man, all races and religions living harmoniously together. Families wore their native dress and spoke their native language; together they organized committees to build playgrounds and get the garbage collected. Parkway Village was Betty's first experiment in an extended family, an idea that she would pursue later in her life and develop into a commune. She brought in the Carters and the Zesersons; the Carters brought in Alice and Harold Mehling. Through the International Nursery School they met two other couples, the Aaron Wassermans and the Tom Wolfs. They were young and idealistic, and they felt they were contributing to international understanding. Hal Mehling was a magazine writer. Dick Carter, a freelancer, later won a Polk award for a book on waterfront crime and wiretapping, and wrote a biography of Jonas Salk. Fred Zeserson would build a medical publishing business. Tom Wolf became a documentary film producer and vice president at ABC News. The six families saw one another constantly. They took care of one another's children and shared houses on Lake George and Fire Island in the summer. They were an extended family under whose protective umbrella rocky marriages could continue to flourish. There would be three divorces and one suicide in the group.

Their lives duplicated those of millions of other young married couples. They relaxed on spare modern furniture—inexpensive Eames plywood chairs, or sling-back canvases: improvisational decor. Carl came up with the idea of cutting down doors and putting foam rubber mattresses on them as beds for the children. They grilled hamburgers on charcoal barbecue grills and dipped their potato chips into the universal dip of the 1950s, sour cream mixed with dried Lipton's Onion Soup. Betty made salad dressing and supervised a maid who cooked. "She [Betty] introduced me to artichokes and avocados and other things I had never had before," Carl said. "I was from the slums. I learned some of the niceties from her." In a secular way, they celebrated Christmas and Passover together, treating Passover as an emancipation, and connecting it with black civil rights. "Betty thought that religion was something that messed up your brain," Gladys Carter said. At a Parkway Village Spring Festival costume party, Betty and Carl went as Senator Joseph McCarthy and Roy Cohn. Betty wore a gorilla costume and waved a roll of toilet paper, ranting, "I have here in my hand..."* Betty saw to it that the group had an intellectual life; she invited people from the U.N. to come and speak about their country. "Betty was a doer," one of the group said. "She had extraordinary intellectual energy. It was just there."

What the group did more of than anything else was drink. In common with the rest of America, where drinking was considered one of the social graces, and people had long liquid lunches before coming home to their cocktail shakers, they sloshed down vast quantities of alcohol. Carl called them the Martini Group. He and Betty drank more than the others. Alco-

---

* Senator McCarthy had a habit of waving pieces of paper around and claiming they were lists of Communists he had discovered in the State Department or some other department. When his power was broken in 1954, he had not discovered a single one.

hol allowed them to indulge their worst impulses and behave outrageously to each other; it blurred the anger and disappointments that were turning their marriage into what a writer would later call "a sadomasochistic free-for-all." At parties, Gladys said, "Carl never let you empty your glass, so you never had any idea how much you were drinking. Everyone was smashed."

. . .

While Betty was pregnant with her second child, Jonathan, Carl began an affair. All these years, he had been carrying a torch for Ruth, the woman he had fallen in love with when he was in the Army. Her marriage hadn't worked; now she was divorced and living in New Jersey. Betty heard the news first from mutual friends. "Your old girlfriend is back," she told Carl. He was electrified. He rushed to see Ruth immediately. "Betty didn't know," he said, but she did, and she was profoundly angry and jealous. Her asthma had returned after she left the *UE News*, and she went back into analysis. She began a flirtation (she called it "a fantasy romance") with Tom Wolf, whose marriage was beginning to fray, but it ended as her other putative romances had: when he became serious, she wouldn't let herself believe he really cared about her, and she rebuffed him.

The affair between Carl and Ruth lasted for two months. "When Ruth came back, I realized how important it was," Carl said, "She was loving and giving, everything Betty wasn't. She was like my aunt Polly. I pushed her to get a job on a magazine. She was two blocks from me at work. She sewed the buttons on my overcoat." But whatever had prevented their marrying in the past prevented it again. This time, Ruth said she didn't want to destroy Carl's marriage and ended the affair. In any event, it is highly unlikely that Carl would actually have gone through with a divorce and left Betty while she was pregnant.

. . .

In Peoria, Betty's mother had decided to liquidate the Goldstein Jewelry Company. She had considered selling it after her husband's death in 1943, but Harry Junior was going overseas then, and she was superstitious, fearing that if she sold the business he might die, too. Betty, Amy, and Harry Junior had each inherited a small amount of stock in the company, and now the Friedans needed the money. Betty no longer had her

$100 a week from the *UE News*, and Carl's career was still rickety. Harry Junior said, "My feeling was that Carl persuaded her—the business had meaning for her, and Mother was taking it all, and Betty should assert her rights. It led to rancor. Mother lived above her means. Carl and Betty resented it. I thought we were fortunate that [the store] was supporting Mother. Betty and Carl thought she was living this high life—'Let us have some, we deserve it.' There was a long period when there was no communication. They [Betty and Miriam] had a very volatile relationship until the last two years of Mother's life."

Betty's relationship with Harry Junior deteriorated also. On a visit to Peoria they had a tense argument about politics and McCarthyism. The argument turned into a shouting match, with nasty accusations and wild threats. Inette, horrified at this assault on her husband, ordered Betty to get out of the house and never come back. Betty's politics had always been a sore point with her conservative brother. It embarrassed him when the *Peoria Journal* ran an innocuous little story mentioning that she was working for the labor press. Attitudes toward labor in Peoria hadn't changed much since Betty went to Highlander Folk School, and wrote (in "Learning the Score") that her father's friends thought their workers ought to be grateful for whatever they got. "Betty was right on the edge of the envelope," Harry said. "She went as far as you could, as far left as you could be."

Betty stormed out of Harry's house, but she had second thoughts. When Jonathan was about to be born, she became frightened. Danny's had been a difficult birth, and, medical opinion being that once a caesarean always a caesarean, she was afraid of being sliced up again. She thought she might die. "She wrote me a letter of apology," Harry said. "A very nice letter. She wanted to clean the slate of her life. She was never one to put out a lot of apologies. She had the wonderful ability of unloading. She never bottled it up, she just unloaded. She apologized for having lost her temper. My wife—it was hard for her to forgive and forget. Betty was so volatile, she [Inette] thought it best that 'never the twain shall meet.' That was her way of surviving unpleasant relationships. So we didn't resume." Betty and Harry kept in touch sporadically—neither wanted to lose the other—until the late 1970s, when Harry's daughter, Laurie, called Betty and brought about a reconciliation.

After Jonathan was born, on November 27, 1952 (by caesarean), Betty began a new career as a freelance writer. She had always felt guilty about leaving Danny. He was well taken care of—he went to the International

Nursery School, and Betty had a housekeeper—but Betty was the only mother she knew who worked full-time, and she worried about the effect her absence might have on Danny. She and Gladys Carter, who taught English as a second language, talked about it constantly, comparing notes on their children. "Betty continued to work because they needed the money," Gladys said. "She had no choice, but she would have anyway. She was attached to the stimulation and the people." She and Gladys wrote a pair of articles that were published in *Charm,* a magazine whose readers were young working women.* Although unrecognized as such, it presaged some of the ideas in *The Feminine Mystique.* In "I Stayed Home," Gladys wrote the housewife's lament: how she had been a happy, busy professional until she had a baby, after which she was confronted with sudden isolation, new dependence on her husband for companionship, diminishing self-confidence, and boring household problems. Still, she felt it was important to be with her daughter. In "I Went Back to Work," Betty wrote: "I was making a good salary in an exciting, responsible job which challenged my abilities." She had been unprepared for motherhood and regarded housework with contempt. But she came to understand "that Danny didn't need a 'perfect' mother, or even one who spent every minute with him."

Many of Betty's freelance articles had the bland, forgettable quality of women's-magazine pieces—light on intellectual content, with upbeat endings, nothing to disturb the miasma of conformity that had spread across America. They would not have been published otherwise. An as-told-to piece with Julie Harris, "The Most Creative Part I've Ever Played," compared the actress's feelings of creativity in imagining her roles with her feelings when her child was born. The comparison between biological and artistic creation was the subject of much discussion at the time, expert opinion being that babies were women's way of being creative, while works of art were men's way. Julie Harris felt more creative when she was acting, but the editors did not think this made fit reading for their readers and changed it. How could they could tell women that there was anything more creative than having a baby? Betty was disgusted but powerless.

As she had been taught at Smith, she did her homework, and most of her stories were overresearched. For "The Gal Who Defied Dior," a piece

---

* In the mid-1950s there were not enough working women to support *Charm.* It merged with *Glamour.*

on Claire McCardell—an important new Seventh Avenue designer of casual clothes for suburban life, who originated separates, pedal pushers, bareback summer dresses, party dresses to wear in the kitchen—Betty discussed the entire fashion industry, all of which was cut. But she was successful with one idea that she came back to again and again—that of a group of people working together to build a community, as she had done in Parkway Village. She did a piece for *Parents* about mothers in a housing project who created a "Day Camp in the Driveways." For *Redbook* (1955), she wrote "We Built a Community for Our Children," about the family that created the community of Village Creek, in South Norwalk, Connecticut. In 1956 she wrote another piece for *Redbook*, "Happy Families of Hickory Hill," about a group of young couples in Tappan, New York, "raising their children together, almost like one big family."

Betty was stymied by the women's magazines in many ways. A combination of traditional male editors and the insidious entwining of advertising and editorial matter ensured that no disturbing new idea could weaken the bonds of family togetherness. Any woman who dared to stick her head out of the kitchen was a threat. An article on Beverly Pepper, the artist, which Betty submitted to *Redbook* in October 1955, was rejected by Robert Stein, the articles editor, with a letter to her agent in which the word "neurotic" was featured prominently. Seven years later, when *The Feminine Mystique* was sent to Stein for possible excerpting, his reaction was the same. "Only the most neurotic housewife would identify with this."

During the summer Betty found beach houses to share with her friends. In 1954, the Friedans took a house with the Mehlings at Hampton Bays, on the south shore of Long Island. Madelon and Bob Bedell visited. The Carters, with the memory of Lake Hopatcong vivid in their minds, also visited. The husbands came out on weekends. Betty always went to a lot of trouble to get herself ready for the arrival of the men. "She was like a schoolgirl when Carl was coming for the weekend. Other people didn't display their emotions, put them on the table like that," a friend said.

"I felt that I would never again, ever, be so happy as I was living in Queens," Betty wrote nostalgically. She thought, watching "how beautiful our children looked, playing in the twilight...that it would last forever." She wrote those words in 1974, after it had all gone wrong and there were too many lost joys, but Betty was made for the larger world; no family, no community was big enough for her. A friend from the Old Left observed, "She was deep into alienation. She was very discontented at that time. Betty seemed to be stuck. She never bragged about her achievements. She never talked about Smith or being cum laude at Parkway Village." It was all in the past. She was disillusioned with the unions, the Left, and the U.S.S.R.; she was home with the kids, unnoticed, ineffectual. Once she had thought of herself as being in the vanguard of the revolution; now the vanguard, not the revolution, had withered away. The postwar world posed the threat of a new war with the Soviet Union and atomic annihilation; and the Red scare, along with the power of America's giant corporations, made the voices of the Old Left less relevant to political realities. Betty had given almost a decade of her life to leftist politics, and there was nothing to replace it.

The dream of an international community was also fading. The U.N., which had underwritten the rent of some of its people, was losing money on Parkway Village and had signed its leases over to banks. The banks, which were not interested in subsidizing interracial housing, were toying with the idea of transforming the Village into a country club. On June 4, 1952, the tenants were notified that their rent would rise by an average of 24 percent—$30 to $50 more a month, too much for many of them. Betty, who was editing the Parkway Village newsletter, formed a tenants' committee with Fred Zeserson, Gladys Carter, and William Jovanovich, the future owner of Harcourt Brace Jovanovich. (Jovanovich did not remain on the committee; he decided that the others were too far left for his tastes.) There were meetings and petitions to save Parkway Village; volunteers set up a cordon around it to frighten away prospective tenants. Betty got publicity for their cause by writing stories for *The New York Times* and the New York *Daily News,* and rallied the troops. "Your executive committee," she wrote in the newsletter, "is working on the assumption, and will continue this report on the assumption, that our entire community has been and shall remain interested not only in individual rents, but equally in the preservation of the community as it now exists." In a semi–rent strike, the majority of the tenants refused to sign the new leases, forcing the bank to negotiate with the tenants' association. The action was successful, partly because people from outside coming to look at apartments thought the rent was too high for the neighborhood. The banks agreed to limit the increase to 8 percent.

The Martini Group stayed on for a few more years. Some of them formed a co-op with some U.N. people and took an option on a parcel of land straddling Ossining and Briarcliff Manor, but the Briarcliff school was not integrated, and the Ossining school had no room for them. Betty and Carl struck out on their own. Their lease was up at Parkway Village, and they needed more space—Betty was pregnant with their third child,

Emily. Betty heard about an old stone barn for rent in Snedens Landing, an exclusive community in Palisades, New York. It was twelve miles north of the George Washington Bridge, in Rockland County, on the west side of the Hudson. Columbia University's Lamont Geological Observatory was just up the hill. The house was owned by Lael Wertenbaker, who was writing *Death of a Man,* about how she had helped her husband, Charles, a swashbuckling *Time* magazine journalist, commit suicide. The Friedans moved in April 1956, a month before Emily's birth on May 23.

The house had stalls for horses and a wall of French doors that opened on the river. Carl, who liked to garden, planted vegetables. "It was a spectacular place," he said. "There was a waterfall nearby. Always, I learned from Betty to have that standard of living." Danny remembered playing basketball in the basement in winter. The rent was low, but the heating bill was enormous. The house had no insulation.

Snedens Landing was old, small, and secluded. All of its roads wound around into dead-end streets. A 1955 book that the Friedans read, A. C. Spectorsky's *The Exurbanites,* described it as a place where "the fetish is non-conformity, individuality, originality." Many of the people who lived there worked in creative fields; their ideas were a force in American business and culture. Katharine Cornell had built a lavish house there in the forties and brought her theatre friends. At one time or another, Noël Coward, Orson Welles, the Oliviers, John Steinbeck, Ginger Rogers, and Maurice Evans had lived there, but it had remained an informal, unpretentious place; people did not flaunt their wealth. "Betty took pride in it," Carl said. "She was proud that she could put Emily's birthplace as Snedens." She told an interviewer, "In some ways it was the most romantic place I've ever lived. I would type with gloves on because every time you turned the heat up, you felt like dollar bills were being burned. The sociology of the place was interesting. There were some very interesting people who lived there, and there were some people whose main claim to fame was living there because of that sort of specialness."

They stayed for a year and a half—one winter of $1,800 in heating bills was enough—and then, in the spring of 1957, Betty found another wonderful old place, six miles north of Snedens Landing, in the village of Grandview-on-Hudson, an hour's drive from the city. They bought it and rented Snedens to the Apsteins—Ted, a writer, and Patricia, who later became a psychiatric social worker. "The day she moved, she had us to dinner with Lael Wertenbaker," Pat Apstein said. "On English bone china plates." (Betty had a live-in maid.) Betty remained friends with the Apsteins. Many years later, when Ted's career needed a boost, she helped him as she did so many of her friends, by putting him in touch with the right people. Of the Friedans' marriage, Pat said, "They got along, but they fought a lot. They had a lot of common interests. He was very supportive of her work. They both liked being abrasive."

The new house sat on a knoll on River Road, a street of Victorian houses that rambled on through foyers and galleries, nooks and crannies, with the river a wide ribbon in front of them. The Friedans' house, at Number 205, was a gabled Charles Addams fantasy with eleven rooms and three baths. It had everything—fanlights, marble fireplaces, sculptured moldings, a wide front porch, French doors, gingerbread trim. There were four bedrooms on the second floor. The house sat on an acre of land with a pool fed by a natural spring, a bank of daffodils, and a boxwood hedge. (When they were very broke, Betty sold the hedge. She had never liked the smell of it, anyway, she said.) They bought the house for $25,000, $2,500 down, on a G.I. mortgage.

During their first year, Betty sanded the fireplace and banister down to their original wood. She and Carl bought furniture at a small auction house in Palisades for virtually nothing—$35 for a carved and tufted Victorian loveseat; $10 for a matching chair. (The twin of the loveseat is in the Museum of the City of New York.) She decorated the living room in warm, rich colors, purples and reds. Some of the rooms had nothing in them. There wasn't enough money to fix up the whole house.

Carl established himself in the advertising and promotion business. Advertising was exciting in the 1950s—in the popular imagination it was one of the most glamorous professions—but it was also a subject of controversy. At weekend parties along River Road, the Friedans and their friends argued about the virtues of art versus the necessities of commerce: starving honorably in a garret or living the good life. Privately, Carl compared his profession to whoring; publicly, the Friedans were proud that Carl hadn't joined one of the large firms and sold out.

Carl had various small clients and a few important ones: the oil dealers associations of New York, Staten Island, and Philadelphia. The oil dealers were engaged in a mammoth struggle with the gas heating people, and Carl created a major confrontational campaign for them. He ran full-page ads in *The New York Times* and other papers with the headline "Why did 15 out of 20 homes on this street rip out their new gas furnaces?" The copy unfavorably compared the prices of gas with those of oil. "The gas people thought it was an unfair business practice," Carl said. "They went to the Better Business Bureau to stop it."

But that was as far as Carl could go. Executives from two major advertising agencies, Doyle Dane Bernbach and Dancer Fitzgerald, called and invited him to join their firms. Carl, who was actually delighted to have been asked, told them, "I don't do that kind of shit." Like Betty, he covered his fears with offensiveness. "I was tongue-tied," he said. "I couldn't talk about my clients. I think I was afraid to compete. I never had the talent to parlay it into something bigger."

Betty made friends easily and generated an active social life. Barbara Keil, a neighbor, said, "She was very good company, she laughed, she had a nice sense of humor. Her house was always open, people were always welcome. It was always fun and very lively. She invited people with intellectual things to offer."

But her parties were sometimes riven with discord. When Bob and Madelon Bedell came back from Europe in 1956, Betty found a house for them and gave a dinner party for them and invited the Zersons. It was an evening that was remembered vividly by all who attended. In Bob Bedell's account, "The women decided to dress for dinner. It was very pleasant, and Betty brought out the main course, a beautiful fish on a platter. Carl said, 'Jesus, Betty, fish, you know I don't like fish.' He took the platter and threw it at her. Betty picked it up, peeling pieces of fish off the walls. Carl walked out and disappeared upstairs. Fred said, 'There are three beautiful children up there. I guess it proves that neither heredity nor environment makes a difference.' Betty just served dinner, as if nothing had happened. Everyone followed her lead."

Betty adored her children and would have deemed her life sadly incomplete without them; yet there was an underlying ambivalence in her pleasure. In many ways she was duplicating the pattern of her mother's marriage: she had not succeeded any more than Miriam had in finding "feminine fulfillment." Twenty-five years later she wrote, "I think of my own uneasiness, being called 'mother' of the women's movement—not because of modesty, but because of the way I felt about being a mother altogether. An uneasiness, an unsureness, a fear about being a mother because I certainly didn't want to be like my mother."

Unlike Miriam, Betty paid little attention to keeping her children well groomed, but she took endless pains with their intellectual needs. Emily recalled, "Once I got a C− in the seventh grade. They immediately wanted to take me to a psychiatrist. They were always thinking about things and having intellectual discussions." Emily's hair may have been unkempt and her clothes disheveled, but other things were more important than ironing or neatness. Betty read to her children and she showed them how to look at things. Joseph Kastner, a neighbor who was an editor at *Life,* watched her: "She started to talk to the kids about a flower. She knew nothing, really, but 'Look at this,' she said, 'and the leaves, how they are attached, and the curve of the petals.' The kids were fascinated." She sent them to the Rockland Center for the Arts for classes in pottery and painting and ceramics, and to camp in summer.

Carl spent a lot of time with the children and got high marks for fathering—and mothering—from their friends. Betty would become so focused on what she was doing that she forgot about everything else. Her ability to concentrate utterly on a single thing was no small factor in all of her successes, but mothering several small children demands a talent for judiciously scattered wits. The children often found traditional mothering at neighbors' houses. Like Parkway Village, Grandview was the kind of community where everyone took care of everyone else's stray children. Once, a policeman found Danny hitchhiking home at one A.M. after a weekend poker game with his high school friends. The cop, who thought it was too late for Danny to be out alone, called Carl. Emily, who had a waiflike air, spent a lot of time at the Keils; their daughter was her best friend. "They were delightful kids," Barbara Keil said. "Jonny was imaginative, fun, with a lovely sense of humor. Emily was a sweet girl. Quiet, nice to have around."

The children coped as well as they could. Danny, who was a genius like his mother, escaped into his mind, spinning out theories on the far side of physics. His territory was the third floor of the house, where he spent hours reading his huge collection of sci-fi books. He was a child prodigy, doing calculus in his head when others his age were having trouble with the multiplication tables. Every Saturday Carl took him to an advanced math class at Columbia University, where he learned to use computers. At fifteen he was accepted at Princeton.

Jonathan, the middle child, who played in the Little League, was perhaps the most deeply affected by the marital discord. He and a friend would sit at the top of the stairs and watch "the Friday night fight," when Betty and Carl indulged themselves in throwing crockery. One night Betty threw a teapot. According to the friend, Jonathan said, "Oh, she's going to be sorry she threw that. She liked that teapot." In the seventies, after finishing high school, he dropped out for several years and lived in a commune.

Emily, surrounded by chaos, developed a critical eye and a strong sense of irony. After Betty began lecturing and traveling, Emily became her organizer and record keeper, efficient and rational, making sure her mother had the tickets and got to the airport before the plane took off.

With the aid of therapy, all three children managed to distance themselves from the emotional fallout of the marriage. Each of them chose professions in the hard sciences—theoretical physics, engineering, medicine: work based solidly on reason and logic—and they married and had children.

Betty always needed to have a big project going, something with grand implications that also made her important. Organizing people was one of her great talents, as natural as breathing. From the Baddy Baddy Club in grade school to the rent strike in Parkway Village, she created groups and drew people to her causes. She would continue to do so all her life. William J. (Si) Goode, a prominent sociologist at Columbia University who became a lifelong friend, said, "My most vivid memories... were the telephone ringing and immediately someone says: 'Here's our plan!' And no identification, no nothing... I always think her story is... the hordes are coming in through the gates, the waters are rising, there's poisonous atmosphere—and she says, 'Here's my plan.'... And she was forever bullying me and nagging me to do things that I didn't wish to do, some speeches at some educational meeting or fussing at some school committee, talking about sex education in a little community that felt there should be none whatsoever under any circumstances, complaining about the priests teaching at the public high school, etc., etc., a long list of indignations that we were forever arguing about." In the Grandview school system, Betty found her next project: the Community Resource Pool.

At nine, Danny had outgrown the local schools. The Friedans had sent him to a better school in Nyack, which was outside their district and for which they had to pay tuition, but he was still bored. He was doing Newtonian experiments at home, dropping balls over the banister, and he had worked up some numbers that seemed to Betty to challenge Galileo's theories. What Danny and other bright children needed, Betty thought, was outside stimulation, from scientists who could imbue them with passion for scientific discovery. She came up with the idea of enriching the entire school system by inviting local experts to talk and teach in a special program every Saturday.

Rockland County abounded in intellectuals. It had been a rural out-post until after World War I, when it was discovered by a group of theatre people—Lotte Lenya, Kurt Weill, Maxwell Anderson. Betty planned to recruit from the ranks of the editors, writers, actors, and professors who lived there and scientists from the Lamont Observatory. They would spend an hour a week stirring up the passions of the mind. Robert Menzies, director of marine biology at the observatory, would explain scientific processes; George Mathews at the history department of Columbia University would talk about the institutions of Western civilization; C. Wright Mills at Columbia would unravel sociology; and so on. The children, middling students as well as bright ones, would get a private school education on weekends.

Betty's timing was perfect. In 1957 the Russians had sent *Sputnik* into orbit, beating America into space. It was a shock to the American nervous system, an insult to the national honor. America was first in everything; this was the American Century, and it was inconceivable that we could lose the space race. The national consensus was that the fault lay in the educational system, which took a lackadaisical approach to science and math. Numberless articles compared American schools unfavorably with their European counterparts and bemoaned the country's wide streak of anti-intellectualism. Betty could not have found an edge more cutting. The Community Resource Pool was the first program of its kind in the country.

The heart of the Rockland community was the Rockland Center for the Arts, housed in an old, ramshackle building in West Nyack. It functioned as a school, forum, art gallery, and concert hall—it was like the local bar where everyone met. The Center was run by the Rockland Foundation, headed by the architectural historian James Fitch, who taught at Columbia and knew everyone. It was to him that Betty went for funding. She and Fitch organized the Community Resource Pool and, over a period of six years, recruited seventy-five of the county's leading scientists, artists, and other creative thinkers. Two years after it started, the CRP got a grant of $13,000, which enabled Betty to take a salary of $2,500, later raised to $3,000—something her co-workers, housewives who volunteered their time, would have been surprised to know.

James Fitch thought Betty was remarkable. "She was brassy. She was always very dramatic. She had a big house on the edge of the river, and she had outrageous taste in decor—orange, red, purple—and dressed like that, too. Betty is an authentic home-grown radical. She represents the same sort of movement in national intellectual life as Rachel Carson and Jane Jacobs—people who were no longer content to accept the orthodox interpretation of what should be done. They entered a field for which they had no formal training and were driven by the urgency of what they saw was needed. Betty was a leader of the county. When you examine the motives of her critics, they think their position is threatened."

One of Betty's jobs was to placate hostile teachers and talk them into cooperating. She saw her project as altruistic, but many of the teachers resented outsiders coming in and tampering with their system, the obvious implication being that they were incompetent. Questions were raised of elitism, of skimming the cream of the children for special treatment. Joseph Kastner, the Rockland Foundation's liaison to the school district, was assigned to monitor Betty and keep her out of trouble. "She offended people, had no regard for their feelings; she had no problem getting personal in an argument. Her language was genital and scatological. Women didn't speak that way in those days. The fear was that she would blow it. She didn't. She was absolutely wonderful. She knew well when to be tactful."

Betty was less tactful with the women volunteers; perhaps she chose not to bother. "Betty was overpowering," one woman said. "She got everyone around her to do the work. She dealt with Joe Kastner, who was a force in the community, on an intellectual level. Why should we have been her handmaidens? We addressed envelopes so she could be the star. There was a secretary who got a pittance, if anything, and after a meeting Barbara Keil said to Betty, 'Let's help her clean up.' Betty said, 'I'm not washing cups.' "

The CRP evolved into something even larger than Betty had envisioned. There were field trips for the students and classes for adults. The teachers, including those who had been so hostile to the "highbrows" at first, asked for seminars on new developments in science, and English departments all over the county began scheduling sessions with the writers. It was an enormous success, and schools around the country copied it.

The CRP brought Betty a measure of fulfillment that had been missing from her life. At a stroke she had launched herself into the company of the elite and come roaring back from oblivion. She was a cultural personage. Her parties were county-wide salons, attended by distinguished people. Her name was in the papers. She had followed her basic blueprint: taking a personal need and developing it into something universal, attaching herself to people who had credentials. Her work could be seen partly as compensation for her lost academic career, partly as a reflection of her need to be at the center of a swirl of people and to make things happen. "She was really attracted to fame," a neighbor said. "She wanted to know every important person in Rockland County. She was an intellectual social climber." To Betty these motivations were all of a piece. She would not have been content to do something that was not uplifting—but it also had to satisfy her ego. As she would do all her life, she left a mixed legacy in Rockland County: a better public school system and a residue of hostility.

6

Feminine Fulfillment

IN THE SPRING of 1957, Betty went to the fifteenth reunion of her Smith class, bringing with her a detailed questionnaire for her classmates. The idea had grown out of the previous reunion, in 1952, when many of the women were living in the perpetually harassed state that comes with having small children. "We were appalled at all these intelligent people talking about baby formula," Maggie Comstock Bayldon said. "We thought there were a lot of wasted lives. We thought we would find out."

Betty herself had been feeling guilty, she later told an interviewer—she hadn't lived up to the glorious future predicted for her, to her "so-called brilliant possibilities. It rankled me that I hadn't delivered on a promise. . . . I still had the reputation at Smith." Betty Goldstein, the star of the Class of 1942, was writing freelance articles to magazine formulas and doing community work. She was a failure.

Betty had invited two other classmates, Marion (Mario) Ingersoll Howell and Ann Mathers Montero, to help her. Each was a rebel in her fashion, less trammeled by convention than most women. Mario, who had been head of student government at Smith, had married a pacifist minister; Betty had marched on the White House with them during the war. Ann, who had married a black man, was an activist in better-government organizations and the Urban League. "It was a proto-feminist questionnaire," Mario said. "Because we'd all three of us been in therapy, we asked questions that were very feminist for that time. Questions that were aware and more outspoken than people were accustomed to." Many of the questions were open-ended: "What do you wish you had done differently?" "How do you feel about getting older?" The most memorable question was also the most frivolous: "Do you put the milk bottle on the table?" The answers ranged from "Of course" to "I hope I never sink that low."

The questionnaire was the psychic and historical germ of *The Feminine Mystique.* Betty became totally absorbed in it and spent an inordinate amount of time brooding over the results, trying to find out how her classmates were managing, whether her own dissatisfactions were echoed in theirs, whether she was a freak. She was finally coming to grips with the either/or choice she had made at Berkeley.

Most of the women professed to be reasonably happy with their lot. If they were not setting the world on fire, they were at least keeping busy. But Betty found underlying dissatisfactions. "I have sometimes found it hard to convince myself that any intelligence I have wasn't wasted on being a mere wife and mother," wrote one woman. Almost half regretted that they hadn't studied harder. To the question "What problem have you had working out your role as a woman?" one woman answered, "My problem is always being the minister's wife instead of me." Another: "Still find housework routine and never-ending in spite of all appliances." Sixty percent did not find fulfillment in their role as homemaker.

There was a *Stepford Wives* aura about the fifties as all the forces of the decade converged to impose a psychological powerlessness on women. After the war a glass curtain seemed to descend, like the picture window that was the pride of so many suburban houses, a window that looked out on nothing. Few women spoke of it. The girdle, which all middle-class women wore from their teens on, was perhaps the best symbol for their lives: the elastic stretched only so far; they were free to move, but only up to a point. Security was the main thrust of the fifties, safeguarded by conformity and hypocrisy, repression and inhibition. Those who went to analysts did so in secret and shame and rarely talked about it. A 1953 movie, *The Moon Is Blue,* caused a furor because the word "virgin" was in the script. Amid this surfeit of family values, the economy produced wondrous new devices, streams of cars and appliances and gadgets for the deprived children of the Depression who might never had had such things, and wanted them—and thus became hostages to them. Working women, sent home after the war, shut away from the world, were regarded with contempt for not being in it and refused admission when they tried to join it.

At first, Betty did not know what she had. She was focused on education. A serious debate was raging in the press on the inferior capacities of women and the folly of wasting education on them. A particularly influential book was *Modern Woman: The Lost Sex* by Ferdinand Lundberg and Marynia F. Farnham, a shrill, Freud-soaked polemic on the theme of anatomy is destiny, one of whose authors, a professional psychiatrist, was a member of that same lost sex. This unfortunate sex was in grave peril, the authors warned; intellectual interests were leading to "the masculinization of women with enormously dangerous consequences to the home, the children dependent on it, and to the ability of the woman, as well as her husband, to obtain sexual gratification." *Life* and *The New York Times* did articles on the subject; the *Ladies' Home Journal* weighed in with "Is College Education Wasted on Women?" by Nevitt Sanford, Ph.D. *Newsweek* published a "Special Education Report on the American Co-ed," asking why girls bothered to go to college at all: "With earlier marriages becoming an American pattern, wouldn't it be simpler all around...if they just trained themselves for such domestic tasks as cooking and sewing and child-rearing?"

Using the questionnaire, Betty wrote an article for *McCall's*, "Are Women Wasting Their Time in College?" College did not educate women to be housewives, but neither did it cause their problems, she wrote. Women were not only wives and mothers, they were individuals, and they needed to work out ways of integrating all of their roles without shortchanging themselves.

The article was rejected. She sent it to the *Ladies' Home Journal*. The editors rewrote it to make the opposite point, and Betty withdrew it. *Redbook* was next to turn it down. After each rejection she interviewed more housewives, sociologists, and psychologists, adding and refining. She had masses of material; what she would later call her "geiger counter" was clicking away, and she knew she was onto something—but what? "I was going to disprove the current notion that education had fitted us ill for our role as women," she later wrote. "...The suspicion arose as to whether it was the education or the role that was wrong."

In 1957 she went to a meeting of the Society of Magazine Writers (SMW), an organization of freelancers, which she had joined to make herself feel like a professional. The speaker was Vance Packard, author of *The Hidden Persuaders*, a best-selling exposé of subliminal advertising practices. Packard had written a book because his subject matter precluded his getting published in magazines. It dawned on Betty that she was in the same position.

Betty's agent, Marie Rodell, suggested that she call George Brockway, the president of W. W. Norton, an old-line publishing house. Brockway was an admirer of Betty's. In 1958 she had written a highly praised article, "The Coming Ice Age: A True Scientific Detective Story," which made the September cover of *Harper's* magazine and was reprinted in *The Reader's Digest*.* Brockway had asked her to expand the piece into a book, but Betty had turned him down. She hadn't researched the article herself; she had popularized a scientific work, with the delighted approval of its two authors (though after the article was published, they turned against her and accused her of making their work *too* popular). Betty wanted to do her own book.†

"She was incredibly ambitious," Brockway said. "The most ambitious woman I had ever met. She said that she didn't know what to call the subject exactly, but that it had something to do with a lack of identity, that women weren't being told ... they aren't being allowed ..." Brockway was intrigued and gave her $1,000 on a $3,000 advance. She thought she could do the book in a year, a chapter a month. It took five years.

Betty wrote part of the book in the Frederick Lewis Allen Memorial Room for writers at the New York Public Library, and part of it on her dining room table. Emily was in nursery school, which left her mornings free. She wrote in longhand on lined yellow pads, and hired Patricia Carter Aleskovsky, who had been secretary of the CRP, to do typing and shorthand for two dollars an hour. The job was filled with little extras. "Unfortunately, she was obsessed," Pat said, "with no regard for my personal family. Usually, on Saturdays, the neighbors got together for cocktails and dinner at different people's houses. She would get a brilliant idea at a party and go to the bedroom and call me, and I was stupid enough to take dictation, even though my family was at dinner. My husband finally said, 'Enough.' I don't think Betty ever thought I was a person. She would probably never admit to certain things that happened. I would go to work in the morning and she would be on the phone, arguing; her six-year-old daughter would be at home with a cold, and Betty would assume I would give her breakfast."

---

* In 1959 it was selected for a new anthology, *Gentlemen, Scholars & Scoundrels: A Treasury of the Best of Harper's from 1850*, which put Betty in the company of William Faulkner, Mark Twain, Aldous Huxley, George Bernard Shaw, Bertrand Russell, and Sigmund Freud.
† The scientists were Dr. Maurice Ewing, director of the Lamont Observatory, and Dr. William Donn, assistant professor of geology and meteorology at Brooklyn College.

Betty was uncertain about the whole enterprise. The years of being a housewife had rattled her confidence. Her colleagues in the Allen Room, important male writers working on important male books, teased her because she was just writing about women. Her book would challenge all the experts, and she didn't even have a master's degree. Without credentials she might be swept aside, ridiculed, in an angry assault of Ph.Ds. So she sought out the authority of the academy to buttress her thesis. Her friend Si Goode, who was working on world changes in family patterns and considered himself a feminist, was one of her strongest supporters. Betty used him as a sounding board for her ideas, and he made available to her research that he and his students had done. A mutual friend said, "He gave her the academic credibility she needed. He gave her work validity." Recalling those days, Si Goode said, "During that same time the book was being done...I was writing my own books...and I had no thoughts that this little housewife couldn't write a book. I thought anybody could write a book.... But I did not think *this* book was coming out. The issues, yes, but not the book, because in my talks with Betty, her astronomical I.Q. was always pushing her tongue quite a bit and the tongue was lagging behind more than a bit and the words were tumbling out, and I didn't think she could actually write a whole sentence in a consecutive way, much less a paragraph or a page."

At home, Betty and Carl progressed from broken china to physical abuse. Her asthma acted up again, and she went back into therapy. Carl could not perceive any interest in his problems on Betty's part. "We had no partnership," he said. "She never gave anything. I was looking for love in other places. She complained to her analyst, William Menaker, that I never came home at night. It was true. I didn't want to. There were slambang battles. I was out trying to screw around all the time." Menaker was one of Betty's biggest supporters. He had been trained in Freudian analysis in Vienna, but his mother had been a suffragist. After years of analyzing women, Menaker had come to the conclusion that there was no such thing as penis envy. He encouraged Betty to take herself more seriously and to concentrate on her work, telling her, "If the patient doesn't fit the book, throw away the book, and listen to the patient."

Betty reacted to Carl's absences with renewed anger. The Friedans were a local spectacle, creating scenes wherever they went. They would leave parties fighting. Once, Carl knocked her down in the road. "Everyone saw," Barbara Keil, their neighbor, said. "People leaving the party helped her up. People talked about it a lot." At another party Betty walked out and crashed her car into a pole at the end of the driveway. It stayed there for days.

Betty would later say that she had hidden her writing "like secret drinking" (Jane Austen also comes to mind), but it is hard to find a reason for this, other than fear that her idea would be stolen. She was banking so much on the book—it would fulfill her promise; it would bring her fame—that she was supersensitive to any hint of encroachment on her theme. One day, Murray Teigh Bloom at the Society of Magazine Writers received a frantic call from her: "Word had gotten out" about her work, she said, and Morton Hunt, a fellow SMW member, was doing a book on women. "It was a ticklish situation," Bloom remembered. "A member had accused another member of stealing her idea for a great, seminal book."* As it turned out, there was no connection.

Betty finished *The Feminine Mystique* in the summer of 1962 and celebrated by painting the living room a color she called "euphoric purple." With all her doubts—feeling, as she said, like a "freak"—Betty was certain that she had written a groundbreaking work. Even before she finished it she told a neighbor, "I'm writing a book, and it's going to be very important." She began to consider her image and bought dramatic new clothes, including an expensive, swishy cape. One day she asked Pat Aleskovsky whether she, Betty, ought to think about a new nose. Carl had been talking about it. It was a recurring topic, and Betty always pointed to Barbra Streisand and Eleanor Roosevelt. "They didn't need surgery," she told Carl. People would accept her for what she was, as they always had. (Betty was tempted, but, like Streisand, she knew she had a unique voice and was afraid the operation would alter it.)

But if she was adamant about her nose, her resolve wavered when it came to her hair. In the summer of 1962, bewitched by a Clairol advertising campaign ("If I have only one life to live, let me live it as a blonde"), she bleached her hair. It was an idea her hairdresser should have talked her out of. The salon couldn't make her blond—her hair was much too dark—but it made her a redhead. On the beach in the summer sun, her hair turned green.

Marie Rodell sent the book to magazines for excerption. The response was negative: *The Feminine Mystique* was, among other things, an attack on women's magazines. One entire chapter was devoted to slicing up their articles and another to dissecting their ads. The book as a whole eviscer-

---

* Morton Hunt's book, *Her Infinite Variety*, was selling well when *The Feminine Mystique* came out. It was a celebration of the female sex. Betty remained unmollified. In a letter to George Brockway, she wrote that it lowered her chances for the Book of the Month Club.

ated the entire concept of "togetherness," which glorified the nuclear family.* *Redbook* declined, saying it was "heavy going...and strident." *Life* criticized its "overstatement." *Esquire* dismissed it as too "sociological," and *The Reporter* found a lack "of humor or proportion." Betty refused to accept these rejections. She saw them as her agent's fault. Marie, she knew, had been shocked by the book; she wasn't presenting it with the enthusiasm that a major work required, wasn't treating it like an important book. Betty fired her, switched to Martha Winston at Curtis Brown Ltd., and started making phone calls. She was determined to get excerpts into *McCall's* and the *Ladies' Home Journal.*

Between 1958 and 1963, when *The Feminine Mystique* was published, many more women had moved into the workforce, and the magazines themselves were in the throes of reimagining themselves. At the *LHJ* the old guard had retired; the new articles editor, Peter Wyden, an aggressive risk-taker who wanted to make his mark, bought a chapter. Another editor there, Betty's college friend Neal Gilkyson Stuart, was also excited about the excerpt. At *McCall's,* Vivian Cadden, an important writer and editor, said that the magazine ran it "because it was such a happening. It was clear it was going to be a blockbuster." Betty had somehow pulled off the impossible: it was an extraordinary coup for an unknown author to have her book excerpted in two major women's magazines. The articles were published at the same time—*LHJ* in its January–February issue, and *McCall's* in its March issue, which came out while *LHJ* was still on the newsstands.†

The book was published on February 19, 1963, during a 114-day newspaper strike in New York. Betty was frantic. There were no reviews, no ads. "I told Betty there had to be more promotion," Carl said. He was enormously proud of her. "I read it on the subway. I went four stops past my stop. So I knew it would be a blockbuster."

---

* "Togetherness" was an invention of Lenore Hershey, a flamboyant personality and one of the top editors at *McCall's.* Betty's original title had been "The Togetherness Woman." "The Feminine Mystique" came from out of the air during lunch with Tom Mendenhall, the president of Smith. Betty said, "I was telling him what I was doing, describing what I was doing, groping...'because it challenged the feminine mystique, the mystique of femininity, the mystique of feminine fulfillment,' and a couple of minutes later he played it back. I realized 'mystique' was the word I'd been groping for. But I thought it was too hifalutin a word, too academic, too sophisticated, and I wanted my book to be read by all women. George Brockway at Norton liked it, and they persuaded me."

† Altogether, four excerpts from *The Feminine Mystique* appeared in magazines: "I Say Woman Are People Too!," *Good Housekeeping,* March 20, 1961; "Feminine Fulfillment: Is This All?," *Mademoiselle,* May 1962; "The Fraud of Femininity," *McCall's,* March 1963; "Housewife Is Not a Profession," *LHJ,* January–February 1963.

George Brockway, who expected to lose money, printed only three thousand copies and ran a handful of small, well-bred ads in *The New Yorker*. Betty felt betrayed. All along she had assumed that George thought the book was as important as she did—a seminal work of social criticism that would have as much impact on the sixties as William H. Whyte's *The Organization Man* and Vance Packard's *The Status Seekers* had had on the fifties. Her book was moving off the shelves without benefit of a famous author or newspaper publicity; women were coming into bookstores and asking for it. It had "struck home," Betty wrote in a long, semicoherent letter to George, exhorting him to get behind it. Norton kept going back to press, but there never seemed to be books in the stores. The Friedans kept haranguing George, and Betty brought him a list of promotional ideas from Carl. "One day," George said, "she told me that Carl wanted to know what could be done to make *The Feminine Mystique* as big a seller as *Gift from the Sea* [Anne Morrow Lindbergh's collection of essays]. Tell Carl, I told her, that he can fly the Atlantic solo."

The Friedans' persistence paid off: Norton hired an outside publicist, Tania Grossinger (daughter of the famous Catskill Mountains hotelkeepers), to arrange an author tour. She and Betty had met when *McCall's*, one of Tania's clients, excerpted the book. "Norton's publicist came to me and asked me to handle Betty," Tania said. "They were not hitting it off. At that time, very few authors went around the country pushing their books. I had done it before."

Tania got Betty on all the best talk shows, and Betty reciprocated by bringing her to SMW meetings where she might find other clients. On the road she looked up Tania's friends in various cities: "I got Jewish-mother letters from her: 'I saw Tony; she hasn't heard from you—write to her.' " Tania had to coach Betty for her interviews—Betty talked so fast it was hard to understand her. "She was impatient," Tania said. "What she had to say was very, very important, and everyone should understand that. She was afraid she wouldn't have enough time to get her message out." Betty sometimes forgot about her coaching. On *Girl Talk*, hosted by Virginia Graham, Betty was one of several guests and could hardly get a word in edgewise. At the commercial break she became the Betty Friedan many other women would soon come to know: "If you don't let me speak, I'm going to say 'orgasm' ten times," she threatened. She was also extremely irritated by Graham's attitude toward her female audience. "Girls," Graham asked them, "what better thing can we do with our lives than to do the dishes for those we love?" In itself the question was a dismissal of *The Feminine Mystique*; it was also a hypocrisy, and Betty spoke out, telling the women that Graham needed them to be housewives, that without them she wouldn't have an audience and maybe not even a career. By the time the tour was over Betty was famous.

The tour and Betty's provocative personality helped to make *The Feminine Mystique* a best-seller. It was sold to the Book Find Club; Dell paid $25,000 for the paperback rights, and it became the number one best-selling nonfiction paperback of 1964, with 1.3 million copies sold in the first edition. (It kept selling. As of November 1970, the year the women's movement became a major social force, 1.5 million copies of the paperback were in print, and Betty had made about $100,000 on hard- and softcover sales.)

In 1964, Random House offered Betty a $30,000 advance for her next book, tentatively titled "The New Woman," about the life patterns of all the women who had thrown off the feminine mystique. When he heard about it, George Brockway, who did not want to lose his newly famous author, invited Betty to lunch at an exquisite French restaurant. After the polite chitchat, the waiter brought dessert, and Brockway brought up the subject of her next book. Betty remembered how she had had to beg for advertising and grovel for attention—how she had been, as she saw it, betrayed—and burst out, "What next book? You're not going to have my next book. George, you made me feel so Jewish for trying to sell my book. Go fuck yourself!"

Betty sent her mother a copy of *The Feminine Mystique,* with a gracious note: "With all the troubles we have had, you gave me the power to break through the feminine mystique which will not, I think, be a problem any longer for Emily. I hope you accept the book for what it is, an affirmation of the values of your life and mine."

The Feminine Mystique

CERTAIN BOOKS BREAK through the thought barriers of their time and reverberate for decades, shifting the social kaleidoscope. In the early sixties, a number of such books came out: *The Golden Notebook*, by Doris Lessing, in 1962; *The Death and Life of Great American Cities*, by Jane Jacobs, in 1961; *Silent Spring*, by Rachel Carson, in 1962; and *The Other America*, by Michael Harrington, in 1962. Another influential book was Helen Gurley Brown's *Sex and the Single Girl*, in 1962 (before that, everyone had pretended that single girls didn't have sex lives). But it was *The Feminine Mystique* that became the opening salvo in the most far-reaching social revolution of the century.

When *The Feminine Mystique* came out, America was not the same place it had been when Betty started writing it. There was a young president who had style, wit, and sex appeal and could do stand-up comedy at press conferences. The civil rights movement was burgeoning. The abandon of rock and roll was replacing the smooth, contained style of the crooner tradition. Sex itself was coming out of the closet; the Pill had inaugurated the sexual revolution. Theoretically, women could be as free as men. "The separation of female sexuality and conjugal love was ... the psychosexual transformation of our time," Benita Eisler wrote in *Private Lives: Men and*

Women of the Fifties. The social code was coming unglued. In 1949 Ingrid Bergman had been branded with the scarlet letter and banished from Hollywood for having an affair with Roberto Rossellini and becoming pregnant with his child. In 1962, the even more public affair between Elizabeth Taylor and Richard Burton, each of whom was married to someone else, aroused no such punitive fury. The repression of the fifties had made possible the deluge of the sixties. The elements were all there, waiting to explode.

There were other stirrings among women. In the early sixties, Dusty Roads, a stewardess with American Airlines, began a long fight to change the work rules, which stipulated that stewardesses had to remain single and that they would be fired in their early thirties (when they were no longer considered young and sexy enough to appeal to male passengers. Something was wrong with them anyway, if they weren't married by then, the airlines reasoned). "In tackling the age and marriage restrictions," Flora Davis wrote in *Moving the Mountain,* "stewardesses assaulted some of society's ingrained assumptions: that marriage was all women really wanted; that it was perfectly natural to judge a woman solely on her looks; and that men somehow had a right to the services of women."

Each year more women entered the workforce. By 1963, over one-third of women held jobs, and one-third of those were married. Women were living longer; after raising their children, they still had half their lives ahead of them. The number of working women was reaching a critical mass. So was the number of affluent, educated women—women with college degrees—who were being offered jobs as lifelong secretaries. Betty had caught the wave. *The Feminine Mystique* was the right book at the right time.

The book begins with a description of the problem Betty had tried to explain to George Brockway, "the problem that has no name":

> The problem lay buried, unspoken, for many years in the minds of American women. It was a strange stirring, a sense of dissatisfaction, a yearning that women suffered in the middle of the twentieth century in the United States. Each suburban wife struggled with it alone. As she made the beds, shopped for groceries, matched slipcover material, ate peanut butter sandwiches with her children, chauffeured Cub Scouts and Brownies, lay beside her husband at night—she was afraid to ask even of herself the silent question—"Is this all?"

In painstaking detail, Betty told women that the feminine mystique required them to renounce their brains and deny their senses, retreat to a childlike state, and immolate themselves on the altar of their family's needs. Only then could they find "feminine fulfillment." The mystique worked exactly like Freudian psychoanalysis (Freud was the book's major villain). It was a box that one could not climb out of: all objections, all criticisms of the theory were a denial of the truth, and those who demurred were neurotic. Should women not adjust to their role, they would be afflicted with the greatest ill that could befall them: the loss of their femininity. "Before all else you are a wife and mother," Torvald told Nora before she slammed the door.

In chapters on psychology, sociology, anthropology, economics, and the mass media, Betty explained that the system was crazy, women were not—that the current definition of femininity was wrong and adjusting to it was sick. She told them that they counted, that they were not just major appliances or service stations, not just somebody's daughter, wife, or mother; they had an identity of their own. Further, she told them that cultural attitudes were ephemeral, and that women themselves could be a force for change. Her great achievement was to provide a coherent explanation for the routine belittlement women had experienced all their lives, the condescension they must already have noticed but had never found a rationale for. Although the book took as its example the suburban housewife (and was severely criticized for that limitation), the attitudes it described were universal. The writing—prolix, repetitive, obsessive—was Betty demanding attention for her passionate belief and her urgent need to get it all out. That passion infused the book with its power.

Of the many influences on the book, the strongest was the theories of Abraham Maslow, which constitute its intellectual underpinnings. Having debunked Freud's views on women, Betty needed a replacement, someone high in the pantheon of psychology. She and Maslow shared a similarly optimistic view of life and became friends during her research. A pioneer in humanistic psychology, Maslow abjured the sick and neurotic, the daily fodder of analysis, and studied psychologically healthy people. Among them he found that once basic biological needs were met, the fundamental human drive was the need to grow and reach one's full potential, or self-actualization. Self-actualizing people usually "have a mission in life; they delight in bringing about justice, stopping cruelty and exploitation, fighting lies and untruth.... They are spontaneous and creative....

They are autonomous, not bound tightly to the customs and assumptions of their particular culture."

One aspect of his theory was particularly appealing: Maslow's idea of "high dominance" women, women like Betty—strong, purposeful, independent women who "do not take the ordinary conventions seriously." These autonomous women, Maslow declared, had great sex; their femininity was enhanced by their independence. For Betty, who had never been able to choke down the accepted standards of femininity, Maslow was her validation. He was, however, also tainted by Freud. He did not believe that most women were capable of self-realization. Indeed, he could find only two—Eleanor Roosevelt and Jane Addams—who qualified. Betty took his theory and applied it to women, showing how they had been prevented from attaining self-actualization. She concluded that the accepted definition of femininity was antagonistic to human growth.

Many of the ideas in *The Feminine Mystique* were already circulating, but the world had not been ready to pay attention to them. In the 1940s, Dr. Jessie Bernard, Ruth Herschberger, and Margaret Mead had each written about the assumption that there was something inherently wrong with women and criticized the arbitrary link between femininity and domesticity. Mead had laid out virtually the entire problem, calling housewifery "semi-voluntary slavery," and advocated shared housework and day care centers. More than any other work, Simone de Beauvoir's classic study, *The Second Sex,* had ranged wide and deep over the same territory, examining the roots of misogyny; how women became the "Other," the object, not the subject, the one etherized on the table. It was a monumental work, literary, philosophical, and historical. Betty, immersed in the inexact sciences, did not scale those heights. Her book had about it the aura of women's magazines (she was, after all, a journalist)—which was one of its strengths: everyone could read it; it was accessible in a way that Beauvoir was not. Several reviewers accused Betty of cribbing from Beauvoir. Diane Ravitch wrote, "Yet, for all her deference to authority, Mrs. Friedan conspicuously fails to give sufficient credit to her major source of ideas: Simone de Beauvoir's 'The Second Sex.' ... Mrs. Friedan's book represents little more than a rehashing and watering down of many of the French writer's ideas." Beauvoir herself was angry, believing that Betty had lifted her ideas without giving her credit.

Betty always denied the accusation, but she was skittish about Beauvoir, and danced around the subject. (Actually, Beauvoir was so comprehensive, Betty could hardly have avoided her ideas.) It was Beauvoir's existentialism that had influenced her, she said, not the book's feminist content. "I read that perhaps ten years before I wrote *The Feminine Mystique.... The Second Sex* gave us a very depressing feeling about the horribleness of our condition as women. I was then a suburban housewife in Rockland County, trying in a small way to do freelance writing. Ms. de Beauvoir's book just made me want to crawl in bed and pull the covers over my head. It did not lead to any action to change the lot of women, which somehow *The Feminine Mystique* did."

It is true that Betty did not credit Beauvoir. The likely explanation is that she wrote out of her own experience and did not believe she had lifted Beauvoir's ideas. Betty did not like *The Second Sex*. It offended her optimistic spirit and pragmatic approach to life. It was too grim. It offered no hope.

Looking back a dozen years later, Betty wrote, "In a certain sense it was almost accidental—coincidental—that I wrote The Feminine Mystique, and in another sense my whole life had prepared me to write that book; all the pieces of my own life came together for the first time in the writing of it." But one piece of her life did not appear—her Marxist youth. She had deliberately buried it, with good reason.

In 1963, the fallout from McCarthyism was still raining down. People were frightened and suspicious; those who had lived through the worst would remain so for decades. In such an atmosphere, Betty would have been crazy to give her book a Marxist interpretation. No one would have listened to her. Moreover, her radical youth was over. She was older and more sophisticated; the daring desire to overturn society had subsided into the more prudent position of analyzing it. If there was going to be a revolution, it would not be the one she had worked for. That ship had already sunk. The one thing Marxism had in common with feminism was an ideal of social justice, and it was the ideal that impassioned her.

Betty went out of her way to distance herself from the discredited left. When she finished the book, she dictated a long list of acknowledgments to her secretary, Pat Aleskovsky, but left Pat herself out. "I'm not including you in the credits because it would be bad for my book," Betty told her. Pat's husband, Nate, a journalist, had been named by HUAC. "Other people were afraid to talk to him," Pat said. "They avoided those who had been named. They were afraid to be connected in any way." In the interests of her book and the movement that followed it, Betty also suppressed the extent of her labor writings, erasing nine years of her working life. On one occasion she described her work as "the usual kinds of boring jobs that lead nowhere." On another, she called it "little writing jobs," and told the reporter she preferred to elide that time. It wasn't "pertinent to NOW." In 1996 she admitted, "I did not in those early years when I was freelancing, make a big point of having worked for labor unions. It would not exactly have been a recommendation."

In trivializing her work and presenting herself as a bit of a dabbler, Betty strengthened her image as a housewife and mother—one of the women she was writing about—who had succumbed to the feminine mystique. She would present herself that way for the rest of her life. Betty lived in the suburbs and was a housewife, but she was not and never would be a "suburban housewife." She understood the importance of the image, how helpful it would be in selling the book, and she polished it. In a *New York Post* interview, she said that the first thing she did after the book was published was buy a dishwasher. A *McCall's* press release had Betty advising women to use every appliance they could to make housework quick and efficient. It ended by describing an unimaginable state of affairs: "But when it comes to weekends, Mrs. Friedan stays away from the typewriter. 'My husband is home then—and he doesn't want me to work when he's around,' she says simply."

Reviews of *The Feminine Mystique* were mixed, but few were indifferent. The headlines revealed the excitement: "Housewives Raked Over Coals," "Book as Bombshell," "Are Women People?" "Men Do the Housework?" John Kenneth Galbraith said that *The Feminine Mystique* "made the conventional wisdom totter." Lucy Freeman, the author of a best-seller on how she overcame her mental illness, panned it in *The New York Times:* "Sweeping generalities, in which this book necessarily abounds, may hold a certain amount of truth but often obscure the deeper issues.... To paraphrase a famous line, 'The fault, dear Mrs. Friedan, is not in our culture, but in ourselves.'" In the *Herald Tribune,* the author and journalist Marya Mannes, who was already a feminist, gave it a rave: "Her book is a damning indictment of the social, educational and commercial pressures in the last 15 years particularly, which have caused a harmful discrepancy between what women really are and what they are told they should be."

Under the headline "To Herd Women by a New Dogma," in the *Boston Herald,* Alden Hoag wrote, "The feminine mystique is Mrs. Friedan's smear word to describe the contemporary doctrine that women's great role is total devotion to the home ... she is 'simply substituting one dogma for another' by telling women to get out of the home."

In *The New Leader,* Diane Ravitch (who in the same piece chastised Betty for not crediting Beauvoir) agreed with her analysis but quarreled with her presentation: the book was

> marred . . . by a pervasive glibness of thought . . . she blames the housewife for almost every conceivable blemish on the American character: passive children; middle-class children who commit crimes for kicks; teenage prostitutes, schizophrenic children; timid husbands, the emotional unhealthiness of suburbia; the failure of American prisoners-of-war in Korea to attempt escape—in short, the deterioration of the American moral fiber."

Certain omissions would come back to plague Betty: for the rest of her life she would be accused of indifference to women who were outside her class and race. Gerda Lerner, the esteemed feminist historian, sent her a letter of praise, comparing her to Rachel Carson, but also criticizing her for her narrow focus. Other, more radical feminists, white and of color, would do the same.

McCall's and *LHJ* were besieged with unprecedented thousands of letters, of every range of opinion, from "I feel like an appliance" to "Balderdash." Some women were smug about their position in the family—no one else could do what they did. A woman in her twenties who had three children and had just suffered a nervous breakdown said she had learned more from Betty's article than from consulting her psychiatrist. Another wrote, "I blame your magazine for helping to promote the complete breakdown of family life in this once great country. Ladies, go to your Priest or Minister and have him refresh your mind on what woman's greatest role is!" Another: "It . . . seems to me that Miss Friedan would not be urging others to follow her out of the home if she had what I have within the home."

By summer *The Feminine Mystique* was a best-seller. On August 4 it was number nine on the *Herald Tribune* list, between *Happiness Is a Warm Puppy,* by Charles M. Schulz, and *Portrait of Myself,* by Margaret Bourke-White. James Baldwin's *The Fire Next Time* was number one.

The reaction in Grandview was fraught with unspoken resentments. Along River Road the women Betty had partied and carpooled with, the women who had worked with her in the CRP, were deeply hurt and very angry. They had been a support system for her while she wrote her book: they had fed and cared for her children along with their own; and she had written that housework was something an eight-year-old could do and that they were living in "a comfortable concentration camp," wasting their time in volunteer work. She had dismissed their lives, made fools of them, and they felt used. One of the neighbors, who had worked on political campaigns and the school board, said, "It was as if she was saying, 'This is your function in life; I am above all this.' It was a very sensitive point. I don't think she was sympathetic to the fact that we were as well educated as she and our careers were at least as distinguished as hers."

Betty's life had changed dramatically. She was touring the country, publicizing her book, accepting lecture engagements, making television appearances, and she could not hold up her end in Grandview. She became persona non grata, and Emily was no longer welcome in the car pool, a development that infuriated Betty. She blamed the women for turning her into a "leper"; in interviews she told of how, when she was on the road, they refused to take Emily to dancing class or art class, even though she offered to pay for taxis when it was her turn to drive,* and no one invited her and Carl to parties anymore. She thought she knew the reason: "*I threatened them because I was acting out the secret desire that they did not yet dare to face in themselves* [emphasis in original]." Either she misunderstood, or she did not comprehend that she might bear some of the blame—or she just didn't care.

Yet she had galvanized some of them, too. Barbara Keil, for one, went out and got a degree in social work. Betty wrote of her victory: "Some years later, long after we had moved to the city, Jonathan went back at Christmas to a party at his friend Peter's house, three doors down from our old suburban homestead. 'Where are the cookies?' he asked Peter's mother, one of those ideal housewives who baked and always kept a cookie jar full for her kids and their friends. 'I'm working,' she said drily. 'Tell your mother we're all working now, more power to her.' "

. . .

In the late spring of 1963, the Friedans went to Peoria, to Betty's twenty-fifth high school reunion. It had been a close-knit class—many of the classmates had married one another, and they had continued to socialize together through the years. Betty's book was selling well; she was in the first heady stage of fame, and Carl was proud of her. She and Carl loved celebratory occasions, and this one would be particularly sweet, considering all the leftover baggage she was carrying like a toxic lump: the

---

* The women remembered Betty calling from New York and telling them that her maid wasn't there, and asking them to pick up Emily.

remembered slights, the bitter memories. Now "they" would have to respect her.

They stayed at Bob and Ruth Easton's house. "Betty and Carl didn't want to see the family," Bob Easton said. She and Harry were still estranged, and now she had raised the ante. Not only was she a flaming radical, she also had written a book that flouted all the received wisdom of civilized womanhood. "I wasn't very happy with her in those years," Harry said. "She was a cross I had to bear. I was a young shining light and I had to live her down."

On the whole, Peoria sided with Harry. Betty's class, which had an unusual number of high achievers in business and the professions, was not overly impressed by her book. A lot of them hadn't even read it, and many of those who had didn't agree with it.

Before the reunion dinner, Bob Easton whipped up a few shakers of his Easton Special—big double martinis, three and a half ounces of gin with three fat olives. Betty liked those; they all had several, and then went on to the Jefferson Hotel and more drinks. The reunion committee had decided against reserved seats at dinner, the idea being that no one should feel slighted. The Friedans found places at a table already filled except for two empty seats. At the table were John Altorfer, an industrialist who was running for lieutenant governor of Illinois; and Betty's old friends Marian Sweney and her husband, Art Szold, who had converted to Presbyterianism. He was sorry, Art explained to the Friedans, but he was saving the seats for another couple. The Friedans erupted. "I was angry at the lack of deference being shown Betty," Carl said. "They had a famous person in their midst; compared to Betty, they were unimportant." To everyone's shock, Betty completely lost control and made a snide remark about Art Szold's conversion. "They were so obnoxious and bombed," Marian Sweney recalled. "They drank and swore. They spoiled it for themselves. She wouldn't speak to Art for a long time after that." The Friedans found other seats. After dinner, John Parkhurst, the toastmaster, went around the room and asked people to stand up and reminisce about high school. Betty stood up and said, "It was not because but in spite of going to Peoria High that I got where I am."

The next morning the Friedans were repentant and tried to mend fences. They even took the children over to Harry and Inette's, but no one was home; Betty thought her brother had deliberately taken his family to the country so as not to be contaminated by her presence. Harry thought it was probably a coincidence. "I would be more than disappointed in myself if I thought I was that cowardly," he said in 1996. But there was another outrage to be faced. When they woke up, the trees around the Easton house were festooned with toilet paper. Betty was indignant: Peoria had insulted her. But the toilet paper was decorating the trees for an entirely unrelated reason: "Our children had come home. It was for them," Bob Easton said. Marian Sweney described the toilet-papering as a celebratory custom: "If someone likes someone, or if there's a birthday, kids throw toilet paper over the trees. It's done all the time. It was in her mind."

8

Death Throes

THE FEMININE MYSTIQUE was the great divide of Betty's life, and its publication the beginning of her historic role. She became a personage, larger than life, her opinion solicited, her presence sought, invited to the White House. Lawrence Lader, an old friend who had been in the Allen Room with her and who was working to legalize abortion, observed her progress:

> Through television, radio, and lectures, she established almost instant communication with an audience waiting to be stirred. Often sharp and overbearing, she grated on many nerves, disturbed and even terrified others . . . women she touched with fire. Particularly on college campuses, and among young professionals, she roused an increasing number to the realization that tidbits of equality would not satisfy the demands of women.

Her success tilted the balance of the marriage. One could almost say that Betty wrote the book as the beginning of a long preparation for leaving Carl. It would take six more years to sever their tie legally; the Friedans spent those years working themselves into a frenzy, pitching the rage higher and higher, until at last there was nothing left but to end the marriage. James Fitch, with whom Betty had orchestrated the CRP, said, "I saw Carl at parties and meetings. I thought he was a perfectly nice guy who didn't know what was happening. He looked dazed. As if he were drifting over the falls. He was not the aggressor. To save herself, she had to jettison baggage—and he was part of it. It had to happen, for her own development."

In the late spring of 1964 the Friedans left Grandview. It was Betty who persuaded Carl to move back to the city. Always on the cutting edge, she sensed that the time of the suburbs had passed. She had wrung Grandview dry. She was, as she said, "the big cultural cheese" of Rockland County, and she would have to leave that, but she wanted to be at the center of things, part of the ferment and excitement. Perhaps, in the back of her mind, she realized it was easier to be a divorced woman in the city than in the suburbs, where everything was done in pairs.

The suburbs were just as glad to be rid of the Friedans, and seemed to collaborate in their departure. Their station wagon disappeared one day—it had been repossessed, and Carl had to scrape up the money to get it back. One night, driving home along a winding road in Piermont, Carl was caught speeding by a policeman. He and Betty had been drinking. Betty screamed at the cop and told him off, and kept screaming as he wrote another ticket. The upshot was that Carl's license was suspended, and he couldn't drive for a few months. He finally hired a lawyer to settle things and got it back. In the city Carl wouldn't have to commute, Betty pointed out, and they could sell the car. The schools would be better, too. Daniel was going to Princeton on a scholarship, and Jonathan and Emily would go to Dalton, one of the best private schools.

With her usual flair Betty found an apartment in a building they normally would not have been able to afford: the Dakota, a legendary brick pile, built like a château around a courtyard, at Central Park West and Seventy-second Street. The Dakota was going co-op, and the owners were going broke—they had too many empty apartments on their hands. Apartment 55, which the Friedans bought for approximately $15,000, had seven cavernous, high-ceilinged rooms, with an entry foyer, a dining room, a den, and two bathrooms. Carl recalls that the maintenance was $1,500 a month, which was very high at the time. The River Road house was still on the market when they moved, and Carl was temporarily low on cash, but Betty had book earnings ($25,000 from Dell and $10,000 of her $30,000 advance from Random House). She told Carl she was going to put the apartment in her name, but he insisted on giving her a promissory note for half. "It made me feel all shriveled up," he said. He paid the note a few months later.

The Dakota was a center of radical chic and the Beautiful People, whose parties were chronicled in the press with love, envy, and spite: "Manhattan's aristocracy of accomplishment, caste and gall..." "New York society is a success society, a talent elite.... It has the appetite of an adolescent vulture for new blood." Celebrated people clogged the hallways—people who ran New York's cultural life. The actor Robert Ryan had an apartment next door to the Friedans'. Carter and Amanda Burden, considered by many to be the chic-est couple in the world, lived there, as did Lauren Bacall and her then husband, Jason Robards Jr.; Susan Stein, the daughter of Jules Stein, the head of MCA; the writer and critic Marya Mannes; the architect Ward Bennett. "At the Dakota, Betty's parties became celebrity parties," said a friend from the Society of Magazine Writers. "The room was filled with distinguished people. She did it with a kind of crazy style. Her place was funky. She had a taste for expensive funky things." It made Carl nervous. He had always had dreams of writing, and Betty had beaten him to the punch, so to speak. He felt inadequate. "We didn't belong in the Dakota," Carl said. "It was all millionaires."

Betty decorated the apartment in the colors she loved—rich reds and purples in the living room, a fashionable silvery paper in a bathroom. In a hurry to get the work finished, she had the paperer come in on Sunday, at double the cost, which was high to begin with because this was the Dakota. She wanted it done when she wanted it done. The Friedans threw lavish parties—a hundred people came one New Year's Eve, and ate food ordered from a Harlem restaurant Betty and Carl liked. The restaurant was famous for its shrimp crackling rice soup—when you put fried rice in it, it crackled. Jonathan played the drums with his band. Betty had a maid who cooked, two children in private school, enormous food bills, and severe cash-flow problems. She was her mother's daughter.

As a well-known writer, Betty was invited to the White House in 1964, along with such prominent women as Ethel Merman and Betty Furness. President Johnson spent an hour talking to them, asking for their support in his campaign against Barry Goldwater. Betty expected to be asked to do something substantive, but LBJ only paraded the women in front of the television cameras. She realized they were just tokens, whose function was decorative merely. The White House visit was one of many activities that took her out of town, and she felt guilty about leaving home so often. Carl had become Mr. Betty Friedan, and he resented it. At parties he would make disparaging remarks: "I'm the bitch's husband," he told one guest; to another he said, "She's kind of doggy, but she's very bright." While Betty was away, Carl found his element.

Rock culture was beckoning to the middle-aged, a siren song promising they could be young again. A new French import, the discothèque, had caught on. Carl met a dancer who took him to the Peppermint Lounge and taught him how to do the twist; he became a regular at Ondine's and at Arthur, a new place run by Sybil Burton (recently divorced from Richard Burton) and Jordan Christopher, her lover. Arthur had been an instant smash, with lines outside every night. One night, after an evening of drinking, Carl took Betty there, hoping she wouldn't notice that he was known. The maître d' escorted them to a long, low coffee table with lit candles and benches. Betty hated it. "I don't like this table," she said, and kicked it over. A bouncer appeared, removed Carl's glasses, took each of them by the arm, and escorted them out. Betty was insulted. "How dare they do this!" she stormed. "They can't do this!" At three A.M. she called up William Fitts Ryan, her congressman, to complain.

According to Carl, Betty was taking diet pills—amphetamines. Amphetamines were legal then; no one understood the effects of speed yet, or how it combined with liquor. As a public figure, Betty was particularly concerned with looking attractive. Photographs show her wearing the little sleeveless shift dresses that were fashionable; her hair was cut smoothly short to her ears, a youthful style that was especially becoming to her. She looked prettier than she ever had, but she had always had a weight problem. Dr. Feelgoods had begun sprouting up, dispensing happiness, and there was one on the Upper West Side who was popular among people she knew. The violence and unpredictability of her outbursts may have been connected to the diet pills.

Her asthma was worse and her rages had started to frighten her. She would black out during fights with Carl and wake up with a bruised face and a black eye. They rarely discussed the violence. "We both repressed it—we were so glad when it was over," Carl said. "Once she said, 'You drive me crazy.'" In 1964 a book appeared that fascinated her—*I Never Promised You a Rose Garden*, by Joanne Greenberg. It was about a schizophrenic who had unpredictable seizures. "She read and reread it, searching for an answer," Carl said. "Her analyst told her that her nerve endings were all on the outside of her skin. She repeated it. She kept reading that book."

Although her marriage was violent, Betty was not what one ordinarily thinks of as a battered wife. She and Carl were a match; she egged him on, and she gave as good as she got. "It's not simple!" she told an interviewer many years later. "If you don't really have enough confidence to claim your own rage and stand up on your own two feet, then unconsciously—

you can't bear the fact that you feel this fury—so what you do is provoke the rage in him, then you have the black eye, then you feel justified in having the rage." Carl showed up for an important job interview with a scratched face. The woman who set up the appointment with him told him that he looked as if he had been mauled by a tiger.

Although Betty felt guilty about leaving home, she found relief on her trips. Carl escaped into what he called his "Walter Mitty life." Even when Betty was home, he sometimes spent the night elsewhere. Marlene Macaro, the creative director of Coty Cosmetics, a business acquaintance and buddy, threw all-night parties that ended with breakfast, and Carl stayed in her floor-through brownstone apartment on East Twenty-sixth Street. He took Betty to one of Marlene's parties, where she promptly got into a fight with Ultra Violet, an Andy Warhol superstar, who aroused instant antipathy in her. Ultra Violet had long curly hair and wore a knitted gold-chain vest with nothing under it. They stood in the bedroom and argued about *The Feminine Mystique*, yelling and shoving each other. During one shove, an antique wooden chime clock went out the window and crashed through the brand-new awning in the garden below, where two men were eating a gourmet dinner on their best crystal and china.

Carl turned to other women for consolation and flaunted his infidelities. Betty would later say, "Carl only struck out at me when he was drunk. He used other women more and more to get at me." But revenge was not Carl's only consideration, and sex was not his only motive. He gravitated to beautiful younger women who were in some sort of trouble—women who took drugs or drank too much; daughters escaping from oppressive families; illegal immigrants needing green cards—women he could rescue. Carl's women depended on him; for them, he could be heroic, the magician who pulled rabbits out of hats. There was no way he could rescue Betty or control her. He could only be the tail to her comet.

Betty and Carl took several vacations to the Caribbean—to Antigua, Guadeloupe, and Caneel Bay, whose peace was shattered by their presence. One hotel invited them to leave. To spend twenty-four hours a day together was impossible. On Fire Island one summer they rented Theodore White's house, and Betty broke a few windows. "They cost a fortune to replace," Carl said.

They made forays into togetherness. "My husband began to treat me much better after the book came out. He knew I'd leave him. So he was very threatened. It would alternate," Betty said. In 1965, during one of their good periods, they bought a five-bedroom house in Lonelyville on

Fire Island, for $5,000 down with a $20,000 mortgage. The house was in a cul-de-sac on the bay side, in a family neighborhood. Betty planted dusty miller. Carl planted trees. They built a deck and threw memorable parties. One summer Carl made a giant clambake in the sand with lobsters and chicken and corn; Betty cooked huge pots of clam chowder, served with endless bottles of vodka.

Early in the morning, when only the fanatical tennis players were out to see her, Betty would roam around, sleepless. "She just walked around," said Ray Robinson, one of the tennis players and a former editor of *Seventeen*. "It appeared she had suffered physical punishment—bloody nose, black eyes. She was obviously drunk. She looked distracted." The Friedans' scenes alternated with truces. People would see them sitting quietly holding hands, calm and happy together. "Sometimes they would go to the beach together, fighting like cats and dogs, and then they would come back together and be nice to each other," said Jay Herman, who had a house near the Friedans' and would later become one of Betty's escorts.

People who visited them never knew what to expect. Greta and Gerald Walker—she was an actress; he was an editor at *The New York Times Magazine*—had a fine time. "They were superb hosts," Greta said. "They were generous and kind and made us feel totally at home and couldn't do enough for us. It was a lovely weekend."

On another weekend a couple from Grandview came with their three small children. Betty had been particularly insistent that they come but had somehow forgotten that they were arriving. "Nobody met us," the woman said. "We stood on the dock and waited and waited and finally decided to go home. Then Carl happened by, pulling a red wagon full of groceries. He hadn't known we were coming. It was way past lunchtime. I said I'd get something for the kids. Betty did nothing. She had maroon or dark green faceted glasses. In the glasses were layers of hardened milk. There was no dish cloth, no soap, nothing. So I ran hot water and got face soap from the bathroom. We had lunch. I think she had dinner for us. We went around to cocktail parties. Everyone walked around holding their glasses, going from one party to another. None of the beds were made. Betty opened this chifforobe and a pile of scrunched-up sheets fell out. She waved her hand. I made the bed. I made beds for my kids. I always thought the sheets were dirty. Then we went to parties and everyone drank. During the night I was wide awake. Carl and Betty were fighting. They were whispering, but in such a rage, a loud whisper—*hissing*. It was vicious. I was terrified. It was the scariest night of my life. The next morning, the groceries they had ordered from the mainland—milk, et cetera—were still sitting in the box. Six kids were hanging around. We went to the beach. And then I said, 'We have to go,' and we went to the ferry."

In the winter of 1966, Betty got an assignment from the *Ladies' Home Journal* to cover the inauguration of Indira Gandhi, the world's first woman prime minister. It had been Carl's idea. As she would do on all her trips, Betty called everyone she could think of to get names and addresses of people who could help her or have dinner with her or who would be entertaining. In this way she enlarged her acquaintanceship all over the world. She collected about a dozen names in New Delhi, one of them being Ambassador Chester Bowles, who invited her to the embassy for drinks and a buffet luncheon and told her what she should and shouldn't eat.

The *LHJ* offered to double Betty's fee if she could get an interview with Indira Gandhi, and to triple it for an exclusive. "I had never been to Europe," Betty said. "We had just begun to go to the theatre—we didn't have any money. I got to India and got her schedule, and I went at five A.M. to a service on the banks of the Ganges commemorating the dead, or the anniversary of Nehru's death. I got there early, and people were pointing at me, because I looked like her. We were roughly the same age; she was a little older, with dark hair and wearing it the same way, and strong features. When she arrived services began, and within an hour her aides came up to me. 'Bet-ty Friedan, Bet-ty Friedan, the prime minister would like to see you' [imitating their lilt]. I brought a copy of *The Feminine Mystique* to give her, and after that I traveled with her by helicopter. The press was so mad—I was the only journalist, the only woman, American, and I traveled with her everywhere."

Betty and Indira got on beautifully. Indira was much taken with Betty's dramatic Rudi Gernreich cape—black on one side and beige on the other with a loop to put one arm through—and borrowed it to have it copied. Betty was thrilled. When she came back to New York she would ask people, "Do I look like Indira Gandhi?" She kept a photograph in her apartment of the two of them huddled over *The Feminine Mystique*.

After her four-thousand-word article (cut from eight thousand words) was published in the May issue of *LHJ*, the prime minister wrote to Betty, "For the first time somebody has tried to portray a person rather than a freak," and sought her out on subsequent visits to Washington. "I really did feel a bond," Betty said. "It was my real first experience of another culture. I loved India. I just loved India. I was so taken with India...it had insuperable problems, but she was a very good leader, Indira Gandhi, and things were happening, and you couldn't look at it through Western eyes. When things got tough in that country [when Indira suspended civil liberties], I refused to lend my name to attacking her."

Betty's forty-fifth birthday fell during her three weeks in India. This was a period when Carl was being more loving toward her; he sent her enough roses to fill her hotel room. On her return, he went to the Fur Vault and bought her a "fun fur," a paws-and-tails mink coat. "Maybe I was a bastard," Carl said. "It may have been my wanting out from the marriage at the beginning. My not really loving her influenced her reactions." The coat was a peace offering. But however pleased Betty was, she was also puzzled and suspicious. Their history together had not inclined her to be trusting, and she had trouble accepting it. Carl said, "There were times when she threw it at me, but she wore it all the time." She wore it to a party in Greenwich Village one wet winter night, over a red silk dress, and was seen in the crowd by Karen Durbin and Hendrik Hertzberg, two young journalists new to celebrity.* "I was thrilled," Karen said. "I was about twenty-three years old." After leaving the party, she and Rick walked along the street and stumbled across Betty and Carl again. "She was lying on her back in a little walkway that led to a brownstone," Karen said. "Her coat was spread open. A man in an overcoat was remonstrating with her, facing into the yard. As we came up to them, we saw these daintily shod little high-heeled feet between his feet. It was so evil. He was saying, 'Betty, get up. Stop this. Stop this right now.' And she was screaming, 'I don't have to get up, you fucking son of a bitch!'" It was a Polaroid of what their marriage had become.

---

* Karen Durbin, after a long career at *The Village Voice,* became its editor; Hendrik Hertzberg became the editor of *The New Republic,* and later the editorial director of *The New Yorker.*

9

Founding NOW

IN JUNE 1966, Betty was invited to Washington to attend the annual conference of state commissions on the status of women. The commissions, along with the Citizens' Advisory Council on the Status of Women, had grown out of a government report, *American Women* (November 1, 1963), which stated that "one of the most pervasive limitations is the social climate in which women choose what they prepare themselves to do." The commissions were toothless entities all, glorified study groups, but they were also precursors of the women's movement: they provided a network for women, and they made sex discrimination a legitimate issue. Other venerable institutions were alive, among them the National Federation of Business and Professional Women Clubs and the League of Women Voters.* The National Woman's Party, which had been founded in 1923 with the sole purpose of passing an equal rights amendment, still lobbied every year to put it on the congressional agenda. These groups worked politely at the margins of power, fearful of rattling the teacups. Feminism had never died; after the vote was won, it had lived on in

---

* The League of Women Voters, however, distanced itself from anything remotely connected to the word "feminism."

reduced circumstances, sitting in a darkened parlor in a condition of impoverished gentility. Some of the women keeping it alive became Betty's mentors.

In 1964, Representative Howard W. Smith of Virginia, an eighty-year-old arch-segregationist of infinite courtesy, was casting about for ways to scuttle LBJ's Civil Rights Bill. When Representative Martha W. Griffiths, a Michigan Democrat, long a fighter for women's rights, urged him to add the word "sex" to Title VII of the bill, he saw her suggestion as the perfect solution. Title VII outlawed employment discrimination based on race, color, religion, and national origin. Smith added "sex" as a joke. He thought the bill would be hooted off the floor, and that would be the end of it. During the debate, the House did indeed dissolve in laughter at this absurd idea, outraging the handful of women who were members. Martha Griffiths then pointed out that "without a sex amendment, white women would be last hired and first fired." They would be unprotected; employers could discriminate against them at will. Griffiths also threatened to have the vote recorded and labeled as being for or against women, and Margaret Chase Smith, Republican of Maine, the only woman in the Senate, threatened to do the same.

After much backstage maneuvering, the Civil Rights Bill passed. The sex clause was never meant to be enforced. However, Title VII had teeth—it set up the Equal Employment Opportunity Commission (EEOC) as its enforcement arm—and this gave women the weapon they needed to fight job discrimination. Ironically, many of the rights that women would gain were based on a joke that backfired.

By 1966, complaints from women were pouring into the EEOC, many of them thanks to Betty, who urged all the women she met on her speaking engagements to file. Women were calling her in the middle of the night and writing to her about their job problems—they had dead-end jobs, they trained men who moved up the ladder ahead of them, they were paid less than men. Nothing was being done. Betty was hanging around the EEOC, talking to people and researching her planned book, "The New Woman," when a young lawyer, Sonia Pressman, pulled her into her office, closed the door, and told her that the EEOC was focusing on blacks and devoting very little time to women's claims. Women needed their own power base, their own NAACP, to fight discrimination.

The idea of an NAACP for women was already in the air. Pauli Murray, a noted black lawyer and a fellow at Yale Law School (she later became an Episcopal priest), suggested it in a militant speech to the

National Council of Women of the U.S. at the Biltmore Hotel in New York. Betty called her, and Pauli Murray put her in touch with Catherine East, the woman who would change her life.

Catherine East was a civil service professional and an organization woman to the core. After twenty-three years in the federal government, she had become the executive director of the Citizens' Advisory Council. "I never succumbed to the feminine mystique," she said. "I had a career and good full-time help." She was an éminence grise—a lobbying strategist for women's groups, a writer of position papers. Catherine had statistics no one had put together before, such as comparative earnings by sex, education, and race. No one had known until then that white women with a college education earned less than black men with a high school education. She had found discrimination in social security, education, pensions, fringe benefits. In family law, only 15 percent of women were awarded alimony. Women had no right to support that could be enforced. "NOW got a lot of issues from us," Catherine said.

Together with Mary Eastwood, a Justice Department lawyer, and a few others, Catherine was a member of what Betty called the feminist underground, women who could do nothing official for fear of losing their jobs. Catherine knew that the old organizations couldn't shake things up; they were too cumbersome and too ladylike. Something new was needed, a leader with fire. She found that fire in Betty—in a woman who was fearless, outspoken, and famous—and chose her to head the new organization, which had yet to be founded.

Over a series of dinners with Betty, Catherine and Mary made lists of women—all the women Betty had met around the country—fed her statistics, and persuaded her of the need for a formal outside organization to pressure the government to take sex discrimination seriously. At first Betty was reluctant to be drafted. Even though she had instinctively created groups all her life, she thought of herself as a writer. Organizations were stuffy, hung up on *Robert's Rules* and bylaws, and they did nothing but talk. Betty would later say that she started the women's movement because her mother was unhappy as a woman. More to the point, her marriage was in tatters and her new book wasn't working. The army of brave new women who had shaken off the feminine mystique and gone out to conquer the world hadn't quite come into existence yet.

Catherine arranged for Betty to be invited to the 1966 conference of state women's commissions, whose theme was "A Time for Action." On the afternoon of the second day, a group of women was bused to the

White House to have tea with Lady Bird Johnson. LBJ, who had once said that he didn't want a stag government, spoke to them in the Rose Garden, quoting an epitaph from an old tombstone: "Born a woman, died a person." He had been well briefed but had not gotten the message: he told the women to return to their homes and continue their volunteer work, to help the unfortunate in their communities. Betty, who had spent other afternoons being patronized in the Rose Garden, resented it.

That night about fifteen women crowded into Betty's smoke-filled room in the Washington Hilton. Catherine East had stage-managed the meeting and told her whom to invite, and Betty had asked a few more. They were particularly concerned that the term of Richard Graham, an EEOC commissioner who supported women's claims, had expired, and he was not going to be reappointed; and that the EEOC was continuing to allow help-wanted ads to be categorized as "male" or "female." They argued for hours about whether to start a new organization. It seemed like such a radical thing to do. Some of the women were hesitant to step out of their accepted roles. It would look selfish for them to push their own agenda; they would be accused of being aggressive, unfeminine. Betty was ready to do it, but she still wasn't sure she was the one to pull it together. The women didn't trust her or one another yet; they didn't know one another well enough. Kathryn Clarenbach, chair of the Wisconsin commission, was "a darling of the Women's Bureau," Betty said, and the bureau was a creature of the White House. Betty suspected that Kay, who was not in favor of starting a new organization, might be a spy for the Establishment.

Betty was irritated, too, by Nancy Knaak, whom Kay had invited. Nancy sat on the floor sipping water and kept raising questions. There were so many organizations already, she said, and she herself had served on too many of them. At about eleven o'clock, Betty had had enough of Nancy Knaak. Betty did not have much patience with negative attitudes unless they led to something concrete. She began a ringing diatribe on the theme "Who invited you?," segued into "This is my room and my liquor," and wound up with a thunderous crescendo: "Get out! Get *out!*" When Nancy didn't move, Betty stormed into the bathroom (there was nowhere else to go) and sulked for fifteen minutes. When she came out, she ignored Nancy, who retired gracefully (and, she hoped, unnoticed) a short time later by slipping out the door when everyone was shouting about something else. The meeting ended with the decision that Kay Clarenbach would present two resolutions to the conference the next, and last, day—June 29: that Richard Graham be rehired, and that the EEOC enforce Title VII.

Kay thought it was going to be easy, but she was turned down. The state commissions on the status of women did not have the status to get a resolution onto the floor. The women were there only to exchange information. Despite its theme of action, the conference had no power to act.

At the luncheon ending the conference, Betty and Kay sat together, scribbling on yellow paper napkins, inventing NOW.* Kay, radicalized by her powerlessness, had reversed herself. "Betty was talking in her loud whispers," said Gene Boyer, a businesswoman from Wisconsin, who was at a nearby table. "In fact, some of the closer tables were shushing her up, but she was not about to be shushed up. It was all happening there." What was actually happening was a preemptive strike against Betty, whose performance with Nancy Knaak must have been alarming to Midwestern sensibilities.

Kay Clarenbach and Catherine Conroy, an official of the Communications Workers of America, had a prearranged plan. According to Mary Eastwood, "Catherine just started speaking. Since they couldn't have resolutions, they would start a new organization. It would be based either in Madison or Chicago, and Kay Clarenbach would be the temporary chairman. All these things were just decided." In their history, *Rebirth of Feminism,* Judith Hole and Ellen Levine suggest the reason for the rush to install Kay:

> Friedan's avowed feminist position coupled with her flamboyant and combative personal style had made her extremely controversial, and, in some corners, greatly feared. Several observers have interpreted the sudden urgency to organize the new action group "on the spot," even before the conference had adjourned, as an attempt to circumvent Friedan, and keep control of any new women's group in less militant hands.

Catherine Conroy and Kay had also come to lunch prepared with a written statement of purpose for the new organization. "Betty and I were shaking our heads," Mary Eastwood said. "They weren't proposing an activist organization—it could be just a study organization." Betty knew they needed an acronym and came up with NOW, National Organization for Women. "Nobody was impressed," Mary said. "They thought of it as a working title. The name sounded blah. But the acronym had an urgency."

---

* Others at the table included Mary Eastwood, Catherine Conroy, Inka O'Hanrahan, Pauli Murray, and Dorothy Haener.

Then, in a flash of inspiration, Betty scribbled the magic words: "to take the actions needed to bring women into the mainstream of American society—now, full equality for women, in fully equal partnership with men." The words were a reflection of Betty—her impatience; her urge to act; her need for men; her passion for justice.

After lunch, the women fanned out to get the word through the crowd; anyone who was interested was to meet in a designated conference room. People ran in, threw their dues on the table, and ran out to catch their planes. Typically for women, it was a low-budget operation—dues were five dollars.

Within a week, Kay Clarenbach and Catherine Conroy had picked a steering committee to organize NOW—and Betty was not on it. Betty was no longer as important to them: she had been useful in lighting the fire, but now they didn't want anyone so abrasive. They were going to launch NOW in the Midwest, with Kay in charge. Kay wanted NOW there because she was doing all the clerical work with her staff. Betty suddenly realized how neatly she had been outflanked. It was to happen again and again in the movement, and she would always feel helpless, but this time she would prevail.

In July, Catherine East and Mary Eastwood, her champions, came to Fire Island for a strategy meeting. Betty called Kay in Madison and raised hell—NOW was her idea in the first place, and why wasn't she on the steering committee? In her best intimidating manner, she informed Kay that the launch would have to be in either New York or Washington, so they could get publicity; no one paid attention to anything that happened in Madison. Overcome by this blast, Kay acquiesced. Betty volunteered Mary to make the arrangements and look after her interests, the main one being that she be president. She also wanted Pauli Murray, the civil rights lawyer, to be the chair, but was talked out of it: Kay, a cool, white Midwestern professor, would go down much better with the all-male WASP establishment than the combination of a Jew and a black.

Betty and Kay had a stormy but symbiotic relationship. They were virtual opposites. Kay, the daughter and wife of a minister, was extremely controlled. She spoke in a voice of authority and approached problems in a cool and logical manner. "She showed very little outward emotion, even when saying something dramatic," said Gene Boyer, the Wisconsin businesswoman who would put NOW on a sound financial footing. "Betty improvised; she was excitable, with sudden mood swings and lapses into bullying. Kay was the real organizer of NOW, the administrator, the one who understood structures and systems. Without Kay, there would have been no organization. Betty would call her up and tell her what needed to be done, and then, after Kay had tried to do it, criticize the way she'd done it. Kay felt beset by Betty. Betty's strengths were in her articulation of the concepts and her writing skills... as a catalyst, in her personal magnetism, in her network that she was able to tap into, in her ability to give inspiring speeches."

Gene acted as their go-between, spending hours trying to explain Betty's behavior to Kay, to get her through the screaming and yelling. Betty had a great deal of respect for Kay, who had academic credentials and therefore outranked her. Kay also had a wry sense of humor. A sign in her office at the University of Wisconsin read: THOSE OF YOU WHO THINK YOU KNOW EVERYTHING ARE A TERRIBLE PAIN TO THOSE OF US WHO DO. Betty had no irony, and her sense of humor did not apply to herself. At the marathon weekend sessions that were NOW board meetings, they both drank prodigiously, partly as a means of opening up to each other. Eventually Betty grew to love Kay—they became close friends—and more important, to trust her. She saw that her fears were groundless: Kay did not wish to wrest control from her and had no interest in sharing the limelight. None of the Midwestern feminists, in fact, were driven by Betty's ambition or media hunger. "It was because Kay was not threatening to Betty as a power player on her own turf that they were able to have a long-term relationship in which they really worked together as colleagues," Gene said.

At first, Betty underestimated the scope and appeal of NOW. She did not realize that she was lighting a match in an oil field. NOW's founders had created an organization before there was a women's movement, and they had created it in their own image—they were middle-class leaders and activists in the liberal tradition. Betty wrote letters to people whose names would impress those in power (NOW tilted heavily toward the professions), inviting them to join the group or its board of directors. The names emanated a power NOW had not yet acquired.* Considering

---

* Anna Roosevelt Halsted, Eleanor Roosevelt's daughter, was one of the first to join. Coretta Scott King joined. Some others: Phineas Indritz, a black civil rights lawyer who worked for the Government Operations Committee in the House of Representatives; Dr. Anna Arnold Hedgeman, a black woman who was coordinator of special events for the National Council of the Churches of Christ; two nuns, Sister Mary Austin Doherty of Chicago and Sister Mary Joel Reed, who later became president of Alverno College in Milwaukee; Carl Degler, a Vassar professor who was a great admirer of Betty's; Jane Hart, the wife of Senator Philip A. Hart (D.–Mich.) and a professional pilot who was campaigning to admit women into NASA's astronaut program; Dr. Alice Rossi, a scholar and theorist who became president of the American Sociological Association in 1983; Sonia Pressman, a lawyer at the EEOC; Muriel Fox, a vice president at Carl Byoir Associates, a public relations firm; Dr. Shepard Aronson, Muriel's husband.

the respectability and qualifications of these people, how could anyone say no? The letters made Betty's position clear: NOW was not going to be a mass organization, she wrote, but a more elite group that knew how to get things done.

Betty also sent out rejection letters. Susan Brownmiller, then unknown, received a misdelivered letter inviting Jane Jacobs to join NOW. Susan and a friend, Janice Goodman, who would become an important feminist lawyer, instantly wrote to Betty, asking to be members. They got back a note saying no, thank you very much for your interest, but NOW is a small group of women set up to lobby Congress.

The formal organizing meeting of NOW took place over the weekend of October 29–30, 1966. It was a no-frills occasion, held in the *Washington Post*'s John Philip Sousa Room, a bare space where community groups met. Thirty-two of the 300 members came. They elected Betty president and Kay Clarenbach chair of the board. Richard Graham, the former EEOC officer, became vice president; Aileen Hernandez, a black woman who was about to leave the EEOC, was chosen executive vice president. Caroline Davis, director of the UAW Women's Department, was elected secretary-treasurer.

Betty had written NOW's first document (edited and emended by Pauli Murray, Mary Eastwood, and Alice Rossi), a stirring five-page state-ment of purpose rooted in eighteenth-century ideals of freedom and democracy, the same basic American ideals that had once led her to Marx-ism and the labor movement. It had the ring of the Declaration of Inde-pendence: "The time has come to confront, with concrete actions, the conditions that now prevent women from enjoying the equality of oppor-tunity and freedom of choice which is their right, as individual Ameri-cans, and as human beings." All of the women felt a sense of history, of being heir to a great tradition. Pauli Murray had brought a medallion that had once belonged to a suffragist who had been jailed and gone on a hunger strike. Alice Rossi told the story of two British suffragists who were trying to bring a petition for the vote to Parliament and had had to resort to hiding it in an apple cart. The women of NOW had picked up the fallen standard.

After the organizational meeting, they held a press conference in New York. *The New York Times* did not consider it important enough to attend. Muriel Fox, the public relations vice president with whom Betty worked closely throughout NOW's early years, sent a letter to Clifton Daniels, the managing editor—Daniels and his wife, Margaret Truman, were patients of her husband's—asking him to send a reporter to interview Betty in her apartment. The interview appeared on November 22 on the women's page, right under a story whose headline was "How to Cook Your Thanksgiving Turkey."

NOW seemed daring and radical at the time, but the founders were a relatively conservative group. They had no thought of overthrowing the power structure; they wanted to join it. They believed that everyone would see the justice of their cause if it was presented properly by the right people. They did not want to be identified with the old feminists, the nineteenth-century heroines who had been demonized and wiped out of the history books. It was important for everyone to understand that this was a new breed of feminist—as Betty wrote, "not battleaxes nor man haters. Indeed, there were men in our own ranks."

NOWs first priority was to impress upon government officials that sex discrimination was important and that important people cared about it. One of the first things it did was to write letters asking for meetings with the top rank—LBJ; U.S. Attorney General Ramsey Clark; and John Macy, head of the Civil Service Commission. Betty always started at the top. It was a waste of time to deal with people who didn't have the power to make decisions. NOW asked for legislation to make child care costs for working parents fully tax deductible, and for federally assisted child care centers, enforcement of Title VII, and more women in policy-making positions.

The women mounted campaigns against newspapers for running sex-segregated want ads and supported Dusty Roads in her fight for the stewardesses. Representative Martha Griffiths was very helpful, writing needling letters to the airline presidents about running a bordello in the sky, but the EEOC was dragging its feet on producing guidelines.

NOW set up a legal committee, headed by Marguerite Rawalt, an IRS lawyer; on behalf of blue-collar women, it brought three suits designed to test whether Title VII of the 1964 Civil Rights Act superseded state protective labor laws.* These laws limited the number of pounds women could lift and the number of hours they could work and barred them from the night shift as well as from many traditionally male occupations. Earlier generations had fought for these laws and had considered their pas-

---

* *Mengelkoch* v. *Industrial Welfare Commission of California and North American Aviation; Bowe et al.* v. *Colgate-Palmolive; Weeks* v. *Southern Bell Telephone and Telegraph Co.* NOW won all of these cases.

sage great victories. In the new social climate, the laws discriminated against women, protecting them out of higher-paying jobs.

Some of the early organizers came out of union backgrounds, and NOW's agenda reflected that bias. The old work issues, the ones Betty had written about in her labor union days, had never been resolved. In the past they had been seen primarily through the prism of the class struggle. The new feminist spirit grew out of the social civil war that was the sixties and was based on women confronting their own daily experience, their condition as women.

NOW's membership quadrupled to twelve hundred in its first year. The original exclusionary policy was swept away in the enthusiasm of younger, more radical women. At the 1967 national conference, Betty, after an initial reluctance, decided to confront the movement's two thorniest issues: the Equal Rights Amendment and abortion. The right to have an abortion was the sine qua non of women's liberation, the rock-bottom condition for autonomy, but Betty, who had made a few referrals in her time, was worried about NOW's dignity. Jean Faust, an early member, said, "It was the kids who led the fight. Kids from Michigan, Ohio, and Texas kept standing up and shouting, 'We've got to have an abortion plank.' " The vote, to adopt a policy of repeal of all abortion laws, split the organization. A group led by Betty Boyer of Ohio left NOW to found the Women's Equity Action League (WEAL), to focus on employment and education.

The ERA fight was more complicated. The union women who had been among NOW's founders were forced to oppose it because their unions wanted to keep the protective laws. The United Auto Workers sent down a slew of women who paid their five-dollar dues at the door, thus becoming instant NOW members and eligible to vote. Another bloc, the National Woman's Party, dedicated to the ERA, also packed the meeting. Dorothy Haener of the UAW begged for one more year until she could get her union to change its position, but the pro-ERA faction won, and the union women had to walk out. (They came back a few years later.)

Independently of NOW, other groups were forming by spontaneous generation around the country. Many of the women founding them were inspired by the black civil rights movement; they had gone to the South to work for voting rights, only to discover that they were ignored in policy meetings and relegated to making coffee. They were handmaidens in the temple: the sexual revolution had freed them to become "chicks," passed around like cookies on a plate. Like the suffragists before them, they found their voice through the black cause. As early as 1964, women in the Student Nonviolent Coordinating Committee (SNCC) had begun meeting in small groups to confront male supremacy.* It was they who first used the phrase "women's liberation." Betty referred to the women's movement as the "movement for equality" and later as "the sex role revolution."

The radical women gave the movement its intellectual structure. NOW's theoretical base was liberal democracy; the radicals rethought and reinterpreted the entire female experience, placing women at the center, producing dazzling new insights and forcing NOW beyond the borders of its legalistic mold. They provided the extremism necessary to revolutions. Starting with their personal experience, they analyzed relationships and the politics of housework, of clothes, of sex, and named patriarchy, built on the unpaid labor of women in the household, as the root of all evil. Women were a class, they argued, oppressed by men. It was a position Betty could never countenance, and she would fight them to the end on it. They started consciousness raising as a tool for political action and invented the slogans that caught fire: "Sisterhood Is Powerful"; "The Personal Is Political." They introduced the word "sexism" into the language.[†] Their bible was Beauvoir, not Friedan.

These two streams, women's liberation and women's rights, flowed together, and when they met they created a torrent. The movement opened the world for women: it changed their sense of themselves and their place in society, and forced men to perceive them differently. Among movement women there is a struggle for the laurels of history, the honor of being named the first, and a reluctance on the part of each side to credit the other. Radical women argue that it wasn't until they became involved that there really was a movement. Betty called them "pseudo-radicals" and disparaged their contribution. "It does not confront the real condition of the majority of women in a two-sex world," she said. "When women have been in the movement a long time, they see that what really created the change is the mainstream of the women's movement, not the extremists." The movement erupted out of *all*

* The first women to protest were Casey Hayden and Mary King, in 1964.
[†] "Sexism" was coined in "Freedom for Movement Girls—Now," an essay written in 1968 and published in *No More Fun and Games: A Journal of Female Liberation*, no. 2 (February 1969), p. 31.

women's need for it, and both sides were essential to its growth; but there was only one national organization, NOW, and one national leader, Betty Friedan. She was the movement's star and personification, its center of excitement, the one who embodied its hopes and dreams, its rages and frustrations. The radical groups had their day and faded, but their issues and ideas—their theories of sexual politics—would become central to the debate.

10

Divorce

IN THE SUMMER of 1967 Betty was having serious doubts about NOW. She had embarked on the greatest enterprise of her life, but her friends on Fire Island were mocking her spindly little organization, which had yet to accomplish anything. Women had things so good, they said, there was no need for them to be liberated. Carl had no use for feminism; his idea of a wife was someone who took care of the house and left the competition to men. In her worst moments Betty even considered dropping NOW. Carl would come home to the Dakota at eleven o'clock at night to find a NOW meeting in progress and yell, "Get the fuck out!" and they would scramble to leave. He taunted Betty with being a lesbian, an unspeakably insulting word, then, perhaps the worst thing anyone could call a woman. After one such exchange, she felt she had to get away from him; she needed a safe place to spend the night, and she called Dolores Alexander, a woman in the movement who had been working as her assistant.

"Carl and I have been fighting," she said, "and I have to get out of here." Dolores turned her down. "I was living in a teeny-tiny apartment on Twelfth Street, and besides, I didn't want to get involved. It was after midnight. Carl picked up the extension and was listening. I heard him say, after I said no, 'See, she's not a lesbian like you.' She was so terrified of the lesbian taint—it was a weapon against her."

Betty invited Dolores to Fire Island for a few weekends and confided in her. "She had blackouts occasionally," Dolores said. "She was deeply disturbed about it. Betty kind of admitted she taunted him as much as he did her. She was very down about the movement; it was causing her aggravation; it was at odds with her personal life. In some blind last-ditch effort to save her marriage, she blamed the movement for its demise."

Betty's position grew more untenable daily. She had dozens of requests to lecture but turned down many of them because Carl objected to her being away, and she felt guilty about leaving the kids. She flew around the country to attend NOW board meetings, which were held in a different city each month. She joined a picket line against job discrimination at a Colgate-Palmolive plant in Louisville, Kentucky. She picketed the Equal Employment Opportunity Commission's New York office and testified there for the airline stewardesses. She wrote long memos outlining strategies for NOW—which direction the organization should take, which issues were primary and which secondary. In public she was leading a crusade for equality; in private she despised herself. "I used to think, what a phony I was in my personal life. I was such a *worm*, such a masochist, unable to face my rage."

So they continued. Among their good friends were Dr. Harold Greenwald, a psychiatrist who had written a best-seller, *The Call Girl*, and his wife, Ruth. Betty phoned them late at night for comfort and advice. They saw the Gittelsons, Natalie, who was special-projects editor at *Harper's Bazaar*, and Mark; Alvin and Heidi Toffler, who were working on *Future Shock*, and Greta and Gerald Walker. "I liked her because she was effervescent and lively and spoke her mind," Gerry Walker said. "She had a nice smile. She was interested in what other people were thinking and doing. She was generous, had an open home, liked company. But it was never very pleasant. There was a lot of rage between them."

In the summer of 1967 Betty and Carl became involved in an anti–Vietnam War action. Gerry Walker and some colleagues at *The New York Times* formed the Writers and Editors War Tax Protest, whose members withheld 23 percent of their income tax, the calculated portion of the federal budget that went to the Pentagon. People who withheld their taxes wrote to the IRS explaining why. The IRS then sent a form letter telling them how much they owed, followed by a succession of letters, each more threatening than the last. Ultimately, tax rebels could expect to have their bank accounts attached.

Betty volunteered her apartment for a fund-raising party. Hundreds came and overflowed into Robert Ryan's apartment next door. Gloria Steinem, who was then a freelance writer, became involved in the party. "She was in charge of vegetables," Greta said. "She sent over bags full of uncut raw vegetables, straight from the grocer. The carrot fronds were waving out of the bag." Carl designed a "we the undersigned" ad for magazines and newspapers around the country, to show that adults, not just draft-age kids, were against the war. Over four hundred writers and editors signed. Gerry said, "We got ads placed; we got seven thousand dollars in six months and placed more ads. We had a surplus of money, two or three thousand, and gave it to Dr. Spock and the Reverend William Sloane Coffin at the War Protestors League, to defend people."

It all seemed such a great lark, but then it got a little scary. The FBI started tapping people's telephones. Gerry's phones were tapped at home and in the office. In March 1968, LBJ decided he could not win a second term and announced that he would not run. Some of the protesters paid their taxes. Bobby Kennedy and Eugene McCarthy, both against the war, were running, so they felt that they had won.

In the Friedan household, the violence escalated as Betty and Carl hacked away at each other. Marlene Macaro, Carl's friend, said, "Arguments would start by him goading her about NOW. He hurt her feelings so badly. He was cruel—he talked about his paramours even when they didn't exist." Betty struck back. Carl showed up at Marlene's once at three A.M. with a big gash on his head. Betty had hit him with a curtain rod. In a perverse way, they were helping each other end the marriage. Neither one had the courage to do it; neither one wanted to assume the guilt and blame.

In 1967 Betty and Carl separated for the first time, preparatory to a divorce. Betty had already begun testing the waters. She dressed provocatively, seeking perhaps from other men the sexual reassurance that Carl was not providing. At a New Year's Eve party she had worn a see-through blouse and nothing underneath. She showed up at a spring party wearing the same dress as Linda Wolfe, a younger writer. "It was a black satiny slinky fabric, short, with a very, very deep plunged neckline. It was so low, I cut the label placket out and sewed it in front." She began an affair with another writer, but it soon ended. Her household was in turmoil; perhaps it was better to keep the family together.

A month after separating, Betty and Carl tried to patch things up with a vacation in Ocho Rios, Jamaica. "Betty was grim-faced," Carl said. "There was nothing going on with us." Back at the Dakota, she slammed a bureau drawer so hard the mirror above it shattered, raining huge shards all over the floor. "I thought I would die," Carl said.

As they careened toward the inevitable end, Carl tightened the screws by presenting Betty with an ultimatum. Unless she gave him control of her money, he would divorce her and destroy her public image as a house-wife: if the leader of the new feminism got a divorce, feminism would be blamed and the fledgling movement would be damaged. In the marriage, money was the language for talking about emotions.

As Betty understood Carl's ultimatum, he considered her money to be his. They would set up a joint corporate account for tax purposes, and all of Betty's earnings would go into it. It would pay for all their expenses; they would live on it. She would not be allowed to have a separate check-ing account. Carl would keep all the money he earned, and he would also be free to spend the money in the joint account—for his office expenses, to take out other women, whatever he wanted. In return for the money, he would maintain the façade of their marriage. Carl wanted to be appreci-ated for all that he had done during their marriage, for what *The Feminine Mystique* owed to him. "She had time to write it because she lived in a mansion on the Hudson River, had a full-time maid and was completely supported by me," he said later.

Considering his conflicting desires and needs, the ultimatum could be seen as Carl's way of helping Betty to leave—or of gaining control so that she would not. In any case, it caught her at a time when she was in a par-ticularly jealous and panicky state, incapable of throwing it back in his face. She remembered his awful letter to his parents before their marriage, saying she wasn't much to look at but she was so bright that he would never have to worry about money. The ultimatum was "like being asked to pay for my marriage," she wrote in disjointed jottings, trying to make sense of it. On the one hand, he was asking for her absolute trust of him with the money; on the other, he was telling her that she *couldn't* trust him because he was going to do whatever he wanted. If she couldn't trust him, they had nothing. She was willing to share her money, but not to lose control over it. She was also aware that Carl, having gained that power, would come to resent her for it, and the arrangement would perpetuate a state of affairs already intolerable. She would have the shell of a marriage and no self-respect.

Betty was demoralized enough to agree to Carl's conditions, but nothing could save this marriage. She was carrying an immense burden of guilt, which she blamed on Carl—guilt for the money she had earned and the fame she had achieved and even for having had the courage to unlock doors for women. Had she allowed herself to contemplate the enormity of her rage, she wrote, "I would have wanted to murder him."

Still she delayed. She had an irrational fear of being alone, and a shell of a marriage was better than nothing. Finally, she made a pact with herself. She had been invited to speak at a conference in Zurich. She had never been to Europe, and she thought if she could travel and stay by herself in a hotel and have dinner alone for a couple of days—if she could manage that—she could overcome her paralyzing fear and get a divorce. She went to Sweden, Finland, Czechoslovakia, and France, where she met with other feminists—movements had already begun in Europe—and made plans for a future international gathering. In Paris she met Yvette Roudy, who had translated *The Feminine Mystique* into French. On her return she wrote to the women she'd met, thanking them for their hospitality and telling them of her plans: she had made the decision to get a divorce, and she felt free—a great burden had been lifted from her. She had even lost weight. The divorce would take another year and a half and another trip to Europe.

There are two versions of their final parting. Betty said she presented Carl with her own ultimatum: "I'm going to the Philharmonic; when I come back, I want your things out.... I sat through the Philharmonic with tears streaming down my face. The loneliness was never as bad as I thought it would be."

Carl said, "There was no ultimatum. That is too simple. She helped me get out. I left because I wanted to leave. The separation was mutual. I was not going to stay, so she said, 'Get out.' " He also said, "She had no alternatives. I never had the strength to pull out."

In April 1969 they signed a separation agreement. On May 14, after giving a lecture at the Episcopal Cathedral in Jackson, Mississippi, Betty flew to Chihuahua, Mexico, and got the divorce. In an interview a few years later, she told a reporter, "I went to a bar and sat and cried, not because I was alone but for all the wasted years."

The marriage had lasted almost twenty-two years. It had not been all black eyes and broken mirrors, although the gratification they derived from their bouts, the freedom they gave each other to behave badly, had surely bound them together. For all Carl's protestations of not loving her, the bond between them was almost unbearably intense. Two decades later, Betty told an interviewer: "I look back now and realize that there were happy times. My marriage had some rich, rewarding textures.... Intimacy is one of the most important things in life." There had been the comfort of habit and the safety of the known. Guilt about the children cemented them, as did Betty's sexual dependence on Carl. Until *The Feminine Mystique* she was a failure; the marriage was all she had. Carl's psychoanalysis had convinced him that he had married his mother, so to him, the fights were a way of getting back at her. Betty had held him together, centered him, kept him from drowning in his insecurities. In the process she overwhelmed him. All his life he would remember her warmth.

C H A P T E R

II

Liberation

BETTY HAD BEGUN to see the the limitations of a small organization very soon after NOW's founding. On Christmas Eve 1966, she and Muriel Fox had been dragged downtown to federal court by the airlines for a nasty session of testimony, and no one was there to picket and make noise in the street. Muriel organized New York–NOW, NOW's first chapter. The first meeting was held in the middle of a snowstorm on February 6, 1967, at 5 East Seventy-fifth Street, a mansion with a marble foyer and a black-and-white-tiled floor. Seventy-two women came, all of them thrilled to be in the same room with one another. They had never acted in their own cause before. They came from IBM, Morgan Stanley, J. Walter Thompson, from journalism and the law, advertising and television, poetry and the theatre. Some were housewives. Jean Faust, elected the first president, was the daughter of a North Carolina sharecropper who had worked her way through college. She was married to a novelist and was an aide to New York City Congressman William Fitts Ryan— the same William Ryan whom Betty had called after being thrown out of Arthur.

The large turnout, the setting and the connections it implied, presaged the chapter's preeminence. It was a euphoric time, suffused with the breathless excitement of creating a revolution. America was in the throes of a "youthquake," making people feel they could be young again and have a second chance. All things seemed possible. "Betty galvanized us," said Betty Berry, who headed the Marriage and Divorce Committee. "She always had ideas. She had a talent for putting the right people together for the task. If there was a question, she would just rise up and say what to do. She was so brave."

Among its many actions, the chapter sued all the major city newspapers to "de-sexify" the help-wanted ads and sent busloads of women to Albany to lobby for abortion rights and equitable divorce laws; its Image Committee mounted a license challenge against WABC-TV for sex discrimination and started a public service advertising campaign to raise consciousness. One of the ads featured a man with his trousers rolled up and the line, "Hire him, he's got great legs." NY–NOW's actions reverberated around the country.

The media were centered in New York, and in those early days NOW lived for media coverage. The movement was born at the moment of television's ascendance and could not have come so far so fast without it. NOW had no offices and no staff. Muriel ran the publicity out of her office at Carl Byoir Associates; Betty made policy in the Dakota; Kay Clarenbach ran the organization from the University of Wisconsin. The media was a mixed blessing, destructive and life-giving; it spread the word, but its methods were ridicule and stereotyping. The idea of females demanding their rights had an entertaining aura of lunacy about it. In this uneasy collaboration, the women created spectacles to attract attention: when they demonstrated at the EEOC, they brought coffins and wore black veils to symbolize the killing of the 1964 Civil Rights Act—and their theatrics further encouraged the press to make jokes of them.

In those first years, Betty and Muriel had their hands full trying to protect the image of NOW and be taken seriously. Muriel was always pleasant, reasonable, and diplomatic, a perfect foil for Betty's volatility. She was one of the founders of American Women in Radio and Television (AWRT) in 1950, and a vice president of Carl Byoir, the largest public relations firm in the world. Betty was impressed with her title and the $25,000 salary—very large for a woman—that went with it. Muriel had written the first press release announcing NOW, and from the beginning Betty had depended on her for advice. Even so, she had been suspicious of this paragon who had suddenly appeared. "She told me that she checked me out with a friend," Muriel said. " 'I'm talking to this woman, Muriel Fox, I'm taking her advice a lot. Who is she? Can I trust her?' "

Muriel's background bore some parallels to Betty's. Born on February 3, 1928, in Newark, New Jersey, she was the family's oldest child. Her father, a Polish immigrant, had a grocery store. She fought constantly with her mother, who had paranoid delusions that were later diagnosed as a chemical imbalance and treated. Muriel's mother had been overwhelmed by housework and motherhood; she had been an A student, but her schooling had ended when she was fourteen. Her father did not think that girls needed any more education.

Muriel had been an ugly child—skinny, sloppy, badly dressed in wrinkled hand-me-downs—who dreamed of being a rich and famous author. She graduated from Barnard summa cum laude, and worked in the Congress of Racial Equality. In 1956, at twenty-eight, she had become the youngest vice president in her firm—but she was paid less than male vice presidents and warned that she wouldn't rise further "because corporate CEOs can't relate to a woman."

Muriel grew up to be beautiful—tall and dark, with brilliant eyes and shining hair, always perfectly groomed. She and her husband, Dr. Shepard Aronson, went to NOW meetings together and held hands. They had two children, a large, sprawling apartment in the East Eighties, and the kind of perfect marriage Betty envied. Muriel had judgment, connections, a sense of strategy; she even had an IQ that almost matched Betty's; but she and Betty never became friends. "I always felt that Betty didn't like me," she said. "I think she resented me. And I was very pretty. I'm sure Betty resented that. Plus, Betty just wasn't very nice to anybody.... I remember just walking into meetings, board meetings, or one thing or another, and Betty'd just never look at me. It was upsetting to me." Whatever antagonism Betty may have felt, she and Muriel were of one mind when NY–NOW began veering off in unseemly directions in 1968 under the new presidency of Ti-Grace Atkinson.

Betty had discovered Ti-Grace (Cajun for "Little Grace"), who was corresponding with Simone de Beauvoir, and thought she was the answer to a prayer. "Ironically, it was I who first pushed Ti-Grace into leadership," Betty wrote. "Her Main Line accent and ladylike blond good looks would be perfect, I thought, for raising money from those mythical rich old widows we never did unearth." Ti-Grace had been one of the women who had convinced Betty to put abortion on NOW's national agenda and had made sure they had the votes. Betty encouraged her to talk to the press, and to learn how to handle herself. A 1969 photograph shows a tall woman with cropped blond hair, stylishly dressed in heels and a tiger-print sheath. Ti-Grace was American aristocracy. Her mother's family were founders of the state of Virginia, and her father, a chemical engineer for Standard Oil, was in *Who's Who* as the creator of the Alaska pipeline. She had graduated from the University of Pennsylvania with a degree in fine arts and was a former critic for *ArtNews*. She was divorced and lived on East Seventy-ninth Street in a rent-controlled one-bedroom garden apartment filled with family heirlooms. Ti-Grace was a feminist theorist—"Vaginal Orgasm as a Mass Hysterical Response" was one of her papers. Like Betty, she was an original.

Betty had no idea how radical Ti-Grace was. During her term as the second president of NY–NOW, Ti-Grace gave a speech attacking marriage as legalized prostitution and a form of slavery (an idea previously voiced by Victoria Woodhull, Emma Goldman, and others). She also sanctioned the Colgate action: in conjunction with NOW's lawsuit against Colgate-Palmolive, women demonstrated for four days in front of Colgate's headquarters on Park Avenue. One of the days featured a "Flush-In," with Colgate products going down the drain of a toilet sculpted by Kate Millett. It was not the sort of thing Betty had envisioned for NOW, and she yelled at Ti-Grace, who cried. Betty also took a dim view of some scholarly research Ti-Grace was doing. She told the NY–NOW executive committee, "I want all of you to realize that what is involved here is something very sick. The [committee] members tell me that Ti-Grace is now doing a study of the Amazons." Betty had no patience with theories of Amazonian glories and ancient goddesses in some prehistoric never-never land. She was interested in ideas that led to action.

Even before these disillusioning activities, Ti-Grace had embroiled NOW in the Valerie Solanas scandal, which caused Betty much grief. Solanas, twenty-eight years old, was a writer and actress who had been in *I, a Man,* one of Andy Warhol's films. On the afternoon of June 3, 1968, she went to The Factory, his studio at 33 Union Square West, and shot him in the chest. About three hours later, she surrendered herself to a policeman directing traffic in Times Square, and handed over a .32 automatic and a .22 revolver. She told the police, "I am a flower child. He had too much control over my life." The police thought she was crazy and put her in a psychiatric ward.

In the name of NOW, Ti-Grace and Florynce Kennedy, a flamboyant black lawyer who had once represented H. Rap Brown, the black power leader, leaped to Solanas's defense. (Flo Kennedy made Betty nervous, too. She was a loose cannon, prone to pungent epigrammatic statements such as, "There are only a few jobs that actually require a penis or a vagina.") Ti-Grace told a reporter that she considered Solanas a "feminist heroine" whose motive was economic—Solanas believed she had been exploited and cheated out of money—but since only men were supposed to get violent over economics, she was considered crazy.

Valerie Solanas might not have become a cause célèbre among feminists had she not also been the founder of SCUM, the Society for Cutting Up Men. SCUM's goals were rather more drastic than those of other women's liberation groups. Its twenty-one-page manifesto declared its purpose to "bring about a complete female takeover, eliminate the male sex and begin to create a swinging, groovy, out-of-sight female world." This goal was to be accomplished through sabotage and murder. As far as anyone knew, Solanas was the sole member of SCUM.*

Betty and Muriel drew back in horror. Their first thought was damage control. On June 14 they sent Flo Kennedy a pompous telegram: "Desist immediately from linking The National Organization for Women in any way with the Case of Valeria Solanis [*sic*]. Miss Solanis' motives in the Warhol case are entirely irrelevant to NOW's goals of full equality for women in truly equal partnership with men." They were a little late. *The New York Times* ran a story linking NOW and feminism with Solanas. Betty was frantic. She called Mary Eastwood, who had a soft spot for Ti-Grace, and asked her to use her influence. "She started to talk about the awful publicity NOW was getting because of Ti-Grace's rash statements," Mary said. "She said, 'You've got to get rid of Ti-Grace, we've got to get rid of Ti-Grace.'" To Mary's ears, it sounded as if Betty was implying, "Get the Mafia to rub her out or something," which shocked her.

Betty had a way of dramatizing things, but her overreaction was probably closely connected to the mayhem in her marriage. All her life she would avoid the issue of violence against women, never joining others to speak out against it, relegating it to a limbo of concerns she would label "sexual politics." In 1968, still a year away from her divorce, she was fearful that her abusive marriage would become public knowledge. People would say the whole movement was crazy. She would be a laughingstock, and NOW would be destroyed.

That fall, Ti-Grace provided Betty with a way to dispatch her. As president of NY–NOW, Ti-Grace was planning to change the bylaws to eliminate the hierarchy in favor of a structureless, rotating leadership that would give all women a chance to lead—and to do the scut work. The idea

---

* SCUM later developed a large cult following. What might be called a bloodless echo of Solanas's sentiments was seen on a T-shirt in the early 1990s: IF WE COULD PUT ONE MAN ON THE MOON, WHY CAN'T WE PUT THEM ALL THERE?

came from radical groups, and it would prove to be a design for chaos. Betty was alerted in advance by Jacqueline Michot Ceballos, one of her new lieutenants, and she and Muriel got on the phone. On the night of the bylaws vote, the room was packed with their friends. The vote was 44–18 against Ti-Grace. Ti-Grace, the ungrateful daughter, resigned, as did Flo Kennedy. NOW was saved.

The Solanas affair was still simmering in September when the radicals finally put the movement on the map with their Miss America "zap action" in Atlantic City.* The movement exploded just as the rest of America was exploding; 1968 saw two assassinations (Martin Luther King Jr. and Robert Kennedy), draft card burnings, campus riots, and the police riot at the Democratic National Convention in Chicago. Until then, Betty had been hanging back, mindful of NOW's image. Earlier that year, NOW women had dumped aprons in front of the White House in a Mother's Day demonstration, "Rights Not Roses." The event scarcely made a ripple. Nola Claire, one of the demonstrators, remembered, "Six or seven of us were in Betty's room in a hotel in Washington. We had plans to chain ourselves to the White House fence. We had chains and locks. We sat there in Betty's room, and she talked us out of it. She wanted to look good—she called certain women up front in the line when photographers came. She couldn't have her demonstration be unladylike. With chains we'd be arrested, and it was too radical. After Atlantic City, she changed her mind."

The Miss America zap had the kind of brilliant craziness that was irresistible to the media. It was orchestrated by Robin Morgan, a former child TV star (she played Dagmar, the kid sister, in *Mama*) who had founded WITCH (Women's International Terrorist Conspiracy from Hell), an anarchic group that specialized in hectoring corporate institutions. She was married to a poet, Kenneth Pitchford, and had a son. Robin was known for "Goodbye to All That," an article in the underground newspaper *Rat,* that included this inflammatory sentence: "So they'll have to make up their own minds as to whether they will be divested of just cock privilege or—what the hell, why not say it, *say* it!—divested of cocks." She later settled down and became the editor of *Ms.* magazine.

In Atlantic City, WITCH crowned a live sheep Miss America, but the symbol that went down in history was the Freedom Trash Can, a receptacle for all the paraphernalia of false femininity—"bras, girdles, curlers, false eyelashes, wigs...any such woman-garbage you have around the

---

* A zap was a onetime guerrilla action centered on a specific event.

house." The myth of bra burning, which would forever haunt the movement, arose from that unlit trash can. Betty thought the concept had "verve and style," but she was never comfortable with the scorn for femininity and its implied hostility to men. Her own desire to be attractive to men made the radical position unthinkable, beyond all reason; and her psychological training had taught her the infinite subtleties of male-female connections. In 1963, after *The Feminine Mystique* was published, *Life* magazine had quoted her as saying, "Some people think I'm saying, 'Women of the world unite—you have nothing to lose but your men.' It's not true. You have nothing to lose but your vacuum cleaners." The women's movement was many things to Betty, but it was never a war on men.

In 1969, national NOW designated February 9–15 Public Accommodations Week. All over America women were denied entry to restaurants at certain hours—or at all times—and forbidden to sit at bars unescorted for fear they would give the place a bad name. In New York they made their stand at the Oak Room of the Plaza Hotel, richly decorated with bronze chandeliers and brown leather chairs, Gothic arches and dark paneling, a bastion of male privilege. Women were excluded from noon to three P.M. Muriel had chosen this castle to storm to redress an old grievance. She had once taken a group of clients and journalists to a business luncheon there and been turned away. Betty, too, had been embarrassed in the Oak Room. In 1964 Clay Felker, the future founding editor of *New York*, who was then a consultant to the *Ladies' Home Journal*, had offered to let her edit a section of *LHJ* and invited her to lunch at the Oak Room to discuss it. Betty had arrived first, but the maître d' had refused to seat her. She had been very rattled—something was wrong with her, she thought; maybe she wasn't dressed right? She couldn't understand it. The incident had so unnerved her that she had hardly been able to believe that Clay was serious about his offer.

On February 12, in the wake of a blizzard, the women stood shivering in the snow with their signs—WAKE UP PLAZA! GET WITH IT NOW!—waiting for Betty. Reporters, drawn by the aura of the Plaza and sick of covering the weather, outnumbered the demonstrators. Muriel had suggested that everyone who had a fur coat should wear it. Fur conveyed a certain image: these were women of substance, women who were the equals of the men inside, not bra burners; there was no reason to exclude them. The furs would also look good on television.

Betty, the star of the event, was out of commission. On the phone she told Dolores Alexander to start the demonstration without her—her face was bruised and she had a black eye. It would be too humiliating for the leader of a movement still the source of endless ridicule and jokes to appear as a battered wife. But Betty was the reason for the cameras, and Dolores sent Jean Faust to the Dakota to camouflage her eye. "She was very matter-of-fact," Jean recalled. "She said nonchalantly that Carl had hit her because he thought it would keep her from going on TV. I patched her up. In the cab we talked about what we were going to say in interviews."

Betty arrived an hour late, wearing the mink coat Carl had given her, and dark glasses. Shep Aronson, Muriel's husband, escorted her inside. Followed by cameras, the women went in and sat down, but the Oak Room waiters had been ordered not to serve them. "We were sitting at a round table in the center of the room," said Diana Gartner, one of the demonstrators. "Four waiters came and lifted the table and walked away with it. We were wearing dresses—we were sitting there with our legs, and the men were looking at us. One of them offered us bread sticks. After a while Betty said, 'It looks like we are not going to be served; we'd better leave.' "

The Plaza sit-in was covered by media outlets as far away as Hong Kong. On the *Today* show Betty, flawlessly made up, her sunglasses removed, pronounced in outrage, "This is the only kind of discrimination that's considered moral, or, if you will, a joke." The action broke down more barriers, but NOW took a lot of flak for those fur coats. "Friedan, the mother of the movement, and the organization that recruited in her image, were considered hopelessly bourgeois," wrote Susan Brownmiller, a founder of New York Radical Women. Betty did not consider such criticisms important; she had her vision, and she knew she was right.

A week after the Plaza sit-in, Betty flew to Chicago to speak at the organizing meeting of the National Association for the Repeal of Abortion Laws (NARAL).* Lawrence Lader, the founding chair and president, had invited her to be a cofounder. Long a crusader for abortion rights, Lader had published a book on the subject in 1966 and was trying to parlay the book into a movement as Betty had done. For this he needed Betty. She could pick up the phone and create disturbances across the country.

Larry Lader was Harvard and family money; like Betty he came out of the Old Left. They had met in her post-Berkeley days in New York, through mutual friends from Vassar. Both had worked for Vito Marcantonio in the forties, although Lader did not recall seeing her then, and he had been working in the Allen Room when she was writing *The Feminine Mystique.* He admired her greatly. She was "a hurricane," he wrote:

* February 14–16, 1969, at the Drake Hotel. After the Supreme Court's 1973 *Roe* v. *Wade* decision, NARAL changed its name to the National Abortion Rights Action League.

She sweeps through meetings, telephone calls, dinners, and speeches with frantic bursts of energy as if each day might be her last. Everything is in motion, not just her words which come so fast she seems to ignore the necessity of breathing. Her hands gesticulate, wave, flail. Her eyes are deep, dark, charged, and violent as her language. Her nose is long, her hair ... often askew. Nothing fits the accepted model of beauty. Yet she exerts a powerful, haunting attractiveness—that special combustion which lights up a few, rare individuals interacting with their audience.

. . .

BEFORE NARAL, BEFORE women's liberation, the abortion movement had been building around the country. There were networks of referral services and challenges to state laws, almost every one of which prohibited abortions except to save a woman's life. Doctors, lawyers, and clergymen were in the vanguard, not women, and their focus had been to make abortion legal for doctors to perform. The essential idea of choice, the connection between abortion and women's rights, eluded them. They were not feminists. At the founding NARAL conference Betty enlightened them. She proposed that the charter contain a preamble declaring "the right of a woman to control her own body [to be] her inalienable, human, civil right, not to be denied or abridged by the state, or any man."

It was not NARAL but the angry voices of the radical women who forced the issue. At almost the same time that Betty was shaking up NARAL, a dozen women from Redstockings were disrupting a New York state legislative hearing.* The committee's list of witnesses consisted of fourteen men and a Catholic nun. Fifteen minutes into the hearing, Kathie Sarachild, a leader of the group, jumped up and yelled, "Now it's time to get testimony from some real experts!" After a shouting match, the hearing was adjourned to another room. The story was covered everywhere and intensified the pressure on legislators.

Betty, NOW, and the radical women's groups endorsed the repeal of all abortion laws, a policy that made the most sense, but it was a pipe dream. Constance Cook, a New York State legislator, introduced a reform bill that came closer to repeal than any other—it legalized abortion, requiring only that a licensed physician perform the procedure. As it usu-

---

* Redstockings was a militant group founded by Ellen Willis and Shulamith Firestone. Its manifesto stated: "Women are an oppressed class." The group was known for its "pro-woman line," meaning that there was nothing wrong with women; it was men who had to change.

ally does, pragmatism defeated principle, and several more clauses were added to the bill. Still, it was considered a very good bill, and Betty and most feminists, knowing it was the best they could get, lobbied for it. But many of the radical women did not. Some of them accused Betty of selling abortion down the river, of declaring victory and pulling out.

Had the women in the movement held out for total repeal, they would have gotten nothing. The new, liberal New York State law produced a groundswell, paving the way for other states to enact their own reforms. After the struggle for abortion rights culminated in *Roe* v. *Wade,* Betty essentially lost interest in the subject.

. . .

IN 1969, BETTY put out feelers to the radical women's groups. She had tried before: at Susan Brownmiller's invitation, she had attended a small consciousness-raising meeting. She had been less than impressed. "As far as I'm concerned, we're *still* the radicals," she said. "We raised our consciousness a long time ago.... The name of the game is confrontation and action." But now the radicals seemed to be the center of energy, conducting speak-outs and sit-ins and crashing hearings that NOW only picketed, and they were getting more publicity than NOW was. Betty was not so starry-eyed as to think NOW and the radicals could all get together in one big happy family, but she thought they could work together on specific issues. She was encouraged in this by Jacqui Ceballos, who was doing publicity for NY–NOW and who acted as a go-between.

Jacqui had been inspired by *The Feminine Mystique* to leave her home in Bogotá, Colombia, and come to New York to follow Betty Friedan. "Betty's book hit me at a time when my marriage was falling apart," she said. "I had formed a successful opera company—it had gone beyond the my-wife-is-pretty-and-she-can-sing stuff. He left home. He was a good husband, a good provider. A friend in Bogotá handed me Betty's book. Everyone else said: 'Go back to him.' This was Colombia. I read Betty's book and thought, 'It's the society.' When I came to the movement I was very passionate about it. I thought, 'This will be for the rest of my life.' It was like a religious movement. I knew Betty was the one."

Betty called the first Congress to Unite Women for the weekend of November 21–23, 1969. Over five hundred women came to a grungy high school on West Seventeenth Street, in what was then the sort of neighborhood where one imagines revolutions are hatched. The women united long enough to pass resolutions on a wide range of issues including repeal of all abortion laws, free twenty-four-hour child care centers, and the passage of the Equal Rights Amendment. On the first night a group of radical women took the stage and presented the crowning event of the weekend—a haircutting session created by Cell 16, a Boston group headed by Roxanne Dunbar, that took the message of the Miss America zap to its ultimate conclusion: women came up on the stage and cut off all their hair. According to Judith Hole and Ellen Levine in *Rebirth of Feminism* (p. 151), the response was "electric.... Although a heated debate followed the haircutting, there was no atmosphere of internecine warfare, a feeling often predominant when politicos and feminists would meet in debate." Betty, who either misunderstood the event's revolutionary depths or refused to credit them, described it in utter disbelief as "a hysterical episode," a deliberate attempt by the women to destroy their looks. They seemed to be saying that "liberated" meant "ugly." She blamed their excesses on their youth. "After they're twenty-five they'll understand; they haven't experienced discrimination in the working world," she told Dolores Alexander.

She was further appalled by the theft of a can of film. Marlene Sanders, one of the few female news correspondents on network television and a friend of Betty's, had been given permission by Congress organizers to bring a camera crew, with the proviso that the haircutting not be filmed. Without Marlene's knowledge, one of her cameramen surreptitiously filmed it but carelessly neglected to cover the little red light on the camera, and soon after they finished, the film disappeared. Betty tried to get it back, but the mood of the evening had turned hostile. The cameraman had violated the rules, and the women told her they saw no reason to behave honorably toward him. The television network was owned by men, after all, and even the women who worked for it were beholden to them. Marlene later learned that Rita Mae Brown, a NOW member who was just beginning her career as a writer, was boasting about having thrown it in the Hudson River.

Betty's flirtation with the radicals left her dismayed, but she did not give up on them. Her next effort would be successful.

. . .

BETTY AND CARL spent years fighting over the disposition of their properties. Her lawyers, Charles Mandelstam and Milton Carrow (Carrow had been the lawyer for the Community Resources Pool in Rockland County), started negotiations for the separation agreement by asking for the maximum: they claimed that Betty owned everything—the Dakota apartment and the Fire Island house—and demanded $100,000. This tactic frightened Carl, who could not afford a lawyer, so he broke into the back door of the Dakota apartment (Betty had changed the locks) to look for papers to prove his part ownership. Betty got a court order to keep him away from her. The agreement they worked out provided Betty with $300 a week in child support for the two younger children (Daniel was twenty-one) beginning April 18, 1969 (the day they signed it), for twenty-six weeks, after which the amount would be reduced to $150 per week for six months, and $100 a week thereafter. Carl would also be responsible for college tuition. Betty did not ask for alimony.

Carl immediately fell behind in the payments and tried to get them reduced. "It was my contention she spent money like water, and it was because of *her needs* that the kids had to go to private school," he said. The children also had therapy bills. On December 19, 1969, seven months after the divorce, Betty went to family court complaining that Carl was approximately $1,500 in arrears. According to the court papers, she had discovered that Carl was living at a fancy address (427 East 52nd St., off Sutton Place), had purchased stock, and had taken a trip to Europe with "his lady friend." She also petitioned that the child support not be reduced. Her petition was granted.

They sold the Dakota apartment for a sum Carl remembers as $80,000, but much of the money melted away, spent on debts and lawyers' fees. There were tax liens on Betty's accounts at the Colston Leigh Agency, her lecture bureau (which took 30 percent of her fees), and at Curtis Brown Ltd., her agent. It took a few years to sell the Fire Island house. They began by asking a price in the low $60,000s, but as time went on, what with renting it out and not taking care of it, the house became run down.

The house had liens up to its roof. Carl had been very cavalier with the IRS. Every time he shrugged them off, they slapped on another lien. Prospective buyers found it difficult to make a deal. "It would be easier to buy the Empire State Building," one lawyer said. People would call Betty to make an offer, and if it was below the asking price she would say, "Do you want to screw around, or do you want to buy the house?" Several people thought they had bought the house from Carl, but Betty said no. Other people thought they had bought it from Betty, but Carl said no. One of the trustees resigned.

After a series of agonizing negotiations, Carl met Betty's terms. The Friedans owed Dalton $8,000, including tuition for Emily's junior and senior years. The school would not permit her to go back for her senior year unless the bills were paid in advance. Carl paid the Dalton bill and the bill for the closing. He paid his share of back taxes, $1,302.40. He paid off all the liens. He paid $5,600 of back child support and put another $5,600 in escrow for the coming year. At the closing the Friedans also had to pay $2149.19 to Milton Carrow, the trustee who had resigned. In addition, there were attorney's fees of 1 percent of the purchase price, a brokerage fee, the balance of the mortgage, interest on the mortgage, local taxes and late charges, and insurance. In 1973, they finally sold the house to a stockbroker for $45,000.

12

The Lavender Menace

After her marriage ended, Betty left the high-maintenance Dakota and sublet another of her serendipitous finds—a four-bedroom duplex with a garden at 33 West Ninety-third Street, just off Central Park West. Nine families had gotten together to create a co-op out of four brownstones that had been scheduled for demolition. Coincidentally, Alice Mehling, Betty's old friend from Parkway Village, also lived there, but their friendship had waned. Other apartments were available, and Dolores Alexander and Ivy Bottini, the new president of NY–NOW, each took one, a move they would regret. Ivy and Dolores knew each other from *Newsday*, where Ivy was an art director. (She had designed the NOW logo.) Ivy was round, good-natured, and easygoing—"When you looked at Ivy you saw a stove," a friend said—a Long Island housewife and mother who had fought against the John Birchers in her daughters' Levittown school, had left her husband, and was discovering her lesbian identity. Betty gave huge parties, including one for Dr. Spock that spilled over into Dolores's apartment. "Emily and Jonathan were with her," Dolores said. "Jonathan seemed troubled. Emily was still young. They both made it clear to me that they were not happy about her reputation as a feminist—groans and moans and facial expressions when the subject came up. I was there a lot."

Dolores was Betty's chief of staff *and* the staff. She was an attractive, soft-spoken woman who had covered the first NOW press conference in New York and experienced instant conversion. She left her reporting job, which paid $10,000 a year, to become executive director of NOW and Betty's private secretary for $100 a week—half her previous salary. Dolores was on call twenty-four hours a day. Together, she and Betty had created the NOW national newsletter on Betty's kitchen table in the Dakota. Their friendship was unusual for Betty, who kept her personal life separate from her movement life.

Dolores met Betty at Newark Airport after her divorce in May 1969 with a celebratory gift of Chanel No. 5. In Dolores's green Volkswagen, they drove to Princeton, where Betty gave an organizing speech for a new NOW chapter. Betty was charismatic—everywhere she went she left a trail of NOW chapters in her wake. Women would come up to her after her speeches and tell her their problems and describe their needs, and she would wave her hand like a wand and say, "Do it!" and they did.

In June Dolores and Betty went to a board meeting in San Francisco and then drove down the Pacific Coast Highway to another meeting in Los Angeles. Along the way they discovered Esalen and stayed for the weekend. Esalen was surpassingly beautiful, high on a cliff at Big Sur, 150 feet above the Pacific. There were eucalyptus trees, redwood groves, gardens, a meadow, and chandeliers of blazing stars at night. The human potential movement, which Esalen had launched in 1962, was a Great Awakening, a parallel to the women's movement in consciousness raising and the search for individual freedom. Esalen was a laboratory for the new psychology—esoteric Eastern philosophies, encounter groups, sensitivity training, psychodrama. It attracted important thinkers: Frederick (Fritz) Perls and Ida Rolf became famous at Esalen. Gregory Bateson, Joseph Campbell, and Betty's idol, Abraham Maslow, had also worked there. It was experimental, free, spontaneous, and therefore scandalous. People sat naked in hot tubs with strangers. "Esalen was a reaction to centuries of repressiveness," said George Leonard, who was vice president of Esalen and *Look* magazine's West Coast editor. "The East Coast regarded it with horror."

Betty was smitten immediately. Psychology was her subject, and here was a new kind of therapy. Only a month had passed since her divorce, and she was in need of comfort. She and Dolores dropped their East Coast inhibitions, took off their clothes, and soaked in a hot tub. They had massages. They attended a workshop given by Virginia Satir, an Esalen star. "I talked about my analysis," Dolores said. "Betty tried to intellectualize hers and put a framework around it." Betty wanted to rejoin the workshop after Los Angeles, but the group voted against her. Dolores spoke for her. "She was a public figure; it was difficult for her to make the request. I said, 'She made herself vulnerable, you can't just throw her out.' They changed their mind. She was permitted to go back."

Betty stayed at Esalen for a month, drawn by Virginia Satir, who was a pioneer in family therapy. "Virginia was large, very vital, dominant," George Leonard said. "She was willful, volatile; she was flamboyant, powerful—so I can see why Betty Friedan would get interested. Betty would like to take on that power as her own.... When people came in the early days they thought they would be transformed forever. We called it the Big Bang Theory. One weekend was an incredibly cathartic experience." Virginia Satir became Betty's teacher. Betty later took Jonathan to her, and they acted out family relationships. She went back to Esalen many times over the years to lead groups, and in the seventies she joined one of its New York offshoots.

. . .

ON HER RETURN to New York Betty began to grapple with a new threat to the image of NOW: lesbians. Well before the lesbian issue became a national one, Betty was calling it "the lavender menace," a play on the "Red menace" of the fifties. In San Francisco, she told Dolores that some of the women looked "dykey." "It was clear there were a lot of lesbians at the board meeting," Dolores said. "Some wore masculine clothing. We were wearing skirts and makeup. The chapter did a demonstration at the Fairmont Hotel, and she didn't want the lesbians there. Betty thought we should keep them in the background where they wouldn't be so visible. But there was no way to keep them out. She tried to steer the press away."

It was natural that lesbians would join the movement. Aside from the obvious reason that they were women, there was no place else for them to go. Early lesbian groups that had tried to join forces with gay men had been rejected. Many lesbians were professional women—NOW's bedrock—who preferred to stay in the closet, the door to which was still firmly shut. It was the others, the militant ones who wanted to make lesbian rights an issue, who set Betty's teeth on edge. She believed fervently, unequivocably, that they were a fifth column, and that they would destroy the movement. She would believe this all her life. A close friend said, "Betty felt we should set aside the homophobia and look at the question of what the damage would be to the women's movement if this became a major issue. What Betty never understood, at least at that point, was that we had no choice. We simply couldn't adopt a feminist position and say that this was out of bounds." Muriel Fox thought the same. She and Betty viewed the lesbians as a public relations problem, and in that regard they had grounds for concern. The media operated on the general assumption that women joined the movement either because they were unmarried and bitter, or divorced and angry, or lesbian. An autonomous woman was an oxymoron.

Betty's personal attitudes were an uneasy jumble of contradictions. She always denied that she was homophobic. She was just "a square from Peoria," she insisted, a reflection of the mainstream. "Betty had no patience with the lesbians," Jacqui Ceballos said. "She covered her face with her hands and said, 'I don't want to hear what people do in bed.'" What people did in bed was, of course, irrelevant to the issue. But there is evidence in *The Feminine Mystique* that male homosexuality had appalled her. Although she had demolished Freud's theories about women, she had swallowed whole his idea that mothers were to blame for homosexuality. Repeating the prejudices of the time, she wrote: "The shallow unreality, immaturity, promiscuity, lack of lasting human satisfaction that characterize the homosexual's life usually characterize all his life and interests. The lack of personal commitment in work, in education, in life outside of sex, is hauntingly 'feminine.'" She saw homosexuality "spreading like a murky smog over the American scene" and considered it "ominous." But it would be unfair to Betty to damn her for something she wrote in 1963. She committed other excesses in the book: she blamed mystique-shrouded mothers for brainwashed soldiers in Korea, and labeled the suburban house "a comfortable concentration camp."

Although lesbians in the movement thought she hated them and hated her back, Betty's concerns extended beyond sexual identity. She needed to belong; she clung to the mainstream as to a life raft. Being a lesbian was like being an outsider and a Jew. Lesbians were rejects, and if she championed their cause, *she* would be rejected. Lesbians were discounted, and if they took over the movement she would be discounted too, driven out of the discourse. Her fear was like the fear of Red-baiting: lesbians would destroy all that she had done, her movement and her life, her achievement and her status, and she would be nothing. In striking at them, she was defending herself.

The story of Betty and the lesbians runs like a fault line through her life. She continued to attack them long after the rest of the movement had embraced them. The use of the word "lesbian" (as Carl had called Betty) had always been the first line of attack against feminists, and Betty was far from the only woman in the movement to fear the label. She saw secret plots, a faceless enemy—and, strangely, she was right. There was a plot afoot, but not quite the one she might have imagined.

Dolores told Betty about it. "It was a major mistake to have said anything," Dolores said. Rita Mae Brown and two other women (both of whom were straight) thought it would be amusing to take over NY–NOW. They would do it by seducing Betty, after which she would be hopelessly compromised and incapable of stopping them. This idea was concocted during a period of great sexual experimentation when many women, caught up in radical rhetoric about "sleeping with the enemy," slept with each other instead, and some indeed found that they preferred women. Such attitudes were proclaimed, accepted, and widely discussed. Rita Mae, who was young and mischievous and had a brazen charm, delighted in shocking the "gray ladies" of NOW. Her idea of a board meeting was to discuss sexual fantasies. She was an orphan, she told people, and when she first came to New York she had lived in a car for a month with a friend and her two cats, Baby Jesus and Beelzebub. Even before Betty learned of the plot, she had told Dolores to get rid of her. The plot was a joke and nothing came of it, but Betty took it seriously. Leadership often has a destructive effect on one's sense of humor. Betty became more nervous about the lesbians in NOW, and her suspicions fell on Dolores. Dolores had hired Rita Mae as an office assistant and had brought Betty the news of the plot in the first place.

By the end of 1969 Dolores, who was constantly at Betty's beck and call, had been run ragged. Betty was also under pressure. She was living through that off-balance first year after a death or divorce, when one's judgment and senses are unreliable. Random House was after her for her unwritten book. She was behind on the rent. And she was facing another change: her term as president of NOW would end in the spring of 1970, and she was ambivalent about continuing for another two years. Tensions developed between her and Dolores. "Betty seemed to be adding an extra level of harassment, engineering the situation so that I would leave," Dolores said. During the month Betty spent at Esalen patching up her psyche, she had called up Dolores and screamed at her: "What do you do with your time? What do you do with yourelf?" Things came to a climax when Betty decided to testify against Judge G. Harrold Carswell, President Nixon's nominee to the Supreme Court.

Catherine East had alerted Betty to Judge Carswell's record, which was antiblack as well as antifemale, and sent names, dates and cases. There was one case that particularly outraged Betty: *Phillips* v. *Martin Marietta*. The company had refused to hire Ida Phillips as an aircraft assembler because she had preschool-age children, although it hired men with preschool-age children. Carswell had ruled for Martin Marietta. Betty's testimony would be the first time a judicial nominee had been challenged on the grounds of sex discrimination.

On January 28, 1970, the night before she was due to fly to Washington to testify, Betty was in her usual last-minute frenzy, getting her speech together. Brenda Feigen Fasteau, a young lawyer recently out of Harvard, was helping her prepare. Dolores, who had been running around the city attending meetings on Betty's behalf, was late. Betty buzzed her into the apartment, then, as Dolores stood at the bottom of the stairs looking up at her, screamed: "Where have you been? You're an hour late!" Dolores, previously meek as a lamb, cracked. "I saw red," she said. "We were dealing with respect for women's autonomy, and she was treating me like her lackey. I yelled, 'Fuck you, lady! When you learn to talk to me like a person, then I'll come back and help you with your speech. I'm going home!' " An hour later, Ivy Bottini knocked on Dolores's door. The speech was too important for personal quarrels, she said, and it still had to be mimeographed. The mimeo machine was in Dolores's apartment. Dolores acquiesced. They worked on the speech until three A.M., when Betty went to bed. Dolores went home, typed the speech on stencils, ran it off, and dropped it off at Betty's front door. She finished at seven A.M. At eight the phone rang. It was Betty, screaming, "Where is that speech?" Dolores told her and Betty slammed down the phone.

Dolores had spoken unforgivable words. After such an assault on her dignity, Betty saw no choice but to get rid of her. It was not as easy as dispatching Ti-Grace, but Betty would not be denied. On February 3, 1970, she set up a conference call with NOW's executive committee and had a monumental tantrum. For the better part of two hours she carried on, insisting that they fire Dolores: she had overstepped her bounds; she was insubordinate; and—here Betty played her trump card—she was part of the lesbian conspiracy. If they didn't fire Dolores, Betty threatened, she would call a press conference and announce that NOW was being taken over by lesbians. She would rather tear down the temple than see it defiled by other hands. Dolores, who was not a lesbian—in fact, she was dating a man—was stunned. So was the board. Despite their unanimous opposition, Betty beat them down, and they fired Dolores.

Betty had zeroed in on their weakness like a heat-seeking missile. The NOW board knew that above all they had to preserve the organization.

Some, like Muriel, gave no credence to Betty's threat, but others thought it was too much of a risk to call her bluff. Patricia Trainor, the acting treasurer, suggested giving Dolores severance pay. "It was the right note to strike. It was removed, passionless, and it was a way for the board to forgive itself for what it had done." The board gave Dolores three months' pay.

There may also have been a subtext to Betty's action. Before confronting the NOW board, she had learned that the NOW nominating committee had drawn up a slate of national officers for the 1970 election, and she was not on it. (In those days there was a single, uncontested slate.) "She made a series of calls," Dolores said, "pressuring people for a spot, but they were irritated and upset with her." Dolores may have been a scapegoat for Betty's anger at the board.

The board had tolerated Betty's histrionics, her kamikaze style, but her temper had driven many women to leave NOW. "Every decision provoked an argument," Dolores said. "The way a meeting is run, the way a press conference is run, any plans you may be forming for something—it had to be done *this* way—*her* way." The board members were professional women; nobody had ever treated them the way Betty did. And perhaps because they could not stand up to her, they had to depose her.

NOW had needed her fiery temperament, her boldness and disdain for the rules, to make its impact; now the organization needed to be broadened, to reach minority women and working-class women. NOW was also too closely tied to New York. Muriel, who thought that Betty could have been drafted to continue very easily, said, "Betty still had insight and vision, but she had already served two terms. She was also making noises that she had to finish her book, it was overdue and all that, which didn't make anybody terribly unhappy." The board changed the bylaws to create the position of chair of the advisory council for Betty (even though there was no advisory council) so that she would have a platform, and chose Aileen Hernandez, a black woman, to succeed her. It was immediately obvious to Betty that she could not contest the selection of a black woman.

Reflecting on her ouster many years later, Betty remembered the decision as having been under her control. "I was a very good leader of NOW, and I was supported strongly. And if I had wanted to stay president of NOW, I would have been elected. The only reason I did step down was that a black woman wanted to run.... I always let myself be outfoxed in that way. I don't consider it a virtue. I think I should have let myself be president of NOW a few more years."

Betty had presided over four momentous years, during which America's consciousness had changed—even hurricanes, once considered descriptive of women, were now being given men's names—and its women had been radicalized. Betty heard from those women all the time. NOW had a hundred chapters and three thousand members in thirty cities. She had lit a candle in the darkness. Her term of office had followed the pattern she had set in Grandview: she had risen to a great height, created a monument, and left the surrounding plain strewn with wreckage.

Betty flew to Chicago for her last board meeting, where she would hand the power and the limelight to Aileen Hernandez and make her farewell speech, an eloquent, Castro-esque, two-hour peroration. Toni Carabillo, a board member and NOW historian, said, "A group of us went out for dessert in the middle of it. We came back, and to our amazement, she was still talking." Betty ended grandly: "I have led you into history. I leave you now—to make new history."

But she was not quite finished. At the press conference to announce the new president, held at the O'Hare Inn in Des Plaines, Betty had an announcement of her own. Out of the blue, without having consulted anyone, she issued a call for a strike on August 26, 1970, the fiftieth anniversary of women's suffrage. The cameras were on her, not on Aileen. She had brought her own thunder with which to steal her successor's. "When she announced it, I almost fell off my chair," Aileen said. The board was suspicious of her motives, but protocol was never Betty's strong point. As she always had, she combined her needs with her cause. It was her saving grace.

She had gotten the idea for a strike from Betty Armistead, vice president for academic affairs at Osceola University in Cape Canaveral, Florida, who had proposed, among many other things, "that on Wednesday, August 26, 1970, the women of America stay home to commemorate Amendment XIX.... How long can America, the Cradle of Democracy, remain half free and half female?" Armistead had been thinking in terms of a boycott: if women were home all day, they wouldn't spend any money. The event would be called the Women's Strike for Equality.

In her announcement Betty proposed a virtual paralysis of the workplace: that women in offices stop typing and answering the phone; that working mothers without adequate child care bring their babies to the office; and that all women who were underpaid, who were not getting equal pay for equal work, simply stop for the day. They would gather in the evening, lighting the darkness with candles, "symbolic of the flame of that passionate journey down through history."

13

"Bliss Was It in
That Dawn to Be Alive"

IN THE SUMMER of 1970, Betty was in the Hamptons sharing a house with friends and trying to raise money for the August 26 event, which was changed to a march. (On further consideration, the idea of a strike seemed impractical.) She was constantly trying to get rich women to contribute to the movement, but their millions eluded her. Despite the best efforts of Betty and Muriel, women's liberation had a terrible public image. A New York *Daily News* article explained it all: women called the feminists "strident, snobbish homewreckers. Men call[ed] them ugly, man-hating harpies." On the other hand, feminists had acquired enough clout to force the resignation of Dr. Edgar F. Berman, Hubert Humphrey's physician, from the Democratic National Committee. Dr. Berman had made some unwise remarks concerning "the raging hormonal imbalance" that made women unfit for important work. Representative Patsy Mink, a Democrat from Hawaii, had helped to engineer his downfall.

Betty convinced Ethel Scull, whom she had once interviewed for a magazine piece, to hold a fund-raising party on August 8 in the sculpture garden of her house on Georgica Road in East Hampton. Ethel and her husband, Robert (he ran her father's taxi fleet, Scull's Angels), were known for their Pop art collection. Ethel was unaccustomed to this sort of entertaining. "We were not allowed to go into the house and use the bathroom," one of Betty's friends said. "She didn't want the trash." (The party was actually too expensive for "the trash"—$25 per person.) Gloria Vanderbilt Cooper was interested in being a co-hostess, but her husband insisted that she stay away. "We had flak from some of the husbands. One man tore up his wife's invitation," Betty told Charlotte Curtis, the women's news editor who reported the event in deadpan prose for *The New York Times*. In the end, two other women co-hosted: Edith de Rham (Mrs. Richard S. Coulson), a socialite and the author of *The Love Fraud* and *How Could She Do That?*; and Gloria Steinem, recently come to the movement, who was then writing the "City Politic" column for *New York* magazine.

The party was memorable for the exhibitionism of Jill Johnston, a columnist for *The Village Voice*, who dove into the pool and removed her shirt. (She was not wearing anything under it.) Betty herself almost had an accident. She had to keep yanking at her new red polka-dot dress, whose low-cut U-neck sank dangerously low during her fund-raising pitch. (Betty later said it was the weight of her women's liberation pin that had pulled the dress down.) She spoke of finishing "the unfinished revolution" and being "liberated from menial housework.... No more of this obscenity of one woman in the Senate...." She demanded "*her*story not just *his*tory." "Herstory" was a new word she had become extremely fond of. According to Betty, the benefit raised $5,000 for the march.

Betty hoped that the march would transcend the differences of all the women's groups. The movement had not yet made a strong enough impression on those in power. A mass display of unity would demonstrate that women were to be taken seriously. With the help of Jacqui Ceballos, she managed to forge the coalition with radical women that she had failed to develop at the First Congress to Unite Women. If anyone else had called the march, nothing would have happened. The radicals, many of whom counted themselves among the lavender menace, joined because the idea was irresistible.

Betty's call to arms galvanized women around the country. Women heard about the march and walked in off the street to their local headquarters and started working on it. New Yorkers ran around the city putting up flyers, carrying buckets of flour and water to mix the paste. Jacqui said, "We met in the Village by word of mouth. Everything was so casual and careless in those days; there was a youthfulness, an ease of movement, a blind faith that we would accomplish whatever we set out to do. It was like a fever. Everyone was doing something. We were having a ball."

The women invented outrageous actions to dramatize the three central demands of the march: abortion on demand and no forced sterilization; free twenty-four-hour child care centers, to be community controlled; and equal opportunity in jobs and education. The media spread the message for them. On August 10, at 10:40 A.M., a group of women liberated the Statue of Liberty by wrapping a banner around the pedestal: WOMEN OF THE WORLD UNITE! Photographs went around the world. They held the island for three hours. The police did not know what to do with them. That same day, the Equal Rights Amendment passed the House of Representatives after having been bottled up in committee for forty-seven years. Teams of women presented "male supremacist" awards to GM, GE, and ATT, among other companies. NOW's Image of Women Committee presented "Old Hat" awards to the advertising agencies that had created the ten most sexist ads of the year. Members of the child care committee demonstrated at the IRS for tax deductions. Banks, the stock exchange, every institution was hit. NOW held a ceremony in Father Duffy Square, calling for the replacement of his statue with one of Susan B. Anthony.

August 26 was Betty's day. Governor Nelson Rockefeller proclaimed it a holiday and, in Seneca Falls, he honored Susan B. Anthony, Elizabeth Cady Stanton, and Betty. Wearing a raspberry shift that she had bought in Finland, and described by a reporter as "looking like a gray-haired combination of Hermione Gingold and Bette Davis," she was lionized in the press, which devoted dozens of column-inches to the march. Its timing was serendipitous—the last week in August is one of the deadest news weeks of the year.

Reporters followed her from her morning hairdresser appointment at Vidal Sassoon through her rounds at various demonstrations in the city. "I don't want people to think Women's Lib girls don't care about how they look," she said. "We should try to be as pretty as we can. It's good for our self-image and it's good politics." At lunch at Whyte's, a formerly all-male restaurant on Fulton Street, she had crabmeat and two whiskey sours with fresh lemon juice and no cherry, and managed to administer a little consciousness raising. A man at the next table wanted to know if the three women she was seated with were secretaries. "That's what I call a male supremacist remark," she shouted, banging the table. "These girls are not secretaries. They're securities analysts." One of the men asked for her autograph. Everywhere she went women came up to her to wish her luck, and she smiled at them and called out, "Join us, sisters, join us." At the end of the long sunny afternoon she took the bus up Madison Avenue and walked to Fifth Avenue and Fifty-ninth Street, where thousands of women were massed at Grand Army Plaza, outside the Plaza Hotel, waiting for her to lead the march.*

Walking with Judge Dorothy Kenyon, a former suffragist who was in her eighties, and her friend Shana Alexander (Shana had brought Helen Gurley Brown, who was unaware that Betty was planning to announce a boycott of her magazine, *Cosmopolitan,* the next day), Betty led fifty thousand women down Fifth Avenue at five-thirty, in the middle of rush hour. The women had been given a police permit for only half the street, but Betty ignored it; they took over the whole avenue. With their banners—DON'T COOK DINNER! STARVE A RAT TODAY!! HOUSEWIVES ARE UNPAID SLAVE LABORERS! UP AGAINST THE WALL MALE CHAUVINIST PIG DOCTORS, EVE WAS FRAMED— they marched to Bryant Park, behind the New York Public Library at Forty-second Street, where Betty and others—Gloria Steinem, Bella Abzug, Eleanor Holmes Norton, and Kate Millett among them—stood in the dark and made speeches. Betty got the loudest cheers and applause. Shouting into the microphone, pumping her fists in the air, she struck the chords of her life and outlined a transcendent dream—she spoke of sisterhood and of overcoming all the divisions created by society and politics, race and class, and creating one giant coalition against violence, oppression, and fascism. She ended as a Jew: every morning men said a prayer thanking God that they had not been born women; but now, women could say their own prayer, thanking God that they *had* been born women.

Betty's achievement had been enormous. In those first few years she had led NOW from victory to victory. The feminists were like a small band of guerrillas who ran around sniping at a target here, a target there, and then watched in amazement as the entire edifice crumbled. Looking back, Betty marveled at their "chutzpah," at how so few had accomplished so much. The sweep of history was with them, the surge of the civil rights movement and the music of the counterculture, and the unbottled rage of thousands of women. It was the Age of Liberation. In the fall of 1967, LBJ had added "sex" to Executive Order 11246, which would penalize federal contractors who discriminated against women and lead to affirmative action. The want ads were desegregated. The airline stewardesses won in 1968, when the EEOC ruled that sex was not a "bona fide occupational qualification" for the position of flight cabin attendant, and the old rules about age and marriage were eliminated. NOW protested the fact that women on welfare, with children, could not get job training and day care,

* Betty had wanted the parade route to start at 110th Street so the women of Harlem would feel included, but it had not been possible.

and a comprehensive child care bill (which did not pass) was introduced in Congress in 1967. In many states the rules exempting women from jury duty were rescinded. Within the next few years women would be able to get credit cards in their own names and bank loans without a male co-signer. NOW attacked sexism in law, medicine, education, sports, religion, and the media.

August 26, 1970, may well have been the most glorious day of Betty's life. Never again would she lead such a united group in such a euphoric spirit; never again would she be regarded with such universal good will. Women said afterward that the march had been the most thrilling thing in their lives. NY–NOW alone recruited a thousand new members. Women in other cities had also marched, and the effect was the same. When Betty went to lecture the halls were packed beyond capacity, beyond anything she had encountered before, and she got standing ovations on Southern campuses and in Middle America.

Betty's personal life had also taken a turn for the better. She was having an affair with a writer, Arthur Whitman, a big, balding redhead with a self-deprecating manner. He was a member of the Society of Magazine Writers and had written several books during the sixties: *Hi-Fi Stereo for Your Home; The LBJ Barbecue Cookbook;* and *How to Use Art in Your Home,* with Jeanne Owens. Another book, *Each Other's Victims,* about his divorce and his son's drug problems, chronicled an affair with a woman like Betty. "He was very brilliant," said Richard Ekstract, a friend of Arthur's as well as of Betty and Carl. "He was not physically attractive. It was a torrid affair. The attraction was mental and developed into a physical thing."

And then Arthur became fatally ill with hepatitis, picked up in Mexico. Betty visited him at New York University Hospital every day and got all their friends to go, too, or send flowers or money. When Arthur needed blood transfusions Betty called everyone she knew at the Society of Magazine Writers to give blood. Nothing helped. He died early in October 1970, when she was at Augsburg College in Minneapolis, about to give a lecture.

A magazine writer who was following her around wrote:

One hour before her lecture, she learns that a man she had loved has died in a New York hospital, despite transfusions of eighty quarts of blood which she had solicited. She sobs with grief and with guilt; she hadn't said good-bye, she hadn't done enough. She takes a deep breath and a quick drink; it is almost time to go on.... She rambles through visions of an emotional Utopia wherein men and women will be free to love one another on an equal, lofty

plane, where no one will die lonely and unfulfilled. People in the audience—
male and female—weep off and on as she speaks, and when she finishes with
a husky call to make love not war, they applaud for seven minutes.

. . .

THE AUGUST 26 march had been such a roaring success that Betty
decided to rally another coalition for a second march. Abortion and day
care were under threat in New York State: money for child care centers
was about to be cut, and the legislature was in the midst of sabotaging the
liberal new abortion law by adding expensive in-hospital requirements,
time limits, and residential prerequisites. The two issues made a nice foil
for each other. The women would demand that Governor Rockefeller veto
the proposed abortion restrictions and take action on child care.

The second march was set for December 12. It would begin at Governor Rockefeller's office, on Fifty-fifth Street near Fifth Avenue, and then
cross Eighty-sixth Street to Gracie Mansion, where Mayor John Lindsay
lived at Eighty-ninth and East End Avenue. Betty was out of town for the
planning sessions; her lieutenants and the coalition committee attended to
the details.

Between August 26 and December 12, a new star had risen in the movement. *Time* magazine had put Kate Millett on the cover of its women's liberation issue and featured her new book, *Sexual Politics,* installing her as the
leading theoretician of the movement: "Until this year with the publication
of a remarkable book called *Sexual Politics,* the movement had no coherent
theory to buttress its intuitive passions, no ideologue to provide chapter
and verse for its assault on patriarchy." (*Time's* writers had apparently not
read the reams of papers published by the radical women.) *Time* labeled
Kate the "Mao Tse-tung of Women's Liberation." The cover picture,
drawn in thick black strokes, was that of a harridan, her long dark hair
hanging down, her face consumed with rage and hate.

Kate's reign at *Time* was brief. On December 14 she was dethroned,
appropriately, in the "Behavior" section. *Time* had changed its mind about
the book and found a critic to rip it apart; he pronounced that Kate had "discredited herself as a spokeswoman for her cause" because she had admitted
at a meeting at Columbia University that she was a bisexual. On a panel of
feminists and gays, Kate had been representing the bisexual point of view. A
woman in the audience, like Kate a member of a group called the Radi-
calesbians, had yelled, "Are you a lesbian? Say it! Say you are a lesbian." Kate
had hesitated. She had married her lover, Fumio Yoshimura, to prevent his

deportation, and the story of their romance, carefully orchestrated, was part of the publicity for her book. She also had female lovers. She hadn't been ready to come out at that particular moment, but the emotional pressure had been too great to resist and Kate was a woman who cared about pleasing people. "The line goes, inflexible as a fascist edict, that bisexuality is a cop-out," she would write. Later, she said that coming out had relieved her of the burden of being a public spokesperson.

Kate was an artist and a scholar who did not even own a television set. She was unprepared for the hot lights of sudden fame and equally sudden notoriety. Brought up a strict Catholic, she was worried about her family: what would her mother think when she read *Time?* Until now, the lesbian issue had simmered privately within the movement. When *Time* took off the lid, certain leaders of Betty's coalition—Ivy Bottini and two other NOW lesbians, Sidney Abbott and Barbara Love, and Gloria Steinem—decided that they had to support Kate, and that the march was the place to do it. No one informed Betty.

December 12 was a bone-chilling day of rain and sleet, and the march was a fizzle; only about three hundred women turned out. Betty, Gloria, Flo Kennedy, and Kate were scheduled to speak. As they stood together on a flatbed truck, huddled under umbrellas, Betty saw women in the crowd distributing lavender armbands. Everyone was wearing one. On the truck, Barbara Love held one out to her. She turned away in disgust. Ivy turned to her and put one in her hand. Betty looked at it for a moment, then threw it on the floor and stamped on it. She was furious. Behind her back, the committee she had appointed had used her name to support a cause she detested.

The lavender armbands aroused Betty's suspicions that the movement had been infiltrated by agents provocateurs. Thinking back, she even saw something peculiar about the haircutting incident at the first Congress to Unite Women. Some insinuating voice must have planted the idea for that folly.

Betty was not alone in her suspicions. Many women assumed the FBI had infiltrated the movement. The Socialist Workers Party (itself an expert infiltrator), which had tried to take over the August 26 march, was an FBI target; the FBI also connected the movement with the Weathermen, a violent offshoot of the New Left. Its members, unsophisticated in bomb techniques, had accidentally blown up a house on West Eleventh Street while they were in it. The women who survived the blast had gone underground, and the FBI was looking for them. The women's movement seemed a likely place for them to hide. Betty later came to believe that

Kate had been virtually blackmailed into announcing her lesbianism, and that perhaps the same dark force behind the haircutting incident was also responsible for pressuring Kate.*

After the December 12 speeches, sitting in a bar with Kate, Gloria, and Ivy, Betty learned that they were planning to hold a "We are all lesbians" press conference to support Kate. She tried to convince them that a press conference could only damage the movement—it would be thrown into disarray by guilt-by-association, and the women who stood up for Kate would themselves be smeared, but she could not talk them out of it. Kate was their sister, and she needed their help. Instead, Betty pulled out of the coalition and threatened to sue if the women ever used her name in connection with any of their activities.

There was nothing Betty could do about the damage Kate or Gloria might cause, but Ivy was vulnerable. In January 1971, Ivy was running for reelection as president of NY–NOW. Jacqui Ceballos was running against her. Ivy, like Jacqui, Dolores, and Muriel Fox, had venerated Betty. "I had traveled with Betty to and from board meetings," Ivy said. "I was incredibly impressed with Betty. She was laying out the issues—why we are doing this—and it was not just philosophical, it was emotional. She had a very deep commitment. There was a period of time when I adored Betty. I would look at her and think she was the most beautiful woman in the world. Like Streisand."

Ivy heard rumors that Betty was mounting a campaign against her, and other, nastier rumors that she herself was lecherous. "Typical stuff," she said. Sidney Abbott and Barbara Love offered to pack the election meeting, but Ivy was too principled and too naive to stoop to such tactics. "I had faith in the membership," she said. In any case, she was not trying to turn NOW into a lesbian organization; she just wanted to air the issue. Betty, however, took no chances. She had called her friends, and the room in the Universalist Church on the Upper West Side where NY–NOW held its meetings was crowded with Jacqui supporters. Betty and Muriel came, their appearance at once a testament to the importance of the proceedings and a symbol of the divisions within NOW, and watched as Ivy was defeated.

Ivy, Dolores, and a few other women resigned from NOW, and the event became known, rather dubiously, as the Lesbian Purge. It was more

---

* Blackmail does not describe Kate's situation. In the lesbian community there was tremendous hostility to her money and fame and the heterosexual façade provided by her marriage. Kate seemed to have everything, but she was not what she appeared to be. For this, she was made to pay.

an effort to put artificial brakes on a revolution. Many lesbians, open and closeted, remained in NOW. However, as the historian Alice Echols observed, "a number of former NOW members contend that the organization's homophobia was not unrelated to the large number of closeted lesbians...who felt they might be exposed as lesbians if the issue were openly discussed."

If Betty saw the parallel between the position of women in society and the position of lesbians in the movement (and of Jews in Peoria), she gave no indication. The issue would worry her for years, until the first American convocation of women—in Houston in 1977—when she would make her separate peace with them.

14

The Commune

AFTER HER MARRIAGE ended, Betty was lonely for the richness and complexity of family life. Even though she was at her peak, famous and sought after, facing life alone after twenty-two years of being half of a couple daunted her. She was not the self-reliant new woman she was having so much trouble trying to write about. "I was forty-nine, had finally gotten divorced, and was afraid of being alone. I was not even thinking about getting married again—to end this marriage had been too terrifying—but I had no sense at all of how I was going to live my life." Groups had always sustained and energized her; she had spent part of the first summer after her divorce in Esalen, and in 1970, making plans for the march, she decided she wanted a house full of people.

Betty called her new group a commune. It would be an extended family, a "chosen family," people she could rely on, rather than her own unsatisfactory relatives. It would be a support system, to help her start her life over again. She told a divorced friend, Arthur Herzog, "We didn't do it right, this marriage thing. We are the type who don't like being alone. What's to keep us from making another mistake and getting married again from sheer loneliness? What will we really miss, not being married, that could open us to that? Not just sex, I think. It's living with someone, being able to sit around the kitchen table in your bathrobe without makeup on, letting it all hang out."

She had met Arthur, a well-known writer (*The Swarm*) at the Society of Magazine Writers in 1966, and again during Eugene McCarthy's run for the presidency, when Herzog was the Senator's Oregon campaign manager. Arthur was dating Betty Rollin, then an editor at *Look* magazine. (They married in 1972.) Her next recruit was Si Goode, the sociologist who had encouraged her to write *The Feminine Mystique*, whose marriage was collapsing. Si was a gourmet cook and a dandy—he had worn a blue velvet suit and multicolored striped shirt to Ethel Scull's party. These four were the founders, the matriarchs and patriarchs of the commune. Each summer they would rent huge old mansions in the Hamptons, owned by prominent families, and invite friends to share. The same people came back, year after year. The commune was a social anomaly. The houses tended to be white elephants, a bit run-down and expensive to heat in the winter, but they offered a way to live grandly without having real money, and a base from which to social-climb. The Hamptons had not yet acquired their celebrity sheen, and it was easy to make connections. Si Goode recalled, "Betty had some casual invitation, or at least, Betty knew a party was going on, and it would be a big party, so we could all go. They would always be delighted. We upped the grade of the party. And we were the smartest, most charming people."

The first year they rented a house in Sagaponack that belonged to a daughter-in-law of Diana Vreeland. Betty's concept was lofty—they would have long intellectual discussions of politics and the way things worked in the world—but as time went on the conversations became less grand. "We had vicious family arguments over money," Betty wrote. " 'My kid is only two, how can you say he eats as much as a thirteen-year-old?' ... 'I was on the Scarsdale diet this week, I didn't eat a thing.' "

The name of Betty Friedan was a magnet. More and more people, most of them professionals on the rise, wanted to become regulars. In the first years the group included Martha Stuart, who produced *Are You Listening?*, the first television talk show on Channel 13, New York's public television channel; Robert Hirschfield, then head of the political science department at Hunter College, who met and married his wife, Muriel, a lyricist, at the commune; Shirley Johnson Lans, an economics professor at Vassar, and her husband, Asher, an international lawyer; Karl Fossum, a psychiatrist who owned two abortion clinics. They were joined by Richard Laupot, a businessman who owned a factory in New Jersey that manufactured lighting fixtures, and Cynthia Epstein, a sociologist, and her husband, Howard, editor-in-chief and publisher of *Facts on File*. Some of these were peripheral; others permanent. Dick Laupot would become one of Betty's frequent escorts. They had met at a party. "We hadn't spoken," Dick said. "We were getting our coats. I said, 'By this time you must be bored with the women's movement.' With these words, we went out for a cup of coffee, and she invited me to the commune." Cynthia Epstein would become one of Betty's closest friends for life. "It was a permanent floating crap game," Howard said.

Betty's ebullience and sense of fun set the tone. The writer Lois Gould, who visited, said, "She was a kind of Auntie Mame, but it wasn't about glamour; it was about a sense of self. It was fun to watch. She was extremely strong-willed and independent of spirit. There were hilarious rules for equal tasks. Everyone had to contribute. One night Betty was assigned the potatoes. Betty, in a caftan, tossed the potatoes over her shoulder into the pot and sailed out of the kitchen. There was a sense of eccentricity which was irresistible. Magnetic, laughter, high spirits. Everyone wanted to be involved in political action. They had a love affair with the notion of social change; they were in tune with the forces of their time. It was heady stuff."

They indulged themselves in wonderful foolishness, mad silly things like being photographed lying on gravestones. It was a little like summer camp for grown-up delinquents. "We drank a lot then," said Arthur Herzog. "One night Betty and I worked out a very intelligent formula about heat and light in politicians—the third law of thermopolitics. She thought it was brilliant and wrote it down. Then she passed the piece of paper over the candle flame, and it burned. The next morning neither of us could remember what this dazzling theory was."

The second year, 1971, they rented Sheldrake Cove, an estate on Georgica Pond that belonged to the Wainwright family. Stuyvesant Wainwright had been a Republican Congressman. There was a lot of writing going on. Betty was still working on the book she owed Random House. Arthur Herzog was writing a novel, and Cynthia Epstein was doing articles. Senator Eugene McCarthy came to visit and walked on the beach with Betty, discussing the possibility that he would run for president in 1972.

That summer, Betty met Susan Wood, who would become another close friend. Susan, a successful freelance photographer who had carved out her career in a male-dominated field, was the kind of tough, male-oriented woman Betty liked. "She adored my guy Joe Haggerty," Susan said. "The first time he met her I was jealous: he was so stimulated by her conversation he could hardly go to sleep." Betty and Joe talked about politics. Their debates got so passionate, they threw glasses at each other that smashed on the floor. Many years later, after Joe had died, Betty and Susan became each other's stalking horses at parties. "Men would covet my body or her mind," Susan said. "We always had a surround of men. We were both single, self-supporting, free. We had a sense of adventure. She was always interested and curious and willing to see and do things she had never done and didn't know how to do. Some of them were beyond her ability, but she would try." Photos taken at Sheldrake Cove show Betty drifting on a kayak on Georgica Pond and playing croquet on the lawn. She wore caftans in vibrant colors and prints that flowed gracefully around her. "She was the Grande Dame," Arthur said. "The central spirit."

Life in the commune was often viewed through an alcoholic haze. As the residents sat nursing their gin and tonics they fantasized plundering the Long Island potato fields and distilling their own vodka. "There was very little activity until lunch," Erica Abeel, a writer who visited, said. "People were recuperating from the night before." Betty's temper began to show itself more and more often. She would come down the stairs in the morning, dressed in her jogging costume, her head down, her face contrite, and announce, "I was bad." Everyone would forgive her instantly. "You had to be made of stone not to melt at the sight of a contrite Betty," Betty Rollin said. "When she was contrite, she was very contrite.... People tended to become Betty's mother. She was such a mess. When she shopped for food, she would usually forget something—the meat, not the curry. She would start to set the table, become distracted ... and then completely forget [about it]."

The commune became famous for its games of charades, played in the evenings and at the annual Labor Day party, in front of an audience of about one hundred people. There were two teams, ten on a team. "Betty threw herself into it," Betty Rollin said. "Her most famous charade was 'botulism'—it killed you if you ate it.* Betty did falling down and dropping dead. She loved doing it. She abandoned herself in physically acting out. She collapsed on the floor and kept collapsing, and each time she collapsed closer and closer to the coffee table. I was afraid she would crack her head open. I was the mother, I was nervous about whether people would hurt themselves and drink too much. That was my role."

As the commune grew, the division of labor, always shaky, began to break down. Betty Rollin, one of the more fastidious members, ennobled each job with a title: "Duke of Dishes," "Queen of Cleanup," "Sultan of

---

* Botulism was in the news. Some cans of Bon Vivant Vichyssoise had been contaminated with botulin toxin and had to be recalled.

Setting the Table." "Everyone had a grand title—anything to get people to work," she said. Betty Friedan and the children were assigned aesthetic labor—flower arrangements and table settings—never cleanup. "We knew there was no way she would clean pots, and we didn't want her to cook—to negotiate with Betty in the kitchen can be daunting."

Guests who came for the weekend were shocked to be handed a bill upon their departure, usually for about $40 per person. Dick Laupot worked out the amount on a slide rule. Gerry Walker, Betty's old friend from their tax-protest days, and his new wife, Joanna Simon, who had rented out their own house and had nowhere to go, said, "At the end of the weekend, Howard Epstein handed me a bill. It was all broken down—electricity, gas, food. I was aghast. We were invited. 'I hope you come back again,' he said. I said, 'Sorry, I can't afford it.' I was paying alimony and child support and I had about twelve dollars a week to spend. The bill was seventy or eighty dollars, pro-rated. Very crude."

In 1972 and 1973 they rented a house on Drew Lane, near the ocean. The house belonged in *Great Expectations*. It was coming apart and had leaky pipes, but it was beautiful. It was owned by the Drews, the great theatrical family, and trunks of costumes from their tours filled the attics. The neighbors on Drew Lane, a most exclusive street, looked down their noses at these motley groupies and their wild parties. "A lawyer friend advised us to give a block party," Betty told a reporter, "so we got hold of every duck liver on Long Island and made pâté." On the night of the party it rained, and the guests moved inside, spreading pâté everywhere. "It was so bad that we had to redo the floors, but we never had any trouble with the neighbors again."

The commune foundered on Drew Lane. No one would say it in so many words, but Betty was becoming very difficult. "The early seventies were a bad time," a member of the group said. "I remember thinking she was not happy. She so much wanted a relationship. In the movement, Gloria Steinem was getting an undue amount of attention. In those days, people said Betty was very tough on younger, good-looking women." In the commune Betty made sudden, unwarranted attacks on people. Cynthia Epstein had to read the riot act to her: "She yelled at people or people's guests. She was not unique about not doing her fair share of the work, but because it was Betty, it was more dramatic." Howard Epstein remembered that Betty wanted a lot of new people to come in—people the rest of them didn't like to begin with, and who would have made the house too crowded. Betty always wanted the best bedroom. She monopolized the phone. One way or another, she was taking up too much space.

The problem was that Betty's was the only name on the lease. It was her rental, and she wanted to rent the house again the following year. "A dissident group got together," Howard said. "Betty Rollin and I were elected to ply Betty with drink and talk her into not going into the lease." It was too much responsibility, they told her; she was too busy and important to bother. They suggested that she be a guest. She seemed amenable, and they thought the matter was settled. But Betty, always sensitive to being excluded, changed her mind. Howard said, "She called the next day and said, 'I've been thinking about last night, and I smell a rat.'"

The upshot was that the commune split from Betty. As one member put it, "Betty went to Avignon." Arthur Herzog and Betty Rollin got another house, on Jobs Lane in Bridgehampton, taking the Epsteins and Erica Abeel and Ross Wetzsteon, a writer for *The Village Voice*, with them. Betty took a smaller house nearby.

Betty was briefly on the outs with the group, but the commune itself was changing. Betty's long-range plan had been that they all live together as a family, and they had tried to buy every house they had been in, but they had never been able to put together enough money. The legal complications of buying collectively were also insurmountable. In the mid-seventies, as people became more successful in their professions and less enamored of adolescent hijinks, they began buying their own houses. Si Goode, the Epsteins, Arthur Herzog, and several others bought. Betty managed to scrape together enough money in 1978 to buy a house in Sag Harbor.

But the spirit of the commune endured. Through the years, people fell in and out of favor with Betty, but her family of choice endured. "She was one of the more active people in keeping things together," one of the group said. "She has a strong sense of communal life and friendships that have a history." They gathered for holidays; they threw parties for each other and supported each other through the crises of their lives—illness, divorce, death. The commune grew into a big squabbling crowd, its bonds cemented by the squabbles, like the family Betty had intended it to be. In 1990, they gathered at Susan Wood's house in Amagansett to celebrate their twentieth anniversary, the arrangements for which had been fraught with conflict about money and food. After eating a buffet supper in the garden and singing "Auld Lang Syne," they reminisced, omitting every unpleasant thing that had happened. Betty, wearing a long red evening dress with matching shoes and a black shawl, said, "What we began was a family. It was a real family of choice. Incredible bonds were created. We have had a lot of joy together.... We bore each other, we know each other's every weakness.... We love each other and we are there for each other."

15

"The Age Demanded an Image"

IN FEBRUARY 1971, Betty was in London the week of her fiftieth birthday, which she dreaded. Betty had a normal interest in cosmetics and clothes, but she had never been particularly concerned with trying to appear younger than she was. This birthday was a dividing line, and she was alone. She cheered up after she ran into a man she knew in the lobby of her hotel, but the prospect of growing old was not the only source of her unease. She was facing the supreme challenge to her leadership: Gloria Steinem, her archrival, the latecomer who would become the polestar of the movement, had begun her ascent.

They had met in the late sixties, their politics having converged in the antiwar movement. Gloria remembered first seeing Betty at a benefit given by a group of writers who were working for Senator Eugene McCarthy. "This was in someone's apartment," she said. "She ordered me—and others—to get food, coffee, clean up, find her purse, et cetera, and we did it. Pronto. My first impression was that she was very disorganized, rude, and quite frightening." Gloria later changed her mind about McCarthy, her second thoughts generated by the very quality that must have attracted Betty—his aloof intellectualism.

Ironically, Betty had sought Gloria out and invited her to be a hostess at Ethel Scull's party, just as she had chosen Ti-Grace for the way she looked. "Betty didn't *think* about Gloria then," Betty Rollin said. "Gloria was palatable, pretty, a good front—she had public relations value."

Betty called her "the Hair." The hair was long, blond-streaked, center-parted, and poufed on top; millions of young women all over the country copied it, as they copied her tinted aviator glasses. It was the Gloria Look. There was a fascination about her, an ineffable quality that made people of both sexes fall in love with her. She inspired the kind of breathless yearning that had less to do with feminism than with the adoration of a fan for a movie star. "The minute Gloria came on the scene," Muriel Fox observed, "the media dropped Betty like a hot potato." The cameras devoured her. All she had to do was stand there. Gloria and Betty were an irresistible force and an immovable object, and their collision would widen the rift between feminists and bring Betty's house crashing down around her.

Gloria was beautiful, and the common wisdom laid the blame for their feud on that doorstep. Newspaper articles openly reinforced it—"Ms. Steinem—sometimes known as 'Gloria is the pretty one...' "—just as people had always reinforced the idea that Betty's sister Amy had been "the pretty one." Gloria may well have inflamed that old, unresolved sibling rivalry, but she was also a formidable opponent who possessed resources that Amy did not. Then too, Betty had many close friendships with beautiful women, among them Cynthia Epstein, Betty Rollin, and Shana Alexander. Beauty was only part of the story. Betty regarded herself as *the* leader of the women's movement, above other women, beyond the need to compete. She had to be the only one.

Gloria was serious competition. "I wouldn't say that I started the movement; it surely is a product of historical forces, but if Betty Friedan weren't alive, she'd have to be invented to see the movement through," Betty told a journalist. She had written the book and founded the organization; she was the indispensable ingredient; and now she watched as Gloria came along and danced away with the credit. Her anger was deep, bottomless. "We all knew Betty hated Gloria's guts," said Jennifer MacLeod, who was a founder and first president of the Princeton chapter of NOW and would work with Betty on the National Women's Political Caucus.

Betty and Gloria had many things in common, none of which served to bring them together. Both were middle-class Midwesterners who had gone to Smith. Neither could wait to leave home; but whereas Betty knew that her brains were her passport, Gloria hoped her legs would carry her. (She was a dancer.) Both had mothers with stunted lives, mothers who had gone to college and become newspaper reporters and had their careers cut short by marriage; and both became journalists themselves.* Gloria was half-Jewish, on her father's side, but religion meant little to her. As teenagers, each had suffered a traumatic abandonment, Betty by her friends and Gloria by her parents, literally and metaphorically: her mother had become mentally ill, her parents had divorced, and her father had left. Both women avoided intimacy. Betty rarely talked about her family to her friends, and Gloria was considered inscrutable. "Nobody knows Gloria," a *Ms.* editor who had worked there for a decade said. Each had a great need for and appreciation of men and made uncommon arrangements with them: Betty could not accept a peer, and Gloria would not make a long-term commitment.

In style and personality they were polar opposites. Both had the inexhaustible energy and charisma essential to leadership, but Gloria was cool and removed, Betty passionate and involved. Betty was brusque, open; Gloria was diplomatic, opaque. Betty was untidy, sprawling; Gloria was neat and contained. Betty gloried in fights; she derived power from them. Gloria shrank from confrontations; they made her ill. She was a peacemaker, patching together impossible compromises between irreconcilable groups; her power came from bringing people together. Betty created scenes, blew up small things into huge nerve-racking dramas, forcing people to deal with her; Gloria salvaged situations, papering over the cracks, even denying that differences existed. She was the bandage; Betty was the blunt instrument. Betty was defenseless—screaming was her defense. Gloria's protection was being nice: she apologized endlessly—for having more money than other women, for wearing miniskirts and designer clothes, for being thin, for dating powerful men. She saw herself as Holly Golightly in *Breakfast at Tiffany's*, an elegant waif. Betty never made excuses for herself. She led armies; she was Joan of Arc.

In their pursuit of power and influence, Betty reached out and took what she wanted; Gloria was passive and waited to be asked, seeming not to care. Betty's leadership style was arbitrary and imperious, in the male mode. Women who expected emotional sustenance from a feminist

---

* The lives of the mothers, the confined, unrealized mothers, were a major impetus to many of the movement's leaders. Muriel Fox's mother was also mentally shaky. Other mothers, like Betty's, were unhappy being women.

resented her for not providing it. If she had been a man, her tactics would have been glossed over; she would have been forgiven because of her brilliant mind.

Gloria's leadership was supportive and cooperative, but she was not a leader in the sense that Betty was: she did not try to run anything formally. Her empire was a magazine ("remedial reading," she called it), not a national organization. Ms. grew out of another small organization, the Women's Action Alliance, a referral service to help local women's groups create shelters for battered women, find local child care, and fight such things as sexist textbooks. Both were run by a handful of people. Gloria was a freelance organizer; groups around the country would call her to help them fight a local dragon, and she would get on a plane and go. She spent many years doing this work and never took credit or sought the limelight for it. "Gloria has all the irritating qualities of a saint—she is a rebuke," said her friend Liz Smith, the columnist. Gloria was a rescuer. Rescue was a driving fantasy and would characterize her work in the movement as champion of the poor and women of color. One of her biographers, Carolyn Heilbrun, wrote that in her childhood "she developed extensive rescue fantasies, in which she would at the last minute save someone from a fatal situation. A man would be lynched; Gloria, arriving in the nick of time, would hold off the lynchers with a shotgun...free the prisoner, and drive away with him. These rescue fantasies were not only her escape from daily life; they were also the dramas in which she saw herself as acting upon the world, as extricating those enmeshed in the world's cruelties."

Within the movement each embodied a central paradox. Gloria, the essence of glamour, identified with the poor and downtrodden. Betty, the founder of modern feminism, preferred the company of men to women.

Gloria was born on March 25, 1934, in Toledo, Ohio; she was the younger daughter of Leo, a feckless father, and Ruth, a mother who had already begun to show signs of instability. Leo, whose family had money and property, owned a resort at Clark Lake, Michigan, where the big bands came to play, and Gloria was raised in a show biz atmosphere. Her childhood was eccentric, unstructured. Some winters the Steinems traveled to Florida or California, living in a house trailer attached to a car. Leo was a junk-food devotee who was six feet tall and weighed over three hundred pounds, which may explain the fear of fat that Gloria developed later in life. One of her friends said, "You could lose ten pounds if you stayed with her. She never ate."

In 1945, when Gloria was eleven, Leo and Ruth divorced. The money vanished, and Ruth drifted further into madness. For six years, those of her adolescence, Gloria took care of her mother, making the decisions, feeding her meals of bologna sandwiches. In those six years of poverty and despair lie the reasons for Gloria's flight from long-term entanglements, her unwillingness to marry or become a mother. If there was no commitment, she could never be abandoned again; if there were no children, she would never have to be a caretaker. As both of her biographers, Carolyn Heilbrun and Sydney Ladensohn Stern, have observed, her one long-term relationship—that with *Ms.*—unwittingly re-created the one with her mother: she nursed a magazine that could not get enough ads and would never be healthy. But there was always an escape hatch. When she started *Ms.* in 1971 she told Clay Felker, her editor at *New York* magazine, "I'll do this for two years, no longer." She was still there when *Ms.* was sold in 1987.

After the divorce, Gloria and Ruth lived in a rat-infested house on the blue-collar side of town. Lillian Barnes Borton, who lived in the downstairs apartment as a child, recalled, "Gloria had a mattress and box spring on the floor and a wooden packing crate for her clothes." She was always immaculately dressed, the pleats of her skirt knife-sharp. Ruth treated her like "a little lady princess." On her bad days, Ruth might barge into Lillian's apartment and turn off the radio, or try to paint their windows black. She threw her clothes out the window, and, when she became frightened, she would call the police to find Gloria. Gloria went to high school with the children of factory and white-collar workers. She earned money as a waitress and by dancing, and was a runner-up in a beauty contest. Gloria wrote: "My ultimate protection was this: I was just passing through, a guest in the house; perhaps this wasn't my mother at all."

Gloria never expressed anger at her parents and would later deny that she had felt it. She did what was necessary to survive, developing what she would call her Great Stone Face. "I could never get behind her eyes," Lillian said. When friends came to her house, she behaved as if everything were normal, ignoring the squalor. If there were no personal confrontations, if everything could be smoothed over peacefully, the façade could be maintained, the fear kept under control.

Ruth sold the house in 1951 so that Gloria could go to college. Gloria graduated from Smith in 1956, fourteen years after Betty, magna to Betty's summa. In 1957, the year Betty began delving into her Smith questionnaire, Gloria was in India on a Chester Bowles Fellowship. The trip was a flight, an escape from an engagement and the life that was laid out for her, the harness of marriage and babies. She was also pregnant, but she managed to get an abortion in London while waiting for her visa.

In India she traveled to primitive villages, helping the landless poor, a profound experience that she hoped, in vain, to replicate in New York when she returned in 1958. But something quite different came up for her. Clive Gray, a contract agent for the CIA whom she had met in India, recommended her to work for the Independent Research Service. The IRS was a nebulously named CIA-funded organization set up to send students to international Communist youth festivals, where they would represent the Western point of view. Gloria also made connections at *Esquire* and became a freelance magazine writer and what was then called a girl about town, meaning that she dated well-known men and was seen at all the right places. She was a minor celebrity before she had actually accomplished very much.

In 1963, the year Betty published *The Feminine Mystique,* Gloria also had a book out: *The Beach Book,* an anthology of beach lore. It was published by the Viking Press, which was owned by the family of Thomas Guinzburg, the company's president, with whom she had begun an affair the previous year. Her life was littered with famous people—the "culturati," Tom Wolfe called them—and the men she was attracted to were powerful, rich, or creative: Theodore Sorensen, President Kennedy's White House adviser; Robert Benton, who would co-write the screenplay for *Bonnie and Clyde;* Mike Nichols, the director; and Herb Sargent, a playwright. Later there would be Jim Brown, the football player and actor; and Rafer Johnson, the 1960 Olympic decathlon gold medalist, who was a friend of Robert Kennedy. In 1966, the year Betty founded NOW, Gloria went to Truman Capote's famous Black and White Ball at the Plaza Hotel (limited to 540 of his most intimate friends), invitations to which were so coveted that people left town rather than admit they had not received one.

But Gloria was also serious and wanted to be taken seriously. She co-founded *New York* magazine and wrote a column, "The City Politic," for it, and used the column to further her causes: the Young Lords, a Puerto Rican gang seeking social change in the barrio; and Cesar Chavez and his grape pickers in California. On March 21, 1969, she went to the sanctuary of Washington Square Methodist Church to cover an epochal abortion speakout held by the Redstockings. Members of the group explained the concept: the personal is political. As twelve women, one after another, testified to their harrowing experiences, Gloria had an epiphany, the "click" that came from consciousness raising. She remembered her own abortion: the fear that her life would be over if she didn't get it; the difficulty of getting it; the enormous relief afterward. And she began to work in the movement. By December 12, 1970, the day of the lavender armbands, she already had a large following. Gloria pinpointed that date as the beginning of Betty's antagonism toward her. The following year, a series of events drove Betty into such a state of insecurity that she simply exploded.

In the spring of 1971, Betty learned that Gloria had been invited to give the Smith College commencement speech. That was a slap in the face, as if her own family had adopted an orphan and loved it more than they loved her. Actually, the senior class, not the administration, had chosen Gloria, and she had not been their first choice, but that was no consolation.

In August, coinciding with the second New York City march, came a *Newsweek* cover with Gloria's face, smiling and sunny. The accompanying article, which anointed her the leader of the movement, was a besotted love letter written in the swooning style that so many pieces on Gloria lapsed into. She was "the stereotype of the Eternal Feminine." She had "dazzling physical gifts." She had "pithy anger: 'If men could get pregnant, abortion would be a sacrament.' " She was "as self-effacing as Ethelred the Unready and as selfless as Albert Schweitzer." "She ... throws herself like a blanket over any criticized or threatened sister." On and on. Somewhere in this cascade of adoration was a quote from Betty, who managed to choke back the bile and provide a gracious comment: "The fact that Gloria is very pretty and chic is nice for the movement, but if that's all she was it wouldn't be enough. Fortunately, she is so much more."

In December 1971, the prototype of *Ms.* appeared, folded into *New York*'s year-end double issue. For years it had been Betty's pet project to start an intelligent magazine for women. She had started thinking about it in 1966, when her piece on Indira Gandhi had been published in the *LHJ*. In May 1966, she had written to Alma Birk, the editor of *Nova*, an English magazine she admired, suggesting that Alma's publishing group start an American edition of *Nova*, which she would edit. She had also approached Helen Gurley Brown of *Cosmopolitan* about the possibility of getting backing from the Hearst Corporation. With Muriel Fox, she had even gone to see David Rockefeller about funding. His daughter Abby was in Cell 16 (the haircutting group at the First Congress to Unite) in Boston. "He was interested in population control and reproductive rights," Muriel recalled. "He wouldn't bankroll it. Betty didn't have a written proposal, but it was a magazine like *Ms.*"

Just as the trial issue of *Ms.* was being published, Gloria appeared on a second major magazine cover: *McCall's* named her its Woman of the Year. If *Newsweek* had anointed Gloria, *McCall's* crowned her. Like the Smith honor, it was another betrayal: Betty was writing a monthly column for *McCall's*. Patricia Carbine, the editorial director, who had asked Betty to do the column, had also been working nights and weekends to help Gloria shape *Ms.* and was considering leaving *McCall's.** She had made the cover decision over the vociferous objections of the corporate hierarchy. David Mahoney, the CEO of Norton Simon, which owned the magazine, did not think Gloria was the sort of woman the readership of *McCall's* would identify with. He wanted Pat Nixon on the cover. Pat Carbine prevailed by threatening to resign. "I believed Gloria was the most influential woman in the country," she said. "I did not see Betty Friedan as a contender. Gloria was describing life in a way that named the issues—domestic violence, sexual harassment on the job. She said, 'We used to call this life.'" In the profile, Gloria was referred to as "the reluctant superstar of the women's movement." Betty was mentioned twice, but only in passing. Gloria had eclipsed her as the most famous feminist in America.

The accumulation of slights, the stabs at Betty's self-esteem, were beyond endurance. She had traveled the country for years, speaking, lecturing, getting out the message; everywhere she went, women thanked her for what she had done for them and sent thousands of letters overflowing with gratitude; she had led NOW to victory and united women in the first march. And this newcomer, with her hair and her empty refrigerator, who had written no book, who had started no organization, had appeared out of nowhere and was suddenly being hailed as the leader of the movement. It was like waving a red flag in front of a wounded bull. Betty rose up and charged.

Betty's first attack came on January 8, 1972. (All-out war would not be declared until eight months later.) Speaking at the opening of Women's Week at Trinity College in Hartford, Connecticut, Betty claimed that Gloria "has never been a part of the organized" women's movement. "The media tried to make her a celebrity, but no one should mistake her for a leader." In the question-and-answer period she accused Gloria and *Ms.* of "ripping off the movement for personal profit." It was not a position she could have defended. By that standard, everyone was ripping off the movement. Women from every corner of the women's movement were busy filling libraries with feminist books and articles.

After the story was reported, Betty had to retreat. In a conciliatory phone call to Gloria, she said her "ripping off" remark had been quoted out of context. Betty's other point—that "the media tried to make her a celebrity"—was well taken, but, as often happened, the sense and solidity of her positions warred with her method and manner of presenting them.

* Pat left the following year, giving up a bundle of stock options and other perquisites.

Many radical feminists also thought Gloria was exploiting women's liberation and resented her fiercely for the way she had been elevated. Echoing them, Germaine Greer later wrote that "the American media created 'stars' and denied the grass-roots character of the movement." The media had trivialized and distorted the movement, turned power struggles into catfights and attached sexual innuendoes to serious issues. It had raised up Kate Millett and dashed her to the ground, and now it had chosen Gloria Steinem as the incarnation of feminism.

Gloria was a natural leader and would undoubtedly have risen to that height in time. She was also in a unique position. As Sydney Ladensohn Stern, one of her biographers, observed, she was constantly on the road promoting *Ms.*, and *Ms.* promoted her in its pages, providing "ongoing visibility and institutional support." But as things stood, the media actually had no choice. None of NOW's leaders after Betty possessed her charisma, and the early feminists were unsuited for national leadership. The radical women, who did not even believe the movement required a leader, refused to talk to male journalists and were even suspicious of female journalists.

Other early leaders were like rocket flares that burned out, consumed in their own fire. Ti-Grace Atkinson had thrown in her lot with Joe Columbo, a Mafia don, and lost all credibility. Kate Millett suffered a nervous breakdown after *Time* got through with her; thereafter, she concentrated on her books and sculpture and refused to have anything to do with the media. Robin Morgan became an editor. Susan Brownmiller decided that her future lay in writing; she produced the extraordinary, groundbreaking *Against Our Will*, which connected rape to violence, not sex, and limited her public actions to specific issues. Germaine Greer, author of *The Female Eunuch*, was a foreigner, an Australian with eccentric ideas who flaunted her sex life and flamed into the public eye at irregular intervals. Bella Abzug, who arrived even later than Gloria, was a politician, and for many years focused her efforts on Congress. Only Betty and Gloria remained, and the media were in love with Gloria.

Gloria always maintained that the mantle had been thrust upon her and she wore it reluctantly. Yet she did not refuse it. She was not an accidental icon. She had an instinct to match Betty's "geiger counter," and it led her to the centers of glamour and power. So many of the best and the brightest were connected to the CIA; the New Journalism was created by her colleagues and nurtured by her editor; radical chic and the Beautiful People were all the rage, and then the new feminist woman was, too. Her purpose was no less serious, her dedication no less complete, but she could not have gotten where she was without her beauty and her aura. Gloria herself could never reconcile the two sides of her life, and it always bothered her that the way she lived and looked invited exactly the kind of attention she said she deplored. As late as 1992, discussing body images, she wrote, "I'm still suspicious of the degree to which I make choices that society rewards.... (I know that, wherever I am, I absorb the going aesthetic.)" Implied criticism put her on the defensive. When a reporter inquired about her low-cut olive wool dress by Rudi Gernreich, she answered with a non sequitur: "But it's last year's."

Reporters did not ask Betty about her clothes, and she did not tolerate other indignities. She was at Denison University in Ohio, about to deliver a lecture, when the president of the school made a few women's lib jokes during his introduction. Standing at the lectern, she demolished him: "I am the serious leader of a serious movement," she said. "If I were Malcolm X you wouldn't dare make jokes.... If there are any more jokes, I shall walk out of this auditorium."

Paradoxically, even as Gloria fit the old feminine stereotype, she was also a "new woman." Her arrival coincided with a historic turning point: for the first time, a generation of young, single women, freed by the Pill, could leave home and seek their fortune, invent their own lives, and have fun—could live as men did. They needed new female heroines, powerful women whose lives they could emulate, and Gloria was the exemplar of that new lifestyle—independent, unencumbered by family, earning her own money, free. She had the life, the look, the men, the clothes. To them, the mystery of Gloria was how she had done it. They were all trying to do the same thing. It was her life they wanted; they wanted to *be* Gloria.

So powerful was Gloria's image that people frequently misunderstood the message she was sending—or perhaps Gloria seemed to be sending conflicting messages. In 1972, Kingman Brewster, then president of Yale, told an audience of graduate women that he could accept the part of the movement represented by Gloria—the part that included men. Sheila Tobias, then associate provost of Wesleyan and a friend of both Betty's and Gloria's, who had been in the audience, later said, "He got it wrong because of appearance and style. Because anyone as beautiful, as charming, as accommodating, as Gloria—as *female*—could not possibly be advocating that men be deposed and the system be destroyed; only disgruntled women—and disgruntled women had only one real reason to be disgruntled, and that was that they were not attractive to men."

Betty could not compete with this. No one could. In print she picked at Gloria repeatedly with one of her favorite stories: "It always amused me," she said in 1996, laughing at the memory. "I didn't see it myself, but there was an anecdote I told; Gloria never forgave me for it." The anecdote finds Gloria at the hairdresser, having her hair streaked by Kenneth and hiding her face behind a copy of *Vogue*. "I think someone must have told me. But here is someone who always dressed beautifully, chic-ly, and all that, and told other women they didn't have to bother to wear makeup or shave their legs."* It was the perceived hypocrisy that inflamed her. It drove her to distraction when Gloria came out with remarks like, "A woman needs a man like a fish needs a bicycle." "I hate that slogan," she wrote, connecting it with "certain women who, in the name of women's liberation, told other women that they don't need men, or love."

So the media chose Gloria, and through their alchemy she was transmuted into the Jackie Onassis of the movement, a figure of endless fascination, utterly unknowable, a star upon whom women could project their fantasies. The image told women they could be sexy and still be feminists, banishing the old suffragist specter of the battle-ax. How ironic for Betty, then, that the emblem of beauty and respectability, the woman she had sought to be the face of feminism, turned out to be Gloria.

---

* Though *Ms.* featured women who did not wear makeup, neither Gloria nor *Ms.* told other women not to look good, and Betty had nothing against hair coloring. She was afraid that if she colored hers, people would throw it up to her, just as she was doing to Gloria. Many years later she told a friend, "It just wouldn't look right. People would say, 'But you're a feminist.' "

CHAPTER

16

"A Fight for Love and Glory"

EVEN BEFORE THE August 26, 1970, march, Betty had sensed the next direction of the movement. She believed that its first phase was over, and unless it took new action its strength would be dissipated. "From now on our thrust will be political," she told a reporter. "This was a necessary stage, but that job is over with. From now on we have no need to stagnate in navel-gazing rap sessions or man-hating.... We are going to run."

It was an astonishing statement considering that millions of women were still absorbing the impact of feminism, and a high-handed dismissal of the radical women and all that they stood for.

Betty was a mover and a shaker, and after she had moved and shaken, after she had accomplished as much as she thought possible, she would pronounce the result satisfactory and move on to the next thing. Through the years she would announce new stages in the movement, declaring the old ones a success, while those who had worked with her stood around with their mouths open. She always looked at the big picture. The details might not have fallen into place, but the outline was clear to her.

In this case, Betty was right: political power was the next logical step. Women were 53 percent of the population, but in the United States Congress there were only 12 women out of 435 representatives and only 1 senator out of 100. She envisioned a caucus, rather like her earlier coalitions, that would include women of both political parties but would operate as an independent pressure group.

At a meeting in the fall of 1970, she outlined the idea, including the name and a strategy. The new organization she would cofound, the National Women's Political Caucus (NWPC), would be the first such political group since women mobilized to win the vote. Almost immediately the NWPC opened a new arena, and thousands of women, who had been put off by the movement's youthful excesses, surged into it. It was a second enfranchisement. "Betty knows what train is coming down the track and how to get on it," Gene Boyer said.

Betty also needed another organization to provide a power base from which to launch her political ambitions. She wanted to be a U.S. senator. The movement had come so far so fast, anything seemed possible, even unseating such a well-funded, well-liked liberal Republican as Senator Jacob K. Javits of New York in 1974. Betty announced her intentions in *The New York Times:* "I've helped and freed a lot of women, and I think I would have their vote; in fact, I don't think there's another woman in America who could muster more votes. And I'd love to be in the Senate. I don't want to sound corny about it, but...well, you know about Joan of Arc and the voices that guided her? I think I hear voices sometimes, too. It is no more than your own sixth sense telling you what is best; but it's like hearing voices."

Among feminists, there was always a disagreement about who started the NWPC, Betty Friedan or Bella Abzug. Betty's enemies, by now legion, credited Bella, a lawyer who had been elected to Congress in November 1970. Gloria Steinem said, "My emotional memory is that it was not Betty's or any single person's idea. It was a spontaneous feeling that there needed to be women in the system and an organization devoted to electing them that would support women's issues. At that point NOW was not doing it and didn't want to. People said, as long as Betty is involved it won't happen. It was the women who were already in Congress who had the credibility. Betty was responding to this."

Bella claimed that she and Betty started the NWPC simultaneously, but Jacqui Ceballos has a different memory. Jacqui, who was then president of NY–NOW, said, "Betty invited Bella to help plan it. Then we heard that Bella was going to one-up us; she was going to jump the gun and announce that she had formed her own political caucus. We rushed to her office in the Village to confront her. Bella said, 'No, I wouldn't do that! I wouldn't start the caucus without you!' And then we saw a press release on her desk." Caught in the act, she brazened it out. "She laughed. 'You caught me!' she said. 'We'll go together.' Betty never felt she could trust Bella. They were at arm's length."

Bella Abzug, with her cartwheel hats and her glass-shattering voice, was first noticed on the women's liberation scene at the Second Congress to Unite Women, in May 1970. (Betty had not attended. The first one had been quite enough.) For Bella, feminism was one more cause on the continuum of her politics: Old Left, anti–Vietnam War, Women Strike for Peace (she was a founder), Committee for a Sane Nuclear Policy, black civil rights. As she went along, feminism came to mean all of those things and more—it became her fight against everything that was wrong in the world. She was a whole-earth feminist, as ambitious and driven as Betty. After winning her congressional seat she announced, "My election goes beyond this district. I think I represent the entire peace movement, the women's movement. I seek to represent women in the entire country."

Betty and Bella were two of a kind, loud and earthy, warm and vulnerable, screamers and bullies, two imperious egos who tried to occupy the same space. Bella shocked Betty by yelling at her on the phone for invading her turf and then slamming down the receiver. "She hung up on me," Betty told friends in disbelief. Hanging up was what Betty did. (Sometimes she called back.) Reflecting on their decades of titanic battles, Betty said, "At one point I had a strong ideological difference with Bella, but basically I fought back against being pushed out.... It was my turf before it was her turf." Bella was to politics what Betty had been as NOW president—a powerhouse, a dynamo, barging in where angels feared to tread. Shana Alexander described her: "Who is this bizarre figure advancing down Main Street at high noon with a blazing six-shooter in one hand and a bowl of chicken soup in the other?"

The press called her Battling Bella and Bellicose Bella, but she had a disarming sense of humor that mitigated the tyrannical (and sometimes violent) way she treated her underlings. One of her critics said: "She ran her office like General Patton. The most important thing was the war. Your grunts, staff, were shit. People quivering with fear. In the war room— that was her working style. Betty and Bella were in the tradition of Carrie Chapman Catt and Alice Paul,* women of single-minded purpose who convinced themselves that they and the cause are one; they are fused with it and powered by it."

---

* Carrie Chapman Catt shepherded the Nineteenth Amendment to its successful ratification. Alice Paul founded the National Woman's Party in 1923 to achieve passage of the Equal Rights Amendment.

But people also adored Bella. She exuded warmth and love toward women and allowed them to see her vulnerabilities. Outside her circle of close friends, Betty rarely let her weaknesses show. Bella inspired lifelong loyalty in those who worked for her. One of them, ironically, was a woman she had met in high school, Mim Kelber, the former Miriam Kolkin, Betty's editor at the *Federated Press*.

Bella grew up in the Bronx and went to Hunter College, a tuition-free school, and Columbia Law School, where she was an editor of the law review. She was pretty and sexy and had the great good fortune to marry a man who adored her and supported her career. When they needed money, Martin Abzug gave up his own freelance writing to become a stockbroker. Their marriage lasted for forty-two years. After he died she wrote of him,

> *From the beginning he did everything and anything to make possible what I was doing. If I had to work eighteen hours a day as a young labor lawyer, he would keep me company reading a book or typing in the room next to my office. On the weekends, he would always say, "You rest, I'll go do the shopping."... When I practiced law he said I was the greatest lawyer that ever was. When I became a member of Congress he said I was the greatest member of Congress and later he said I was the greatest stateswoman. He never felt competitive—only proud.*

Bella found her clients among fur cutters, restaurant workers, longshoremen, many of them victims of the 1950s witch hunt. In the early fifties, when lynchings were not uncommon in the South, she took on a famous case—she defended Willie McGee, a black man who had been accused of raping a white woman. Bella was seven months pregnant at the time. She lost the case and the baby.

The first pre-organizing meeting of the National Women's Political Caucus took place on June 9, 1971, in Bella's congressional office, decorated with a framed copy of the poster "And God Created Woman in Her Own Image." It was the first thing you saw when you walked in. The Big Four of the caucus were there: Betty, Bella, Gloria, and Shirley Chisholm, the first black congresswoman. Shirley and Representative Patsy Mink talked about how to get organized. Shirley thought the caucus needed a program before rallying the women. Patsy talked about a charter. Betty got up and waved her arms. "The hell with all that," she said. "We've got to do it and do it now. There's an election coming up. We need an organizing conference at the end of the month! And task forces."

Betty went home to her West Ninety-third Street duplex and got on the phone. The NWPC was another NOW, a new call to arms, with Betty on horseback at the head of the troops. All her friends came to her purple living room with its settees and curved chairs, its brightly colored banners hanging over the staircase, to make phone calls to every woman they knew in America. Letty Cottin Pogrebin, author and publicist, who had worked for Bella's election to Congress, remembered: "It was frenzied. It was grandiose and without regard for any perceptible limitations. 'We'll do this, do that, we'll go to Washington, we'll take over the hotel'—I had never heard anything like it. It was an epiphany for me that this was the way it worked. I didn't understand that you could start something like that from scratch. I felt I was present at the creation."

Gloria allied herself with Bella. She had met Bella marching outside the Pentagon and had at first been put off by her brassiness. "She frightened me. I had never seen a woman that forceful. Later I realized that was my problem, not Bella's. She just refused to be restricted by the prison of being ladylike." They would need each other in the colossal battles for control of the NWPC. Gloria could smooth the roiling waters; Bella could face Betty down, could carry off the confrontations that made Gloria's stomach sink. Ronnie Feit, the director of the caucus, said, "Gloria had a mother-daughter relationship with Bella. It gradually became clear that Gloria was dependent emotionally and checked in with her." Politically they were on the same wavelength; together, they could short-circuit Betty. "Betty was so serious and had such a quick trigger, it was easy to set her off," said one caucus staffer. "At a meeting on Capitol Hill in a House committee room, where the point of contention was the plum job of who would speak to the press and what she would say, Betty was screaming so hard she almost leaped across the table. Bella sat tipped back in her chair, so far back that her hat slipped off, laughing—to infuriate Betty more."

The anarchic organizing conference at the Statler Hilton Hotel in Washington on July 10–11, 1971, was filled with women who were new to power, new to politics, united as women but, like any political party, divided by race, class, sexual orientation, and generation. Myrlie Evers, the widow of the murdered civil rights leader Medgar Evers, was there, and Fannie Lou Hamer, who was running for Congress in Mississippi. Welfare-rights people came, as did others whom Betty hadn't invited. Gloria said, "Betty was angry about my bringing in Flo Kennedy—'How could you? How could you? She will Mau Mau us.' " Betty brought in her friends, among them LaDonna Harris, who fought for Indian rights, and Shana Alexander. Bella and Gloria objected when Shana brought in Liz

Carpenter, who had been Lady Bird Johnson's press secretary. "They didn't want her because she was associated with LBJ and the Vietnam War," Shana said. The caucus had the impossible task of trying to unify all these disparate interests virtually overnight—a job tailor made for Gloria's talents. "It was a kind of a raucous caucus," Liz Carpenter said, "but there was a shock treatment in it, and a lot of truth. And it made people stop and listen. And you know, women like myself just decided that we're not going to let the theatrics turn us off anymore."

Betty had come prepared. She had brought in NOW veterans who, she thought, would support her in her bid for leadership of the caucus, and enlisted Kay Clarenbach to chair the opening session of the organizing meeting. In a letter to Kay she wrote that she was worried about the purists and extremists who inhabited another world and whose die-hard stands only served the cause of polarization. Kay, who could get along with both Betty and Bella, said, "Each of them thought she was going to be the keynote speaker and kept sending lieutenants to me to ask how she was going to be introduced." Kay solved the problem by not having a keynoter.

Bella and Betty were like the North Vietnamese and the Americans fighting over the shape of the table at the Paris Peace Conferences. They fought over strategy, public statements, structure, bylaws, procedures, the next meeting, everything. Bella was a politician to the bone; she understood, as Betty did not, that politics was about twisting arms, not breaking them. Jane Pierson, one of the three caucus staff founders,* said, "Betty would tenaciously grab an idea or a position and had very little ability to negotiate with other people, so she always found herself in a box on the other side of Bella. She would create a great disturbance, and things were organized around her. She was the rock in the pond. Betty would shop an idea on the phone to three or four people and it then needed to be on the agenda, to be talked about. She was very smart. She beat away on things. People wouldn't give her power—she was too unpredictable. The problem for Betty always was, if she didn't get her way she stamped her feet and started yelling."

Beyond their jockeying for position, there were real ideological differences between them. Bella and Gloria wanted the caucus to be a voice for humanist values. In *Bella! Ms. Abzug Goes to Washington*, Bella wrote, "You know, it's nice to say that by 1976 we're going to have two hundred women

---

* The other two were Doris Meissner, who became head of the Immigration and Naturalization Service under President Clinton; and Virginia Kerr, who became a lawyer. Jane Pierson became a management consultant.

in Congress, but do we want the kind of women who are going to vote for missiles and Vietnam wars? Or do we want the kind of women who are going to put our tax money into housing and health and child care centers and abortion clinics and things like that?" Betty thought attention to such issues as Vietnam and welfare would interfere with the main goal, which was electing women. Her basic issues remained, as they always would, equal pay and equal rights and the situation of ordinary working women. She was an equality feminist.

The caucus served to define the two main factions of the movement, but all sides agreed on its main purposes: it would form local chapters and help women to run for office; and it would pressure local officials to appoint more women to public positions.

Betty had her followers, but they were not powerful enough to spare her a bitter defeat. At the NWPC council meeting, she campaigned hard to be the caucus's spokesperson, the one the media would deal with at the Democratic convention in Miami. She wanted the position desperately, but the council chose Gloria, who had said she did not want it and had deliberately stayed away from the meeting. Betty was convinced that Bella had outmaneuvered her, but others thought that Betty had outmaneuvered herself.* Nikki Beare, a NOW ally of Betty's, said, "People didn't want Betty for two reasons. When Betty talks, she has a tendency to ramble—she can't cut to the gist of it without walking around it twice. The media want sound bites. And Betty had her own agenda, and nobody knew what it was. There was a time when she was homophobic." In Gloria's view, "People didn't trust her to speak for the group. She always spoke for herself." Gloria believed Betty's failure to win was one of the reasons for Betty's later attacks on her. "She never forgave me for that," she said.

. . .

IN THE SPRING of 1972, while she was organizing the NWPC, Betty took the first step toward realizing her political ambitions. She ran in the Democratic primary as an Upper West Side delegate for Shirley Chisholm, the first black woman to run for the presidency.† Gloria and

---

* If, indeed, Bella and Gloria knocked Betty out of the center ring, they could not have done it without Betty's help. Gloria did not have to be present to be elected spokesperson. Betty was so prickly, so intemperate, she undid herself.
† The primary system then in place listed the names of delegates to the presidential conventions on the ballot. Voters elected delegates pledged to a particular candidate, and the delegates would then vote in their party's convention.

Jacqui Ceballos also ran as delegates for Shirley. Golda Meir and Indira Gandhi were then the prime ministers of Israel and India, respectively, and a Gallup poll indicated that 66 percent of American voters would be open to the candidacy of a qualified woman.

Shirley Chisholm, forty-seven, whose slogan was "Unbossed and Unbought," did not expect to win. Hers was a brave and quixotic run, a concept candidacy; she was bucking the party structure to make a statement. She presented her candidacy as a coalition of the have-nots. Those politicians who accused her of being on an ego trip and of taking votes away from the liberal pool did not think she would last more than six weeks. Shirley may not have expected to win the Democratic Party nomination, but Betty expected to be elected as a delegate, and she was not happy with the support she was getting from Shirley's campaign headquarters. "Her concern was that she and her candidacy were not given enough exposure," said Ludwig Gelobter, Shirley's campaign manager.

To remedy that oversight she hired a public relations firm, Simon and Geltzer Ltd., and formed a Committee to Elect Betty Friedan. She distributed literature and flyers at subway stops and threw a fund-raiser for herself, instructing her secretary to inform her guests of their responsibilities: they would have to pledge either time or money to her campaign. Friends contributed: Barbara Seaman, a cofounder of the National Women's Health Network and the author of *The Doctors' Case Against the Pill*, $250; Alvin Toffler, $500; Gerold Frank, the author of *The Boston Strangler*, $200; Dick Laupot, $500; Martin Peretz, owner of *The New Republic*, $250; Harold Wit, an investment banker at Allen & Company, $500. Betty's use of her resources created bad blood with Shirley's managers. The Chisholm campaign, which had an extremely limited budget, was incensed that someone like Harold Wit, in particular, who had access to enormous sums, was funneling money to Betty and not Shirley. The contributions at Chisholm fund-raisers were pitifully small.

Some of Betty's flyers bore a picture of her wearing a jacket and a blouse with a ruffled jabot, dangling earrings, and shoulder-length hair, very Upper West Side. "Betty Speaks Out for Women! You Speak Out for Betty on June 20," they read, and below that, "Support the Chisholm slate—unbossed & unbought." Betty's campaign material focused on herself, as if Shirley were a second thought.

She held a press conference on June 7 at eleven A.M., early enough to make the television evening news, at the Ginger Man, her favorite restaurant, around the corner from her apartment. They always gave her a good table and whiskey sours with fresh lemon juice, which she loved. Betty stood for having women included in all policy-making decisions and appointed to the Supreme Court and Cabinet; for abortion, day care centers, income-tax deductions for child care and household expenses, divorce reform laws, the ERA, enforcement of sex discrimination laws, and extending the minimum wage and overtime pay to household workers—the NOW agenda. She would be committed to Shirley on the first ballot at the convention. Feminists would enter the smoke-filled rooms at last.

The Chisholm people viewed Betty's efforts as an exercise in self-promotion at the expense of the candidate. She did not speak to specific black issues. Ludwig Gelobter said, "In the black community twenty-odd years ago, being associated with the white women's movement was not necessarily the best thing for Shirley in attracting black support." Fraying race relations exacerbated the situation. The old alliance between blacks and Jews, who had championed civil rights, was unraveling; the new black power groups supported Yasir Arafat's Palestine Liberation Organization and its terrorist arm, al-Fatah. Blacks themselves were divided on the question of whether a black woman should be running for office; after centuries of being held back, the men thought *they* should come first, and many black women agreed. It was one of the reasons black women had not flocked to join the movement. "There were a lot of snide remarks from campaign workers," said Jacqui Ceballos. "Betty did not seem to be aware of them."

On her own, without discussing it with Shirley, Betty made plans to rent a Hertz truck, fill it with watermelons, and hold a rally in Harlem. A press release announced her "Traveling Watermelon Feast." It is difficult to imagine what she could have been thinking of. Betty had always supported black civil rights—at the dinner table in Grandview she had impressed on her children the importance of the civil rights movement, and she had chosen to live in Parkway Village, an interracial community. After the 1972 Democratic convention she would go to Mississippi to campaign for Fannie Lou Hamer. Blacks were certainly part of her larger vision, but they were out of her direct line of sight. She got into one of her terrible fights with Barbara Lamont, a black journalist who was married to Ludwig Gelobter. "I told her that bringing watermelons to Harlem was political suicide," Barbara said. "She saw nothing wrong with it. She said some of her best friends were black, and I didn't know anything about being black. She told me I had no right to tell her what to do."

In the end, Betty did go to Harlem, but she did not bring watermelons. "This was a blind spot," Ludwig said. "In other ways she did lend a lot of support to the campaign."

Betty and Gloria and Jacqui all lost their bids to be a delegate. Beyond doubt, their skin color was a cause of their defeat, as was their timing. The Gallup poll notwithstanding, in 1972 neither New York City nor the rest of the country was ready for a black female presidential candidate—or a feminist one. Betty went to Miami with press credentials from *McCall's* and continued the fight there, trading on the influence of the caucus and the power of her own name. She would attend every presidential convention as a member of the press and use her entrée to speak for women.

17

Political Initiation

BETTY ARRIVED IN Miami a few days before the convention without a clear role in the caucus. She was separated from its power center by her location: *McCall's* had reserved a room at the Fontainebleau, far from caucus headquarters at the Betsy Ross, a dismal eight-dollar-a-night fleabag plagued by stalled elevators and a clogged switchboard. Bella had emerged as the floor leader for the caucus delegates, and Gloria was the spokesperson to the press. Reporting for *Esquire*, Nora Ephron wrote, "The day before the Democratic Convention is to begin the National Women's Political Caucus is holding a press conference. The cameras are clicking at Gloria... and there is Betty, off to the side, just slightly out of frame. The cameras will occasionally catch a shoulder of her flowered granny dress or a stray wisp of her chaotic graying hair or one of her hands churning up in the air; but it will be accidental...." She had been sidelined.

Betty had a simple, straightforward strategy: the caucus should unite behind Shirley Chisholm and bargain as a power bloc for Cabinet jobs, a voice in the party, day care, abortion, etc. New guidelines had opened the Democratic Party to women and blacks; 40 percent of the delegates were women, as against 13 percent in 1968. Many of them could be expected to vote with the caucus. George McGovern, the leading candidate, would be forced to deal with them.

But Betty did not have the power to impose her strategy on the caucus. For pragmatic reasons, the NWPC had not endorsed Shirley's candidacy, even though she was one of its founders. Although all four principals were Democrats, the caucus itself was bipartisan and did not want to be identified only with the Democratic Party; it was also split between ideological support for its own and political reality. "Shirley was furious about it," Jennifer MacLeod said. "She was fit to be tied. And there were mixed feelings about her. She was pretty far left, not mainstream. And black. She was not getting black support, either. And no one had money. She was very angry about it, and that turned people off."

Bella and Gloria led the more practical strategy—to bargain with the strongest candidate in return for the caucus's support, and then reap their reward. This approach was somewhat compromised because McGovern, who wanted to pull out of Vietnam, already had their support. In fact, Bella and Shirley MacLaine cochaired the women's committee of his campaign, and Gloria had backed both Chisholm and McGovern in the primaries. In those states where Chisholm was not on the ballot, she had campaigned and raised money for McGovern. "He was the best white male candidate," she said.

Both strategies were doomed. Shirley had only a handful of delegates, and McGovern knew he had control of the convention anyway. In his speech to the caucus he talked about Vietnam, not women's issues. His nomination was safe from the beginning. The women had no bargaining chips, nothing to make a deal with; they could not deliver anything. They were neophytes, undergoing their initiation rite. Most of them were seeing the inside of a convention for the first time, and in the electric atmosphere, the excitement of proximity to power, they made the mistake of thinking they, too, had power. Betty finally figured it out: "The McGovern . . . strategists . . . never intended us to have real political power. They counted on our inexperience and our traditional passivity to do whatever they told us to, in gratitude for just being there, as the ethnic blocs used to do."

Betty's feud with Gloria was common knowledge. Nora Ephron wrote: " 'I'm so disgusted with Gloria,' she [Betty] would mutter on her way to a NWPC meeting. Gloria was selling out the women. Gloria was ripping off the movement. Gloria was a tool of George McGovern. Gloria and Bella were bossing the delegates around. Gloria was part of a racist clique that would not support Shirley Chisholm for Vice President." Nothing the caucus did was to Betty's liking. Introduced at a press conference at the Deauville Hotel as "the mother of us all," she said grumpily, "I'm getting sick and tired of this mother-of-us-all thing." It was no longer a tribute; it was more like being passé.

Betty was not one to be ignored with impunity. She was beside herself at Gloria's ubiquitousness, at how she always seemed to be on camera. Germaine Greer, covering the convention for *Harper's* (in this year of women's political breakthrough, the magazines finally sent women to cover politics), noticed it too: "Gloria's relentless prominence in all affairs began to disturb me, and most of all her occasional wistful mentions of 'the smoke-filled rooms where the decisions are made.' " Betty wanted a little relentless prominence too. Her frustration became so great that she tried to unseat Gloria: she told Gwen Cherry, a black legislator, to make a fuss about not having been elected spokesperson, her reasoning being that Gwen was a member of the Florida State House of Representatives, and the convention was being held in Florida. Gwen refused. "Betty's way to keep power was to have an alternate candidate," Jane Pierson said. "Betty was always trying to keep Bella or Gloria or any other luminous figure from having power over her."

A few days before the official opening of the convention, Betty announced that she would campaign to make Shirley vice president. No one was aware at the time that Shirley had absolutely no interest in being vice president. She had not yet arrived in Miami. The ballroom of the Carillon Hotel rang with shouts and cheers, and Betty got a standing ovation. But the NWPC council thought it politic to wait and make a list of other possible candidates. On the list were Frances (Sissy) Farenthold, a member of the Texas legislature (she had recently run for governor of Texas and come in second in a field of seven candidates), Representative Martha Griffiths—and Bella and Gloria.

Betty was agitated in the extreme. She had seen her power disintegrate, her strategy ignored, and her vision for the caucus distorted. So when she ran into the woman who had suggested Gloria for vice president, Jane Galvin-Lewis of the National Council of Negro Women, her reaction was irrational. They met in the lobby of the Deauville Hotel, where they had gone to greet Shirley Chisholm on her arrival. According to Nora Ephron, Betty accused her of "play[ing] both ends" against the middle. "What kind of black are you anyway?" she asked offensively. Jane had no idea what Betty was talking about. "You didn't even want to support Shirley Chisholm," Betty told her, her voice getting louder and

Miriam Goldstein and her three children:
(left to right) Amy, Harry, and Betty.

COURTESY OF HARRY GOLDSTEIN JR.

Betty's father, Harry Goldstein.

COURTESY OF JONATHAN FRIEDAN

One of Betty's elementary school classes in Peoria, posing for the camera. Betty is in the first row on the far right.

COURTESY OF JONATHAN FRIEDAN

Betty stole the show with her performance as the mad Mrs. Rochester in a high school production of Jane Eyre.

FROM THE PEORIA HIGH SCHOOL YEARBOOK, CLASS OF 1938

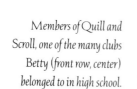

Members of Quill and Scroll, one of the many clubs Betty (front row, center) belonged to in high school.

FROM THE PEORIA HIGH SCHOOL YEAR-BOOK, CLASS OF 1938

Betty's high school
graduation picture.
Her classmates expected
her to be a writer.

FROM THE PEORIA
HIGH SCHOOL YEARBOOK,
CLASS OF 1938

The editors at <u>SCAN</u>, the Smith
College newspaper, caused major
upheavals on campus. Betty is
fifth from left.

FROM THE SMITH COLLEGE
YEARBOOK, 1942

Betty's college graduation picture. The
school had never seen anything like her.

FROM THE SMITH COLLEGE
YEARBOOK, 1942

Betty and Carl Friedan on their first wedding day, June 12, 1947. Due to circumstances beyond their control, they had to get married twice.

COURTESY OF CARL FRIEDAN

Betty and Carl at the beginning of their tumultuous life together, 1947.

COURTESY OF CARL FRIEDAN

Gladys Carter, Betty's confidante, at Lake Hopatcong, summer 1947. After sharing a house with the Friedans, Gladys and her husband, Dick, decided never to repeat the experience.

COURTESY OF RICHARD CARTER

Betty and Carl's eleven-room Charles Addams house in Grandview-on-Hudson, where she lived her suburban-housewife days and conceived The Feminine Mystique.

Betty and her three children, Emily, Daniel, and Jonathan, on the banks of the Hudson River, being photographed for a spread in Life, *1963. She had just become famous.*

With Dorothy Haener (left)
and Kathryn Clarenbach
(right), discussing strategy at
a 1967 NOW board
meeting in Madison, Wisconsin.

COURTESY OF MARY EASTWOOD

Speaking to 50,000
women after the first
women's march,
August 26, 1970.

PHOTOGRAPH © BY
BETTYE LANE

Communards entertaining Senator Eugene McCarthy (on Betty's left)
at lunch, summer 1971: (from center) Ross Wetzsteon, Betty Rollin,
Arthur Herzog and his son, Matthew. McCarthy consulted Betty
and Arthur about running for president in 1972.

Addressing the National Women's Political Caucus during the 1972
Democratic National Convention in Miami while her two rivals,
Bella Abzug and Gloria Steinem, think their own thoughts.

Betty's pendant, the female biological sign crossed by an equal sign, was a replica of the one she gave Pope Paul VI during a 1973 audience with him.

PHOTOGRAPH © BY BETTYE LANE

Leading a small march to present 894 resolutions to the U.N. International Women's Year conference, Mexico City, 1975. Jacqui Ceballos is in the second row, far right. The women were barred at the door.

COURTESY OF JACQUI CEBALLOS

Speaking for her candidate at a NOW convention in 1975
during the organization's first serious power struggle.

On the dais, being honored at NOW's tenth-anniversary dinner, flanked by Mary Jean
Tully (left) and Muriel Fox (right). Betty and the other founders were not invited to
NOW's fifteenth-anniversary dinner.

Taking her exercise in Sag Harbor, 1976.

Mulling over a speech to be given before the National Women's Conference in Houston, 1977. It would mark a 180-degree turn in her lifelong opposition to lesbians. Jean O'Leary, a prominent lesbian leader, is at left.

Four of Betty's leading *bêtes noires*—Ti-Grace Atkinson, Florynce Kennedy, Gloria Steinem, and Kate Millett—at a matriarchy conference in 1978.

PHOTOGRAPH © BY BETTYE LANE

Flying with a group of Hamptons friends to Washington for an ERA march, 1978. Linda Francke is at right. PHOTOGRAPH © BY SUSAN WOOD

With her lover, David White, mid-1970s.

*In the pool at her Lincoln Plaza apartment building with
Barbara Seaman in 1978, before their friendship dissolved.*

PHOTOGRAPH © BY HENRY GROSSMAN

With Kurt Vonnegut, a good friend from Sag Harbor.

Disco dancing at Studio 54 with an unidentified friend from California.

Three old warriors at Betty's Labor Day party, Sag Harbor, 1994:
Jacqui Ceballos, Betty, and Mary Jean Tully.

louder. Jane tried to explain that she had suggested Gloria's name only for the caucus's list and so Betty should stop screaming at her, but Betty wasn't listening. "I'm going to do an exposé," she shouted. "I'm going to expose everyone. If it's the last thing I do, I'm going to do it. I'm going to do it."

After the convention opened officially and the delegates began voting on the party platform, Betty redeemed her honor in the fight over the abortion plank. A masterpiece of euphemism, in whose paragraphs the word "abortion" did not appear, it was referred to as "the human-reproduction plank." (*Roe* v. *Wade* was still six months away.) Breaking his promise to the women, McGovern and his campaign manager, Gary Hart, had let a right-to-lifer speak against abortion. The women were split on whether to have a roll call or a voice vote. Shirley MacLaine was strongly opposed to having any vote at all, on the ground that it could only damage the candidate. Bella and Gloria thought a voice vote would be less humiliating to women when the plank went down to its inevitable defeat. Betty insisted on a roll call and lobbied for it, and women in many state delegations agreed with her. The pro-choice votes quickly mounted; suddenly, telephones shrilled across the convention floor, and the delegates began to rescind their votes. George McGovern was not about to campaign against Richard Nixon and his Silent Majority with this scarlet letter hanging around his neck. Feelings ran so high that fistfights broke out on the floor. The plank was defeated, but only by 466 votes out of 1103. McGovern was to show his power in the same way again—phoning his delegates to take back their votes—when caucus delegates appeared to be winning their challenge to the seating of the South Carolina delegation, which had not met the 40 percent guideline for women.*

On the night McGovern was nominated, Betty finally confronted Gloria. Her cup of bitterness was running over. Although she had succeeded in her effort to make Shirley Chisholm the caucus's choice for vice president, she was apparently unaware that Shirley had rejected the offer. After choosing Shirley, the caucus was to have held a meeting of women delegates to support her; instead, Sissy Farenthold had suddenly emerged as the leading candidate. Betty yelled at Gloria for having called off the

---

* McGovern's betrayal of the women was a parliamentary maneuver to avoid having to challenge the California delegation later. California also had less than 40 percent women delegates, but the state operated under the unit rule (majority takes all), and he had its votes. He did not want to upset his applecart.

meeting and accused her of single-handedly replacing Shirley with Sissy. According to Betty, after she shouted at her, Gloria "said sweetly, in effect, that I had to get out or else."

As with so many long-ago meetings, time has blurred the memory of this one. Twenty-five years later, Gloria, who did not remember the encounter with Betty, said, "We waited to get word from Shirley about whether she wanted the vice presidency. The [caucus] meeting never took place because everything was so chaotic, it was impossible to get hold of people." Betty remembered the confrontation but not its content.

For Betty, the crucial question was whether the caucus had conferred with Shirley before choosing Sissy Farenthold as the nominee. Evidently, the caucus had. In a 1997 interview, Sissy said, "Someone called me and said, 'Shirley has decided not to run.' It was always with that qualification." Faced with the fait accompli in 1972, Betty told Sissy she wanted to nominate her on the convention floor. "I said no," Sissy said. "I knew I was creating enemies, but it was a gut reaction, and seldom have I been that direct. I just said no. I felt like I was being put in a position I would rather not be put in. It wasn't anything personal. Because I didn't know Betty."

At a meeting in a hotel ladies' room ("for privacy," Gloria said), it was decided that four people would nominate Sissy: Fannie Lou Hamer; David Lopez, a young Hispanic lawyer; Allard K. Lowenstein, a Democratic gadfly who had been a protégé of Eleanor Roosevelt; and Gloria. In the voting, Sissy did so well—coming in second, with 408 votes, to Senator Thomas Eagleton, McGovern's choice—that McGovern again had to call out his troops to stop her. "McGovern's people were so angry with me they took my telephone away from me," Sissy said. Because of the lengthy nominating speeches for Sissy, McGovern wound up giving his acceptance speech at two A.M., after most of the country had gone to sleep. The spectacle of different groups pushing their own agendas served to loosen the delicate skein of accommodation that had held the Democratic Party together, and prompted Eric Sevareid, the *CBS Evening News* correspondent, to joke (prophetically, it turned out, considering the future emphasis on identity politics), "Who's going to represent the left-handed Lithuanians?"

Betty had become profoundly suspicious of everything Bella and Gloria were doing. For some women, she thought, the caucus had been a front for personal ambition—or worse, a deliberate attempt to undermine the group's effectiveness. (Turning this conspiracy theory around,

Betty's enemies could have said the same of her and her aspirations for the Senate.) Martha McKay, who had grown up in North Carolina politics and was one of Betty's allies, agreed with her: "Bella and Gloria had sold out to McGovern because Bella wanted something." In this scenario, what Bella might have wanted was a position in the administration; she had been gerrymandered out of her congressional district. But there is no evidence for Betty's assertion. The NWPC was a bid for power, personal and political, and everyone involved wanted it. Bella and Gloria were playing politics, a game Betty was not good at, and they believed women would be more powerful with the mainstream candidate. The unbearable frustration of that week in Miami, of being so easily outmaneuvered by her opponents, may have led Betty to draw a more sinister conclusion.

Betty went back to Miami in August for the Republican convention, without Bella and Gloria. This was a Nixon crowd, a hats-and-gloves tea party compared to the noisy, unruly Democrats, and few of the women were sympathetic to the movement or to Betty's brand of advocacy. Jill Ruckelshaus, one who was, had been chosen by the NWPC to be its spokesperson to the GOP convention. A party insider, she wrote speeches for the Republican National Committee and was married to William Ruckelshaus, the first director of the U.S. Environmental Protection Agency. She was pro-choice and just the sort of person Betty had had in mind when founding the caucus.

Betty was scheduled to speak at a preconvention seminar. Her topic was fairly innocuous—that women didn't have to wait until their husbands died to run for office—but her reputation had preceded her. The Republicans had scripted the convention down to its last spontaneous demonstration, and they were afraid of her, of her talent for disruption. At the last minute, Pat Nixon was prevailed upon to visit the group of women Betty was planning to address, and Betty was disinvited. It was a futile exercise. Betty was a one-woman guerrilla force. She attended another seminar (on pollution, drugs, and child care), chaired by Jill Ruckelshaus. In the middle of the proceedings Betty stood up, went to a floor mike, and began to make a scene, launching into a discussion of the most controversial subject she could think of: "I am here now to raise the issue to urge women to fight for the right to control our own bodies, to fight for the right not to die by a coat hanger abortion." Alarm bells rang in Jill Ruckelshaus's head. She ran down down the aisle to Betty and whispered, "C'mon Betty, this isn't fair. You're out of order." Betty ignored her. They wrestled for the mike, Betty edging away from Jill and dragging the mike with her as she went on talking, Jill circling around, trying to seize it from the other side and shut it off. The seminar was saved by a large, imposing older woman, Natalie Moorman, a New York City delegate, who walked toward them saying, "This lady and I have reached the point where abortion has ceased to be an issue." Betty bowed to necessity and left, but she was quite positive about her role: "The amount of sheer discussion on the issues is the important thing," she would write.

The infighting that marked the caucus's first steps toward the smoke-filled rooms pales to insignificance next to its success. At the convention, abortion had been debated on national television and a woman had run for vice president, making a strong showing. Another woman, Jean Westwood, had been chosen to be chair of the Democratic National Committee, the first one to hold that position, and a plank supporting the nomination of a woman to the Supreme Court had passed. In the November election, five new congresswomen—Yvonne Brathwaite Burke, Marjorie Holt, Elizabeth Holtzman, Barbara Jordan, and Patricia Schroeder—went to Washington, and dozens more were elected to state legislatures. Women had become engaged in politics.

Between *The Feminine Mystique* in February 1963 and *Roe v. Wade* in January 1973, the essential work was done, the groundwork laid, the nation's consciousness changed. The next thrust would be expanding and protecting that base, fighting to keep what had been won and dealing with new problems. Betty was always in awe at the swiftness with which the movement had taken hold. "How did we get the chutzpah," she marveled. They had battered down the gates and invaded the sacred groves, but the relative ease of their success had been partly due to a certain attitude toward them. At first, the movement had been a fascinating new phenomenon that offered all sorts of ideas to play with. To the centers of power, feminists were like children, amusing the adults with their antics. And perhaps because of the sexual bond, the men had given in to their demands—for a while. They were only women and did not have to be taken too seriously. They were not dangerous. After *Roe v. Wade*, after they won something of enormous significance, the backlash would begin in earnest.

Betty had been devastated by press accounts of the Democratic convention. They were salt in the wound. The media had zeroed in on the contretemps between Betty and Bella and Gloria, and had sided with Bella and Gloria. Betty was particularly aggrieved by two stories: Nora Ephron's "bitchy" piece in *Esquire,* and one by a Florida columnist "who sneered that I was 'jealous' of Gloria Steinem, because she was blond and pretty and I was not (illustrated by one of those monstrous ugly pictures of me, mouth open, fist clenched).... Gloria is assuredly blonder, younger, prettier than I am," she wrote plaintively, "though I never thought of myself as quite as ugly as those pictures made me."

But Betty had other resources. All through the Democratic convention she had harbored a secret, an antidote to all the gall and wormwood she was being forced to swallow. She may have been outfoxed in Miami, but she wasn't going to fade quietly into the background without a fight.

"Female Chauvinist Boors"

ONE WEEK AFTER the Democratic convention, on July 18, 1972, at the Biltmore Hotel in New York, Betty stood on the dais in a room full of reporters, trying to explain why she had denounced Gloria and Bella as "female chauvinist boors" in her *McCall's* column. It was not her finest hour.

The *McCall's* article was the first of many attacks Betty would launch over the years, faulting the movement and its leaders for taking positions she regarded as extreme. The movement was getting away from her; it was going too far in the direction of the "outs," and she was trying to hold back the tide. The column sounded Betty's theme—"equal partnership with men"—and redefined feminism as a sex-role movement, part of her vision of human liberation. She was sure that men were unhappy within the confines of the masculine mystique and would be delighted to change their own sex roles.

At the press conference Betty tried to take the high ground. She had written the piece, she explained, because she was worried about a backlash against female chauvinism. It had taken her months, she told the reporters, to decide whether to write the article because "it has been our practice up to now to keep to ourselves differences within the movement and present a united front. But the movement has become too big to hide or dismiss these differences." Betty went further, taking issue with the latest turn of feminist thinking, the idea that men and women were engaged not only in a sex war but also in a class war. In this struggle (a variation of the Victorian pedestal theory), men as a class belonged to a lower order of the species; women as a class had the upper moral hand. Although Betty told reporters that she was criticizing feminist theory, not personalities, in her article she accused Gloria of equating marriage with prostitution, citing a speech Gloria had made to the League of Women Voters.*

As for Bella, Betty thought it was female chauvinism for women to support female candidates on the basis of their sex when an equally qualified male was running. Betty was referring to Bella's recent primary campaign to capture the congressional seat of William Fitts Ryan. Although many people considered Ryan too ill to run, he was pro-woman and very well liked, and Betty supported him. Bella lost in the primary, but Ryan died, and she was appointed to his seat.

Bella hit back: "Once again Betty Friedan is exercising her right to be wrong. I never asked anyone to vote for me solely because I am a woman." Gloria had an attack of laryngitis, and *Ms.* magazine issued a statement on her behalf: "Having been falsely accused by the male Establishment journalists of liking men too much, I am now being falsely accused by a woman Establishment journalist of not liking them enough."

Gloria could not stand up and attack Betty publicly. It was not in her. Betty would talk of having been outfoxed by Gloria; Gloria would say that each time she held out a hand to Betty she was left with "a bloody stump." She was also wary of the media's tendency to pounce on disagreements among women, labeling them "catfights." Long afterward, wondering if she might have done things differently, Gloria said, "I always made it clear there was no penalty. I didn't encourage any behavior change. If I had responded to Betty in a tougher way, she might have behaved better. The problem is, it just makes my heart sink; I don't have the energy for it. I can fight with the right wing, but not with other feminists."

Gloria did retaliate in other more subtle ways, however. In all of *Ms.'s* history, there was no major piece on either Betty or NOW. Mary Thom, a *Ms.* editor, said, "There was no policy. There didn't need to be, because of the *McCall's* piece and the attacks." (On the other hand, any profile of Betty would have been critical of her, exposing Gloria and the magazine

---

* Gloria had actually said, "Most of you are only one man away from welfare yourself," and estimated the value of housework at $9000–14,000 a year for a 99.6-hour week, "not including part-time prostitution privileges."

to charges of revenge or worse—trashing a sister.) Occasionally, one of Gloria's partisans took a shot at Betty. In "Behind the Scenes at Houston: Four Days That Changed the World," an article discussing press coverage of the first national women's conference in America, Lindsy Van Gelder wrote, "While prime movers...were virtually ignored, easily recognizable but noninsider personalities were seized upon. For example, Betty Friedan—who told me herself that she was 'not involved' with the planning of the conference and wasn't even 'sure why we're having it'—was before the cameras every day." Among those who were disillusioned with her, the standard view of Betty was that of a microphone hog.

Gloria also stayed away from NOW. "Betty sent a message: if I ever showed up at a NOW meeting she would condemn me in public." But Gloria was not interested in NOW. As she had said years earlier, "I was not attracted by the substance—Betty and Muriel Fox as professional women; only march in your fur coats. What spoke to me was not NOW but abortion meetings, small groups, radical feminists. They were speaking to my experience."

Gloria's public statements and writings had the effect of whittling down Betty's image and importance. In *Outrageous Acts and Everyday Rebellions,* a book in which Betty is mentioned only twice, she wrote, "Despite the many early reformist virtues of *The Feminine Mystique,* it had managed to appear at the height of the civil rights movement with almost no reference to black women or other women of color." She blamed this omission for journalists' perception that the movement was confined to white middle-class women.

Even during her darkest days, in the mid-seventies, when she had been accused of being a CIA agent and Betty was doing her best to publicize the charges, Gloria was silent. She was aware that she was just pulling the covers over her head, but she did not get up her courage to hit back until the 1980s. In a 1983 *Us* interview to promote *Outrageous Acts,* Gloria shunted Betty aside and rewrote history, saying that Betty's period of activism had been the mid-sixties and she was "an old-style person." As she explained her theory later, "All women have been damaged. Younger women of the New Left reacted by saying they had never had anything, so no one else would, either, and refused to credit individuals for their work. Older women responded like Betty, saying well, this is the first thing that I've had of my own, so I own it. I invented it, I own it, it's mine."

In 1988, at the first *Ms.* Awards, a fund-raising affair at the elegant

Rainbow and Stars nightclub, Gloria reverted to wimpdom. "Betty called at the last minute and asked to come for no money, something board and staff couldn't do—and we let her. She sent someone to ask that I introduce her when listing people in the room—and I did."

In public, they followed separate tracks and disagreed on many issues but were photographed together supporting some of the same people and causes: Bangladeshi women ostracized by their families after being raped; the Three Marias, Portuguese poets threatened with excommunication for their unseemly writings; Anita Hill, slandered for her testimony against Judge Clarence Thomas. They campaigned in New York for Robert Abrams against Alfonse D'Amato.

Privately, they were almost never alone together. On the rare occasions when their paths did cross, something unpleasant usually happened. People noticed that Betty walked out of rooms when Gloria walked in. One Christmas they found themselves in Bonwit Teller's together, in the men's shirt department on the first floor. In the spirit of the season, Gloria said, "Betty, Merry Christmas." Betty glared at her and turned away. There were icy encounters in airports, coming and going, and once they were on the same plane. Betty was in first class (Betty always flew first class; it was written into her lecture contracts), Gloria in tourist, and a flight attendant innocently offered to move Gloria, assuming she would want to sit next to her friend. "I didn't have the heart to disillusion her, so I moved. Betty said hello, but not a word for the rest of the trip."

Gloria's mother inadvertently stepped between the combatants and was caught in the crossfire. Ruth, an agoraphobic, had been coaxed into attending a National Women's Political Caucus reception in Washington, where Betty was introduced to her. Betty didn't remember what happened next, but according to Gloria, Betty smiled and held out her hand—and then she heard the name Steinem. She flung away Ruth Steinem's hand, said something that Ruth could never bring herself to repeat, and walked off. "My mother didn't go to a public event for a long time afterward, and when she did, she would put another name, not Steinem, on her name tag."

In the mid-eighties, Betty began to make sporadic, if ambivalent, efforts to patch things up. In the 1985 introduction to the paperback reissue of *It Changed My Life*, she wrote that Gloria "certainly became a devoted feminist in the women's movement and contributed much of wit and style and shrewdness.... I think it was important for young women to have an attractive role model like Gloria Steinem who chose not to marry and have children." But even those condescending words stuck in her throat. In the next paragraph she lambasted *Ms.* for encouraging women to throw away their razors and stop shaving under their arms.*

Shortly after that, when Betty was working on her book about age, a bizarre rumor went around that Gloria was so madly in love with her current lover, Mortimer Zuckerman, that she was trying to get pregnant to please him. She was over fifty at the time and had never shown the slightest interest in becoming a mother. Among certain New York feminists it was the rumor of the century. To Betty it was irresistible. If Gloria were to have a child, it would be a confirmation of all that she, Betty, had been saying for decades about the importance of families. She would have defeated Gloria. Although they had barely spoken to each other for fifteen years, Betty called her. "Is it true?" Betty wanted to know. Amazed by the call, Gloria sidestepped the question. Betty persisted: "So you're not going to get pregnant?" "Not unless there's a star in the East," Gloria said firmly.

After almost a quarter of a century, old wounds still throbbed. In her 1991 review of Naomi Wolf's book *The Beauty Myth,* Betty managed to repeat her old apocryphal story of Gloria hiding under the hair dryer at Kenneth's. Finally, at the twentieth-anniversary party celebrating the NWPC's founding, held in a Washington hotel in 1991, Betty said to Gloria, "We should bury the hatchet." But Gloria, in whom the hatchet had been buried many times, had stiffened her spine. "After twenty years I finally got up the courage and said, 'If you accuse me in public you have to apologize in public.' " Betty could never do that. Their feud has no ending, only a cooling of passion with time as Betty's other activities gradually took her away from the heart of the movement.

. . .

SEVEN MONTHS AFTER the Democratic convention, on February 11, 1973, Betty went to Houston, where the NWPC was holding its national convention to elect officers. The Rice Hotel, the group's headquarters, was still so steeped in tradition that it would not allow women to be paged on the loudspeaker—being paged was not ladylike.

Two experienced politicians ran for president: Sissy Farenthold, supported by Bella and Gloria; and Martha McKay of North Carolina,

---

* Like Gloria (and virtually everyone in public life with an image to protect), Betty had a tendency to rewrite history. *Ms.* had no policy on hair. Betty frequently used "hairiness" as shorthand for "anti-man, anti-marriage, anti-motherhood pseudo-radicals," which in turn was her characterization of people she considered outside the mainstream.

Betty's candidate. They had differences about the structure of the organization: should its power reside with local grassroots groups, or be centralized? Betty thought that the issues on which women would run should be decided locally. Bella thought that national headquarters should make the decisions, for the sake of visibility. There were some—Betty among them—who thought Bella wanted that visibility, and the power it commanded, for herself. As usual, Bella and Gloria were solicitous of the minorities, Betty and Martha of the mainstream. Jane Pierson observed, "Martha and Betty were convenient for each other. Betty didn't want Bella's choice. And the issues—they were perfect for each other."

The caucus had not yet outgrown its chaotic origins. During the campaign, signs were posted in the hotel elevator saying that Martha was a racist. Sissy won, and Betty again complained about being outflanked by Bella and Gloria, whom she accused of forcing Sissy to run and thereby compromising Sissy's political future. Being associated with feminism was death in Texas. Sissy said, "I went against all the advisers I had. They were right." She was badly defeated in the 1974 gubernatorial campaign, and she did not run again.

Betty ran for the national steering committee, which was elected separately. Her name was loudly cheered, and she felt confident of winning. She had good reason to feel secure in her popularity. She had worked hard for women in the state caucuses, traveling around the country, speaking, lending her name to them. Previously, she had seconded Bella's nomination for the steering committee, noting that although she and Bella had fought "bitterly," she still wanted to work with her. She had gotten a standing ovation.

After the vote, she flew back to New York, sure of her victory. Sissy phoned to tell her that she had won—the first tally made her one of the ten at-large members of the steering committee, and she had more votes than anyone else. Then something odd happened: Betty's name was somehow left off the list of winners. Sissy ordered a recount. In the recount, Betty lost. Sissy, a veteran of South Texas voting irregularities, impounded the ballots, locked them in the trunk of her car, and called Betty to tell her the bad news.

The original count had been flawed, but the recount compounded the errors. There was a mass of unsigned ballots that no one could explain. Some of the voting had been done by polling state delegations, which submitted one state ballot; some members had been polled individually. The count had been done by hand; there was no adding machine. On February 19, the caucus asked Lucas and Tucker, a Washington accounting firm, to tabulate the ballots. The firm came up with the same list of winners as the NWPC had in its recount, although the numbers were not quite the same. Betty did not make it.

After learning that she had not been elected, Betty began to hear disquieting stories from various NOW women: during the vote "someone had announced" to the California and Missouri delegations that Betty had withdrawn from the race. She was also told that the written record of the convention, taken by court stenographers, had disappeared, and so had their tapes. It looked like vote fraud, and she was convinced that it was a plot.

Betty retained Sally Katzen of Wilmer, Cutler & Pickering, one of the big Washington law firms, to investigate the entire process. It was agreed the firm would not charge her more than $1,000. After an extensive investigation, which created havoc in the NWPC offices, Sally Katzen found the explanation: while the votes were being tallied, it became obvious that Betty had more votes than anyone else, so her name was put to one side. Then, in their rush to compile the list of the other steering committee winners, the ballot counters forgot about Betty. When this was discovered, the women started worrying that the whole vote might be challenged. So Sissy ordered a recount, but this time the votes were counted in a different way. Sally Katzen uncovered more improprieties, including some ballots that linked the first name of one candidate to the last name of another. She recommended setting aside the election and holding a new one, but the national board of the caucus decided against doing so. To everyone's relief, Betty accepted their decision.

The question of whether anyone deliberately tampered with the ballots has never been resolved. One can imagine some misguided soul with a grudge against Betty taking advantage of the confusion, but no one has stepped forward. In 1998 Jane Pierson said, "To this day I believe there was no organized vote fraud. It was not possible. People were looking over each other's shoulders. In the movement, whenever anyone didn't get what they wanted, there were charges of vote fraud or arm-twisting. But—maybe we all were hoodwinked? If we were, it was a random act."

Once again, Betty found herself on the outside, evicted from her own house, so to speak. Once again, she had helped create a powerful national organization, and her vision of what it could and should be had slipped out of her control. She would pour out her anger and suspicions two years later in *It Changed My Life*, telling a tale of breathtaking perfidy and Borgian backstabbing masterminded by unknown villains, the identity of whose instruments was nevertheless perfectly clear to her.

Betty was so angry at Bella that she did not support her when Bella ran for senator in the 1976 New York Democratic primary. At a party for Ramsey Clark, Betty's candidate, a reporter asked her why she hadn't come out for Bella, and quoted this reply: "Because I hate her guts."

In truth, Betty's feelings for Bella were far more complicated than that. She had enormous respect for Bella, who was one of the few women who could meet her on her own ground, who could confront her and deal with her and not let her get away with her outrageous statements. They were both Jewish, both mothers; they had Old Left backgrounds and used some of the same techniques to overcome opposition. Years later, Betty was incredulous when she was reminded that she hadn't supported Bella in the 1976 primary. "I always supported Bella," she said. In her mind she had.

Betty's own plans to run for the Senate had evaporated. "As one of my male political friends put it," she wrote, "I see the shadow of a certain large-brimmed hat." Betty feared that shadow and knew she could not escape it; indeed, she wrote that Bella was "determined to blot me out of existence" politically. Bella had risen on the tide of the movement, Betty's movement, and Betty's talk of running for the Senate had only aggravated an already bitter conflict. Her only choice, she thought, was to keep her distance from both Bella and Gloria. And that meant removing herself from politics.

19

Treading Water

THE SEVENTIES WERE a time of setbacks and disappointments for Betty. Doors were slamming on her, and she seemed to have lost more than she had gained. Carl was reneging on the support payments. She had no man. Random House was pressuring her for her unwritten book. She still had—would always have—an enormous grassroots following, but her role in the movement was no longer on the cutting edge. More than anything she feared losing her place in history, a fate tantamount to losing her identity. Her friends were worried about her. Susan Wood, her photographer friend from the commune, said, "At that time Betty didn't trust her optimism." She needed to re-create her life.

In her beleaguered state she sought to reassert her primacy in an article for *The New York Times Magazine* recounting her personal history of the movement. It was one of many bombshells she would explode, each one creating a wider rift, until the crater was too broad to cross. In the article, "Up from the Kitchen Floor," she took credit for every movement accomplishment and ranted against the lesbians and man-haters who had taken over and distorted her movement. Her secretary, Ann O'Shea, who typed her articles and did some editing, tried to get her to soften the piece. "She was furious at me," Ann said. "It was a huge battle about what she should or shouldn't put in. I told her she was alienating people and creating political difficulties in the movement. She didn't care. She felt very hurt about not being honored sufficiently. Gloria was taking center stage."

Betty attacked the radicals and the lesbians, labeled early movement papers on clitoral orgasms a joke, and took swipes at individual women. She was certain that the CIA, with its near-perfect record for destabilizing distasteful governments, was behind the movement's difficulties. "I never told anyone, but very early, Ti-Grace Atkinson took me to lunch in Philadelphia with the wife of a top CIA official, who offered to help us." Betty wrote that she had rejected the offer.

The article brought the wrath of movement leaders down on Betty's head. A meeting was called to denounce her, and the *Times* was inundated with hostile letters. Mim Kelber called her "a solipsist" and "a woman-hater." Robin Morgan, who had founded WITCH and led the Miss America action, chastised her for "her deliberate misrepresentations of the radical feminist wing (more than half the Movement), and insensitive blindness to the needs and demands of Third World women." Ti-Grace, "stunned and outraged," wrote, "As for Mrs. Friedan's libel against me— the CIA luncheon about which Mrs. Friedan 'never told anyone.' No such luncheon ever occurred; no such 'other' woman existed; no such offer made; no such offer refused." Betty (who did not think Ti-Grace was a CIA agent) stuck to her guns concerning the lunch. In 1997 she insisted that it had taken place exactly as she had described it.

The CIA ran through Betty's discourse like a serpentine river that overflowed its banks periodically, whenever she thought the movement was veering into a swamp. She would fling wild accusations at people, leaving the impression that she was paranoid. She probably was, but by 1973 paranoia was becoming America's dominant mind-set. Rooted in the Cold War, it had bloomed with the assassinations of the sixties and the unfolding drama of Watergate. The country was awash in bizarre conspiracy theories. Two years later it would all come out, the story of FBI and CIA surveillance, wiretapping, and infiltration of the movement. To this day, no one knows the names of the agents or how much trouble they actually caused. In a general sense, it could be said that Betty was ahead of her time.

. . .

IN HER PRIVATE life, Betty was still attending to old business. After the sale of the Fire Island house, peace had not descended. Carl was angry about stories that had come back to him of Betty telling people that he hadn't made any money and had given her a black eye every time she had to go on television. In 1971, just after Betty turned fifty, Carl finally got his say, a long, bitter blast in a widely read interview in *The Washington Post*. He had married a younger woman in August 1970, and her picture accompanied the article. Norene was the ultimate revenge. She had the look of the moment, the long, streaked-blond hair parted in the center, and a wide smile, as if she were having fun. "It stuck in Betty's craw that Carl married a good-looking woman," a close male friend said. Juxtaposed with this vision was one of those ghastly pictures of Betty that photographers seemed to stockpile, this one in three-quarter profile; her face was haggard, her forehead lined, her hair stringy.

Most of the interview was devoted to Carl's version of their marriage. In a sweeping generalization, he lumped Betty together with the militants and extremists in the movement, characterizing all of them as man-haters. Over half of them were lesbians, anyway, he said. Asked about Betty's statement that "Carl hated my success," even to the extent of tossing her papers around the room,* Carl denied that he hated her success; the marriage became rockier because he was working out his own problems and standing up for himself more. Betty, he said, had never been a housewife; she had "never washed one hundred dishes during twenty years of marriage." He thought her independence was merely a façade, that underneath the bravado Betty was just "a dependent little girl." He blamed himself for having married "this activist type of woman"—he had been "neurotic" when they married. Only ineffectual men could make such a marriage work. He still went to group therapy, and he thought penis envy was valid. "Someone once said, there are two kinds of women—boring women and hysterical women," he said. As for Norene (who he said belonged in the hysterical category), "she makes chicken soup, and that's love. She shines my shoes sometimes." Carl and Norene separated in 1972, two years after they had married.

Carl had stopped paying child support ($100 a week, plus tuition) in 1971, and Betty was overwhelmed with money problems. In the nine years since the publication of *The Feminine Mystique*, the book had netted her a total of $109,280.01 in hardcover and paperback. All of it had been spent. Foreign royalties dribbled in—in 1971, $1,965.95 from Germany; in 1972, $52.80 from Italy. But her lecture fees ran between $2,000 and $4,000 per engagement, a respectable amount. She had moved into a new apartment

* This last was later confirmed by Emily.

across from Lincoln Center. It was on the fortieth floor, and the building had a swimming pool. It was expensive. Emily would be starting Radcliffe in September 1973; her first-year tuition was $7,755.00.

(Ironically, Radcliffe had not been Emily's first choice. She preferred Wesleyan. "It would have been better for me," she said. "It was very, very important to Betty that I go to Radcliffe. Status symbols are very important, and outward appearances—some." Just as Miriam had steered Betty to Smith, so Betty insisted on Harvard for her daughter.)

Betty's extravagance, her carelessness about money and her lack of interest in keeping track of it, had contributed to her financial crisis. Being broke was not sufficient to prevent her from living in the style to which she had always been accustomed. A friend, Arthur Dubow, a venture capitalist whom she had met in East Hampton through the commune, remembered running into her in Boston. "Every time she opened her purse a wad of lire fell out. She had been to Italy months before. I explained to her how she could go to the bank and exchange the lire for dollars." For her parties, which were frequent and lavish, she would send Ann O'Shea to Zabar's, the Upper West Side omni-delicatessen, with her credit card. "It was carte blanche spending on food," Ann said. "Hundreds of dollars." (Betty's extravagance had its underside. She was also a cheapskate who resisted paying her maid for overtime.)

Ann came in every day, opened and answered the mail, kept Betty's appointment book, and paid the bills. "The accountant was tearing out his hair—for taxes, she took boxes of papers and receipts and dumped them on his desk. She carried loose checks around. There was no way to balance her checkbook. There were fights with Carl about child support, in and out of the courtroom. Betty couldn't hold on to money. She had Mexican baskets with piles of mail—bills, articles, projects. She was always trying to get some teaching position. She wanted to have a chair named after her, anyplace. She started teaching at Temple. She went once a week—sometimes by seaplane. And then she would wonder where her money went."

She was also generous to her friends. Jacqui Ceballos, who worked for Betty at the same time as Ann O'Shea, was raising two daughters on very little money. She had started a feminist lecture bureau, which wasn't doing too well, and Betty switched her bookings to it to help her. Jacqui had a great deal to offer Betty. She was good at getting her organized so that she could function (the same role Emily had taken on). Ann O'Shea said, "Jacqui would give Betty ideas, tell her what to do and say, and Betty would say, 'That's stupid,' and then do it and take the credit. Betty realized this, but she was too insecure to give anyone credit."

In 1972 Carl petitioned Family Court for a reduction in child support to $25 a week, and for the next few years he and Betty were in and out of court. Carl argued that Betty was a world-famous woman who had the ability to earn unlimited amounts of money. The government had taken almost his entire share of the sale of their Fire Island house, and the escrow account was empty. He had moved from his office at 420 Madison Avenue to avoid his landlord.

Carl was $13,300 in arrears and he hadn't paid Emily's tuition. He had a chip on his shoulder about fancy schools and didn't see the point of Harvard. Hunter College, he thought, would be quite satisfactory. "It was all Betty's snobbery," he said. After he lost in Family Court on August 26, 1974, Betty filed a complaint against him in New York State Supreme Court. She asked for a total of $26,055 in child support, including attorney's fees of $5,000. Carl then went to the press with a mischievous story that his ex-wife, the great feminist who believed in equality of the sexes, was suing him for alimony. It was extremely embarrassing for Betty; reporters gathered at the courthouse, and she had to sneak out by the back stairs to evade them. Bella Abzug suggested to Gloria that she cover the story, but Gloria said, "I didn't have the heart."

Carl claimed that he couldn't pay. He had lost his big oil accounts. There had been a dramatic shift in international power politics, and the Organization of Petroleum Exporting Countries was holding the world for ransom. Oil prices—the prices of everything made with petroleum—were soaring, and the oil dealers associations no longer needed his services. In March 1975, however, the judge ruled in favor of Betty, and she got a court order for the money. She never collected it, and she finally dropped the case.

Emily, who lived with Betty during some of the most difficult years of her mother's life, bore the brunt of the quarrel. "It didn't matter that she was Betty Friedan or a feminist," Emily said. "What came into play was the immense amount of self-involvement it takes to change the world." Emily ran away a few times, and wrote a letter to *The New York Times*—never sent—denouncing her mother. Still, she knew Betty would take care of her schooling. A decade later she told a reporter, "I lived with her alone during my teen years. She was away a lot. . . . But that was a good thing— we needed our own space. When we lived alone, we were both in bad shape. Often, she wasn't there mentally. She was so wrapped up in hate, the divorce."

There were no tuition problems for Daniel or Jonathan. Daniel had had scholarships. After a year at Princeton, he had dropped math and physics and majored in English. For his senior thesis he wrote a novel that never saw the light of day—he wouldn't even let Betty read it. (Or perhaps especially not Betty.) He then earned his doctorate at Berkeley in theoretical physics.

Jonathan had had a harder time. Through no fault of his own, he had been rejected at Harvard, Stanford, and every other school he had applied to. He and Betty and Carl believed that Donald Barr, the headmaster of Dalton, had deliberately sabotaged his applications with a damning letter of recommendation. Jonathan was a perfect candidate—a classic leader, smart, clean-cut, president of the student body. During his senior year, a group of parents, Betty included, revolted against Barr, whom they considered reactionary, and tried to get the school to fire him. According to Cathrael Kazin, a classmate of Emily's, "He took it out on Jonathan. The sense everyone had was that Barr was punishing Betty." Jonathan believed his politics were the cause. In the late sixties, college students were liberating their campuses and curricula—Columbia had even called in the police—and admissions boards were carefully scrutinizing applications for signs of revolutionary fervor. Barr was angry that Jonathan had involved the students and faculty in a protest against the invasion of Cambodia.

In a 1997 interview, Barr said that Jonathan "had political and personal demons that made him edgy." At first he denied having written the letter to Harvard (Jonathan's first choice), but then admitted having "input"; he also insisted that the letter had been laudatory. Betty, however, had a friend on the Harvard admissions board who told her he had read the letter and that it had "intimated that Jonathan was this wild leader AND the son of this revolutionary." Jonathan went to Columbia, but dropped out after a year to live in a commune on Lummi Island, which is in Puget Sound.

Betty and Carl fought one more round. In 1975, still obsessed and seething, Carl brought a damage suit against Betty. She had written an article for *New York* magazine, part of which described, in glowing terms, the early years of her marriage. Accompanying the article was a picture of Betty and Carl as proud parents, with Betty holding an infant Danny. Under the First Amendment Carl would have had no case, but the magazine had advertised the issue, using the photograph on television. His lawyer advised him that there was a legal distinction between publishing an article and advertising it. Claiming that his picture had been used without his permission, Carl sued for invasion of privacy. In June 1976 the judge dismissed his suit, ruling that the material was a matter of "public interest," to which Carl's right to privacy should be subordinated. By then

Carl had moved to New Jersey, where he supplemented his advertising income by renting big houses and letting rooms in them. "That kept me going," he said.

Betty found other ways to augment her income. She was a historic figure, and her papers were important. In August 1970, she had approached the Arthur and Elizabeth Schlesinger Library on the History of Women in America at Radcliffe, which had offered her $1,000 for her papers, money she considered sharing with NOW. Meanwhile, Smith had also become interested in the acquisition for the Sophia Smith Collection, and matched Radcliffe's offer. Betty, who saved everything, requested that someone come to her apartment, sort through her fifty-odd cartons, and pull out the material she needed to write her next book. Smith could not spare anyone for the task, but Radcliffe sent someone immediately, and so won the papers.

There the matter stood until February 1974, when Betty was casting about for a way to pay Emily's tuition. Radcliffe had physical possession of the papers, but was vulnerable because no legal agreement had been signed. Patricia King, the director of the Schlesinger Library, wanted a binding arrangement so that Betty would not, to put it crudely, peddle her papers elsewhere. Betty wanted to barter her papers for Emily's tuition, but Radcliffe refused. Instead, she called her lawyer, Charles Mandelstam, who entered into protracted negotiations and came away with $15,000 for her. Emily's tuition was assured. (Radcliffe considered the deal a bargain.)

In her need to earn a living, Betty turned to her first love, academia. She was looking for the status of a permanent university base, an appointment that would cut across disciplines, but school after school turned her down—she didn't have the credentials. The place where the Ph.D. should have been throbbed like an amputation. As always, her ideas were grand. She wanted to set up an "Institute for Sex Role Study," in which graduate students and scholars could do research, under her direction. She applied for Guggenheims, Fords, and Rockefellers, but no one would fund her.

Instead of something permanent, Betty was offered a series of visiting professorships for a few semesters each. At the New School for Social Research, she taught a course called "Women in the City" in which she relied heavily on guest lecturers, including Congressman Edward Koch; Eleanor Holmes Norton, chair of the New York City Commission on Human Rights; Ira Glasser, executive director of the New York Civil Liberties Union; and various NOW members to talk about women in business. She took another position at the College of New Rochelle, at its campus in Co-op City, in the Bronx.

In 1972 she got an offer from Temple University in Philadelphia to be a visiting professor of sociology. She started in the fall, right after the political conventions, teaching an undergraduate course, "Contemporary Social Issues," and a graduate seminar, "The Sex Role Revolution: Stage II." The latter was a pioneering course about obsolete masculine and feminine roles. Its theme was the uniqueness of the women's movement—it was neither Marxist class warfare nor sexual politics nor sex-class warfare—and how it would lead to the restructuring of institutions.

Her reading list was formidable, ranging from Alvin Toffler's *Future Shock* to heavy sociological texts to her own notorious "Female Chauvinist Boors" article. She ran a lively class, referring to herself once as "the wicked witch of Salem." One of her favorite teaching techniques was having the men act out a male beauty contest.

Her students gave her mixed reviews. They were not the best audience for her. Temple's standards were not Smith's, and the students were not the intellectual heavyweights she was accustomed to. Many of them had jobs, and many were Vietnam veterans. And she was in something of a generational rut, still referring to "the unliberated housewife."

In the fall semester of 1974 she was at Yale, teaching "The Sex Role Revolution: Stage II," one afternoon a week, for one credit. She put forty-five books on the recommended reading list. This time the class was small—eighteen students, pared down from the 150 who had applied. They sat on leather sofas drinking soda and puffing on cigarettes, trying to get a word in edgewise. "The students thought she lectured too much and didn't give them a chance to 'interact,' and they told her so," a reporter wrote.

The following year, 1975, she took her course to Queens College in a building like an airplane hangar, reverberating with the noise of jets taking off from nearby Kennedy Airport. Cynthia Epstein, her fellow communard and an associate professor of sociology at Queens, got the position for her. Her Manhattan–Queens taxi fare probably made a large dent in her salary. Twice a week she taught "The Sociology of Sex Roles," asking her friends Barbara Seaman and Jacqui Ceballos to fill in for her when she went out of town to lecture.

During these years, while she was teaching and writing, Betty was much in demand as a speaker. The intellectual world from which she had so reluctantly torn herself in 1943 was her true home; the exchange of ideas was the thing that excited her most. She became absorbed in conferences, seminars, symposia, and think tanks, attending and convening them. Her life was frenetic; she had a schedule that two people would have found difficult to maintain.

In 1971, Betty met the fund-raiser she had dreamed of. Mary Jean Tully was a rich, attractive Westchester matron with a large family, a corporate wife who had been dragged around the world to her husband's postings. Her family tree went back to the *Mayflower*. She was smart, sophisticated, and as formidable as Betty in getting what she wanted. Her talents were primarily administrative. She had started the Westchester Chapter of NOW and moved on to the NOW Legal Defense and Education Fund, of which Betty was a board member. In a few years she institutionalized the fund, raising money from the Ford Foundation, the Rockefeller Family Fund, and the Equitable Life Assurance Company, among others. For fund-raising parties she commandeered the $28,000-a-year Drake Hotel suite maintained by the Celanese Corporation, where her husband was an executive. Avon was her prime catch: in 1974 the LDEF moved into luxurious offices at 9 West Fifty-seventh Street, Avon's headquarters. Mary Jean became one of the few people from Betty's feminist life who crossed the line into her personal circle.

Mary Jean worked closely with Betty in creating the Economic Think Tank in 1974. Betty loved getting important people together to crunch ideas. Her conferences helped keep her in the limelight and provided funding for her, and they were safe enough not to alarm corporate donors. The 1970s were the era of the liberal think tank, and money was available. Betty was moving away from grassroots feminism into the rarefied heights of intellectualism, where the players were people like Amitai Etzioni, Robert Reich, and Theodore Kheel. "Betty was involved in so many organizations and was so good at knowing what the next issue would be and getting people together," Cynthia Epstein said. "It's an extraordinary quality she has. She excites people. She can pull it together. She distills the essence of an issue, and it goes beyond the personal."

The Economic Think Tank conference came about as a result of the 1974 recession—the same recession that took away Carl's main clients—and the energy crisis that caused it. The women's movement had flourished in a time of expansion and affluence, but now Betty was concerned that the gains women had won would be lost. Thirty-five million women were in the workforce, but most of them had been the last hired and would be the first fired. She was also deeply impressed by Alvin Toffler's predictions of automation in the workplace. The think tank would be a catalyst to explore new approaches to these problems. In her opening statement she said, "We must begin to give serious consideration to such things as new concepts about hours of work, split jobs, overtime, putting everyone to work, educational sabbaticals for work.... The next stage ...

will not be male/female confrontation, but a cooperative restructuring of roles and responsibilities to benefit both sexes."

After the conference President Gerald Ford invited Betty, as president of the think tank, to participate in a special briefing on his Whip Inflation Now (WIN) program in the Old Executive Office Building, along with William Simon (secretary of the treasury), Rogers Morton (secretary of the interior), William Seidman (assistant to the president for economic affairs), and Sylvia Porter (chair of the Citizens Action Committee to Fight Inflation).

Ann O'Shea, who had left Betty for another job, had come back briefly to help her with the think tank. "I stayed for a week afterward to do the clean-up and follow-up with letters," she said. "And I told her I was leaving again. She was furious, irrational; she had temper tantrums—'You can't leave me in the middle of this.'" A few days later Ann found out that Betty was spreading accusations that she had taken money and was a CIA agent. "The money part didn't bother me," Ann said. "But my father was destroyed by the CIA, and all kinds of bells went off. I called her: 'If you don't stop telling people I'm in the CIA I'll sue you.'" Confronting Betty with her behavior was the best way to make her change it. "She stopped," Ann said. Betty does not remember this incident and calls Ann "a wonderful woman."

In more than one way, the Economic Summit—as Betty liked to call it—was a blueprint for her future. As Dick Laupot observed, "She is self-creative. At some level she is her own best PR person. She also gets into political things which keeps her name out front and gets her lectures. So there is an overall gestalt in the way she does things that enables her to make a living." In addition, all her conferences and seminars attracted the kind of men she liked—academics, men who traded in ideas, just as she did, who would be impressed with her brain power and like her for it. She was at ease with them, secure in her ability to interest them. She had also generated a new career for herself. For the rest of her life she would continue to search for concepts that applied feminism to the larger society—such as redesigning living spaces for working families—keeping the dialogue going.

She had begun to accept some of her limitations. She couldn't join other people; they had to join her; and she had to be in a position to reject, not to be rejected. "I wasn't good at maneuvering," she said. "What I was good at was the vision, and inspiring people.... What I've done over the intervening years is concentrate on the vision—as a writer and even when I was teaching, I always spent a good part of my energy organizing a think tank, something that would bring leaders together—a vision beyond NOW."

Global Expansion

BETTY HAD BEEN thinking about an international movement since the NOW board relieved her of her presidency in 1970. During her trips to publicize various translations of *The Feminine Mystique,* she had seen feminism generate spontaneously in Europe, and she had a plan: an international day of confrontation, August 26, on which women all over the world would assert their power simultaneously, to be accomplished through the use of satellite television. She deputized Patricia Burnett, the former Miss Michigan who had started the first Michigan NOW chapter, to start an international NOW and convene the world.

In the name of Betty Friedan, Patricia organized twenty-five loose-knit affiliates, drawn from the upper echelons of society, in twenty-one countries, and got special nongovernmental organization (NGO) status for NOW with the U.N. When they needed a place for the meeting, Betty called the president of Harvard, who found space, at nearby Lesley College. On December 3–5, 1973, she convened the first International Feminist Conference, which was attended by Arab, Israeli, and even Soviet women. There were plans for future meetings, but they were stymied by politics within the conference and by a change in administration in NOW. It may have been that the board was nervous at the idea of Betty building a new power base, one not under their control. In any event, NOW tossed out the fledgling international groups.

Meanwhile, she was making frequent international forays on her own, and she got star billing wherever she went. In the summer of 1971, she and Jacqui Ceballos flew to Bogotá. The occasion was a national feminist celebration arranged by a wealthy, ambitious woman who wanted to run for office. Betty was the centerpiece. Just before leaving, she went to the hairdresser, which made them late for the plane. Jacqui recalled, "Our plane was on the tarmac. Betty stood there and yelled, 'Stop the plane! Stop the plane! Don't you know who I am?' "*

In Bogotá they stayed at an elegantly furnished three-bedroom apartment belonging to Jacqui's ex-husband. "Betty looked around and said to me, 'You mean, you left this?' She advised me to go back to my husband." The climax of their visit was a day-long barbecue with thousands of people, dozens of political speeches, ovations for Betty, and stories about her in all the newspapers.

In October 1971, Betty took Emily to Brazil for the publication of *The Feminine Mystique* in Portuguese. Betty was a big hit in Brazil. Stories of her threat to macho culture were splashed all over the front pages. One newspaper ran a front-page editorial that said, "Go home, Yankee lady! Stop stirring up our women!"

In 1972, the Associazione Culturale Italiana, a major intellectual organization, invited her on a five-city speaking tour. She was the first woman chosen for this honor, and thousands of women packed the theatres to hear her. In Milan, the translator got cold feet when Betty was talking about political power and abortion, and the women in the audience, realizing they were getting the wrong message, called for another translator. Joan Marble Cook, her old college friend, who had preceded her as editor of *SCAN* and now lived in Rome, said, "Betty stopped. She had no idea what was going on. Then Lucretia Love, a glamorous, beguiling blond starlet, literally crawled up out of the audience and did a hilarious translation. Then Betty said the pope should get married. They finally rang the curtain down."

In Rome, Betty almost caused a riot at a big pro-abortion rally in the Piazza Navona. A group of fascists and right-wing priests invaded the crowd and acted as agents provocateurs. Motorcycles roared among the tables. Joan whacked some of them with her umbrella while Betty braved the threat of violence and stood up on a café table to speak.

---

* Betty would chalk up a lifetime of near misses. When she was in her seventies she would sit in a wheelchair while an attendant raced her through the airport.

Betty had high expectations for Israel, where she went in June 1973 to speak at the biannual meeting of an international organization of women writers and journalists. "I would see the future," she wrote, "and know that it works." Golda Meir was a heroine to American feminists. In an advertising campaign for job equality, NY–NOW had chosen her face to adorn a poster with the copyline "But Can She Type?" As many Americans did, Betty thought of the kibbutz as a new nonsexist way of living, with men and women sharing the work, indoors and out. She was disappointed. Equality for women in Israel was as elusive as it was everywhere else. She was inexplicably delayed at the airport and missed Golda's speech, which was extremely uncomplimentary toward the women's movement. Further, the prime minister ignored Betty's presence entirely and refused to grant her an audience. The rebuff must have dismayed Betty. Here was another Indira, another head of state she might have bonded with, the more so because they were both Jewish. Arlynn Nellhaus, one of the Americans, recalled, "I never knew the details, but Friedan flounced...out of the meeting room just moments before she was to speak. There was an inordinate amount of hostility toward her."

The meeting lasted for two weeks, ending in Bat Yam, a kibbutz. In the interim, Betty rose above the unpleasantness and came through for the women. When she wasn't fixated on protocol and the importance of her position, she was every inch the inspiring leader. Arlynn Nellhaus wrote, "I remember how impressed I was by the way Friedan handled the meeting (the Bat Yam hotel gave us a comfortable room with lots of couches on the ground floor) and guided the women. She described nuts and bolts of action. And instead of sounding like a famous authority, she was down to earth, interested in learning how their situation differed from American women's and was tremendously supportive."

In October 1973, Betty went to Rome to see Pope Paul VI, on assignment from *McCall's*.* She had always been keenly aware of the role of religion in the lives of women and had a following among American Catholics; indeed, two nuns had been among NOW's founders. It is obvious why Betty would want to have an audience with the pope, and there are several reasons why the pope was willing to see Betty. Harvey Cox, the eminent theologian at Harvard Divinity School, explained, "The pope was very concerned about opening the Church to intellectual and political currents. He was caught in a cross stream—he inherited the tumult

---

* *McCall's* had not renewed her contract for her column, but she had a new one-year contract for individual articles, beginning May 1, 1973, and she was on the masthead as a contributing editor.

after Vatican II. But he did not retreat into a fortress mentality. He wanted to be informed about the modern world."

Rome had condemned the sexual revolution and the new consciousness; in particular, it had not modified its stand on contraception, and its credibility had been undermined. There was unrest among priests and nuns: nuns wanted a larger role in the Church, and many priests, no longer wishing to be celibate, were leaving in record numbers. The meeting with Betty was the message.

Betty was a little apprehensive of this new role as emissary from the women's movement. Harvey Cox advised her to talk about equality, fairness, and human rights, and suggested that she bring a present. At the audience, Betty gave Paul VI a chain with a gold-plated women's equality symbol—the female biological sign crossed by an equals sign—and said, "When the Church comes to terms with the full personhood of woman as it [has] with the personhood of man, many problems that have long oppressed women and are now tormenting the Church will be seen in a different light, and can be solved." The pope advised her not to expect anything to happen quickly, and gave her a jewel box with a bronze medal embossed with his likeness.

After seeing the pope, Betty flew to Paris. Another important interview had come through for her, with Simone de Beauvoir. She had been trying to get the appointment for over a year. Beauvoir apparently felt more in tune with other feminist leaders—Kate Millett corresponded with her, and Gloria Steinem visited her.

Betty approached her interview as an acolyte in search of wisdom. She believed the movement had taken a diversionary direction—anti-man, anti-marriage—and she did not know what to do.* She may also have thought that Beauvoir could shore up her own declining fortunes. "I thought she was truly brilliant," Betty said. "I thought, the two of us together could say we have to deal with the realities of modern women who are combining profession and marriage and motherhood. We would need new institutional changes to do that, and to help women to have a larger and larger role in society."

When they finally met, they did not like each other. Beauvoir looked "prim," Betty wrote; her salon was "self-conscious[ly] Bohemian," her language "an abstraction." The interview did not go well. Betty was voluble; her questions were little essays. Beauvoir was detached, aloof, at times

---

* It is difficult to say where the movement actually was at that point. It was everywhere, and different groups had their own ideas of what it meant. In terms of media coverage, Betty was right, and it is certainly fair to say that housewives were denigrated.

monosyllabic. Two huge egos were in the room, neither willing to give an inch. Beauvoir advocated that women opt out of the system entirely, not accept high-ranking jobs: "to refuse bureaucracy and hierarchy has the advantage of trying to make each human being a *whole* human and breaks down the masculine idea of the little bosses." Women shouldn't try to make a name for themselves, shouldn't sign their articles. But Beauvoir exempted herself—she would continue to sign her own name. Betty believed in winning all the prizes. Beauvoir thought society would be changed from the bottom, not the top. She advocated a communal system; women should not have the choice to stay home and raise children. The family was the source of oppression, the maternal instinct a myth: "As soon as a girl is born, she is given the vocation of motherhood because society really wants her washing dishes, which is not really a vocation. In order to get her to wash the dishes, she is given the vocation of maternity." Betty thought she was throwing out the baby with the dishwater.

Betty was actually appalled by Beauvoir. "She was against mother-hood!" she said later, her eyes wide with disbelief. "You can't be against motherhood, you know. I mean, how are we going to reproduce the race? And she drew a picture of a commune on the banks of the river, everyone washing everyone else's socks. She renounced motherhood and marriage, and there was no more abject and humiliating a relationship than hers to Sartre." Beauvoir was a Maoist; Betty was a liberal Democrat. These two minds could never meet.

In 1974 Betty went to Iran, a controversial move that caused many feminists to despair of her. Iran was enjoying its imperial moment in the sun, but American newspapers were filled with stories of secret trials and torture, uncovered by Amnesty International. At "An Evening for Impris-oned Iranian Artists and Intellectuals," Frances FitzGerald spoke about the situation. Vida Hadjebi Tabrizi, a sociologist at Tehran University, had been arrested by SAVAK, the secret police, tortured, and sentenced to seven years in prison for doing research on the living conditions of the country's peasants. Reza Baraheni, a poet, had disappeared. American feminists were trying to put pressure on the government to help these women. It was a familiar problem, which bedeviled U.S. foreign policy: human rights versus oilpolitik.

"I thought about it," Betty said. "Two years before, I had been invited to Spain. The people who came to see me were like the Ford Foundation in Spain. Franco was not yet dead. They asked me if I would talk about women's rights. They said fascism was going to go, we want to get some new thinking about women. I decided to go—if they are able to organize women even within a repressive regime, it will help something new to replace the regime. There was an incredible turnout—such a hunger for a social movement."

Betty had been invited to Iran by Mahnaz Afkhami, the leader of the Women's Organization. The titular head was Princess Ashraf, the shah's twin sister, who was also Iran's ambassador to the U.N. The U.N. had designated 1975 International Women's Year, and the princess had offered to fund the ensuing conference. As a global personage Betty certainly wanted to participate, but she had no organizational base to connect her to the U.N. NOW had disbanded the international affiliates. "It was pragmatic," Betty said of her trip. "The main thing was that this was the way to organize internationally. Each U.N. conference fed the process of international networking and organizing of women in the Third World." Germaine Greer and Helvi Sipila, the U.N.'s assistant secretary general, whom Betty had met in Finland, were also going.

In Iran Betty was granted interviews with Empress Farah (whom she called a feminist) and with Shah Reza Pahlavi. The shah told her, "No one in the world has done more for women than I have. Myself. When I created the White Revolution, women were still in the category of the criminal, the felon, the insane. They did not have the right to vote.... Women have equal rights in Iran."

Betty understood that whatever the shah had done for women, he did as a by-product of his push to modernize his country, not because he thought it was the right thing to do. Yet she seemed snowed. The reportorial savvy, the skepticism she had once displayed for the labor union newspapers, was curiously absent in the article she wrote for the *Ladies' Home Journal*, "Coming Out of the Veil." She was full of optimism, uncritical of what she was told, ready to ignore what she did not want to see. "I am taken aback, in my own sense of myself as revolutionary, that this Emperor of Emperors would even allow me to advise his women," she wrote. Betty knew and did not know what was going on in Iran. She knew the poor were being hidden from her; she noticed that there were no beggars on the streets. She noticed that even women who did not wear the chador covered themselves in public—a kerchief, stockings, long sleeves—even though it was May and hot. In deference to local sensibilities, she wore stockings and shoes instead of bare legs and sandals at night. Betty wrote—this was her insight—that for all the Iranian women who grew up under the veil, "there is that same sense of irreversibly repressed energy, same invisible wall of restraint between self and world, same residue of diffidence, self-contempt, self-effacement, lack of self-confidence that is left by that veil. There is still a sense of basic shame, a taint about being a woman." Yet, for all that, she ended on an astonishing note: she tried on a chador. "I look at myself, draped in the chador . . . and realize that piece of cloth is easier to throw aside than those invisible veils trapping our spirits in the West."

The informal moments of the trip were recorded by Germaine Greer, who twitted Betty mercilessly. "When Betty Friedan arrived at the Hilton in Teheran, she announced that she would see nobody, nobody, not even the Shah himself, until she had recovered from the flight. . . . Betty refused to take calls, and no one dared to pound on her door." She had the hospital send one of its few respirators to her room, for her asthma.

Germaine and Betty spoke at meetings and women's associations:

> *"The world will never be the same again," she [Betty] barked. "Women want to make pahlicy, naht coffee!" The thoughts poured out higgledy-piggledy . . . a torrent of unfinished sentences raced past. . . . The night before we were due to leave Iran, we were given a party . . . a tremendous scene broke out in the courtyard below. Betty was standing screaming in front of our Cadillac, "Dammit! I want, I deserve, my own car. Get me my own car. I will not travel cooped up in this thing with two other women. Don't you clowns know who I am?"*

The attendants were "shaking with fright." Betty "was furious that the various dignitaries and ministers of state had their own cars, while the guests of honor traveled in a single car like a harem. She just stood there in her spangled black crepe de Chine and kept on yelling. 'No! No! I will nutt just be quiet and gettinna car. Absolutely nutt!' . . . After a good deal of stifled giggling, it was decided that one of the ministers would lend his car for Betty."

"Don't believe what Germaine Greer wrote about it," Betty said some years later, waving away this account. "Germaine kept wanting to talk about abortion. I didn't think abortion was the main issue. After the ayatollah came, almost the first thing they did was take away women's rights, and put on the chador, and I held a press conference on the steps of the [New York Public] Library to protest."

On her return to New York, Betty sought to involve Princess Ashraf in a few of her projects. She wrote excitedly to the princess about plans for a futuristic international conference on design and architecture that would explore new kinds of living spaces, and enclosed the stock offering for the First Women's Bank, which she had helped organize. She and

Martha Stuart, the television producer in her commune, were also planning a World Network of Women, a series of broadcasts for International Women's Year, and hoped to be working with the princess on it. They would meet again in August 1974 at the World Population Conference in Bucharest.

In Bucharest, the regime honored Betty by giving her a room on the fifth floor of the Athenée Palace; the fifth, she learned, was one of two floors reserved for people who were considered dangerous. Betty managed to snare a separate room for rap sessions, and she and Margaret Mead and Germaine Greer lobbied successfully for various resolutions, but she could not get permission to hold a press conference. Betty, however, knew how to use her anger the way a diplomat used persuasion. When she found out that right-to-life groups were having a press conference, she threatened to make a scene and got her way. She would use the same tactic in Mexico City the following June, at the 1975 U.N. conference.

. . .

IN FEBRUARY 1975, shortly after her fifty-fourth birthday, Smith College at last overcame its better judgment and decided to recognize its distinguished alumna. The college administrators were extremely upset that Betty had given her papers to Radcliffe, and the discussion about her was heated. But Betty had a little help from a friend on the board of trustees: Dr. Jane Wright, her former classmate (she had been the only black woman in the class) and an old drinking buddy from Fire Island, had pushed her name through. Betty was awarded an honorary doctorate of letters. She was thrilled. It was Smith's centenary, and the college had planned a feminist weekend around the theme of "New Roles, Old Stereotypes," awarding degrees to Maya Angelou, Nikki Giovanni, Katharine Graham, Dixy Lee Ray, and Elisabeth Kübler-Ross. Betty was the only alumna on the list to get a degree rather than the medal Smith ordinarily gave its graduates.

None of Betty's grand plans worked out. Princess Ashraf did not become her patron, and the World Network did not come into being. But in only a few years she had strengthened the cause of women on the world stage and become an international player.

Mexico City Thriller

BETTY WAS IN Spain on May 9, 1975, when *[MORE]*, a journalism review, was holding its annual "Countercultural Convention" at the Roosevelt Hotel in New York. Two *Washington Post* reporters, Bob Woodward and Carl Bernstein, had recently toppled President Nixon; in the fallout, investigative reporting was transformed into a knight-errant occupation, a giddy combination of noble deeds and scandalous insider gossip. Hundreds of reporters from all over the country came to the convention. It was the perfect place, the members of Redstockings thought, to unveil their own investigative report—an extraordinary document of such stunning implications that everyone would have to take notice.

Late in the afternoon of the second day, they held a press conference and distributed a sixteen-page release accusing Gloria Steinem of "a ten-year association with the CIA stretching from 1959 to 1969 which she has misrepresented and covered up." When Kathie Sarachild, a leader of Redstockings, was recently asked what results the group had hoped to achieve with the release, she said, "Coverage! We felt people should know this information so the movement could decide what it all meant and what to do about it. Steinem had this bubble of untouchability around her. I do think we pricked it a bit."

The timing of the release was also opportune for Redstockings. The release was part of a book, *Feminist Revolution,* which the group was planning to self-publish in a few months. Although Redstockings believed they would be pilloried for attacking Gloria, it is fair to say that the publicity generated by her name could only have helped sales.

To the surprise of Redstockings, none of the major news outlets picked up the story. It was old news. In 1967, *Ramparts* magazine had published an article disclosing that the Independent Research Service (IRS), for which Gloria had been working in 1959, had been secretly funded by the CIA. The IRS had paid for American students, most of them from the non-Communist left, to go to Soviet Youth Festivals in Vienna in 1959 and Helsinki in 1962 to counter Communist propaganda—and generate some of their own. (In those days the CIA's reputation had not yet been seriously tarnished; indeed, J. Edgar Hoover referred to the agency's personnel as "parlor pinks.") The IRS was a typical CIA venture, a front masquerading as a cultural exchange. Although few of the students knew where the money was coming from, Gloria and the organizers knew. As they said in the trade, she was "witting."

When the *Ramparts* story broke, Gloria spoke openly to the press, telling a *New York Times* reporter, "I was happy to find some liberals in government in those days who were far-sighted and cared enough to get Americans of all political views to the festival."

The Redstockings release took a different perspective. It was a vicious attack filled with innuendoes; it contained errors, and it leaped to unwarranted conclusions. It left the unmistakeable impression (never stated) that Gloria was a mole in the movement. It also strongly suggested that she had provided the CIA with political dossiers on American festivalgoers. Gloria denied it absolutely.*

Betty was fascinated. Perhaps she thought that Gloria, too, had something to hide, like Betty's own Marxist youth. To someone of Betty's generation, coming out of the thirties and having lived through McCarthyism, it was easy to believe that Gloria was a CIA agent. Her natural inclinations reinforced that belief.

---

* Carolyn G. Heilbrun, a Steinem biographer, exonerated her unequivocally. Sydney Ladensohn Stern, another biographer, wrote, "She had not been hired to report on people—her job had been getting them to the festivals and generating prodemocracy propaganda.... She had gone to fight international Communism, not to report on other Americans' political affiliations." Gloria's written response to the release, published in the feminist press, was inadequate, couched in ambiguous language, and left many questions unanswered. She thus remained open to further suspicion. The CIA files are still closed.

As soon as she heard about it, she sent her secretary to Kathie to get a copy of the release. It was, in a way, a gift from the gods, a conjunction of two obsessions. After years of dark speculations she had finally found someone with an actual connection to the CIA—and it was Gloria. The idea had crossed her mind before: Gloria seemed to have gotten the money to launch *Ms.* far too easily for the funding to have been above-board. Betty now began to pursue Gloria with the same intensity that she focused on her causes. In a movement already jittery about betrayal, Gloria stood to lose everything if she were unmasked as a CIA operative.

Kathie Sarachild, who had pioneered consciousness raising, and Betty Friedan, who had called it "mental masturbation," were unlikely allies. Kathie had not really liked *The Feminine Mystique.* It seemed to blame women for "the problem without a name," which *did* have a name—it was called male supremacy. Betty had never been particularly interested in Redstockings; her new friendship was more a matter of "The enemy of my enemy is my friend." Both women supported equality with men and opposed the movement's focus on lesbianism, and both had conspiratorial minds, but beyond that, they had very little in common—except resentment of Gloria.

Kathie Amatniek grew up in Hastings, New York, in an Old Left family—her father had been in the Lincoln Brigade and had an FBI file—and attended Radcliffe, where she wrote for the *Harvard Crimson.* "She always had a cause," said a less political contemporary. "She was extremely intense and confident she had all the answers. She had a lot of boyfriends. She was into men." Later she became a film editor, apprenticing on *Bonnie and Clyde* at the age of twenty-three. She worked on her career only six months of the year and spent the other half in the movement. She wrote anti–Vietnam War articles early on and went to Mississippi with SNCC, whose militant leaders inspired her to work for women's liberation. When she became a feminist, she took her mother's name, Sara, and added "child." She was one of the most important theoreticians of women's liberation. The slogan "Sisterhood is powerful" was hers. Ironically, it was at the Redstockings abortion speakout in 1969 that Gloria had discovered her feminism.

The early Redstockings had dissolved and reconstituted itself, and in 1975 the group claimed support around the country, but it was secretive—it could be reached only through post office boxes and telephone answering machines—so no one quite knew the extent of it. Rosalyn Baxandall, an early member, recalled, "It was very hard to work with Kathie. She couldn't work with anyone as an equal." Kathie was angry at the media for rendering her invisible, but she had made a serious miscalculation. Ros Baxandall said, "She always said, when asked for an interview, 'My writings are enough.' " Kathie could not come out into the public arena. As much as she wanted public recognition as one of the movement's true leaders, she needed even more to remain hidden.*

In Redstockings' view, the radical women were the authentic founders of the women's liberation movement, and *Ms.* had written them out of it, as if they had never existed. "*Ms.* arose," Kathie said, "well after the movement had mushroomed, capitalizing on the enthusiasm sparked by the women's liberation organizers. *Ms.* was always a mystery, as was Steinem a mystery. She...appeared. They kind of appeared. It seemed like this great gift, even though you didn't know where it came from exactly. And it just oozed power and connections with the powerful." Kathie had a theory that took Betty's suspicions one step further—that the CIA, as it had done in many countries, might have set up *Ms.* as a parallel operation to undermine the authentic movement.

Betty could not stop talking about Gloria and the CIA. She brought it up at parties, everywhere she went. "Betty was not rational about it," her friend Sheila Tobias said. Like Kathie, she wanted the news spread across the front pages. She called Susan Brownmiller. "It was sort of semi-naive," Susan recalled. "She said, 'Susan, I've been following the things Redstockings has been saying about Gloria—don't you think this deserves a full airing?' She wanted me to air it."

In mid-June, a few days before the official opening, Betty left for the U.N. women's conference in Mexico City. Redstockings asked her to hold a press conference there denouncing Gloria, and she decided to do it. Her friends were aghast. Barbara Seaman, who was also a friend of Gloria's, tried to mediate: "She was in a very crazy frame of mind. Gloria was willing to meet, and Betty considered it, but in the end she decided against it. But she promised me she would not hold a press conference. People who cared about her didn't want her to do it. It clearly wasn't going to help her, either." Holding a press conference would look like a personal move against Gloria. Betty was also under pressure to keep quiet. "Just before Mexico City," she said, "one of my friends had been told to call me and tell me that it would be bad for my health, that I would be in danger, unless I did something—to say it is not acceptable for any feminist to discuss this."

---

* Kathie later said that neither she nor Redstockings sought publicity; rather, her concern was historical accuracy, so that women, understanding the past, would be armed for the future.

Betty was big news in Mexico City. She did not have to call a special press conference. Ingrid Stone, a New York feminist, distributed copies of the Redstockings' press release; then, when reporters asked Betty the inevitable questions, she expounded at length.

Meanwhile, in New York, the first story based on the release finally came out, in the *Daily News*. The editors had refused to run it without a few quotes from famous feminists, and Betty had supplied one: "I was very troubled by the Redstockings' statements, and so were a lot of other people I know.... I don't see how she [Gloria] can ignore these charges. She can't ignore them." Once Betty's name appeared, the story was picked up everywhere. (The only other feminist who gave a quote was Elizabeth Holtzman, a friend of Betty's. In 1972 Betty had encouraged her to run against Representative Emmanuel Celler, an entrenched Democrat in her Brooklyn district, and she had beaten him.)

The atmosphere in Mexico City was poisonous. Police were everywhere, and strange groups of women appeared who had been primed by their governments to disrupt meetings and shout anti-American slogans. In the days preceding the ceremonial opening of the conference, Betty heard that UPI had received a false tip that she had had a massive coronary. An anonymous caller hinted obscenely of a sexual scandal. People phoned and cabled warnings for her to keep silent about Gloria and the CIA—sisterhood was at stake. In her interpretation, she was the heroine of "a James Bond novel," the center of intrigue, surrounded by menacing figures, ignorant of her peril.

By the first weekend, when she went to a house party in Tepoztlán, Betty was already so unnerved that all events seemed inexplicably sinister to her. Oddly, one of the guests was an attractive man who had sat next to her on the flight down to Mexico and who seemed to know Carl. At the hacienda, a mysterious woman materialized out of a thunderstorm at midnight and issued a warning: Betty must stop talking about Gloria and the CIA. Betty was rattled. How could this woman possibly have known how to find her? She hadn't mentioned to a soul where she was spending the weekend. Was the woman a CIA agent? Was everyone a CIA agent? But Betty's hosts knew the woman, and the likely explanation is that they told her Betty would be there. The man on the plane no longer seemed quite so attractive. He had asked her to go hiking in the mountains with him—but now it occurred to her that he could shove her off the edge of a cliff. Thoroughly frightened, she called the Del Prado Hotel in Mexico City and reached Patricia Burnett, the woman who had started international NOW. Patricia offered to rescue her, but Betty did not exactly know where she was or how to get there. She finally decided to ride back to town with another guest and the thirteen-year-old grandson of her hostess. A thirteen-year-old had to be safe.

The historic International Women's Year (IWY) conference, the first of its kind, opened on June 19, 1975, and lasted for two weeks. Six thousand women from eighty countries attended, their numbers proclaiming the success of the movement. They were part of the Tribune, the nongovern-mental organizations (NGOs) attached to the U.N.; they had power only to lobby and make suggestions to the official conference. The NGOs were headquartered at the medical center, at the opposite end of the city from the official conference at Tletalolco, one hour away by bus. The purpose, as at all such conferences, was to amend and ratify a "World Plan of Action," promulgated in advance, which each country would then imple-ment. The plan was a document to transform the world: it said that women should have equal rights and status with men in every area of life, politi-cal, economic, social, and moral.

While the Tribune held workshops and passed resolutions to strengthen the plan, the official conference merely moved all its quarrels from the East River to Tletalolco. The buzzwords of the day were "development" and "New Economic Order," meaning that the haves should transfer some of their wealth and power to the have-nots. Arabs and Africans equated Zion-ism and racism. Communists pushed for peace and an end to the arms race. Latin Americans condemned Yankee imperialism. In the grand scheme of things, the women were pawns in this gathering of the forces of international ill will. The two main figureheads of the official conference were Imelda Marcos, whose passion for shoes had not yet been made known to the world, and Princess Ashraf of Iran, who gave a personal check for $1 million to Kurt Waldheim, Secretary General of the U.N., whose Nazi past was still hidden in the archives. (Although it had proclaimed IWY, the U.N. had not voted enough money to hold the conference; hence the princess's contribution.) Delegations were headed by wives of heads of state and dominated by men. To outrage feminists further, a man, the Mexican attorney general and leader of the Mexican delegation, Pedro Ojeda Paullada, won the presidency of the conference by acclamation. He also ran the Mexican police.

At a conference attended by such vocal feminists as Germaine Greer, Bella Abzug, Ti-Grace Atkinson, and Florynce Kennedy, Betty emerged as the giant, creating order out of chaos. She just took over. Her goal for the two weeks was to organize the Tribune women into groups to write their resolutions and present them to the official conference to be incorporated into an amended world plan. A platoon of NOW women, who were wizards at organizing, did the actual work. (Ronnie Feit of the NWPC and Jan Peterson, a New York activist, coordinated the working committees.) Noel Riley Fitch, author of *The Erotic Life of Anaïs Nin,* said, "There were late night sessions doing brainstorming and planning. People sitting on floors of hotel rooms—all the auditoriums were taken. It was so exciting. It was the first time ever there were international sessions on crimes against women. Now it's everywhere. Women would line up at the mike to talk about violence in their countries, and about clitoridectomy."

As the conference progressed and Betty's visibility increased, Attorney General Paullada became more and more nervous. The American ambassador, with whom Betty and Catherine East, who was there as an adviser to the U.S. delegation, had breakfast every morning, told her that the minister of interior security had phoned him and told him to keep her quiet. The ambassador had replied that any effort on his part would be "counterproductive."

Midway through the conference, Betty realized she was being followed. Catherine noticed two men watching them one night when they were having a late drink. They followed Betty back to her hotel, where the clerk, seeking to reassure her, drew her attention to a man sitting quietly in the lobby, saying he was there "to protect" her. The man only frightened her further. She had seen him before. She had seen him every time she had entered or left the hotel. He was watching her. She fled upstairs in a panic and locked the doors and windows. She was completely alone, out of touch with everyone. Her phone was dead. Terrible pictures ran through her head, visions of shootings, stories she had read of terrorism and kidnappings. If she were kidnapped, she thought, "Who would ransom me?"

No one was trying to kidnap Betty. The attorney general, who was having her followed, was more afraid of her than he was of the terrorist who was a member of the official PLO delegation. The Palestinian was a known quantity; he didn't know what to expect from Betty. Rumors had reached him that she was planning to lead a march to demand that he be removed as president of the conference, and he sent for her. Betty was actually far more interested in getting a big space for the women to meet in than in leading a march. She saw the march as a bargaining chip, and they came to an agreement. In exchange for a press conference denying the march rumor, he would see that she got the auditorium at the medical center for her group to meet in.

In a stunning display of unity, the women approved 894 resolutions that Betty and her committees had worked on. Betty wanted to present them with a flourish, in person, to the official conference, and then address it, but the rules forbade her to enter. Ignoring the rules as well as her promise not to march, she led about a hundred women to the conference hall, and a few of them actually managed to get inside (briefly) before the guards slammed the doors on the others. "It was a Betty Friedan grandstand press play," Ronnie Feit said. "It was only because Betty was a celebrity that we got away with anything. She used her celebrity very well."

The next day, the planning session was disrupted by hundreds of unregistered men and women. As women rose to speak, a group of Marxists in the balcony began yelling *"Fascista! Fascista!"* drowning them out, and the meeting dissolved into chaos. Men carrying guns marched up and down the aisles. Television cameras, alerted in advance, pinned Betty in their spotlight. In the nick of time, Dorothy Haener of NOW and two of her friends appeared and dragged Betty away, hiding her in an office, fearful she would be shot.

Betty was distraught. All the work, all the unity, had been shattered in violence. She didn't understand it, and she felt somehow responsible. For two weeks in Mexico, she had been on an emotional roller coaster between panic and euphoria. She had been vilified by the Mexican press, which had called her a racist, an elitist, and "a malicious woman," and had accused her of insulting the attorney general and planning to take over the Tribune. She had also run roughshod over too many people, hogged too many microphones, and tried to maneuver others out of the limelight. She was wounded and contrite, and she needed a catharsis. On a sunny afternoon she sat with a group of NOW women in the courtyard of the Hotel Cortés and said a mea culpa. She had been deeply hurt by the newspaper stories and stung by complaints that she was a devious operator who sought control and publicity, and she had taken out her anger on the other women. She spoke honestly and cried as she spoke, but she was also aware in the back of her mind that her tears would assuage them.

Although Betty regretted some of her behavior, she had performed impressively. She had unified a large multicultural group of women, many of whom were deeply suspicious of American influence in Latin America. Helena Doukidou, a Greek journalist who interviewed Betty, said, "The amazing thing to me was that she said she realized she was playing a divisive role, and she had changed her mind totally. I was taken by surprise that she criticized herself. This is a person who is not afraid of change."

No one was certain who all the strange women were who broke up meetings, or why, but theories abounded of international plots.* Betty thought that President Luis Echeverría of Mexico was trying to use the conference to become U.N. secretary general. Of even greater interest to her was the fact that he had been named by Philip Agee, in his book *Inside the Company*, as a CIA contact.

The 894 resolutions were lost in a tidal wave of U.N.-babble and America-bashing. The delegates had been too busy fighting over imperialism, colonialism, neocolonialism, et cetera, even to debate them. Mainly because of the resolution equating Zionism with racism, the United States refused to sign the plan. But Betty went home happy. The battle had been everything. The power of women had manifested itself.

---

* Joye Swain, an Oklahoma participant, recalled attending pre-conference meetings of a "fanatic" anti-abortion group whose members said they had been trained in Rome.

CHAPTER

22

It Changed My Life

BETTY CARRIED THE jittery atmosphere of Mexico City home with her. The movement was already permeated with it, inflamed by the revelations coming out of Washington. A journalist wrote, "The movement today is a bit like the London of the 1890s where, according to Ford Madox Ford, every Russian revolutionary émigré had a Russian secret agent assigned to him." Women reported phone taps; NOW was in the midst of a ferocious power struggle, and all disagreements became cause for suspicion. Small everyday things were interpreted as signs of intrigue. Jacqui, who lived in Betty's Lincoln Plaza building and was her most loyal lieutenant, said, "When we got back to New York she screamed at me and accused me of being a CIA agent and of stealing papers from her apartment. She called me. 'Where are my papers? You took my papers! You took my papers!' Later she found them. She thought I had arranged things with the Mexicans to follow her. She was paranoid."

Outside the feminist press, the brief flurry of interest in the Steinem/CIA story was dying down, and it gave no sign of becoming a front-page scandal. Gloria zealously protected her image and reputation. She was not destined to be a fallen idol. When *The Village Voice* wanted to do a story, her lawyer sent a letter threatening to sue. Betty did her best to keep interest from flagging. During television appearances she threw out little zingers: "Don't ask me about Gloria Steinem and the CIA," she would say, "I don't want to talk about it," and her host would say, "What about Gloria Steinem and the CIA?"

Betty heard from Kathie Sarachild again when Redstockings sent her a copy of its new book, *Feminist Revolution*. The group had raised money to publish five thousand copies and sent some of them to movement journals and papers for review. *Feminist Revolution* contained articles, historical and theoretical writings, and discussions of how the movement had been watered down by the media and liberal and Establishment women—by one woman in particular and her magazine, *Ms.* One chapter consisted entirely of the press release. Betty called Kathie immediately. The book had sold well, and Kathie hoped Redstockings could get a major publisher. Betty suggested her own publisher and had a copy sent to James Silberman, her editor at Random House, who signed it up. Betty gave the book a blurb; Random House vetted the manuscript and was nearing publication when Gloria, with the help of her lawyers and connections, managed to have the offending chapter removed, along with some other material. Redstockings was in a quandary. Should they publish or pull out? "Betty Friedan was very helpful in encouraging us to publish," Kathie said. "We called her—'What should we do?' She said there was other important material in the book." *Feminist Revolution* was finally published in 1978 but did not make a splash.

. . .

SINCE THE EARLY seventies, Betty had been trying unsuccessfully to finish the book she had contracted to write. How could she top *The Feminine Mystique?* The book's title had changed from *Woman: The Fourth Dimension,* to *The New Woman,* to *Herstory.* The contract had been signed on January 24, 1964, and she had received a $30,000 advance, $10,000 a year until 1966, when the book had been due. In 1965 Random House had licensed the paperback to Dell. By 1970, feminist books were becoming a cottage industry—people could scarcely write them fast enough—and Random House became more persistent. Their author was the movement's founder; her book would be important. All along, Jim Silberman had been sending her polite little nudging notes, to no avail; now he sent Charlotte Mayerson, another Random House editor, to try to draw the book out of Betty. Mayerson's efforts were unsuccessful. Betty was then trying to recover from her divorce, and the anguish of her marriage poured out, pages and pages of it, all inappropriate.

After months of effort with Charlotte Mayerson, it became clear that the book, as originally conceived, was out of date. At that point, Betty proposed (or possibly it was Jim; he said it was her idea, and she said it was his) a collection. It would be a way to get Betty back in the public eye as an author. The book would be called *It Changed My Life*, a title that came from her following, from the thousands of women who had written to her or come up to her after her speeches and lectures, to thank her for what she had done and tell her how she had changed their lives.

On September 5, 1974, Betty signed a letter of agreement with Random House. The book would be a running history of the movement and her life told through her articles and lectures, and she would write an introduction to each section and add new material. Random House would pay her $750 for the cost of collecting and transcribing her lectures, and Betty would deliver them in two and a half months. If she did not deliver, she would repay Random House all the money it had advanced her. A paragraph at the end of the agreement stated that "if the parties cannot reach a mutually satisfactory agreement...our advance of $750 shall be charged against your share of earnings under our agreement dated January 24, 1964" (for the unwritten and unworkable book). This meant that if Betty did not deliver, she would owe Random House the original $30,000 advance plus $750. Betty turned in some of her articles and lectures on February 4, 1975, and got a new contract for 80,000 words with a $25,000 advance, bringing the total amount she had received to $55,750. The book was published on June 28, 1976.

It Changed My Life was a fascinating failure. It was suffused with Betty's passion and commitment to women, her vision of a more just world. Parts of it were moving and inspirational, filled with stirring speeches and high drama. Other parts were as mean-spirited as "Up from the Kitchen Floor" had been. The book reasserted Betty's primacy as First Feminist. It told the world that she, Betty Friedan, did it, and no one else, and furthermore, everyone else was wrong. In the chapters on the National Women's Political Caucus and the Democratic Convention of 1972, Betty repeated and extended her earlier accusations; now she insinuated that the CIA or FBI had been pulling her opponents' strings. (She had already hinted at these accusations in her *McCall's* columns, but more obliquely.)

The caucus considered suing her, but no one had the time, energy, or money. Instead, Audrey Rowe Colom, the national chair, wrote to Robert Bernstein, president of Random House: "It is disturbing that [Betty] now deems it necessary to explain her 1972 NWPC Steering Committee defeat by implying that a [*sic*] FBI–CIA–NWPC cabal conspired to deny her victory." Colom also noted dryly that Betty was still on the NWPC's advisory board and contributed money to the organization.

Bernstein also got a second letter signed by twenty-six NWPC members, saying that the book was

> *too marred by factual errors, self-serving fiction, racist assumptions and character assassinations of almost every nationally-known feminist or feminist organization to serve as any factual source on the women's movement or on the spirit and ideas of feminism. . . . For our part, we prefer to remember the author for her journalistic work of thirteen years ago, The Feminine Mystique, which pioneered in reporting the then little-known dilemma of the well-educated white middle-class housewife, and was a constructive contribution to understanding one group of American women.*

The language of the last sentence was pure Gloria. It diminished Betty's role and confined her influence to a neat suburban lawn. Gloria would repeat her judgment in interviews; it was taken up by her followers and published in *Ms.* Other enemies, some of them NOW women with whom Betty had fought, would go further, crediting Kathryn Clarenbach with inventing NOW and relegating Betty to the symbolic role of the figure on the prow. "They want to disappear me," Betty later said, afraid they would succeed, and redoubled her efforts to remain First Feminist.

Most reviews of the book and articles about her ran from lukewarm to hostile, as if all the people she had offended had decided to get back at her at once. There were contemptuous headlines: "Betty Friedan: Don't Snicker"; and "A Few Kind Words for Betty Friedan," followed by: "Her gray hair was wild, as usual, and her dress struggled to encompass her diet-proof figure, as usual. . . . She was taking rapid, voluminous notes in a small spiral notebook and her face with its Witch-of-Endor profile which has been cruelly caricatured in countless cartoons was glowing with interest. She looked extraordinarily alive and yes, pretty."

The Christian Science Monitor said, "It has all the omissions and confusion of an eyewitness who was in the accident." The *Newsday* (Long Island, N.Y.) reviewer criticized her for not exploring her psyche: Betty did not say what the movement was like for *her,* how it had changed *her* life (implicitly raising the question of whether it had), or discuss what it was like to live as a feminist. The *New York Times*'s daily reviewer, who found the book repetitive and filled with undocumented accusations, wrote, "Though Miss Friedan labors to give credit elsewhere whenever it is due, she often ends up sounding like an egotistical Joan of Arc."

In the all-important *New York Times Book Review,* Stephanie Harrington devoted almost an entire page—most of the review—to the National Women's Political Caucus section, which she said was "filled with innuendoes of dirty tricks that it would take a special prosecutor to investigate." She dismissed Betty's complaints as paranoid, writing that Betty lost because Bella and Gloria were more skilled at political infighting.

Betty considered Stephanie Harrington's review "vicious" and solicited friends to write letters defending her. The *Times* printed one, from Shana Alexander, who said that it had all happened exactly as Betty said; Shana had been there, and she had "resigned from Organized Sisterhood" because of it. "Friedan's own withdrawal from Organized Sisterhood," she wrote, "was painful and prolonged, as her book movingly describes. But it led her from narrow feminism to a deeper humanism; it was the high road, and millions have followed her.... Friedan's life is a testament to the fact that sisterhood is every bit as difficult to achieve as brotherhood."

Random House sold the paperback reprint rights to Dell in August 1976 for $100,000, but the hardcover did not do well. Muriel Fox said, "The reason her book never sold was because feminists who would have given it good reviews were so horrified by what she said about Bella and Gloria. None of the feminists who would have given it a good review would go near it. She always shoots herself in the foot."

Betty was disappointed and at first blamed herself, but then she decided the book's commercial failure was really the fault of Random House. As she saw it, her publisher had not gotten behind the book, had not spent enough money on advertising and promotion, and she thought she knew why: it was a deliberate act of retaliation against her editor. Eight months before Betty's book was published, Jim Silberman had left Random House after a run-in over a personal matter and had gone to Simon & Schuster, Random House's arch-competitor, where he was received with great glee.

Her grievance was such that she decided to leave Random House. Not only was Jim gone, but Neil Nyren (her line editor, who had also edited *The Feminine Mystique* at Norton), had also left. She no longer felt that anyone in the company cared about her or her book. Random House had also withheld a reserve of $7,000 against returns, an amount Betty considered too high.

Betty left Random House in April 1977 and signed a contract with Jim at Summit Books, his new fiefdom at Simon & Schuster, for *The Fountain of Age.* She got a $100,000 advance. Six months later, in November, she learned that Random House had deducted $30,000—the amount of her original 1964 advance—from her share of *It Changed My Life*'s Dell paperback sale, and she decided to sue. Normally, when an author does not deliver a manuscript and she gets a new contract with another publisher, she returns the advance. This situation was different: the S&S book was not the one she had originally contracted to write for Random House. In her affidavit, Betty asserted that not only was Random House conducting a "vendetta" against Jim, getting back at him through her, but it was also "attempt[ing] to 'punish' me for changing publishers, and specifically for going with Mr. Silberman to his new company."

The case hinged on two points: whether *It Changed My Life* was the same book Betty had contracted to write in 1964, and whether Random House had waited too long to try to recover its $30,000 advance. There was a six-year statute of limitations. Betty claimed that one book had nothing to do with the other, and that the statute of limitations had run out. The clock had started ticking in 1971, when she and Jim both realized the book couldn't be written. After January 1971 (when Charlotte Mayerson made her editorial efforts), Random House had done nothing for nearly seven years to get the advance back. Random House claimed that it had not tried to get its money because it was still pursuing the book. As proof it submitted a file of a dozen letters, correspondence between Betty and Jim, dating from 1968 to 1974.

Betty really had no case. In a nutshell, she had taken an advance of $30,000 for a book she did not deliver and then cried foul when Random House deducted the money from a second book. The deduction was standard operating procedure in publishing. In 1979, the New York State Supreme Court ruled in favor of Random House.

23

Love Again

ON THE NIGHT of Friday, July 15, 1977, Betty was in Phoenicia, New York, at the Center for the Living Force, sitting quietly in her room, waiting to be called for her therapy. All the unresolved conflicts of her life—Peoria, her parents, men (one man in particular), the movement, her fame and the way she used it—had converged on her. Gloria and the new younger leaders controlled the movement, and the louder she shouted, the deafer they became. The center had moved, leaving her stranded. Asked by a reporter about her own liberation, she had been uncharacteristically uncertain: "It's not complete. It's so hard to liberate one's self from self-denigration, from the scars of dependency...." The disappointing sales of *It Changed My Life* seemed another sign of her waning power. Her anxiety deepened to panic as she watched the fame that was her very identity, without which she would be nothing, slip away. Her asthma was acting up (she took pills and used an inhaler), and she dreamed of heart attacks. She was in a depression.

Her lifelong strategy was unraveling. "They may not like me now, but they're going to look up to me," she had once vowed, and built herself a pedestal to stand on, demanding that homage be paid to her "big head," as she called it. Now the drawbacks of that choice were becoming evident.

She had become a prisoner of the celebrity mystique. As she waited, she wrote an autobiography of her emotions, reliving her estrangement from her mother and the self-loathing it had generated, pouring out her disgust with the old power struggles, the emptiness of her fame, the depth of her loneliness.

Betty had continued with her therapy after her first visits to Esalen. She had returned often, sometimes to lead groups, and there she had met Dr. John Pierrakos, a bioenergetic therapist. Pierrakos and his wife, Eva, had founded the Center for the Living Force, a compound on three hundred wooded acres near Woodstock. There they provided physical and spiritual healing. Eva was a medium; her teachings came through an entity called the Guide while she was in a trance. The theory was that psychic problems were caused by certain bottled-up energies that would be released by exercises. As physical blocks were overcome, emotional blocks would be, too. By going through the exercises, as well as group therapy, fasting, etc., you would reach your core. After plumbing the depths, feeling and accepting all your mean and hateful feelings, relinquishing your illusions about yourself—a trip to hell and back—you would be able to accept and love yourself. The process was familiarly known as "the pathwork."

Betty had been doing the pathwork since the early seventies, slipping off to a loft in SoHo where a group met once a week. By 1978 she was going to Phoenicia two and three times a month, but in seven years she had been afraid to surrender to the therapy. She had stood back and applied psychology to her problems, rather than deal with them. Her quest for fame had placed her in a paradoxical situation. She needed it, wanted it, courted it, and fought to the death when anyone threatened it—but the focus and urgency that had propelled her to the top of the hill and kept her standing there, warding off all comers, had estranged her from her feelings. The persona she had developed had taken over the person. It protected her from competition, but it also demanded constant care and feeding, separating her from what she truly craved—love and intimacy. And she had come to a crisis in a long affair with a man she had considered marrying, David Manning White.

She had met him at a Cape Cod conference in 1970, in a workshop on alternative family lifestyles. He was an academic, about Betty's age, married for over twenty-five years to a biochemist, teaching and living in Boston. A friend of Betty's said, "He glowed a little. He looked a little as if he was on stage." He had straight, silvery white hair and courtly Southern manners. He was a former dean of the school of journalism at Boston

University. His fields were mass communications and popular culture; he wrote about them frequently and taught at various universities around the country. In 1957 he had co-authored *Mass Culture*, with Bernard Rosenberg, and he had worked on and written the introduction to a popular book on meditation, *The Relaxation Response*, by Herbert Benson, a scholar at Harvard. Barbara Seaman, one of Betty's confidantes in the affair, said, "She was always saying they were great in bed together. He had a beautiful, wealthy wife, tall, thin, dark. She looked like Olivia de Havilland. Betty said he would never leave her because he was devoted to his children and the money."

Betty did not take the affair too seriously at first, but she soon began to find reasons to go to Boston, and David visited her in the Hamptons. Her sex life at this time was sporadic and unfulfilling. Arthur Dubow, Betty's venture capitalist friend from East Hampton, said, "She had men friends staying for weekends, not only David. There were others who followed in her thrall. They were pleasant, not terribly accomplished—a convenience. She was never *involved* with any of them. And people out here were her escorts. She is such a strong character. All these guys, they are just doing something—refilling her drink."

In 1973, when she was on her first trip to Israel, a double crisis in David's life brought their relationship to a turning point. He discovered that his wife, Catherine, was also having an affair, and he had a cancer scare. (It turned out to be gout.) Under the circumstances, he told his wife about Betty, and he sent her a letter breaking it off. "She was just crushed," Ann O'Shea, her secretary, said. "She was like a teenager losing her boyfriend. She was so fragile in some ways. She was sitting and sobbing." But David and Catherine came to an accommodation, and the three of them had lunch. Although Betty participated in this effort to be civilized, it went against her grain; afterward she went home and threw up. Jacqui, who was as traditional as Betty in these matters, thought Betty felt guilty about going with a married man. However, not long after the lunch, Betty invited another man, also married, on a trip to Italy. But it was no good; he was afraid they would be discovered, and he wanted to stay married.

After Carl, David was the most important man in Betty's life. He brought out her domestic side, which she had virtually abandoned in her slapdash life. Betty even wrote an article about rediscovering the joy of cooking: "I've come out the other end of women's liberation—to make my own soup.... That Spanish soup with 20 cloves of garlic and a raw egg. Fish soup with saffron and a little white wine—I wonder how you make aioli. I'll buy a big tureen and some large bowls. And then with bread and salad and cheese and wine, I could have people over to dinner again. It can't be that difficult, running a blender...why should I deprive myself or be ashamed of the sensuous joy I have been secretly snatching, scrambling ambrosiacal eggs for a man I specially love, or plying my long lost son with chicken soup."

(The article was only ostensibly about making soup from scratch. Betty was working hard for the passage of the Equal Rights Amendment and trying to counter the right wing, which was telling women that the ERA would destroy their marriages. The piece presented a warm and fuzzy Betty Friedan and told the world that feminists were not man-haters, that she, the mother of them all, was cooking for both her man and her son, just like any housewife.)

Betty flaunted David as her consort, taking him on glamorous trips during which, as the honored guest, she was treated like royalty. In April 1976, they flew to Fairbanks, where she was special events speaker at the University of Alaska, and then went on to Anchorage and Juneau. They were fed moose dinners and taken dogsledding, and Betty was interviewed on radio and television. They met the governor, Jay Hammond; she was introduced in both houses of the Alaska state legislature, and attended a luncheon with lawmakers.

In November, they went on a much grander trip to Vienna, where the Austrian government had invited Betty to address a large gathering of opinion leaders. The trip was marred by an asthma attack, a signal that all was not well between them.

In January 1977 she took David to Jimmy Carter's inauguration ceremony. She had campaigned for Vice President Walter Mondale and had become good friends with his wife, Joan, and the Mondales had made sure that she and David had good seats. Betty had been alienated from government by Watergate, but her hopes were restored by the ceremony. Even David, who was more cynical than she about politics, sang "The Star-Spangled Banner." Although she was disturbed by the note of religion in the proceedings, she felt the majesty of the occasion and wept as Fritz Mondale took his oath "to preserve, protect, and defend the Constitution of the United States."

Unexpectedly, the center of power shifted. Catherine, who had a more European view of marriage, wanted to be included in their relationship. "I didn't mind sharing David," she said. "I couldn't fulfill all of David's needs any more than he could fulfill mine. He had Jewish guilt, so it bothered him more than it bothered me. He was a dominating person. They [David and Betty] were very much alike. He would set a mood for the whole house. I was glad when he took a week or a weekend off."

David, who had no intention of leaving his wife, began pressuring Betty into a threesome. Betty, who became growly when men she had once dated began to take out her friends, found herself in the worst possible position: the things she shared with David, the life of their romance, would now be Catherine's property, too. David would still belong to Catherine, while she, Betty, would inhabit the periphery. Her friends warned her off. "This is insane," Barbara Seaman and the Tofflers told her over drinks, but Betty was unwilling to give him up. "He was very much in love with me," she said, speaking of it many years later. She stayed with them in Boston and visited David at his home in Richmond, Virginia. "We saw each other four times," Catherine said. "She was always upset when she was around me. I was not here when Betty stayed in Richmond. I worked out an itinerary for them which they followed." Betty was afraid that this was her last chance for love, that she would never have another sexual relationship, and she was desolate at the thought. She was in her late fifties, the age when women suddenly notice that men's eyes are sliding over them as if they didn't exist. Betty was a woman who loved men. "When it's really right, there's really a glow that's the essence of happiness," she said. The things she wanted so much she found in David—"or to be more accurate, only with David in bed," she wrote.

Yet, as much as she yearned for intimacy and love, Betty's fear of getting into another marriage like the one she'd had was stronger. All along she had had her defenses up. Years later she said, "When I look back, it wouldn't take a shrink to tell me that I, in a sense, used the relationship so that I wouldn't have to face the risk of getting married again." She did edge away a little from David. When she was invited to be a guest lecturer on the *QE II,* she decided to take Emily rather than David. It would also be easier to meet other men if he weren't there.

Despite her desperation at the thought of losing him, Betty must have known that the affair was bound to sink under the weight of its psychological baggage. Looking at it without sentimentality, with the kind of sangfroid Catherine could muster, the romance was clouded by all the fancy trips and special treatment, the famous people who came to Betty's parties. Perhaps David was using her. Perhaps, given the circumstances of Betty's life, it was inevitable that anyone would.

In the late seventies, David almost lost a hand in a freak accident. He and Catherine were bicycling to work in Richmond at eight-thirty A.M., during rush hour. As they passed beneath a bridge that was being spray painted, some of the paint dripped into his eyes. He swerved into a truck, catching his hand between the truck and the handlebar, almost severing it. It was hanging by a nerve and some skin. The doctor told him to give up teaching for the rest of the semester, but he returned to his classes the next week. Like Betty, David refused to be defeated by physical afflictions. He had five operations and lost two fingers, but the hand was saved. Betty had a moment of superstitious fear. One of her friends said, "She thought it was a sign, that he was a sinner, cheating on his wife."

Betty and David finally broke up in the early eighties. She had already begun having "a small involvement" with someone else. Afterward, David called her again and, although she was still lonely, she decided not to see him. The reasons were various, depending on the person explaining them. "He disappeared," her old friend Dick Laupot said. "She took a dislike to him in the end. It had to do with a feeling of lack of respect for her on his part—intellectually." According to Catherine, "David ended the affair. It was because of fear of AIDS. She was going with someone from San Francisco who had an artistic side, and David thought he might be AC-DC." According to Betty, it was because David was married. In 1997 she said, "I realized that it was wrong to put all that emotion into the relationship. At the time, I was all over the place, organizing the women's movement. It filled my emotional needs without interfering with my life that much. But I miss him. We had a lovely thing together. He had great joie de vivre."

David White died in December 1993 after fifteen hours of open-heart surgery. He and Catherine had been married forty-nine and a half years. She sent Betty her Christmas card of that year, which bore a picture of a family reunion, and told her the date of the memorial service. She wrote, "His heart was big enough to love more than one." The day of the service was forbiddingly icy, which prevented many out-of-town people from coming to Richmond. For whatever reason, Betty did not attend.

24

The Last Battle

The Equal Rights Amendment:
"Equality of rights under the law shall not be
denied or abridged by the United States or
by any State on account of sex."

"REMEMBER THE LADIES," Abigail Adams had written to her husband, John, who was at the Constitutional Convention, but none of the founding fathers had; until suffrage, there was no mention of women in the Constitution. The Equal Rights Amendment had passed the Senate in 1972, and in a surge of enthusiasm, thirty states had ratified it that same year. It needed thirty-eight states to become law. In 1974, only three states ratified. The reaction had begun; galvanized by the Senate vote and by *Roe v. Wade* in 1973, the right wing marshaled its forces and started its climb to power. By 1978 the amendment was becalmed; not a single state ratified it that year, and it was defeated in six. Only a handful of states had not yet voted.

Betty's major political goal in the mid- and late seventies would be to secure its passage. Without the ERA, all the new laws the movement had won could be swept away in the courts as easily as they had been passed. The only other constitutional recourse, the Equal Protection Clause of the Fourteenth Amendment, had proved unsatisfactory, its application to women capricious, depending on judicial interpretation.

If the ERA was to pass, she knew, she needed the united strength of NOW, but NOW and Betty were not on the best of terms. The organization was consumed by a bitter and probably inevitable power struggle. The fruits of success—power, influence, visibility, and a fat treasury of over half a million dollars—were prizes too tempting to resist. NOW was also divided ideologically.

At NOW's national convention in 1974 and again in 1975, Karen DeCrow, a young lawyer in her thirties from Syracuse, a woman whose life Betty had changed, won the presidency, defeating Betty's choices. Styling themselves the Majority Caucus, Karen's followers adopted a new slogan: "Out of the mainstream, into the revolution." Sidney Abbott, a NOW member long out of the closet, said, "I was not on the side of the Majority Caucus. Karen had a frightening cadre of lesbians from D.C., like Nazi storm troopers, fighting, screaming, yelling on the floor. It was chaos." Afterward, a group of women reporters who had covered the election got together and swore they would never write a word of what they had seen. Betty believed that corporate or CIA money was behind the extremists, and that they had been sent in to divide NOW and prevent it from fighting effectively for the ERA. The lesbians were "guerrillas," she fumed on Tom Snyder's talk show. NOW was *supposed* to be a mainstream organization; that's what it was about.

In the midst of this convulsion, on October 29, 1975, at a time when the economy was slow and jobs were scarce, NOW called an ill-conceived national strike, "Alice Doesn't" (doesn't work, cook, clean, parent), which was ignored by most women. Betty later wrote: "The women who had marched and done all those crazy actions were busy being lawyers and getting Ph.D.s and doing serious work. They were part of the system. They had too much to lose. And there was no real reason to strike." The following month, ERA state referenda in New York and New Jersey were defeated. The campaigns against the amendment played on fears of job loss and the end of alimony and child support. It was a stunning defeat.

Dozens of articles viewed these setbacks as a sign that the movement had had its day. "Is NOW on the Brink of Then?" was the headline in *The Village Voice*. In response to NOW's Majority Caucus, Betty formed a new group with the unfortunate name of Womensurge. Early in November 1975, a few of the old guard—Muriel Fox and Mary Jean Tully among them—met secretly at an airport hotel in New Orleans with the idea of influencing NOW to return to its original goals. NOW's priorities, they believed, should be to face the economic crisis and work out a strategy to deal with the backlash. They were careful to call Womensurge an "operation," not an organization. They sent out reams of paper, but in the end their plans came to nothing. They could not start a fifth column, and it was out of the question to organize another NOW.

Meanwhile, Betty worked tirelessly for the ERA, enlisting her friends in high places. Led by Sey Chassler of *Redbook,* the editors of thirty-six magazines published pro-ERA articles simultaneously. The *Cosmo* Girl endorsed the ERA. Abe Rosenthal, the executive editor of *The New York Times,* invited Betty to discuss the amendment with the *Times* editorial board, and the paper ran a front-page series on it. "Please make sure that we give some decent quotes from Betty Friedan in our ERA series," Rosenthal told James Greenfield, a senior editor. "For one thing she inspired us to do it, and secondly, she really is, still, a paramount figure in the woman's [sic] movement and one who, I believe, is a bridge among many women and men." Abe and Betty had a mutual admiration society. In "The Men I Most Admire," an article in *Parade* (August 12, 1984), Betty would name him as one of her media heroes, along with David Wolper (who produced *Roots*), and Norman Lear (*All in the Family*). Their friendship later gained her virtually unlimited access to the influential *New York Times Magazine.* "I like her nonauthoritarian way of putting forth her ideology," Rosenthal said. "She didn't make people feel that they had to do it right away. And on choices—the right to choose or not choose a career. Some people were categorizing women. She didn't do that. She had a considerable amount of warmth of soul. I enjoy being with her. She makes me feel warm and welcome—she has an open quality."

In 1977, the ERA was stalled just three states short of ratification, with less than eighteen months to go before the deadline of March 22, 1979. Betty, desperate for money for the campaign, decided to raid the treasury of NOW's Legal Defense and Education Fund. She was a member of its board and knew that the fund's tax-exempt status barred it from political action, but drastic measures were necessary. The LDEF was sending out a fund-raising letter and needed a big name for the signature. Gene Boyer, who was then president of the LDEF, said, "I discovered that Betty wanted some quid pro quo for her signature. She wanted all the money we were going to raise with that direct-mail letter to be earmarked for her ERA project. I finally convinced her it was unreasonable and she signed. . . . I had never run into anybody who was a negotiator like that. . . . Betty's idea of being in control was to have a poker chip she held in her pocket until you put out three. She found out what you wanted and withheld it."

Betty, however, did not give up easily. She was the draw at an LDEF fund-raiser in Chicago, scheduled to give a speech and then attend a reception. According to Gene, instead of giving a little "boost-the-LDEF" speech, Betty lost her temper in front of a whole group of potential donors and said, 'I'm going to report you to the IRS for raising money under false pretenses.' Then she stalked out of the room." She and Gene did not speak to each other for some time. Betty denied that she was going to make such a speech and said, "I would never have made that kind of threat."

In 1978, crisscrossing the country for the ERA, Betty went back to Peoria. It was the fortieth reunion of Central High School's class of 1938. It is unlikely that Betty would have gone to it, considering the disastrous twenty-fifth in 1963, but the local NOW chapter promised her an ERA march. A thousand people paraded by torchlight, a number far beyond their expectations. "A thousand for Peoria is the equivalent of a million for New York," Betty wrote.

After her visit, Betty wrote a long piece for *The New York Times Magazine,* an outpouring of affection for Peoria and her old friends who, bathed in the glow of nostalgia, all seemed to have married happily and led lives of singular accomplishment.

It had been an extraordinary high school class, filled with future movers and shakers—doctors, lawyers, politicians; the president of Caterpillar, Peoria's largest industry; the president of a steel company; a ringmaster of the Ringling Brothers and Barnum & Bailey Circus; a naval commander and diplomat; the guru of a religious cult—even a CIA agent. Her "oldest and best friend," Harriet Vance Parkhurst, who was pro-ERA, was a Republican state committeewoman and had six children. Harriet's husband, John, who was anti-ERA, was a conservative lawyer and state senator. John Altorfer had developed an industrial park and run for governor. Paul Jordan, who had started *Tide* with Betty, was chief of surgery at Baylor Hospital in Houston. Most of the classmates who'd stayed in Peoria lived in enormous houses on the Bluff and ran the city. Betty envied the women: she sensed about them an aura of confidence, a self-esteem based on the high regard in which Peoria held them. Power emanated from them. She was still the outsider looking through the window, yearning to be inside with all the happy couples who had managed their lives so well.

Betty saw something she didn't have and had always wanted—the closeness of family, the long, mellow relationships—but she would have died of claustrophobia had she stayed there. She was a world figure who lived to change things, visiting Brigadoon.

Peoria did not feel the rosy glow for Betty that she felt for it. Bob Easton, Betty's "first beau," who had become a pediatrician, said, "Even though people in Peoria are proud of her, a lot of men feel she changed the macho way of life—the way their wives look at them and their children's loss of respect. Most of the women in my generation never had a paid job after they were married. A lot of women think she is perhaps responsible for the breakup of the home."

The greatest pleasure of her visit must have been the disappearance of an old barrier. On the last day of her visit, her brother Harry took her to lunch with his family at the once restricted Peoria Country Club. She thought it was courageous of him to invite her, "his black-sheep sister," into this symbol and stronghold of those who belonged.

Harry had prospered; he was the president of Cohen's, having been favored over his wife's brother, and had two daughters and a son. Miriam was long gone from Peoria. She had outlived two more husbands after Harry Senior, and was living in a retirement home in Laguna Beach, California, where she had become a duplicate bridge manager—a career she had taken up after the age of seventy. Amy had become a teacher in Queens and an artist. Harry had become more philosophical: "Life moves on, and what was not accepted yesterday is accepted today," he told a reporter.

Betty and Harry's family had recently reconciled. Laurie Goldstein, Harry's younger daughter, had become fascinated with Betty, and Betty had gotten her a job working for the ERA. Harry said, "Betty was very good to her, and Inette was very appreciative of that. It softened her up."

Laurie brought out Betty's maternal instincts, as younger women frequently did. They had an affinity for each other. "I was destined to pursue a connection with Betty," Laurie said. "I had similar yearnings and burnings in my soul as Betty. Peoria was love-hate for both of us. A place to be from and not to live in. When you are a freethinker and pursue different kinds of truth, you want to be in an environment that is conducive to that."

Laurie moved into Emily's vacant bedroom at Lincoln Plaza. "It was fabulous," Laurie said. "She opened my eyes to the world. I'd been perched ready, spiritually, emotionally, mentally, everything. She was rigorous, dynamic. She is a visionary. She would read the paper, make a remark.... She included me, took me everywhere. A big black-tie affair at Lincoln Center, and we were leaning out the window watching. Her writer friends in Sag Harbor—'The key is here, just come.' An extended family. We had dinner, hung out together. Betty loved Japanese food—we would go to places and sit on the floor. Theatre, concerts, movies—she was a great playmate."

The ERA fight strengthened the right wing immeasurably. Of all the demands of the movement, only two, the ERA and abortion rights, granted women autonomy, legally and personally, challenging the hidden premises, the unspoken prejudices and unexamined dogmas, that ruled society. These two issues served as a rallying point for the reaction, a means of raising money and consolidating the power that would culminate in the election of Ronald Reagan in 1980. The movement was stunned by the ferocity of the attack against it. In particular, it was completely unprepared for Phyllis Schlafly, the superstar of the backlash, and at a loss as to how to deal with her. Betty debated her several times. "I remember one of my first debates with Betty Friedan," Phyllis said. "She became so incensed she shouted that I should be burned at the stake."*

Phyllis Schlafly tended to provoke that sort of reaction among feminists. She scored high on Betty's hypocrisy meter: she was an accomplished professional who preached that other women should stay home and cultivate their femininity. Although she was an author who got $1,000 a lecture, had a twice-weekly commentary on CBS radio, published a monthly newsletter, and was active in Republican politics, she insisted that marriage and family were her real career. Ironically, she owed her law degree to the movement: in 1975, when she was fifty years old, she was a first-year student at Washington University Law School in St. Louis, Missouri, an endeavor she was unlikely to have been engaged in before NOW made it possible for her to do so. Betty strongly suspected that the Eagle Forum, Phyllis's organization, was funded by the Ku Klux Klan, the John Birch Society, the Christian Crusade, and other right-wing groups, but although she tried, she was never able to prove it.

Phyllis Schlafly looked like a corporate hostess, circa 1955, who had everything under control. She was tall, immaculately groomed, with upswept blond hair, and an intimidating manner that served her well in television debates. In willpower, ability to dominate, and sheer perseverance, she was another Betty. She inspired women, and they loved her. At every turn, Phyllis popped up with her ladies in granny dresses, bearing gifts to legislators of home-baked bread and homemade jam, wrapped in ribbons, with cute, girlish cards: "To the Breadwinners from the Breadmakers." These tactics were a sort of revenge of the feminine mystique, of the housewives who preferred to remain housewives, the women who had been ignored and denigrated during the movement's youth.

Phyllis established a monolithic presence on television; she was the lone warrior, always pitted against a different opponent. Compared with her, the feminists were amateurs. As a debater she was diamond-hard, organized, and disciplined, and she had no compunctions about exploiting people's fears of vast uncontrollable changes in their everyday lives. She was all the

---

* Offstage they found common cause, congratulating each other on their brilliant sons, who were both studying at Berkeley.

more effective because there was a real problem explaining the effects of the amendment. No one knew what they would be. Phyllis claimed to know. Her STOP ERA primer, "What the Equal Rights Amendment Means," warned that wives would "be legally responsible to provide 50% of the financial support of her family" (not true); women would be forced to hold jobs (not true); women would be drafted (true); women would no longer enjoy "preferential Social Security benefits" (there were none); protective labor laws would vanish (they already had); women would lose "protection from sex crimes such as statutory rape and forced prostitution" (not true); and, finally, bathrooms would become unisex (not true).

Betty was so focused on the ERA that anything else seemed a diversion. When the National Women's Conference was called in Houston in November 1977, she could barely comprehend that women were working on other projects. It was "an artificial happening, a pseudo-event, an unnecessary event, a media event," she wrote. Houston was a White House–sponsored conference, two years in the making, initiated by Bella Abzug. It was the first government-financed convention for and about women in American history, and it had a plan of action to further the goal of equality. Every feminist of importance was there, as were three First Ladies—Lady Bird Johnson, Betty Ford, and Rosalyn Carter—along with 2,000 voting delegates and 20,000 other women.

The conference was organized by old movement hands from both sides—Catherine East and Kay Clarenbach of NOW, and Gloria, Bella, and Mim Kelber, Bella's aide. Each played her role: Kay was the administrator; Gloria was the peacemaker, redrafting resolutions and bringing together minority groups; and Bella was the limelight person, the presiding officer. Gloria drew the cameras like a magnet, but the conference belonged to Bella. "She was ubiquitous in her big flop[py] hats and matching outfits. Everywhere she went the women would come at her, pull at her, tug at her arm, her jacket, her skirt," a reporter wrote.

Betty had not been completely ignored. She was an appointed delegate-at-large, and she participated in the torch relay ceremony. The ceremony opened the conference and symbolized the link between Seneca Falls, New York, the site of the first women's rights convention in 1848, and Houston. But amid the euphoria, Betty's only possible role was that of dissenter. She held a press conference and dashed cold water on the plan, which contained twenty-six planks to be voted on. The only relevant issue was the ERA, she said. "I had made a resolution to be sweet. But it's been too easy for them to tell us not to express our differences because of the fear of the right wing. It's the same as fear of Communism in the McCarthy era."

The planks addressed homemakers' rights, child abuse, child care, battered women, employment, credit, health, education, the media, minority women, older women, rape, reproductive freedom, sexual preference, military spending and nuclear weapons, and the ERA. They outlined a New Deal for women, with equality and humanism as national policy. Because the $5 million for the conference had come from Washington, an antifeminist contingent also participated, including men from Mississippi who represented Mississippi women. Some of them carried signs—KIKES FOR DYKES and ABZUG, FRIEDAN, AND STEINEM ARE ALL ANTI-CHRISTIAN JEWS. There were other banners: KEEP 'EM IN THE CLOSET. The sexual preference plank (also known as the lesbian plank), which stated that homosexuals were entitled to the same civil rights as heterosexuals, was not going to sail through.

In the ladies' room, Betty ran into Dolores Alexander, the woman she had drummed out of NOW so long ago. It had been years since they had seen or spoken to each other, but Betty knew all about Dolores, knew that she and a friend, Jill Ward, had started Mother Courage, a restaurant in Greenwich Village, and that Dolores, like some other women in the movement, had chosen to become a lesbian. Impulsively, Dolores asked Betty to speak on behalf of the lesbian plank. Betty refused—she was committed to the ERA for the next year, she said. Dolores pressed her: "You can say that the ERA will do nothing to help lesbians; that will take the lesbian stigma away from it, and you can speak on our behalf." "That's brilliant! Brilliant!" Betty said, and agreed to speak.

The moment was charged with history and hedged with misgivings. Lesbian groups were distrustful of what Betty might say and skeptical that she had agreed only in order to be relevant again. Betty was worried that the debate would go on for hours and that the media, which were broadcasting it nationally, would highlight lesbianism to the detriment of the ERA. On the other hand, if she supported the sexual preference plank, it would pass quickly. But these were minor quibbles. When Betty took the microphone to speak, there was an expectant hush. Beyond the old quarrels and the ill will, she was still Betty Friedan, the mother of them all, the most important feminist voice of her generation, and her raspy voice mesmerized the hall. In the spirit of sisterhood she said, "I am considered to be violently opposed to the lesbian issue in the women's movement, and I have been. This issue has been used to divide us and disrupt us and has been seized on by our enemies to try and turn back the whole women's movement to equality, and alienate our support. As a woman of middle age who grew up in middle America—in Peoria, Illinois—and who has loved men maybe too well, I have my personal hangups on this issue. I have made mistakes, we have all made mistakes in our focus on this issue. But now we must all transcend our previous differences to devote our full energies to get the Equal Rights Amendment ratified, or we will lose all we have gained. Since, contrary to the lies of the John Birchers, we know that the Equal Rights Amendment will do nothing whatsoever for homosexuals, we must support the separate civil rights of our lesbian sisters."

Betty brought down the house. Her speech was one of the most emotional moments of the conference. The plank passed, and a group of lesbians in the balcony released their balloons labeled WE ARE EVERYWHERE. "Every camera was on her," Dolores said. "She got a lot of press time. She left Houston happy. I felt vindicated. Finally she was saying, 'I'm sorry for what I did, and I am making it up to you'—as if it was a personal message to me."

Betty hadn't exactly been saying that, but the ruthlessness with which she had disposed of Dolores seems to have weighed on her. In an interview when she was seventy-five, Betty remembered that she had learned about the lesbian plot in NY–NOW from Dolores and said, "It was probably a blame-the-messenger thing, now that I look back on it."

Betty received many letters of praise and congratulations after her lesbian-rights speech. The writer Alix Kates Shulman, who was one of the first radical feminists, wrote:

> I was moved to tears when you delivered your speech in support of the sexual preference resolution. All around me women held their breath and felt the tears overflow as you said you had made a mistake (the same mistake made by so many). It meant so much to have you, the Mover, once again take an irrevocable step toward what we all desire; to see you move to close the wound, putting yourself, as always, in jeopardy for the sake of all of us.

(This moment of reconciliation was not all-encompassing. In an article in *The New Republic*, Betty went on at length about how "Gloria Steinem and others" managed to control the floor using floor whips so that the planks went through without debate.)

. . .

LATER IN THE conference, the ERA plank passed overwhelmingly, celebrated by a spontaneous snake dance through the coliseum. A year after Houston, women could point to new gains: the passage of the Pregnancy

Discrimination Act, which prohibited employers from discriminating on the basis of pregnancy, childbirth, or related conditions; training for displaced homemakers; improved inheritance status for farm widows; the Amateur Sports Act; part-time career and flextime bills for federal employees; a bill providing money for pregnant teenagers. However, expensive programs—child care and Social Security coverage for homemakers—remained in limbo, partly because of high inflation and soaring interest rates.

Houston notwithstanding, Phyllis Schlafly had the last laugh: the ERA passed into limbo in 1982, three states short of ratification. The causes of its defeat ranged from pressure by conservative business interests—there was evidence in some states of bribery—to a generalized fear of the unknown. After the excesses of the counterculture and a decade of challenges to authority, people were wary of how the amendment would affect their private lives. As Jane Mansbridge suggested in her book *Why We Lost the ERA,* "The only possible way to have persuaded three more state legislatures to ratify the ERA would have been to insist—correctly—that it would do relatively little in the short run, and to insist equally strongly—and correctly—on the importance of placing the principle in the Constitution to guide the Supreme Court."

After the defeat of the ERA, the last great unifying cause, the women's movement ceased to be a movement. Women continued to fight as before, and new groups formed—primarily around single issues like pornography—but no fiery new leaders emerged. The liberal political ethos was discredited, and the age of liberation passed. The new problems younger women faced grew out of the successes they had been bequeathed. "So diverse have the choices and patterns of women's lives become," Betty wrote, "that there is no single issue now that could hold us all together as firmly as the battle for our constitutional equal rights."

25

Apostasy

IN OCTOBER 1978, Betty bought a small, two-story, white clapboard house on Glover Street in Sag Harbor for $102,000. The least expensive Hampton, charming rather than imposing, Sag Harbor was an old whaling town whose main street curved around into a sunny harbor that was packed with tall-masted boats in the summer. Most of the houses were like Betty's, built close together, slightly tilted; some had widow's walks. Journalists and other literati, rather than socialites and nouveaux riches, congregated there; it was a mini–media center, and the ideas exchanged at parties frequently found their way into influential publications.

Betty's double parlor was filled with her carved period furniture, covered in bright print fabrics, cheerful and casual. Abstract paintings by her friend Syd Solomon hung on the living room walls, and a sampler near the fireplace read, A WOMAN'S PLACE IS IN THE WORLD. Slanting down to Sag Harbor Cove was a spacious backyard, where she entertained and where Emily and Jonathan would each be married a few years later. Sag Harbor would become her real home, the center for family gatherings and commune Thanksgivings, the place where she put down roots. She talked about being buried in the Jewish cemetery there.

Betty drove around in a secondhand jalopy she called Herman, the opening and closing of whose doors defied expectation. She had let her license lapse, and she enlisted a young friend, Kathleen Brady, who had written a biography of Ida Tarbell and was a journalist at *Time*, to help her pass the test. "She was inept," Kathy said, "but she was undeterred. She kept at it until she got it. She was not frustrated or angry. She was just focused on the fact that she was going to do it." After several failures, she got her license. Her eyesight had deteriorated, and she could barely see; she drove leaning on the steering wheel, as close to the windshield as she could get, but she knew where the stoplight was. Still, she often depended on friends and houseguests to chauffeur her around.

Betty had begun work on her new book, *The Fountain of Age*, the idea for which had been sparked by Dr. Robert Butler, a gerontologist who had introduced the word "ageism" into the language and was the founding director of the National Institutes of Health. "There were issues that predominantly affected women—Social Security and Medicare—and I didn't hear boo from the women's movement," he said. "Equal rights meant equal Social Security. I admired her, and I called her. We liked each other. I was hoping she would write about it and try to put it on the public policy agenda through the movement." In 1979, she got a $60,000 grant from the Ford Foundation for a project at Columbia University on the study of the aging process and changing sex roles.

She had scarcely begun when Sey Chassler, the only male feminist editor of a women's magazine, invited her to lunch at the Four Seasons and suggested that she write a series for *Redbook* on man, woman, and the family, a subject that could not have been closer to her heart. "That developed into her book *The Second Stage*, he said. "That was my title. She had 'revolution' in the title."

Betty stopped work on *Age* and got another contract from Jim for *The Second Stage*. It was 1979, when passage of the ERA still seemed possible, and she wanted to get her book published before the 1982 deadline for ratification. "I wrote with the feeling of a gun at my head," she said. "I wrote this book with one thought—that maybe it would help bring about that miracle, and if it doesn't, it will leave us in better shape not to go into another 50-year sleep if we lose the ERA."

There had been extraordinary changes, landmark lawsuits, enormous victories, a seismic shift in consciousness—but in some ways nothing had changed. The underlying social structure had held. The domestic sphere was still regarded as female territory. The new problems were the same ones working-class women had always had, the ones Betty had written about in her Marxist days. In the 1980s fewer than 7 percent of Americans were living in Norman Rockwell families; 43 percent of American wives with children under six were working, but America still had no parental leave policy, no flextime, and no system of child care. Once, Betty had thought, naively, that the idea of simple justice was enough. It had become clear to her that domestic issues had to be made men's issues. Women did not have the clout to make further changes themselves.

While working on the book, Betty wrote several important pieces on this theme for *The New York Times Magazine*, which was presided over by Edward Klein, Abe Rosenthal's handpicked editor. The articles received wide play, but they seemed to bolster a new antifeminist line that was appearing in the media: assertive women were being blamed for all the social ills of America—in particular, for a serious problem that had just been discovered—male impotence.

A few months before *The Second Stage* was published, Betty was given the cover of the magazine, which ran a six-thousand-plus-word excerpt. She was photographed in her apartment, sitting on her carved Victorian sofa, looking like a benign guru with her silvery hair combed softly around her face in a pageboy, wearing a long black cotton dress trimmed with stylized red and white Indian patterns. She was in the spotlight again, but now she was a cheerleader for beleaguered men.

In *The Second Stage* Betty laid out a new direction for the movement, to address the problems that its success had generated and to reclaim the issue of the family, which the right wing had preempted. In the process, she defanged feminism. The first stage "has come to a dead end," she wrote; "the problems are insoluble," and women must now turn their attention to the family, "the new frontier" of the future. In this endeavor they needed to enlist men. In fact, men "may be at the cutting edge of the second stage"—solutions would be found if men demanded them. Both work and home had to be restructured to meet human needs. In the workplace, Betty had already seen signs of a new "Beta" leadership, a feminine, nonlinear style, which men were adopting and calling their own. For the home, she called for new forms of housing—cooperative housekeeping, with common areas for eating, child care, laundry, and gardening. "Feminists today have been concentrating too exclusively on equal rights with men," she wrote. Women's issues, she now saw, were special interests that had to be subordinated to larger social problems. Feminism's first stage had been too selfish: in demanding priority for their own needs, women had placed themselves in opposition to the family. She blamed the radical women for having emphasized careerism.

In some areas, Betty seemed to have stepped into a swamp of Victoriana. "Such slogans as 'free abortion on demand' had connotations of sexual licentiousness...implying a certain lack of reverence for life and the mysteries of conception and birth which have been women's agony and ecstasy and defining value down through the ages.... Being 'for abortion' is like being 'for mastectomy.'" Betty did not renounce abortion rights. She would continue to fight when they were threatened, but she changed the terms of her acceptance: "I am not *for abortion*—I am for the *choice to have children*," she wrote, which is rather different from the choice not to have them. The irony was supreme: the woman whose book had launched the movement, who had presented the traditional housewife as a brainwashed blob, a person of little status and less respect, now championed her; the woman who had fought for equality and careers for women and had slammed the radicals for diversionary sexual politics (and did so again in this very book) now censured them for the impasse in which her own reform feminism found itself.

Reviews for *The Second Stage* were mixed. On the favorable side, Erica Jong wrote in *Saturday Review:* "Friedan criticizes the women's movement with the desperate concern of a loving mother. Her insistence on psychological truth rather than political polemicizing...her refusal, in all instances, to throw out the baby with the bathwater, make the reading of this book a supremely optimistic experience."

In *Vogue*, Mary Cantwell wrote: "In The Feminine Mystique, Ms. Friedan spoke to the mainstream; in The Second Stage, she is the mainstream.... When Ms. Friedan is discussing, wisely and well, how American thinking must be restructured towards flextime, parental leaves, and guaranteed child care, she is proceeding from the realities of modern American life."

Webster Schott, reviewing for *The Washington Post*, said, "Betty Friedan's The Second Stage is the right book at the right time.... [It] is intelligent, compassionate, and pertinent. It's an education. And it provides a course of action, especially for men. If we don't want for our mothers, wives, and daughters the freedom we have, why is it worth having? If we are not partners with women, what are we?"

But the negative responses were caustic. Simone de Beauvoir threw the book across the room in disgust. According to Deirdre Bair, her biographer, "she thought, as everyone else did, that Betty was taking back everything she said in *The Feminine Mystique*."*

Angeline Goreau wrote in *Newsday* (Long Island): "Friedan blames...the 'young radical women' of the movement who stole the media limelight from the founders of the National Organization for Women (including Friedan herself, presumably) and publicly 'gave vent to their rage in a rhetoric of sexual politics....' " Goreau also noted the ironic contradiction between Betty's defense of men and her ex-husband's refusal to pay child support.

The most scathing critique by far came from Ellen Willis, the radical theorist. Discussing Betty's restructuring proposals, she wrote:

> *In fact, they are a reductive and vulgarized rehash of arguments radical feminists have been making since the 60s, when the women's liberation movement first suggested—to the dismay of Friedan and her fellow responsibles—that careerism and room-at-the-top liberal integrationist politics were a dead end.... [The] suppression of women's sexual and personal freedom in the name of "family survival" and "the values of life" is the first law of sexism.... To associate herself with radicalism was to exchange the marginality of a housewife for the marginality of a rebel. But to ignore it was to risk being left behind, relegated to marginality.... To allow the logic of her perceptions would mean facing down her fears—of alienating men, offending Peoria, standing alone.... And so her second stage becomes a hodgepodge of pseudo-radical global optimism, modest reformism, and craven appeasement.*

In the daily *New York Times,* John Leonard, chief cultural correspondent and a shining light at the paper, panned the book. "Oddly, Miss Friedan blames the victim [for the backlash]...Let's back up. Has the women's movement, at whatever stage, come to a dead end just because Miss Friedan thinks so? Ask your 15-year-old daughter. Revolutions of sensibility and structure require more than two decades." Referring to Betty's discussion of "Alpha" and "Beta" styles of management, he wrote, "Licking the hand that batters you is neither Alpha nor Beta." The review so outraged Abe Rosenthal and his cultural editor, Arthur Gelb, that they

---

* A decade later, Susan Faludi placed Betty squarely in the backlash, writing that she was "yanking out the stitches in her own handiwork" and that "her book is punctuated with the tantrums of a fallen leader who is clearly distressed and angry that she wasn't allowed to be the Alpha wolf as long as she would have liked.... This solution puts the burden on women; the need for men to change barely figures in Friedan's new plan."

relieved John Leonard of his daily reviewing slot. Gradually they marginalized him, and a year later he left the paper.

Many of the reviews attacked Betty personally. All the royal pronouncements, the tirades against radicals and lesbians, the attacks on Gloria and Bella, were so many chickens coming home to roost. With *The Second Stage*, Betty had written herself out of the movement. "Betty felt awful about the reception of the book. It was a dark chapter," her friend Alida Brill said. Arthur Dubow said, "She felt people were drifting away from her. It was painful for her." *The Second Stage* did not make the *Times* best-seller list. With a second book that hadn't done well, she had a nagging sense that she was passé. She was deeply hurt by the personal attacks and by what she perceived as a misunderstanding of her meaning. She did not seem to realize that much of what she had written read like a recantation. "It was as if people criticize it without even reading it," she said. "There's not the slightest sense on my part of turning back on anything of the women's movement. In fact, every word I say in *The Second Stage* indicates how important I think the women's movement has been for women."

To cheer her up, Mary Jean Tully, who had just been named director of Marymount Manhattan College's new Midlife Institute, threw a party for her, held at the Park Avenue apartment of Elinor Guggenheimer, a founder of the Women's Forum, the network of professional women. At first, Betty was grumpy about her party. "We asked her for a list of women to invite," one of the organizers said, "and she said, 'I'm not going. If you're not inviting men, I'm not going to be there.' But she realized she was unhappy because of all the dumping on her, and she apologized." About eighty people gathered to celebrate her. Betty, wearing a low-necked gown in an antique tapestry fabric, gave a nostalgic speech about the young and crazy days of the movement: "I can think of all those scenes, planning sessions, in this apartment, and I can say if you were around you would have seen what appeared to be only a few sane people."

As the smoke from her burning bridges filled the air, Betty moved on to the next stage in her life: she was leaving for Cambridge on February 1 to be a fellow at the Institute of Politics at Harvard's John F. Kennedy School of Government. There she would lead a study group called "Transcending Sexual Politics" and continue to work on her book on aging. "I don't think this book can be seen separately from *The Feminine Mystique*," she told a reporter. "It's the other half. But I think *The Feminine Mystique* without *The Second Stage* would not be complete either. I feel that this completes my job in that sphere. Now, I can go on and live my life."

Alarms and Excursions

WHEN SALLY RIDE rocketed into space in 1983, her mother exclaimed, "Thank God for Gloria Steinem!" In the eighties, Betty Friedan virtually disappeared as a factor in organized feminism. For her, the decade began with endings—the break with David White; the negative reception of *The Second Stage* and its rejection by the movement; and the defeat of the ERA. She was getting old; she couldn't face her next project, which meant facing her own aging, the loss of power, loss of faculties, the long slow slide into a condition of not mattering. "When my friends threw a surprise party on my sixtieth birthday, I could have killed them all," she wrote. "Their toasts seemed hostile, insisting as they did that I publicly acknowledge reaching sixty, pushing me out of life, as it seemed, out of the race.... I was depressed for weeks after that birthday party, felt removed from them all. I could not face being sixty." The last place Betty Friedan wanted to be was out of the race.

Betty took refuge in the consolations of family. The children had scattered, but they began to see more of Betty after they married and had their own children. Jonathan, who had returned to Columbia after having dropped out and was now a graduate student in engineering, was the first. On October 25, 1981, he married Helen Nakdimen, who taught nursery school and later became a rabbi. The wedding was held in Betty's backyard at Sag Harbor. Bob Bedell, the Friedans' old friend from the early days of their marriage, reported: "My son, Ben [Jonathan's childhood friend], went to the wedding. There were speeches, and Carl got up and said, 'Well, Jonny, I hope you followed my instructions; you should never marry a woman you can't lay flat with one blow.' Everyone stood around and said, 'How gross can you be?' " (Jonathan and Helen produced Betty's first grandchild, Rafael. Betty took him to Hamptons fireworks parties; she crawled on all fours into low-pitched tents at his beckoning, and generally behaved like a besotted grandmother.)

Emily was married on June 10, 1984, also in Sag Harbor. She had graduated from Harvard Medical School in 1982, and was a resident in pediatrics at Boston City Hospital. Her husband, Eli Farhi of Buffalo, was also a doctor. It was a blistering hot day, and the huppa was wilted. Betty had spent days looking for a dress, but because of the weather she didn't wear it. She wore a sari-like dress she'd had for years. One woman appeared in a bathing suit with a skirt wrapped around it. "Carl brought a chick with long blond hair who went around snapping pictures," one guest said. "Everyone tried to look through her, around her. At the reception, which was held at the restaurant on the Sag Harbor dock, Carl made a speech about how wonderful Emily was. 'It was all due to'—we held our breath— 'her wonderful genes.' "

Daniel, the firstborn, did not marry until 1989. His wife, Ragnheidur Gudmundsdottir (nicknamed Agga), also a physicist, was a native of Iceland and had two children from a previous marriage. After the wedding, Carl gave a party for them in Teaneck. Betty came, escorted by Dick Laupot.

. . .

AT HARVARD IN 1982, Betty plunged into the fearsome subject of gerontology. The university installed her in an aerie, an apartment on the nineteenth floor of Mather House with ceiling-high windows that overlooked the campus quadrangles and the Charles River. She enlivened the nondescript furniture with her own paintings and pillows, Indian and Moroccan rugs, and a screen from Haiti painted with jungle animals. She was still overweight and her asthma was acting up, but she had begun taking better care of her health: she went to an exercise class and jogged two mornings a week.

She became interested in evolution and audited two courses: Stephen Jay Gould's course on the history of the earth and E. O. Wilson's on the evolution of life. In Betty's worldview, feminism was becoming smaller, less central. In the introduction to the twentieth-anniversary edition of *The Feminine Mystique* (1983), she wrote, "I became increasingly convinced that the whole process—breaking through the feminine mystique, and the women's movement for equality, and the transition to this second stage, as female values begin to be shared by the male—is not really a revolution at all, but simply a stage in human evolution, necessary for survival." Her optimistic outlook on life was such that she managed to find a progressive lesson in evolution, a theory informed by neither an ethic nor a higher purpose.

The intellectual atmosphere at Harvard stimulated her; she made new friends and recovered her zest for life. Still, she had never reconciled herself to being alone. She disliked going to the movies and traveling by herself. "One unfinished thing I'd like," she told a reporter, "I'd like to live with somebody again and make it work...but there's this damn public persona that makes it, I don't know, so hard."

Christmas was particularly difficult. She usually tried to get away to avoid the end-of-the-year doldrums, enlisting friends who were also in need of companionship. In 1983 she persuaded Arthur Dubow, who had separated from his wife, to spend the postholiday week at Rancho La Puerta, a spa in Tecate, Mexico, where she had been invited to stay as a guest several times before and give talks. "She reached out, she made an effort," he said. "And before I remarried, she would always call—Do you want to do this? Or this?—making sure I was not depressed. She does this for lots of people. She keeps track of people."

During the 1984–85 holiday, she went on an eight-day journalists' tour of Sandinista Nicaragua, arranged by Abbie Hoffman and his wife, Johanna Lawrenson. It was an odd sort of trip for her to be making. Anything even vaguely connected to Marxism repelled her, and in the past she had turned down many invitations to Russia, China, and Cuba, knowing that she would be circumscribed by officialdom. Perhaps she was intrigued by the adventure. Betty whiled away the time on the bus imagining who among the company might be in the CIA.

Her sixty-odd traveling companions included Jonathan Kwitny, an author and investigative reporter for *The Wall Street Journal*; Glenn Horowitz, a rare-book dealer, and his friend M. G. Lord, a political cartoonist for the *Los Angeles Times* (they later married); Art D'Lugoff, the owner of the Village Gate, and his wife, Avi, who were friends with Betty;

and Robin Reisig, a writer on assignment from *Newsweek,* whose asthma medicine Betty borrowed. Others she characterized as "some old left types and religious do-gooders who irritate me just as much as they always did, etc." Some of those she denigrated were not impressed with her, either, noting that at times she seemed tipsy. "Betty poured vodka into her coffee in the morning," Jonathan Kwitny said. "She carried it in a crumpled brown paper bag. It was never far from her."

Betty was skeptical about the Sandinistas. She asked every official she met if women were included in the literacy programs on an equal basis with men. But she also seemed to be off her stride, forgetting the lesson she had learned in Mexico City: the needs of Third World women were different from those of the First. One of the journalists observed, "We were talking to Fernando Cardenal, a famous priest and social theoretician who had been in exile from Somoza. The atmosphere of social reform was very exciting—women's programs of child care and nutrition, and sewing machines. A sewing machine was a huge technological leap. Women had a minimum of education. Betty reared up—'Why teach all this child care stuff? Why not teach computers?' She was very aggressive about it. She looked at them as though they were Westchester housewives. She wasn't asking them what they wanted." Betty probably did not look at Nicaraguan women as Westchester housewives. Her frame of reference was certainly larger than that. Her idea of computer training for women who needed help in basic survival was completely unrealistic, but she was probably thinking of ways to get them out of the domestic sphere and into the world, where computers, not sewing machines, were the cutting edge. Once again, however, her reputation had preceded her.

. . .

IN 1984, WHEN Betty's old friend Walter Mondale ran against Ronald Reagan, a group of feminist leaders decided it was time to have a woman on the ticket.* They settled on Geraldine Ferraro. Betty liked Ferraro's record. She particularly liked Ferraro's pro-choice stand: Ferraro, a Catholic, did not believe in abortion herself. (Betty had always treasured Catholic Women for Choice; its existence was a sign that the movement appealed to all kinds of women.) On July 4, a group of twenty-three feminists, including Ann Richards, then the treasurer and later the governor

---

* Among them were Judy Goldsmith, NOW president; Eleanor Smeal, former NOW president; Gloria Steinem; Bella Abzug; Frances Lear, founder of *Lear's* magazine; and Carol Bellamy, president of the New York City Council.

of Texas, and Marlene Johnson, the lieutenant governor of Minnesota, met with Mondale at the Radisson Hotel in St. Paul, Minnesota. Betty spoke eloquently and convincingly of the historic importance of having a woman candidate and its significance to all those in the country who were excluded from the political process.

At the July convention in San Francisco she was overcome with emotion; for the first time she was seated officially, as a Mondale delegate from New York, and thus spared the necessity of having to wangle press credentials to push the feminist agenda. The agenda was part of the platform. "All through this day of exultation...," she later wrote, "I cry for joy and pride at the power that we women have found in ourselves and given to each other to make this moment possible.... The famous lines from the ancient scholar, Hillel, come to my mind: 'If I am not for myself, who will be for me? If I am only for myself, what am I?' "

But Mondale was defeated, and the Reagan victory signaled the continuation of trends that alarmed Betty in the extreme. With the Sunday *Times Magazine* as her pulpit, she tried to rally younger women who seemed unconscious of the dangers facing them as Reagan whittled away at abortion rights and antidiscrimination laws. She laid out a ten-point program to revitalize feminism. It included consciousness raising (the value of which she now apparently accepted); forgetting about the "dead end" of pornography and focusing on "the real obscenity of poverty"; changing the divorce laws; and infusing "values based on female sensitivities to life...in[to] every discipline and profession."

Hers seemed to be a voice in the wilderness, flinging a challenge in the face of the Greed Decade and the religious right, attacking the dramatic shift to mean-spiritedness as a guide to public policy. Emboldened by the anti-abortion, anti-ERA stances of the administration, the lunatic fringe of the pro-life movement had progressed from waving around pickled fetuses in jars to bombing abortion clinics and painting swastikas on synagogues. As a corollary to the new alliance between church and state, anti-Semitism was on the rise.

It was here that Betty found a new mission. The American Jewish Congress enlisted her to fight the hate and made her the chair of its Commission on the Status of Women. The arrangement was mutually beneficial: the congress needed a headline getter; Betty needed a forum. In 1985, when Ronald Reagan went to a memorial ceremony at Bitburg cemetery, where members of the SS were buried, the congress organized another memorial, at Perlacher cemetery in Stadelheim, this one to honor Christian students of the anti-Nazi underground. Betty was one of fifty official mourners.

Betty's attitude toward organized religion had not changed since she told Gladys Carter, so long ago, that it messed up your brain. In Peoria, her mother had run the temple Sisterhood and been the principal of the Sunday school, and Betty had been confirmed when she was thirteen, but the experience had left virtually no impression on her. She had already found God wanting: "I announced to the rabbi a month before my confirmation that I no longer believed in God. And he said, keep it to yourself until the confirmation is over. So, actress that I am, I gave the flower offering, raising my eyes to the heavens." Feminism had strengthened her aversion: as in all patriarchal religions, women could not enter the male hierarchy and were still forbidden to participate in the holiest rites. She was an outsider in her own religion. Yet her experience as a Jew in Peoria was unquestionably a mainspring of her passion for justice, and she had never abandoned her heritage.

In July 1984, Betty went to Israel for a dialogue on the status of Jewish women, "Woman as Jew; Jew as Woman, an Urgent Inquiry." The consuming issue of the day in Israel was the fact that the birth rate among Jews was lower than that among Palestinians. The politicians wanted women to forget about careers and go home again, to sacrifice their own needs for a larger cause without a corresponding sacrifice from men. On opening night, Betty was one of the keynote speakers, and the audience gave her a standing ovation. She was in her element. A reporter wrote, "Every inch the high priestess was Betty Friedan in her flowing tent-dresses, in the imperious gesture with which she swept back the fall of her long-bobbed gray hair, in the small smile with which she acknowledged the constant stream of accolades from the speakers' platform." Betty's answer to the problem was the one she had been advocating all along: bridging the either/or of work and family by restructuring work, home, and community.

At meetings during the next few days, Betty unified the women, following a pattern she often used with groups: dominating the women, threatening those who disagreed with her, and making a list of demands that culminated in a dramatic action. She did not necessarily always get what she wanted, but she always got something; and she always stirred people up and forced them to act, leaving something positive in her wake. During her threats phase, many people were offended by her autocratic manner and her shocking rhetoric: she threatened to tell Jewish groups in America to cut off aid to Israel if the women's complaints were not heeded. Then, on the spur of the moment, she led the women on an exhilarating march to the King David Hotel to present their grievances to Shimon Peres (Labor

Party) and Yitzhak Shamir (Likud), who were negotiating the fine print of their proposed unity government. In front of the television cameras the two men promised to consider the women's demands. If they did so, nothing came of it: their proposed new government did not include a single woman. The women at the conference, however, established the Israeli Women's Network, and the Knesset created a commission on equality.

In July 1985, the American Jewish Congress sent Betty and Bella Abzug to Nairobi for the third U.N. world conference on women. Their mission was to prevent anti-Semitism from becoming the centerpiece it had been at the previous U.N. conference, held in Copenhagen in 1980. The heroine of Copenhagen had been Laila Khaled, who helped skyjack an El Al plane. In Nairobi there was a safety valve—the Peace Tent. The blue-and-white-striped tent had a conflict resolution center, where women could hash out violent political disagreements.

Betty was intrigued by an African village custom of sitting under a tree and philosophizing. When she learned that it was the men who sat around while the women worked in the fields, she decided to adopt the custom. Every morning at eleven-thirty, on the dusty quad of the University of Nairobi, she went to her tree. Its spreading, leafy branches provided enough shade for about thirty people. Sitting cross-legged on the ground, she was the Great Mother, the fountain of wisdom, the historic monument. Nikki Beare, a NOW member who was there as a U.N. reporter, said, "It was awesome. All these women from all over the world listening to her, and Betty loving every minute of it. She was talking about how the movement got started in the U.S., organizing it, how women could make a difference." By the end of the week, a reverent semicircle of about a hundred women were drinking in her words and telling her the outrages of their lives. One question came up constantly, asked by Arab, African, and Asian women: how could they begin to say that they didn't want eight children, and they didn't want their husband to have three wives, without being ostracized? Betty did not tell them what to do; she told them that whatever they did, they had to do it together, and their voices would be heard through the power of their unity. One day the Iranians came, shrouded in black, surrounded by their male guards, and occupied the tree, nailing a picture of the Ayatollah Khomeini to it. Betty moved to another tree. The next day, both trees had been appropriated, and so had the space between them. Betty moved her people into the sun, telling them, "This is the way women have to move in the world now. We move ahead, we are pushed back, we must regroup."

Betty wouldn't have been Betty without some sort of contretemps, and she had one on the first day. At lunch, she attacked a Mexican woman who told her the conference should deal with U.S. foreign policy toward Latin America. Betty considered women who put national issues first to be pawns of their male governments and told the woman so. "You are not a feminist," she said. The Mexican woman started to cry and left the table. Betty explained to the others why she was right and the woman was wrong, but she regretted the incident later and wondered about the connection (if any) between U.S. feminism and imperialism. She also berated herself for being "arrogant."

Betty and Bella almost had a food fight in the Peace Tent, but basically, they were on the same side. Bella also had a tree, and relished it as much as Betty. Ten years later, Rosalind Harris, the finance officer of the NGOs, said, "Bella reminds me frequently how she sat under that tree in Nairobi and the women were all at her feet." But Bella's great triumph came on the afternoon she took over the conference, commandeering the largest auditorium for her three-hour workshop, "What If Women Ruled the World?" Delegates from the official conference played hooky to hear her.

After the official delegates finished attacking U.S. foreign policy, they moved on to women's issues, and a plan of action was adopted by consensus. It included parental leave and day care, the sharing of household work, recognition of the economic value of housework, and equal pay for comparable work. Largely through the efforts of the Kenyans and the Egyptians, the resolution equating Zionism and racism was removed. Ever optimistic, Betty said, "A decade that began in acrimony in Mexico ended with success in Africa." The great thing was all those women talking to each other.

. . .

In 1986, Betty turned sixty-five. She was deep into research for *The Fountain of Age,* still trying to come to grips with her own aging, and very grumbly about the planned celebration, but such a milestone could not be ignored. Mary Jean Tully orchestrated the party, which was held in the Mike Todd Room at the Palladium on East Fourteenth Street. The Palladium was the latest in spot, a vast Art Deco club built into the shell of an old theatre and owned by the former owners of Studio 54, Steve Rubell and Ian Schrager, who had recently gotten out of jail. Almost three hundred people attended. The celebration included a roast (a light toasting, really) and songs and skits. One was an impersonation of Jim Silberman, Betty's editor, creaking across the stage on crutches, waiting for the book.

Marlene Sanders, the television news correspondent, emceed. Jonathan Friedan, who was getting his engineering degree from Columbia, gave a speech that began, "In our house, breakfast was not a regular meal," and reminisced about the morning he and a friend were leaving to go on a hitchhiking trip. All they wanted was the money Betty was going to give them for the trip, but that morning she was fixing breakfast, standing at the stove and waving a spatula in the air, trying to keep them from going.

Elinor Guggenheimer, a New York City consumer/child care advocate who had once written a musical, *Potholes*, wrote the lyrics to the songs, which were sung to well-known tunes:

"I Like Boys" (sung to the tune of "I Hate Men")

> *I like boys*
> *I'd rather play with them than with my toys*
> *The average little boy, he may be crude and like a peasant*
> *But evenings when the moon is full or even just a crescent*
> *I find that boys have something that can be extremely pleasant*
> *So I like boys.*
> *I love men*
> *Too well, although not wisely now and then*
> *At times they may be serious, at other times they're toying*
> *In either case I'm apt to find them pretty damn annoying*
> *But they have something I don't have that I have been enjoying*
> *So I love men.*

Another song, about Betty's Sag Harbor parties, was sung to the tune of "Enjoy Yourself":

> *Her parties in Sag Harbor, they are known for chic and style—and*
> *She starts by asking one or two then ends with half the island....*

> *There's usually a house guest who's distinguished, also famous,*
> *The party is for him but no one knows just what his name is,*
> *They're told he's intellectual and very virile looking,*
> *But no one ever meets him—he is in the kitchen cooking.*

Mounds of well-wishing telegrams arrived, in particular a flattering one from Gloria Steinem:

From *The Feminine Mystique* of the 1960s to the Masculine Mystique of the PEN Conference, I thank you for always being there.* I thank you for giving all of us the gifts of your energy and caring. I would be dancing in your birthday at the Palladium tonight, but I'm at a long-planned benefit for Meals on Wheels. After all, you and I both may be radical old ladies who need Meals on Wheels to give us energy for our next demonstration. When I passed fifty, I realized that fifty is what forty used to be. But watching you, I think that sixty-five is now what forty used to be. I wish you a long life and the great pleasure of seeing the difference you have made for so many. In sisterhood.

In return, Betty sent Gloria a conciliatory letter.

* At the January 1986 International PEN Conference, run by Norman Mailer, a group of women led by Grace Paley protested the lack of women on panels and in decision-making roles. According to *The New York Times* (Edwin McDowell, "Women at PEN Caucus Demand a Greater Role," January 17, 1986), Betty "assumed an informal leadership role in the caucus." However, one of the women in the caucus said that "Betty came in, gave a rousing speech and got coverage. She wasn't around for the women's group that formed to talk about reform."

27

Sag Harbor

BETTY WAS IN her glory in Sag Harbor. The days of drunken parties and duck pâté were gone; she was an important social force, central to the celebrity culture. Her doings and those of her friends were chronicled in the local papers, one of which was an endless society page. She would come home, check the answering machine, and count the invitations. "Among our friends, she is one of the few who goes to benefits without paying. She is invited as a guest," a commune member said. Her old college friend Joan Cook, who came from Rome to visit during the summer, called her "the Madame de Staël of our age."

She entertained constantly: lunches, dinners, book parties for friends. She favored buffets, served on a long table in the backyard. At Sunday brunches Craig Claiborne mixed the Bloody Marys and Gael Greene scrambled the eggs. One guest described a last-minute party for forty: "With only a week's warning, she gave a wedding reception for Susan Wood and Joe Haggerty. It was Memorial Day weekend. Jeep-y kinds of cars converged on her little street from all directions with people carrying food. Inside the house, Betty is waving a drink and welcoming guests. Everyone else is burdened with food; her houseguests are putting it in the oven or the fridge. And Betty is wandering through the party. She is waving at the bar. She never did anything other than greet people. Her guests were working their butts off, dealing with all this stuff."

Her fans and regulars were a group of about forty or fifty people, well connected to the media, not all of whom agreed with her politics. It was more important to Betty for her guests to be interesting and successful— or celebrated—than to be feminists. The group included Elaine Benson, who owned a famous Bridgehampton art gallery; Helen Rattray, editor and publisher of the *East Hampton Star*; E. L. Doctorow; Kurt Vonnegut; and William Gaddis. Others were Abe Rosenthal, Wilfrid Sheed and Miriam Ungerer, Richard Reeves and his wife Catherine O'Neill, John and Jacqueline Leo, Ina and Robert Caro, Linda Francke, John Scanlon, Robert Heilbroner, Larry Rivers, Budd and Betsy Schulberg, and Mortimer Zuckerman. Selma Shapiro, a publicist and the wife of Jim Silberman (the couple were weekend guests), said, "She did things so effortlessly. You weren't under any pressure or obligation, but everything she planned was such fun, you wanted to do it—whether it was the beach or shopping or a party or just sitting in the living room talking. You always felt comfortable in her house. You never had a feeling of 'Oh my God, where does this cup belong?' You were part of her team, her family."

Parties were Betty's lifeblood. The fear of being left out had never deserted her, and she was rarely alone. She often butterflied around to three or four parties a night, before and after dinner, whirling through overlapping circles of writers and artists, academics and doctors, editors and financiers, the Manhattan elite whose competitive careers provided an edge to the occasion. She sometimes had big fights with people at parties; she was frequently bored and could be seen sitting by herself, ignoring and ignored, but she was driven to go. "She had fears for her position," said Dick Laupot, her old standby. "One summer she was anxious about whether she had been dropped off the A list."

As always, people were lined up like armies, for her and against her. Shana Alexander said, "She is adored out here. If you have a party or a benefit, it's important to invite her." But she also displayed a legendary rudeness toward women, a breathtaking incivility for which she was fiercely resented. She did not care. She did exactly as she chose. She invited distinguished men to her parties without including their less accomplished wives. She turned her back impatiently on women, sometimes when they were in the middle of a sentence, if she decided they were boring. Legions of women complained that they had been introduced to Betty dozens of times but she never recognized them or remembered who they were—unless she needed something from them. Her female friends notwithstanding, she became known as the feminist who did not like women. Her friends made excuses for these lapses. It was usually the same excuse—her eyesight was so bad she didn't recognize people. This was true as far as it went, but somehow she recognized the men. "I have the ur-anecdote about Betty," a male Sag Harbor friend said. "I was talking with a woman at a party, and Betty came over, turned her back to the woman, and said, 'I want to invite you to a dinner party I'm having.' The woman stood there, slack-jawed." Whether she was adored or deplored, Betty's stature and social power carried the day, and even those she angered accepted her invitations.

When Betty was not on parade, when she focused on people, she was a generous friend. For years she pushed Ina Caro to move out of the shadow of her husband, Bob, and write her own book. (Ina finally did, in 1994.) Through her extensive network, Betty helped her friends' careers. One summer she arranged a show at Elaine Benson's gallery of the sculptures of Robert Cook, the husband of her old college friend Joan. When friends were ill, she haunted the hospital. She was particularly generous about giving blurbs for books. Lorraine Dusky, who wrote *Birthmark,* said, "The book is about how I gave a child up for adoption. She 'got it.' She understood how terrible it was for me to give the child up. She came to the book party at the top of the Time-Life Building. A lot of the women I had interviewed were there. They were thrilled and asked her to sign the book, too. She was embarrassed about it. She came to me and asked, 'What should I do?' She was aces."

Betty packed her house with guests; she had affairs and one-night stands and, when there was no one special, a group of men to take her to parties. Her frequent escorts included Ed Gifford, a widower, who did theatrical public relations; Joseph Machlis, the author of a book on music that sold steadily for years; and Arthur Prager, who had written a history of *Punch* and ran the Irish Georgian Society, a small historic preservation group. Not long after she bought her house, she became friends with Nelson Algren, who was living across the street from her. He was ill and indigent, but he had once been Simone de Beauvoir's great inamorato, a connection that must have made him particularly desirable. Betty had told their mutual friend, Kurt Vonnegut, that she wanted to meet him, but he was gun-shy: Beauvoir had betrayed him by writing about their affair, and he was not anxious for another such involvement. One afternoon he heard Betty's car rattling by, and he decided that anyone who drove a car like that couldn't be all bad. He became Betty's escort.

One day they went into town together, Betty driving at her usual cruising speed of fifteen miles an hour. As she turned left onto Main Street, the car door swung open and Nelson fell out. He got up, ran to the car and jumped back in, and said, "Goddammit, Betty, you have to be more careful." She said, "This is hard enough without your goddamn jokes." He died not long after.[*] "Betty told the story as if she was the one who was responsible for his death," her friend Dick Reeves said.

Betty began to invest in new relationships, cultivating younger women as older people do, as a way to keep herself young and to stay abreast of new ideas. In the late 1970s, at about the same time she was mothering her niece Laurie Goldstein, Betty became friends with Alida Brill, a writer and editor who was one year younger than her son Daniel. Alida's mother had been one of the women whose lives Betty had changed: within months of reading *The Feminine Mystique* she had gone out and gotten a job. Betty and Alida shared a passion for clothes and went on marathon shopping sprees, daring each other to buy things. They had eccentric tastes—long dresses with different prints on each sleeve, unusual patchwork patterns. "She has a wicked sense of humor—fabulous," Alida said. "A take on something—one sentence or three words and you'll howl. She felt we were girlfriends. For me she was another mother. We stayed up late talking about literature, everything. I love her." They worked on political campaigns, and Betty advised Alida during her affair with her future husband, Steven Scheuer, who was in the middle of a messy separation from his wife. In 1981, when Betty was in the Hamptons, Alida had a stroke. "She took a helicopter into town," Alida said. "She didn't have much money. I have seen her not be narcissistic."

. . .

IN 1986, BETTY became aware of a community of successful black professionals who lived in their own section of Sag Harbor and had never mingled with the whites. At a party in the city at Larry Lader's (the cofounder of NARAL), she had met and become friends with William

---

[*] There are several versions of this story, which has been lavishly embellished with each telling. According to one, "They were bombed out of their skulls. They left a party and drove around a circle. It was a foggy night, and Betty couldn't see how to get out of the circle. She was nattering away and didn't notice when the door opened and he fell out. She went around the circle, and he got back in as she came around again." Betty said that when Nelson Algren was a guest on Studs Terkel's radio program, he told the story as if she had pushed him out of the car, and when she went on the program, Terkel asked her why she had done it.

Demby, a black novelist (*Beetlecreek*) and screenwriter, to whom she is reported to have said, "Why don't we ever see you?" That meeting was the genesis of her next project, the Sag Harbor Initiative, a dialogue between the races intended to include local issues.

It was vintage Betty Friedan, grandiose in concept, addressed to weighty issues—the political, economic, social, and cultural divisions in America—and packed with names, and it made a big splash. Some sessions were televised by News 12 Long Island and picked up by C-Span. In addition to Betty and William Demby, the prime movers were E. L. Doctorow; Bob Hirschfield, a commune member who was the director of television programming at the City University of New York; and William and Patricia Pickens. Bill Pickens, who owned an international management consulting firm, was a grandson of one of the founders of the NAACP. According to an announcement of the first meeting, the Initiative would "consider some disturbing economic, political and cultural issues of contemporary American life.... The problems our society faces are not subject to traditional solutions. This is a town meeting, in the spirit of democracy." The idea was to have a weekend of discussion, find solutions, and stir people to action. Although the Initiative provoked some eyeball-rolling among Betty's crowd, everyone participated.

Some of the early newspaper coverage was highly skeptical. Betty was furious about it and shut out a reporter who scornfully labeled the dialogue radical chic all over again:

> It was a day for the haves to talk to the haves about the have-nots.... The weekend-long brain trust was the brainchild of Betty Friedan, who is widely regarded as a feminist, a notion that can only be taken on faith by many women who have actually had dealings with Betty Friedan.... "Enough of tennis and softball," said Friedan, who has never been known to play either one.... And so it went, people with extra homes clucking about the state of the homeless.

Betty also had her usual problem of turnover with assistants, several of whom left in quick succession. "Betty would call me up and yell at me. It was extremely unpleasant," said one. Another found herself becoming Betty's chauffeur and taking her clothes to the cleaners, among other items of maintenance.

The original idea of integration was lost as Betty's vision expanded into the lofty realm of social philosophy, to the detriment of local issues. After the October 1987 stock market crash, she held a special economic symposium with her friend Amitai Etzioni, who had done the first Economic Summit with her, almost twenty-five years before. Betty headed a panel, "The Retreat from Equality," which considered special-interest groups, the courts, blacks, women, labor, speech and dissent, and the question "Why have liberalism, humanism, feminism, civil rights and social welfare become dirty words in America?" In an interview with *Dan's Papers*, a free Sag Harbor weekly, she spoke of "people having to step over the bodies of the homeless on the beaches of Los Angeles and the streets of New York as they enter restaurants that charge $100 a dinner.... There is an increasing meanness of standards of living forced on many people underneath, not only new polarizations but hidden ones."

The Initiative lasted for three years. "Its failure to attract the black community...was painfully evident," said an article in the *Southampton* (N.Y.) *Press.* "About five percent of the audience accommodated in a 300-seat auditorium were black. It also seemed as if year-round residents...most notably those of the working class, were absent." Some local people viewed the Initiative as a cocktail party that had little connection to their issues.

Arthur Prager said, "Betty didn't understand. She thought they [black Sag Harbor residents] were not being included. But blacks don't want to see whites. They are doctors, lawyers, judges, important professional people. They want to see their friends on weekends. Years ago, John Steinbeck had a big lawn party to raise money for LBJ. No blacks came. He was very hurt. There was no enthusiasm for the Initiative, that's why it died. The old Saggies laughed at it."

· · ·

BETTY'S MOTHER DIED in 1988, not long after her ninetieth birthday. Betty, her brother Harry, who had a house in Palm Springs, and Laurie, who had moved to Los Angeles, had celebrated the birthday with Miriam at lunch at the Ritz Carlton Hotel there. Miriam's health was deteriorating, and they had talked about moving her to a nursing home. That night, Betty had a severe asthma attack, knowing that her mother wanted nothing to do with nursing homes. For over twenty years, Miriam had been living an active life at Leisure World, her senior community. She and her third husband had moved there from Chicago when she was in her early sixties. (He had died when she was seventy.)

At eighty-seven, Miriam broke her leg, but carried on as usual. Then she tripped over a telephone cord in her room and broke her hip. She recovered; abjuring crutches, she walked with a cane, but the trauma had jarred her. Harry received a call: Miriam was refusing to show her ID, as required, for meals. Leisure World was not equipped to handle people who could not fend for themselves. Not long after her birthday lunch, Betty and Harry took her to Milwaukee, where Harry's second daughter, Nancy, a psychotherapist, found a nursing home.

While they were getting Miriam settled, Betty finally made her peace with her mother, her "great unconscious impetus." "God knows, I had been fighting against my mother almost all my life; it seems that love-hate never dies," she wrote. "But I had come to admire her guts, her survivor's strength. Before she left Leisure World, and now again, this last time in Wisconsin, I was able to put my arms around her and say, 'I love you, Mother,' and mean it. And she said, 'I know you do, darling, and I love you too.' I knew I would never see her again. She died a week later, just didn't wake up one morning."

Miriam was buried in Peoria, and Betty spoke at the funeral. Amy, who was estranged from the family, came with her two sons. She had written to Betty now and then, wanting to get together, but Betty had not been interested. Amy had lived and taught for many years in Long Island and had become a successful artist—her paintings were exhibited in New York—and then she had stopped painting and started writing poetry. If any of the old competition between the sisters remained, Betty saw the obverse side. In 1997 she said, "All her life she was just obsessed, kind of blaming, a lifelong obsession with jealousy of me. She shouldn't have been. She is a very good artist. But she stopped painting. She decided she would write the truth about our family. She is still obsessed." Harry said, "She became very bitter toward us. She vacillated between anger and wanting a warm relationship. We have a nonrelationship." Amy refused to be interviewed.

Betty would return to Peoria six years later (1996) to eulogize Harriet Vance Parkhurst, a role model she could never emulate, who had been ill with cancer for many years. Barbara Van Auken, who had started the first NOW chapter in Peoria, said, "Betty loved Harriet with all her heart. Harriet really *worked*—charities, politics. Betty hit on that—Harriet was a loving, generous person, what everyone would like to be. She never made you feel bad because you weren't as good as she was. Betty said she was her inspiration."

28

California

IN JANUARY 1986, one month before her sixty-fifth birthday party, Betty began a new life in Los Angeles. Her asthma had been bothering her, especially in the winter; she had been making too many trips to hospital emergency rooms and taking too much cortisone. For the next seven years, until she finished *The Fountain of Age,* she lugged her overstuffed carpetbags and boxes of notes back and forth, from coast to coast, spending four winter months at the University of Southern California. Dr. Robert Butler, her guide through the morass of age research, helped her get a position as a visiting scholar at the Andrus Gerontology Center. Betty found an apartment at the Sea Colony, a building with a heated pool at the beach in Santa Monica, and furnished it with a mixture of bought, borrowed, and rented furniture. (She leased a different apartment each year.) The freeways terrified her. She walked wherever she could and cadged rides when she couldn't.

At USC, following her lifelong pattern, she immediately became involved in several things at once and began generating new organizations. Alida Brill had put her in touch with Judith Stiehm, who ran the Institute for the Study of Women and Men in Society (SWMS) at the social work school, and there she started the think tank she had tried to establish for so many years at other universities.* In addition, Betty held the post of visiting distinguished professor at the journalism school, and during her last two years she was at the business school's Leadership Institute, giving a series of lectures and doing workshops with executives on feminist issues, corporate culture, and aging. Warren Bennis, who ran the Leadership Institute and with whom she became friends, said, "She is full of energy, extraordinary energy. She is extremely generous to friends. She homed in on and was very responsive to my personal dilemmas. I was going to do something very self-destructive and self-defeating, and she argued me out of it, and she was right. When she starts paying attention, she is phenomenally insightful."

For the think tank, Betty found another Kay Clarenbach in Madeleine Stoner, a professor of social policy at the school of social work, who organized and moderated it. The think tank ranged widely over feminist issues, including such new ones as surrogate mothers and the wisdom of taking hormones at menopause. Although Betty welcomed new ideas, she was adamant on certain subjects, and hormone treatment was one of them. She was totally opposed to it. "Betty had read, not the empirical studies, but the analysis of them," Madeleine Stoner said, "and told off Dr. Susan Love, the co-director of the foremost breast cancer program at UCLA. Dr. Love had quoted data that the results are mixed." But Betty did learn something about the sexual issues she had always scorned. "Members of homosexual couples gave a lot of insights on intimate bonding among equals in our sessions on intimacy," she wrote. "I began to realize also that the issue of sexual harassment strikes a deep chord among women, increasing perhaps as men's rage increases with the erosion of job security."

Some of Betty's friends participated in the sessions: Marilyn Bergman, the first woman to be president of the American Society of Composers and Performers (ASCAP), and the founder of the Hollywood Women's Political Committee; Barbara Boxer and Dianne Feinstein; Anne Taylor Fleming; and Norman Lear. Barbra Streisand, for whom Marilyn Bergman and her husband, Alan, had written songs, came to a session on sexuality. Streisand was interested in the same problem Betty had: how successful and talented women could have a sexual relationship with men without being used.

---

* Diana Meehan, director of SWMS, created and funded the Betty Friedan Think Tank. Diana would also fund the Vermont Economic Summit, which Betty attended, to work out a feminist agenda for Bill Clinton shortly after he was elected president in 1992. His executive order mandating family leave was the Summit's prime recommendation.

For perhaps the first time, Betty confronted the issue of violence against women. For obvious reasons, she had always avoided it, and she scorned the prevailing feminist line of women as victims. Indeed, because of her known position, she had been blackballed as a speaker at the Women Against Violence Against Women march, during the 1992 Democratic Convention in New York. Inside the convention she had been a star; women surrounded her and asked for her autograph as she made her way across the floor to greet the Mondales. At her seat in the gallery, a constant stream of delegates, guests, and media people came to honor her. Outside, she had been ignored.

Betty had blamed Barbara Seaman for blocking her from speaking. Their friendship had waned long before, and she and Barbara were quarreling at the time: Barbara was in the middle of a nasty divorce, and Betty had run into her husband and accepted his invitation to dinner. Barbara had felt betrayed, but she insisted she had had nothing to do with Betty's exclusion. Others involved in the march said that Women Against Pornography, the group that invited most of the speakers, had had the final say, and Betty had trashed them.

Although it was a big departure for Betty to discuss violence in public, she focused not on physical abuse, but on guns, which were being advertised to women. In 1993, with grants from the MacArthur Foundation and the California Wellness Foundation, she held a three-day gun control summit at Mount St. Mary's Doheny campus in South Central Los Angeles. The theme was that women don't become equal by imitating men's behavior. Rabbi Laura Geller, the first woman rabbi of a major urban congregation, led the group. (Many years before, the rabbi had called on Betty for help: she had been invited to a conference in Arizona, a non-ERA state, and could not decide whether to go. If she stayed away, she could accomplish nothing at the conference. Betty had suggested that *she* be invited and that they hold a rump convention. "The entire conference came to hear her talk," Rabbi Geller said. "We demonstrated at the Arizona state house. Male rabbis joined us. She is an electrifying speaker. She made a connection between feminism, Judaism, and being an outsider.")

People from all over the country came to Betty's gun control summit: mothers of gang members; women whose children had been victims, national leaders in gun control and public health—everyone, it seemed, but representatives of organized feminism. Ann Reiss Lane, a member of the Los Angeles Police Commission, said, "The League of Women Voters, NOW, NWPC—the amount of animosity [toward Betty] in those organizations! They are filled with the walking wounded. A call from Betty wouldn't elicit much response." Ann became coordinator of Women Against Gun Violence, the organization that grew out of the conference. WAGW was a broad coalition whose members ranged from the Pasadena Junior League to mothers of South Central gang members.

Despite her successes, Betty's irrational outbursts continued to ruin many occasions. In the last year of the think tank she was not allowed to talk to the secretaries. When her fit of temper had blown over and she had moved on to the next thing, some of those she had wounded were surprised to get a call from her asking for help. She phoned one woman she had attacked and asked her to put together the gun violence conference. The woman turned her down. "I didn't want to work with her. She started to scream at me. She had no time, she was busy, no one was supporting her, no one appreciated how busy she was, she was editing her book—and she slammed down the phone. Later, I discovered she was going to a spa."

The think tank ran its course and ended in 1994. As a finale, some of its sessions were published in the *American Behavioral Scientist*. Betty's classes at the journalism school were more problematic. Jack Langguth, the professor who brought her in and had become her friend, said, "We had a lackluster leadership and director. They didn't see what Betty brought to the program. The mothers of the young women in the class were excited that she was there—and parents are the ones who are paying for it—and C-Span televised her conferences." Some of the students took offense at her abusive style, others who required a structured situation had difficulty with her freewheeling methods. "Betty can be a little bit impatient," Jack said. "She is a perfectionist, and expects things to be done promptly and to her liking. She would get a little testy. Some of the students wanted to quit. I talked to them and told them the tirade was not personal. When they found that out, they began to feel a great deal of affection for her and she for them."

In 1988, Betty and Nancy Woodhull, the founding editor of *USA Today*, started a new seminar, "Women, Men and Media" (named after Betty's course), to examine the way women were portrayed in the press, on TV, and in the movies. During the early days of the movement, media images (wife/mother, secretary/assistant, or sex object) had met with intense scrutiny and protest, but women were no longer paying much attention to the subject. Eventually, Women, Men and Media operated primarily on a grant from the Gannett Foundation. For the first few years Betty earned $40,000 a year for doing panel discussions in New York, Washington, and Los Angeles. Her subjects included the economic scapegoating of women, the coverage of Hillary Clinton as an example of the right-wing backlash, the feminist emphasis on sexual issues and victimhood, and the glorification of anorexia in fashion.

In the course of Women, Men and Media, Betty renewed her old friendship with Marlene Sanders, the television correspondent whose film had been stolen at the First Congress to Unite Women. Marlene, who had been the first female vice president of network news (ABC), became the organizer of the panels and gradually, of Betty's life. She found new secretaries for Betty when the old ones quit and helped her move from city to city. Betty stayed with Marlene on visits to New York when her Lincoln Plaza apartment was sublet and she had no place to go. "She depends on me because I am the best-organized person she knows," Marlene said. "She takes you to expensive dinners and pays back that way."

. . .

DESPITE ALL HER activities, despite being surrounded by people, Betty could not assuage her loneliness. In an alcoholic moment, she bemoaned to a friend that she never should have divorced Carl even though he had hit her. She became interested in Dr. Roy Walford, who was a professor of pathology at the UCLA School of Medicine and the physician for the Biosphere 2 team.* Betty's friend Gloria Goldsmith, a playwright and screenwriter who had been president of Women in Film, said, "She once brought him to a dressy party at my house. He wore a tie-dyed suit. He was a disappointment to her. She wanted to go to parties—he wanted to be with his biosphere people." Nevertheless, Betty invited him to be her guest of honor at Sag Harbor in the summer of 1994, where she served a buffet of life-prolonging foods, saturated with sweet potatoes in various forms, from recipes created by his daughter Lisa. Marian Burros, reporting for The New York Times, wrote, "There was cold, soggy 'pizza,' mushy, cold 'lasagna,' salad dressed with vinegar and 'chocolate' cake that stuck to the roof of your mouth." One guest called it "Fido food." Another guest, asked by the reporter about the food, said, "I can't tell you or I'll never be invited back to Betty's again." A third guest said, "It was a typical Hamptons scene—the guests were trashing the hostess, who was standing two feet away from them."

Betty was careful about her health, swimming and exercising regularly, and walking distances that most Californians would have driven. Three

---

* Biosphere, an experimental controlled environment, was an artificially created ecosystem in the Arizona desert.

nights a week she took complimentary classes at the Pritikin Longevity Center that included meals and lectures. "P.M." (evening) offered two tracks, advanced and slow, and after being checked, Betty had been put in the slow one. She was extremely upset about it, and had a tantrum on the exercise floor. Sheila Savage, Pritikin's in-house troubleshooter, had dinner with Betty and calmed her down. "She accused them of ageism, said it was a sleazy place, and how dare they! Her indignation was so strong." A male stripper, hired to celebrate someone's birthday, was performing in the dining room, and Betty had to laugh in spite of herself. Sheila drove her home. "She invited me inside, and we talked. I got a picture of a woman desperately hanging on to her youth. She was in her 1959 head and refused to leave it."

Betty had many old friends in Los Angeles: Natalie Gittelson; Al and Heidi Toffler; Ted and Pat Apstein, to whom she had rented the barn in Snedens Landing; Norman Lear; and her Sag Harbor neighbors Dick Reeves and Cathy O'Neill. Harry wintered in Palm Springs, and Arthur Dubow had a ranch outside Tucson. She was at the center of several overlapping coteries of people. She worked with Marilyn Bergman's rich, star-studded Hollywood Women's Political Committee, where she helped write campaign speeches for Barbara Boxer and Dianne Feinstein. Another group went to Sunday evening movie screenings at Norman Lear's. A third grew out of the journalism school: Jack Langguth; Joe Saltzman; Ed Guthman, who had the distinction of having been on Nixon's enemies list; Marcia Brandwynne, a broadcaster; Anne Taylor Fleming and her husband, Karl; and Norman Corwin, who had written classic radio plays in the 1930s. "We had hilariously raucous, opinionated dinners, mostly at Jack's house," Anne Fleming said. "We were a little gaggle of people, and we yelled a lot and laughed a lot." At a birthday party Betty gave at her apartment, then on Sunset Boulevard and Alpha Loma Drive, Jack gave her a sexy bright red chiffon teddy and a boa trimmed in maribou feathers. "She loved it," Anne Fleming said. "She put on the boa and swished around."

After a while, Betty began to wear out her welcome, as she often did. It was as if all her discontents had caught up with her. Sometimes alcohol set her off, which seemed to be the case with her explosions at one of Madeleine Stoner's dinner parties. The party was an elegant, catered affair for fourteen with two tables, one in the den and one in the dining room. Betty, who had earlier been called by the newspapers for comments on the Lorena Bobbitt court decision, was discussing the case when another guest interrupted with her own opinions.* Madeleine Stoner said, "The woman was very pretentious, without reason, and uninformed. Her opinions were banal and sexist. Betty's were correct." Betty was not clear about what happened next, but according to Madeleine, she moved into the second room, where she exploded again. "This time, Betty was wrong," Madeleine said. "She was not hearing right. She was so irritated she couldn't think straight." At the second table, where dessert was being served, one of the men praised a Supreme Court ruling against racially segregated Mardi Gras floats in New Orleans; it proved, he said, that the Constitution was a living, evolving document. Another guest at the table said, "Suddenly she burst out, 'How dare you insult the Constitution!' She turned to Madeleine and said, 'I don't like your friends. I'm never coming to your dinner parties again. My friends in New York would never talk this way. They're much more intelligent.' " The man told Betty he didn't care to sit at the same table with her and went to another room. The other men at the table soon followed him. Betty phoned to apologize the next day. "I don't know what it is, all my conservative friends..." she said, somewhat incoherently. The next night she went to the Tofflers' and the same thing happened. "She is not invited as much as in the past," Madeleine said. "To large events, yes. Not small dinners."

Like so many others before them, Betty's Los Angeles friends had long discussions about her behavior and came to the same conclusion: having changed the world for women, she was entitled to an enormous amount of space in it. "She is an icon," Madeleine said. She has the kind of personality that can fight and forge ahead and make demands. She is also involved—she brings action to the party. And she has charisma. She can be one of the dearest people in the world. And giddy and silly." This judgment was not shared by the feminist leadership; the pedestal Betty stood upon was constantly being chipped at, and her presence was regarded as an obstacle to the power and validation of many who had come after her.

At the end of the eighties, abortion rights were in serious trouble. Throughout the decade, feminists had fought against vicious and increasingly successful attacks on abortion rights, and there were deep fears of losing *Roe v. Wade*. In the spring of 1989, *Webster* v. *Reproductive Health Services*, a pivotal case, was being considered in the Supreme Court. *Webster* challenged a Missouri law that prevented abortions from being performed in public hospitals and clinics. The law also required tests for fetal viability. George Bush's solicitor general, Kenneth Starr (later to achieve notoriety as the independent prosecutor during the Clinton presidency),

---

* Lorena Bobbitt was a battered woman who had snipped off her husband's penis.

appeared before the court as an amicus curiae and took the case one step further, arguing for overturning *Roe*.

Faced with the ultimate catastrophe, the apparently moribund movement sprang to life. NOW and other feminist groups organized a March to Save Women's Lives, and over 600,000 women, men, and children came to Washington on April 9. NOW invited every prominent feminist to speak—except Betty Friedan, a founder of three of the organizations that ran the march. Betty was beside herself. Ann Reiss Lane said, "She had just been named by *Life* as one of the one hundred most prominent thinkers, but she was crushed because she had not been asked to speak at the abortion rally in Washington." Bella Abzug was so appalled that she offered to give up part of her time to Betty. "That hurt. That really hurt," Betty said of her rejection. "Molly Yard [NOW president] told Bella the lesbians would boo—but the lesbians wouldn't have booed."

This was not the first or the last time National NOW would deliberately snub Betty. Noreen Connell, president of the New York State chapter, who ran interference for Betty, said, "I was always in a fight with National NOW about getting Betty invited. They said, 'She'll keep on talking; you can never tell what will come out of her mouth.' It's an attempt to hide her role in the creation, to rewrite history." Betty was bitter at these slights, but it is hard to separate the personal reasons from the political ones. She had slammed every president of NOW to succeed her—in particular, the powerful Eleanor Smeal, the Pittsburgh housewife who had taken over in the late seventies, rescued NOW when it was falling apart, and put it on a professional footing.* On the phone before the twenty-fifth anniversary party in 1991, Betty had even insulted the doctor who was running the event, mistaking the woman for a secretary.

Betty went to Washington with Gloria Goldsmith and marched with Emily. When she appeared at the Hollywood Women's Political Committee breakfast she was quoted in the papers. She was under no illusions about why NOW had disregarded her. "When I speak I get quoted. I am who I am. I had a vision and I have an ongoing vision, so I am asked. They can't take away my place in history. But"—she laughed—"they would just as soon I were dead. It's mother-bashing. If it had lasted, I really would have felt bad. But I turned my energies to *Age* and to my think tank, to help thinking evolve beyond gender focus. I am very committed to that."

---

* Betty's stalwarts, Jacqui Ceballos and Mary Jean Tully, as well as Noreen Connell, all point to Ellie Smeal as the chief culprit. She was reported to be extremely upset that Betty got most of the media attention at the twenty-fifth anniversary party.

With or without NOW, Betty spoke up on the big issues. In October 1991, she was in the thick of the fight surrounding Clarence Thomas, the U.S. Supreme Court nominee who had been accused of sexual harassment by Anita Hill, a former employee at the EEOC. For her pains, Hill had been branded a slut by the pro-Thomas members of the all-male Senate Judiciary Committee, and she became a cause célèbre among feminists. Betty, who was lobbying the committee to hold hearings on Hill's charges, was one of several feminists to get into a fight with Senator Alan K. Simpson, one of those who had smeared Hill. Refusing to shake hands with him, she was reported to have snapped, "I hope that you will be opposed by a woman and defeated by a woman."

. . .

IN MAY 1992, Betty went to her fiftieth reunion at Smith. It still rankled the administration that she had given her papers to Radcliffe, and her reception was lukewarm. At the welcoming cocktail party in back of her house, Mary Maples Dunn, the president, read aloud old headlines from *SCAN* and talked about the achievements of the class. She mentioned Betty only in passing, and inadvertently mispronounced her name—"Fryden." Betty had a hard time with the stairs at her house and suffered an asthma attack. She was ready to go home. Susan McKeever, a classmate, tried unsuccessfully to rally the class, but Betty was a prophet without honor in her own land. "It was a very conservative class," Susan said. "A number of women did not like what she had been doing."

Betty wanted to hold a seminar to talk about *Age*. It seemed an appropriate thing to do. Unfortunately, she had arrived without having bothered to make reservations and demanded to be housed with her classmates anyway. This highhanded behavior created an uproar among the reunion organizers, some of whom had never liked her and saw no reason to humor her. Liz Shaw, a classmate, said, "Several other things were going on, including two lesbian clubs meeting, which were on the official program. But they couldn't fit her in. She was furious. She threatened not to speak at dinner as scheduled."

Her supporters finally arranged a conversation with Betty for Sunday afternoon in the library. About a third of the class came. Mario Ingersoll Howell, a pacifist who had been president of the class, said: "She was wonderful. She asked questions—'What has come into your life recently that is new or different or satisfying or fulfilling?' We talked about the excitement of surviving and the heady freedom of being yourself and not trying to measure up to anyone else's standards. She drew people out." The weekend was redeemed at commencement. Liz Shaw, who walked with Betty in the parade, said, "Lots of undergrads recognized her and photographed her. People were excited to see her. She liked it."

. . .

THAT SUMMER IN Sag Harbor, Betty got caught up in a strange stalking episode and had a face-to-face encounter with the FBI. This time they were on her side. ("They were very good," she said later, with a straight face.) She had been receiving a series of frightening letters, unsigned, bearing vague threats. Oddly, most of the letters had Betty's address and another addressee. They seemed to be intended for Marilyn Fitterman, a former president of New York State NOW, who lived in Noyac, next to Sag Harbor. In addition to the letters, Marilyn was reported to have gotten more than fifty phone calls over two and a half years. "I am going to get you both," one letter said. "I saw you at the deli the other day. You might be a problem." Another letter: "You both are going to pay I can see my warnings are not taken seriously you need a brick to hit you too [*sic*]."

Betty at first thought the stalker might be a woman who had called her for help and with whom she had been " 'a bit brusque,' suggesting she call Fitterman instead." Later, she realized the stalking "was a vendetta against the other woman. I was only brought into it to get attention." When a letter smeared with blood came, Jonathan insisted that she call the police. A friend said, "She was fearful for her life. She asked various people to spend time with her at the house through most of the summer."

Finally the letter writer sent an ultimatum, and the FBI organized a stakeout. On a moonlit August night, Betty and Marilyn, wearing bulletproof vests, sat in the front seat of a sedan parked on the Sag Harbor dock. An armed FBI agent crouched in the back. When the stalker arrived, a wireless microphone would transmit their conversation to a nearby van packed with agents and police. The stalker didn't show up, but the FBI traced the phone calls to a young woman named Kathleen Higgins, who apparently was deranged, and arrested her.

. . .

IN MAY 1993, during her last, hectic, end-of-the-semester week in Los Angeles, Betty woke up one smoggy morning and couldn't get her breath. Assuming the trouble was an asthma attack, she tried to ignore it; she spoke at a Women, Men and Media panel and went ahead with her plan to hike in Yosemite with friends. By the time she got to the park she could barely drag herself from tree to tree. The clinic in Yosemite told her she was in heart failure and gave her diuretics to reduce the liquid around her heart. The prednisone she had been taking for her asthma may have masked the symptoms.

Back in Los Angeles, she called Emily (whose husband, Eli, was a cardiologist) with the idea of lining up a specialist in New York. She was planning to visit her brother in Palm Springs for the weekend before flying home. Emily would have none of it, and insisted that she see a specialist immediately. Betty, who always listened to Emily, was shipped by ambulance to Good Samaritan Hospital. Her aortic valve was infected, rendering it useless, and her body was filled with fluid. After the fluid was drained, she had open-heart surgery and the valve was replaced with a pig valve, a standard operation. She learned afterward that she had been given only a 50 percent chance of survival. Most of her friends had expected her to die.

Betty's heart rejected the pig valve. She bravely joked that it was *trayf* ("filth": not kosher), but her life was still in danger. The hospital could not locate a human valve to replace it, and her flesh had been too weakened by the infection to support an artificial one. Not one to languish at the bottom of a waiting list, Betty began calling various well-placed people she knew. By 1993, many of the women who had worked in the National Women's Political Caucus and other feminist groups had high government positions and were part of an old-girl network. One friend, Sarah Kovner, whom Betty had known since their anti-Vietnam, pro–Eugene McCarthy days, was special assistant to the secretary of Health and Human Services. Sarah got on the phone, and within a few hours Dr. Phillip Lee, assistant secretary of Health, was on the job. In less than a day Betty had her choice of two valves—one from a fifty-two-year-old man and one from a seventeen-year-old girl. Betty chose the seventeen-year-old, who turned out to be a boy. The surgeon opened her up for the second time in two weeks, and this time the operation was successful.*

Her room was jammed with flowers, telegrams, and people; there was an enormous outpouring of love from her children, her students, her friends, her enemies, and women in the movement. Bella called and sent flowers. A bouquet arrived with a get-well message jointly signed by Glo-

---

* In 1997 the infection recurred, and Betty underwent the same operation a third time. This time she was given an artificial valve.

ria Steinem and Barbara Seaman, a feat engineered by Mary Jean Tully. (Betty later told Mary Jean she knew right away it was her doing.) Alida, who was in the room when the flowers arrived, said, "Betty was thrilled: the leadership were concerned. Politics are politics, but this was something else."

The children had told Carl that Betty might die, and he flew out to see her. He had moved to Sarasota, bought a house with a swimming pool, and was semiretired. He had recently had prostate surgery. Like Betty, he was making a difficult adjustment to aging. He still preferred twenty-somethings and had had two facelifts (one for business purposes). Betty had made overtures to him after the grandchildren started arriving, and they had had an emotional reunion in Sarasota when she was visiting friends over New Year's 1992. Even so, his visit was unexpected. "She was shocked to see me," Carl said. "She was silent."

Betty had some bad moments. "I knew this would happen," she told Alida. "I finished the book, and now I'm not going to be able to enjoy it." But Betty was an expert in denial. She could not really believe that she would die.

Dick Reeves and Cathy O'Neill offered her their house in Pacific Palisades to recuperate in. Emily, who had been with her through the operations, and her niece Laurie stayed with her. She also had a visiting nurse. She spent long hours on a deck chair on the lawn, gathering her strength for Memorial Day weekend. Simon & Schuster had arranged for her to address the American Booksellers Association convention in Miami. She had a book to sell. Only death would have kept her away.

Emily was furious, but this time Betty did not listen. The day after she left the intensive care unit, she had vowed to go. "She was hilarious," Gloria Goldsmith said. "She was planning her speech at the same time as she was planning her funeral, writing down who should speak. She'd be ready either way." Before leaving, she went shopping with Cathy O'Neill and bought a jacket, shoes, and a straw hat. Emily flew East with her.

Betty appeared at the ABA convention in a wheelchair. The infection had lodged in a spinal disc, and she was in pain. But she summoned her dramatic instincts and delivered an animated speech, repeating her joke that her "Jewish heart" had rejected the pig valve. "I want as many people as possible to read this book, so there's no way I'm going to spend ten years writing it and then not get out of the hospital and come talk to you." Not to have come would have nullified her thesis. The audience stood up and cheered her.

29

The Fountain of Age

THE FOUNTAIN OF *Age* was published in September 1993 and stayed on the *New York Times* best-seller list for six weeks. The publicity was staggering, as if Betty had risen from the dead. Almost every Sunday magazine of every major newspaper ran a long profile and put flattering pictures on the cover. Age became her. There was a majesty about her head; she looked elegant in her long flowing dresses and jackets, with her white hair. She had been around long enough to be accorded a new level of respect; she was now a wise woman, a dignified matriarch, theoretically above the fray.

The germ of *The Fountain of Age* had been embedded in the final footnote of *The Feminine Mystique:* "The new studies of aging in humans indicate that those who have the most education and who live the most complex and active lives, with deep interests and readiness for new experience and learning, do not get 'old' in the sense that others do." *Age* was a bookend to *Mystique:* women and the old, each defined by male experts, had been labeled helpless and incompetent and consigned to the fringes, the reality of their lives denied. The books shared a basic premise: that people were living longer and had to find new ways to enrich their lives. Betty considered *Age* to be another groundbreaking book, but she had taken too long to finish it; aging was already in the air. Helen Gurley Brown came out with *The Late Show: A Semiwild but Practical Survival Plan for Women Over 50* at about the same time, and other books would follow quickly. Simone de Beauvoir had, of course, beaten everyone with her grim, depressing *The Coming of Age*, not the sort of book a death-denying American public wanted to know about.

For Betty, the struggle had been to conquer her dread of aging. She had held her nose and jumped into the research—Alzheimer's, nursing homes, when to pull the plug—and discovered that most of the statistics on aging came from hospitals and nursing homes and thus drew on only a small percentage of the population. She therefore revised the prevailing view of decrepitude. Age need no longer be seen as a time of regret for lost youth; it was a new stage of human development, another adventure—the one Betty was embarked upon. The recipe for a vital old age was Betty's own rich, many-layered life as she was living it—the bonds of intimacy and extended families she had created; staying involved with life; having choices about whether to retire or continue working; and "generativity," which she defined as using one's life in a way that would "pass on some legacy to the next generation." She also discovered a "crossover" in gender traits—women became more assertive and men more sensitive as they grew older, thus transcending the battle between the sexes, the polarities between the oppressed and the oppressors.

Age was essentially an inspirational book. The fine-tuned fury that gave *The Feminine Mystique* its compelling power was gone, replaced by optimism and uplift. *Age* suffered from some of the same nearsightedness as *Mystique*—Betty assumed that her readers had the money and education to widen their horizons at will. Ultimately, *Age* was about staying in the game, refusing to shuffle off the stage. The book was a way of denying her aging while appearing to deal with it. Betty had mainstreamed old age.

Most of the reviews were good. The Sunday *New York Times Book Review* gave her a respectful, if dull, front-page writeup, which she shared with another book on aging, *Old Friends* by Tracy Kidder. *Time* ran an excerpt. In the *Boston Sunday Globe*, Doris Grumbach wrote, "With this well-researched and most thoughtful book, she may well instigate another popular revolution.... I want to say at once that this is an important book, as significant to those of us in our 60s, 70s and 80s as 'The Feminine Mystique' was to younger women who needed to recognize and then rebel against their place in a patriarchal world."

In *The Washington Post*, Judy Mann, one of Betty's admirers, raved:

[This book] will liberate us from the tyranny of youth as surely as "The Feminine Mystique" liberated women from the calcified gender role of mother/sex object.... She torpedoes the cultural fixation on infirmities of old age.... Thanks Betty. Once again, thanks.

A handful of important reviews, however, were highly critical. For the daily *New York Times,* Christopher Lehmann-Haupt wrote the sort of review that had lost John Leonard his job:

The fragments of a powerful, inspiring message are scattered among the more than 600 pages of Betty Friedan's cleverly titled new book, "The Fountain of Age[.]".... Unfortunately for readers ... the flaccidity of her prose is reflected in the poor organization of her ideas, which are so ramblingly presented that one is shocked awake upon encountering a lucid one. At least half the book could have been cut.... The unrelievedly upper-middle-class milieu from which she draws most of her samples is severely self-limiting.... Finally, you can't help feeling that ... she seems to wish away the tragedy of being human, which is that we get old and die.

In *The New Republic,* Mary-Lou Weisman wrote:

Betty Friedan's metaphorical fountain of age spouts research, observation, conjecture, evangelical fervor, revolutionary rhetoric and denial. The result is a pool of optimism in which the mother of the woman's movement examines the unlifted face of age and finds it lovable.... Wrinkles have character. Shriveling brains: the brain can compensate. Depression: rage at age turned inward. Worn-out body parts—medical technology has a lot to offer. Impotence—cuddling can be more intimate than orgasm ... This is no conversion. It rounds out the odyssey of the woman whose personal crises have fueled public revolutions.

The book was marred by small factual errors that probably would have been attended to had Betty not been so frail in the six months preceding its publication. She also seems to have taken a little dramatic license here and there, angering many people who complained about the way they or their dead husbands had been portrayed. Betty had credited Michael Braude, the founder of Quadrangle Press, with thinking of the title. In *Age,* she referred to him as "my friend Mike," without a last name, and described him as "look[ing] older than his seventy-odd years, a red-faced, overweight, wheezing, retired Chicago builder who refused to quit smoking and drinking when his doctor said he should." His widow, Lillian Braude, was furious. "We always thought Betty was a very good friend of ours," Lillian said. "My husband was nothing like what she portrayed. He never had a heart attack, he wasn't red or wheezy. He was sick in the last year; he had an aneurysm, but *not* when he gave her the title."

Madeleine Stoner was unhappy, too. Betty had been worried about Madeleine's divorce, particularly the economics of it—"She was more concerned about me than my mother was," Madeleine said—and then blamed Madeleine for it in the book. "She is a difficult friend," Madeleine said. Echoing Joan Didion, who once wrote, "Writers are always selling somebody out," Betty told Madeleine, 'Writers write; they use their experience, how they see it—not accurately if it will make it work.'" The historian Blanche Wiesen Cook said that Betty had misrepresented her attitude toward her breast cancer, writing inaccurately that she was trying to keep it a secret. Betty's facts had also been wrong about the illness of Joe Haggerty, Susan Wood's husband, but, Susan said, "The spirit is there; the spirit is right." The spirit was what Betty had tried to get at.

The biggest dispute arose over material from Barbara Seaman. "I read the chapter 'The New Menopause Brouhaha,'" Barbara said, "and thought, She completely agrees with me! I was thrilled—'I could have written this,' I thought—and I *did!* Two pages are clearly recycled from my book *Women in Crisis.* Eighty percent is my view—that doctors are defining normal processes as disease processes. When I was developing it twenty years ago, she poked fun at me." Betty had also attributed a quote of Barbara's to another source, Kathleen McPherson, a nursing school professor. The misattribution was probably inadvertent—Betty had quoted a secondary source, not realizing that the words were Barbara's originally. Betty made the correction in the next edition, but Barbara remained unconvinced. "We, the feminists, did our books first and then the academicians did theirs, and theirs stayed in print because they were used in the schools. So, I think there are other examples like mine. She ignores original ideas from feminists. Is it unconscious? Conscious? An idea is more convincing if it comes from academicians."

Betty's menopause chapter was the source of a great deal of controversy among feminists. In the eighties, such well-known women as Shirley MacLaine and Gloria Steinem had celebrated their fiftieth birthdays publicly, thus opening the way for this formerly taboo subject to be aired in the media. In the early nineties, both Gail Sheehy and Germaine Greer produced books on menopause. The Sheehy book, in particular (*The Silent Passage*), a best-seller, removed the stigma of it.

Betty was interested in the implications of hormone therapy: "There seemed to be a suspicious coincidence of the demographic emergence of this incredible market—50 million women hitting menopausal age—with the revived definition of menopause as disease." She called it "menopause mania."

Betty had spoken to many women who told her their change of life had been a nonevent, and she believed this to be true for women who had broken through the feminine mystique.* Betty herself had barely noticed her own change and used that as a selling point in speeches on her book tour. "I remember dripping with sweat, August 1970, when I was planning the [first] march," she said at the Boston Public Library. This cavalier dismissal of menopause led to a falling-out with Gail Sheehy, who believed in hormone replacement therapy and in thwarting the depredations of nature whenever possible. Linda Wolfe, a friend of both women, said, "Gail and Clay [Clay Felker, Gail's husband] have a salon and Betty has one, and they used to invite each other. They don't anymore. I was there when Betty tried to apologize. She was patronizing. She publicly yelled at Gail. Afterward, Betty tried to start a conversation with Gail, and Gail turned her back."

Although she was still frail, Betty worked hard to sell her book. In July 1993, six weeks after her second heart operation, she entertained Joan Smith, a British journalist, at Sag Harbor for an interview to run in *Harper's & Queen*. They sat in the living room, with its pale pink walls and white lace curtains at the windows, and all went well until Joan Smith asked a question guaranteed to send Betty over the edge: Did she still believe what she had written about homosexuality in *The Feminine Mystique*, that it was "spreading like a murky smog over the American scene"? Betty accused Joan of trying to sabotage the interview, denied that she had written any such thing, and told her to get out. Joan then read the entire damning passage to her. Betty was stunned. At this stage in her life, it was ancient history. After thirty years, she could hardly be expected to remember one paragraph. Furthermore, in *Age* she had written approvingly of the intimacy of lesbian and gay couples.

Trying to make amends, Betty showed Joan pictures of her grandchildren and drove her to Bobby Van's, one of the in places, for lunch. But the damage had been done. In her article, Joan contrasted the rosy picture of vital aging that Betty had drawn in her book with the reality of a fragile Friedan whose lurching car betrayed her dim eyesight, whose hearing was

---

* A commonly accepted theory about menopause is that overweight women have fewer symptoms because so much estrogen is stored in fat cells.

drastically diminished, and who was "a living rebuttal of the arguments she put forward" in her book. A few weeks later Betty had a similar run-in with Carol Sarler, another British journalist, who came to interview her for *The Sunday Times* of London.

In November 1993, braving chest pains and asthma, Betty went on the Jewish Book Fair tour in upstate New York. She performed like a trouper—within limits. In Buffalo, where she drew a thousand people, an unusually large crowd, she refused vehemently to mount a few steps to the stage to deliver her speech. The women who organized the tour were forced to set up a chair and microphone for her in the pit in front of the stage. People could hear her disembodied voice but not see her. Afterward, she further cooled an already frosty relationship by grousing that the car to take her back to the hotel hadn't been parked close enough to the curb. When the driver got out to open the door for her, she resented being treated like a cripple. Betty, of course, would not acknowledge that anything was wrong, but she was probably frightened at being sick again and so found fault with everything. She must also have been aware of the irony, another cause for irritation. As an author who followed her on the tour said, "She was having a physical breakdown. It was cruel—a woman touting a book that features the virtues of age, age is no impediment—confirmed all our worst stereotypes about how debilitating it is, and how you become crotchety and can't do things."

Betty's debilitation passed, and soon a new "gentleman friend," as Betty called her men, appeared in Sag Harbor. Michael Curtis taught political science at Rutgers and lived in Princeton. He had nursed his wife through cancer before her death in September 1993. "Betty was very warm and comforting and helped me get over it," he said. Their affair followed her usual consort pattern. Betty introduced him to all her famous friends and took him everywhere—on the rounds of Hamptons parties, to a Bill Clinton Renaissance Weekend in Hilton Head, and, in March 1994, to Australia on a two-week book-and-lecture tour.

The Australia trip was a bonanza for her. The state governments of New South Wales and Victoria, which were launching a new health program that took a positive approach to care of the aging, invited her as their guest. The accommodations were royal: she and Michael had a double-size penthouse suite with dramatic staircases. Unfortunately, Betty caught a virus and then slipped on the stairs and sprained her ankle, but she soldiered on.

Betty was honored and fêted wherever she went. Her days were filled with lunches and dinners; she took a seaplane trip to a literary luncheon thirty miles outside Sydney, and she met with a group of parliamentarians. Before audiences she was off-the-cuff and down-to-earth, as if holding a conversation with them. John Cody, her publishing escort, steered her to the best restaurants. In Melbourne she was given a grand reception at the university and asked to open its new women's health center. An older-women's network welcomed her with a revue of songs and sketches. The publicity was dazzling. One newspaper spread a photograph of her across a third of a page, showing her standing in front of the fountain of youth in Hyde Park, sprays of water like ostrich feathers pluming behind her. Her energy was unflagging, even though she had to hobble around with a walking stick for a few days. In the evenings, she and Michael went to The Basement, a well-known jazz club in Sydney. "She praised him," John Cody said. "He had introduced her to jazz and opened her to a whole new area." As always, she was an icon; women surrounded her, thanking her for having changed their lives. When the trip was over, *Age* had sold an extraordinary 19,000 copies.

And yet, those who had made the arrangements and smoothed the way were amazed at the contrast between Betty's treatment of them and the high public regard in which she was held. "It was challenging and stretching, and I was very pleased when it was all over," John Cody said. "She is one of the most self-centered, self-serving, uncaring human beings—she is *the* most selfish individual I ever met in my life. She treated everyone she met either as someone who was there to do something for her or as irrelevant and not to be given any consideration at all."*

Michael, too, had some difficulties. The gracious Sag Harbor hostess he knew had metamorphosed into a Personage: imperious, peremptory, demanding. "One morning they had a bruising fight in the hotel," John Cody said, "which was continued in the taxi, over a forgotten minor matter. She snapped at him to bring things, get things, do things; did you remember to do this?..."

The affair continued for some months after their return, becoming rockier as it went along. According to several of her confidantes, Betty was giving much more than she was getting, and Michael had begun socializing on his own with some of her friends. She and Michael arranged a meeting to discuss their relationship, but he called her instead

* Book tour escorts in the United States had the same story to tell. Tales circulated of shouted obscenities in airports and other abusive behavior. Betty was nominated for the Golden Dartboard Award, given to the most arrogant and obnoxious authors. (Previous winners included Jeffrey Archer, Martha Stewart, and Faye Dunaway.) She would have won had not one member of the nominating committee, mindful of what Betty had done for women, insisted on scratching her name.

and broke it off. She ran into him at a party at the house of a friend she had introduced him to. She was not pleased to see him. "What are you doing here?" she said.

Betty too, had changed. She still managed to find men wherever she went, but her libido was diminished. Even before the Michael Curtis affair she had written,

> There came a time when I simply stopped having the old sexual fantasies. I no longer even dreamed of remarrying.... And I didn't let myself feel the panic: would I never know true intimacy again, would I ever take off all my clothes, be completely there with another being again? And sometimes I felt such a yearning, such a sense of loss, that I desperately tried playing the old game again. But it no longer worked. I couldn't do it. I couldn't risk the shame. Better to face the fact that this part of my life was over and take what pleasure I could in children and friends, women and men, without wanting or expecting it to end in bed, much less romance or marriage.

The Lioness in Winter

BETTY'S ASTHMA, THE plague of her days and one of her main reasons for going to California, had virtually disappeared after her heart surgery, and there was no reason to stay on. She had had reservations about Los Angeles, anyway. "The basic problem was the freeways," she said. "If you don't drive... There was no there there for me." As always, she had a new plan waiting in the wings.

In her eighth decade, her zest restored, Betty resettled herself in Washington. "Betty knows how to move on," Natalie Gittelson said. "She did what she did, and you could say that she passed the torch or the torch was wrested from her, but whatever happened she didn't fall down in her tracks. She moved on." She had a new city to conquer, a new audience for her ideas, new friends, a new fight to wage. She had reached the honored-but-ignored phase of her life; she was a living monument, but she was still afraid of losing her place on the celebrity ladder. She couldn't stop. "She needs constant validation of her status," Marlene Sanders said.

In 1994, she had been awarded a fellowship at the Smithsonian Institution's Woodrow Wilson International Center for Scholars, and she had a teaching position lined up at George Mason University in Fairfax, Virginia. The affiliations gave her life a structure that had been lacking in

New York. She had also been offered twice as much money in Washington as she had been making in California.

Washington was the right place for Betty. Bill Clinton was the first president to hold office after the World War II generation had had its run, and the first whose wife had her own career. One of his first acts was to issue an executive order lifting the gag rule that prohibited clinics and hospitals receiving federal money from talking about abortion to pregnant women. He instituted a family leave policy and nominated a feminist, Ruth Bader Ginsburg, for the Supreme Court. The government was filled with power feminists and the city with feminist networks trying to influence social policy. Betty knew dozens of people and was in demand on C-Span as a talking head. Hillary Clinton solicited her ideas. "My advice is very welcome, and I talk to her from time to time," Betty said. "I talked to her and to her people about my concerns about the real needs of families and children, and downsizing."

At the Woodrow Wilson Center she inaugurated a series of seminars, "The New Paradigm." In many ways, America was recapitulating its robber baron era, and some of Betty's proposed solutions to social problems were versions of century-old socialist ideas, things she had been talking about for years: a shorter work week, and flextime as an alterative to downsizing. But if her solutions were not new, the problems were real, and her seminars attracted historians, academicians, policymakers, heads of organizations, futurists, and think-tankers. Many of them were friends from a previous life: Alvin and Heidi Toffler (who had, bizarrely, been lionized by Newt Gingrich, their political opposite); Amitai Etzioni at Georgetown University; and Milton Carrow, the lawyer who had represented her during her divorce and negotiated with the Schlesinger Library for her papers. Betty also began working with neworks of younger women: Heidi Hartmann, an economist and MacArthur fellow, who headed the Institute for Women's Policy Research; and Linda Tarr-Whelan, head of the Center for Policy Alternatives. In 1997 Betty published *Beyond Gender*, a book based on her seminars. It speaks volumes that one of her blurbs came from a member of the American Enterprise Institute, a conservative think tank in Washington. The feminism she had fought for now seemed too narrow, the old organizations stuck on out-of-date agendas. Betty was trying to find solutions that worked for everyone, but the larger the picture, the more indistinct the finer lines become: in her all-encompassing vision, women are reduced to a separate special-interest group. Her new concerns were the enormity of corporate power, the gap between rich and poor, the disappearing middle class—and the weakness of labor unions.

Betty had come full circle. "I have a really good historic 'geiger counter,'" she told an audience of labor union revivalists at "A Teach-in with the Labor Movement" at Columbia University. "We must transcend all the movements—women and gays and blacks—for a common good and social purpose. Something really dangerous has been going on in America, dangerous income inequality. None of us will be advanced much farther unless we start ... *a new movement!*"

In 1998, the Ford Foundation crowned her work with a million-dollar grant, to be used to conduct twenty conferences on her new paradigm over a period of four years. Cornell University's School of Industrial and Labor Relations, which is dispensing the money, appointed Betty distinguished visiting professor. She had been waiting half her life for this academic acknowledgment. "For the first time a woman is head of the Ford Foundation," she observed.

Betty slipped easily into the Washington social circuit and its television extensions. She popped up at screenings, book parties, dinners, and major celebrations. In November 1994, she was at *The New Republic's* eightieth birthday party, held in Decatur House. Martin Peretz, the owner, was an old friend. In December, she was on William F. Buckley, Jr.'s *Firing Line*, whose topic was "Resolved: The Women's Movement Has Been Disastrous." One of her opponents, Arianna Huffington, talked about the need for less government, and Betty demolished her. "If you think politics, government, is so useless," she said, "why did you let your husband spend eighty million [it was actually reported to have been $30 million] running for the Senate?" On New Year's Eve, Betty was one of about 175 guests at Ben Bradlee and Sally Quinn's black-tie party, with dancing to rock-and-roll oldies. Among the journalists present were Bob Woodward, Maureen Dowd, Sam Donaldson, E. J. Dionne, and Sidney Blumenthal; political types included Alan Greenspan, General Colin Powell (who danced at midnight with Lauren Bacall), Lloyd Cutler, Vernon Jordan, and James Carville. Al Gore, who came with his wife, Tipper, was the centerpiece. When he went over to Betty, she experienced a momentary memory lapse. "I'm Al Gore," he said. She said, "I'm Betty Friedan." He responded, "I know who *you* are." "Betty felt she was part of the inner circle," a friend said. "It was a great validation for her."

In 1995, she remained at the Wilson Center as an adjunct scholar and got a new position at Mount Vernon College in the School of Business, Communication, and Policy Studies. Mount Vernon, which was on the verge of bankruptcy (it was later taken over by George Washington University), needed her prestige, and paid her well over $50,000. She gave up her New York City place and bought an elegant three-bedroom apartment not far from Embassy Row. In its center, between the living room and the dining room, a large black-and-white tiled gallery with a white column in each corner created a sweep of space extending the length of the apartment. The living room was filled with her carved Victorian furniture, upholstered in reds and blues, and the walls were covered with her modern paintings. During trips to New York, she would stay with Marlene Sanders or Linda Wolfe or her current "gentleman friend."

In September 1995, Betty went to Beijing for the fourth U.N. conference on women. A few months before the conference, the Voice of America had sent her to China on a five-city tour to explain what the women's movement was all about (China was one of the few countries where it had not penetrated). "I was treated like a bomb that might go off at any minute," she said. The Chinese were even more nervous about the conference, and its infusion of subversive ideas. The 30,000 NGO women were isolated in Huairou, an hour's drive from central Beijing, and were filmed, followed, and harassed by the secret police. Translations were cut off mid-word; shuttle buses disappeared; rooms were searched; and people were kicked out of their hotels in the middle of the night. Maureen Dowd wrote, "The Beijing police are so afraid that half-naked foreign lesbians will run through Tiananmen Square that they have stocked up on white sheets, as Reuters put it, 'to throw over any scantily clad protestors.'"

None of this had the slightest effect on the conference, and may even have contributed, in a perverse way, to its success. The U.S. delegation was filled with feminists. Hillary Clinton and Madeleine Albright, speaking to the official conference, lambasted the Chinese for the heavy-handed security and condemned their policies of forced abortion and sterilization.

Betty had press accreditation from the U.S. Information Agency and did commentary for the Voice of America. She also ran several workshops on her new paradigm and another for UNESCO on cultural changes in the lives of women. She was a particular bête noir to the Chinese. Her New York literary agent had arranged to have her books available to be sold in Huairou, but the Chinese sales representative hadn't been allowed inside. Betty could not get in touch with her, and later learned that the police had taken her in and warned her that if she ever saw Betty again, she would be jailed and her business shut down.

Betty and Bella were the heroines of Beijing. Everyone wanted to interview them and be photographed with them. Women lined up to meet them and touch them. Bella, who had heart disease and difficulty walking, ran her group from a wheelchair. She and Mim Kelber had cofounded the Women's Environment and Development Organization (WEDO), a global network that worked with U.N. organizations to advance economic and political power for women. In Kate Millett's description, "She goes to U.N. meeetings and sits behind the male delegates and scribbles little pieces of paper and shoves them in front of them and says, 'Say this.'" Bella was largely resposible for shaping and wording the conference's final "Platform for Action."*

There were, of course, the usual transgressions. The USIA was unable to provide Betty with sufficient staff, so she dragooned people into helping her and then lost her temper with them. Such matters aside, Beijing was the best of the U.N. conferences. The women ran the show and rose above factionalism, and the delegates reached a consensus that women's rights were human rights. Even the Vatican, which went so far as to send a woman to lead its delegation, was outflanked. The Platform for Action addressed political representation, literacy and inheritance rights, domestic violence, lesbian rights, human rights generally, and bank credit. Perhaps the surest sign of change was an announcement by the World Bank that it was rethinking some of its large-scale, all-male policies: it was setting aside $200 million for loans to poor women for micro-enterprises.

After Beijing, Betty flew to Tokyo and stayed with Walter Mondale, who was the ambassador to Japan. She then went to Germany, where *The Fountain of Age* was being published, and continued to Paris, where Ambassador Pamela Harriman gave her a book party, delivering on an old promise. On one of Betty's previous trips, for a UNESCO meeting, the ambassador had phoned her out of the blue for help: she had to deliver a speech about feminism in America and asked Betty to tell her what was going on. "She gave a great speech," Betty said. "People wondered, how did she know all these things?" The book party was the payback.

Betty seems to have been very favorably impressed with the ambassador. "She was very intelligent. She was one of a group of British women—I've known a number of them—who were uneducated. Their parents didn't send daughters to college, so they always had an inferiority complex. Sure, she was beautiful, and her looks got her a lot of places, but Pamela was quite serious. As an ambassador, if there was a treaty, she would call up the president and ask questions, and he would tell her not to bother about it, to let her adjutant do it. But she studied it. She was no fig-

---

* In 1998, Bella died from complications after heart surgery. She was seventy-seven.

urehead." Discounting the fact that Pamela Harriman's life had been the antithesis of feminism, Betty later told a group of Washington journalists at lunch that she thought Pamela was "a good closet feminist."

Betty returned to Sag Harbor every summer and immersed herself in her Madame de Staël life. By now, the Hamptons had acquired a Hollywood glaze and been overrun by yuppies and day trippers; the streets were clogged with them, and even Sag Harbor was less of a refuge than a tourist attraction. Her own small house bulged at the seams, jammed with the cots and sleeping bags of her children and eight grandchildren. One room was so tiny it had space for only a bed and a chair. In 1994, enriched by what her friends said was a big Japanese advance for *Age* (Betty denied it. "I certainly didn't make any millions of dollars," she said), she expanded the house, building another bedroom and bath for herself, facing the water. Her children, who were by then more comfortable with the fact of having Betty Friedan for a mother, had done her proud. In 1987, when he was thirty-eight, Daniel had won a MacArthur Award, a "genius grant" of $245,000, for his work on string theory, which posits that matter is composed of strings of energy. Rutgers University had wooed him away from Princeton and set him up with his own physics department. Jonathan was a partner in his engineering firm in Philadelphia. Emily was "my daughter the doctor." In 1993, Betty took her whole family to Virgin Gorda over Thanksgiving.

Betty never found the boy who would like her best, but she never gave up the search. In 1996, at an age when most women might have stopped bothering, she dated a man in Washington and another in New York. Ironically, the New York man, Dr. Irving Schwartz, was the widower of one of her former antagonists.* Betty referred to him as "an eminent doctor" and was always careful to introduce him as "Dr. Schwartz." None of the men lasted very long, and no one had ever replaced Carl. "I feel a sense of failure about my marriage," she told a reporter. "Even now, there's still a feeling of loss, of sorrow.... I envy people whose marriages have evolved rather than dissolved. I also envy my friends who have made good strong ties in their second marriages."

Betty began calling Carl for dinner when she had speaking dates in Tampa or Sarasota. He, too, had had heart surgery, but he still had an advertising account with a paint company. Carl began staying with Betty at Sag Harbor for visits with the grandchildren. Betty introduced him to her friends, straightforwardly, as "the father of my children." She was so warm

---

* Felice Schwartz, the founder of Catalyst, a corporate advisory group, invented the phrase "mommy track," a concept that relegated working mothers to second-class status.

and considerate, he thought she wanted to get together with him again, but Betty was beyond that. "Getting together, that's not— No," she said.

Betty's friends noticed that she had mellowed. In 1995, Arthur Dubow said, "She used to always be late. It used to drive people nuts. She had excuses—her cab broke down, she was stuck on the phone. That changed five years ago. I had a long talk with her about consideration for people. So did other people have this long talk. People plan dinners, theatre, etc. She just wasn't focusing on it. She is much, much better. She is much happier now. Her book was a terrific experience—the research and writing—and her kids are married with their own kids. And for the first time in her life she has enough money. She doesn't have the stress of hustling in a non-structured situation. She is a sweeter, calmer, happier person. She has a very wide group of friends. She feels fortunate." Betty even put her finances in order; one of her tycoon friends saw to it that her earnings were invested with money managers.

The old demons had retreated, their pain muted. Betty had accepted herself, judged herself, and forgiven herself. "To be able to feel good about being a woman is something wonderful. I've accomplished that for other women. It's finally happened to me, too!" she told a reporter.

Age had brought a need for reconciliations. Betty had gathered her family together, and now she tried to make rapprochements with those she had fought. On the occasion of a celebratory dinner for Kate Millett in 1998, Betty recalled the lavender-armbands incident and her opposition to the press conference in support of Kate that had followed it, and amazed her listeners by saying that "it probably strengthened the movement."

When Letty Pogrebin, who had left her for Gloria long ago at the National Women's Political Caucus founding, asked her for a special favor, Betty was more than gracious. Letty's mother-in-law, who was dying of cancer, was president of the Jewish Forum at her senior residence and wanted the prestige of having the author of *The Fountain of Age* speak to her group. "It was a freezing cold January night, ice all over," Letty said. "Betty delivered a speech as if she were in Madison Square Garden. She put in so much for all these old people, in wheelchairs, who couldn't read, who certainly weren't going to buy her book. She made the evening. They paid her with a bottle of wine and taxi fare. She spent two and a half hours there, no headlines, no money, no credit."

Betty and Bella, having settled into their respective turfs, found their way to each other at Alida Brill's annual July 14 fireworks party in East Hampton. People stood and watched from a distance as they sat together in lawn chairs, absorbed in their conversation. When Betty was unable to attend a dinner honoring Bella, she sent a message, which was read aloud: "It is a fact that the two of us are stormy gals. I always admired and respected you. And I love you. I wish I were here to give you a kiss on each cheek...."

Closing the books on Gloria and Barbara Seaman was a more elusive proposition. At Betty's 1994 Labor Day party, Betty told Jacqui Ceballos, "I tried to make up with them. No woman should be at odds in the movement. I didn't have dinner with her [Barbara's] ex, except I was trying to get him to make up with Barbara. After all, he lived on the floor just under me. I even tried to make up with Gloria...." ("There were lots of hand gestures here," Jacqui said, telling this story.)

Betty praised Gloria in an interview with *Playboy*, finally disabusing herself of the notion that glamour had been Gloria's main achievement. "But now, in my wise maturity, I see that all of it contributed. Gloria is a survivor and a fighter. She contributed a lot. She is a good role model for women who choose not to marry or have children. She showed that it is possible to have a good life. I don't think that most women want to go that path, but it's important to have a model for those who do. She also has made a real contribution to the women's movement with *Ms.*"

Yet traces of the old animosity still lingered. David Sloan, a producer at *20/20*, recalled going to Lincoln Plaza to pre-interview Betty for a program, "Boys and Girls Are Different": "She made several disparaging remarks about Gloria—there were traces of bitterness about the beginning, which was a quarter of a century before. The gist of it was, Gloria's message got greater play than hers because Gloria was more telegenic than she. Gloria always got on TV and she didn't." As things turned out, Betty was prophetic: David ended up using Gloria and Bella on the show. "Betty never really focused," he said. "She rambled—disconnected anecdotes without a point. I was looking for eight-second soundbites. Gloria was more seamless." Gloria would remain forever beyond Betty's reach.

In the end, the three giants of the movement all found their place. Bella, who had cofounded Women Strike for Peace and wanted to run the world, wound up as a gadfly at the U.N., shaping policy behind the scenes. Gloria, who had had an epiphany in India among the poor, did missionary work among the powerless in America and later went to Botswana to help the N/oakhwe people, whose land was being taken from them by the government. Betty, whose passion for ideas paralleled her passion for justice, taught in universities and held conferences, injecting those ideas into the vast circulatory system of America. If the three of them had not quite turned the world upside down, at least they had given it a good shove and tilted it on its axis.

. . .

ON FEBRUARY 4, 1996, Marlene Sanders, Cynthia Epstein, and Linda Wolfe gave Betty a seventy-fifth-birthday party at Marlene's apartment in New York. The food was eclectic. Cynthia brought a ham from Zabar's. Marlene made chopped liver from her mother's recipe. Betty, with her silvery hair and majestic head, sat enthroned in an armchair as more than sixty friends showered her with presents and extolled her virtues. Linda Wolfe remembered Betty's instinctive ability to brush aside barriers, even on a small scale, and enable others to do the same: "I'd been trying to capture a source [in Florida] for a book I was working on... and the source was stalling and saying he'd come to New York. Betty said, 'What's the matter with you? Why don't you just go down there?' So, with a little push, I went and got the story." J. Anthony Lukas called her "a self-generated engine of civic outrage.... In an era when all too many of us are ready to give way to the pull of apathy, in the face of [Newt] Gingrich, [Philip] Gramm, and [Patrick] Buchanan, and unfortunately Clinton's effort to appease them, Betty is there to remind us of the inequality and injustice that still thrive in American society.... She's a national treasure." Robert Caro praised her brilliance, originality, and "remarkable convictions. The thing about her is that she's held to those convictions.... When she's thought something through, she will stick to it.... Nothing deters her." And he told a story that was a metaphor for Betty's life, how at Sag Harbor she would swim across a channel to get to the bay, through a narrow inlet between two sandbars that was well traveled by boats. She always swam straight across and back, never dipping her head, never watching for the boats, because Betty thought the boats should look out for her.

She was a force of nature, as indomitable as the movement she had helped to found. Neither would disappear from history.

Notes

ABBREVIATIONS

BF:	Betty Friedan
BFC-SL:	Betty Friedan Collection at the Arthur and Elizabeth Schlesinger Library on the History of Women in America
CA-SC:	College Archive, Smith College
FM:	*The Feminine Mystique*
FOA:	*The Fountain of Age*
ICML:	*It Changed My Life*
MC:	Marcia Cohen
MCC-SL:	Marcia Cohen Collection at the Schlesinger Library
SL:	Schlesinger Library
T-COHP-SL:	Tully-Crenshaw Oral History Project at the Schlesinger Library
SS:	*The Second Stage*

Almost all of my research took place between 1993 and 1998. Throughout that period I conducted extensive interviews—sometimes going back to the same person three or four times as new information came to light. Most people spoke on the record. Betty Friedan consented to be interviewed four times, in 1996, 1997, and 1998, each time for about an hour and a half. With very few exceptions, I have not included quotations from my interviews in the Notes. The exceptions are cases where the source of a quotation is unclear, or where the source has repeated something that was previously published.

The numbers in the left-hand column refer to page numbers in this book.

CHAPTER 1: Roots

5 "All in all": BF, "Through a Glass Darkly," high school class paper, 1938 (BFC-SL).
6 "I grew up feeling a mixture": Transcript of MC interview with Amy Goldstein Adams, mid-1980s (MCC-SL).
7 "Betty was so cute": Ibid.
7 "Our mother always looked": Ibid.
7 "She's been sloppy": transcript of MC interview with Harry Goldstein, mid-1980s (MCC-SL).
8 "want[ed] success and fame": BF, "Through a Glass Darkly," high school class paper, 1938 (BFC-SL).
8 "the hypocrisies and phoninesses about my mother": Transcript of MC interview with BF, mid-1980s (MCC-SL).
9 "She was a fearsome person": Transcript of MC interview with Harry Goldstein Jr. mid-1980s (MCC-SL).
9 "If there was a serious discussion": Transcript of MC interview with Amy Goldstein Adams, mid-1980s (MCC-SL).
11 "My father, provoked by my mother": Ibid.
11 "a boy to like me best": BF, personal writings (BFC-SL).
12 "There's nothing bad enough": Author interview with Mildred Arends, BF classmate, May 4, 1994.
14 "If you wanted": Transcript of MC interview with Amy Goldstein Adams, mid-1980s (MCC-SL).
15 "They may not like me": BF, "The E.R.A.—Does It Play in Peoria?," *The New York Times Magazine,* November 19, 1978, p. 39. Also in a slightly different form in Cohen, *The Sisterhood,* p. 57.
15 "I adored being in plays": Transcript of MC interview with BF, mid-1980s (MCC-SL).
16 "There once was a": BF, *Opinion,* undated copy. The Central High library has some copies of *Opinion;* others are in BFC-SL.
17 "the biggest thing in my life": "The 'Tide' Comes In," Smith College paper (BFC-SL).
18 "pompous pretentions"; "the numbing influence": BF, "Education for the Masses," unpublished article for *Tide* (BFC-SL).
18 "the new international dictator": *Opinion,* May 27, 1938.

CHAPTER 2: The Passion of the Mind

20 "We want a diamond": Smith College yearbook, 1942.
22 "an old maid": BF, "Smith Portraits, #13, The Character" (BFC-SL).

24 "a strident voice haranguing": Daniel Horowitz, "Rethinking Betty Friedan and *The Feminine Mystique:* Labor Union Radicalism and Feminism in Cold War America," *American Quarterly,* March 1996, p. 9.

25 "since it would be impossible": *Smith College Associated News (SCAN),* December 6, 1941, p. 3 (SA-SC).

26 "The atmosphere of the meeting": Ibid., October 21, 1941, p. 1.

26 "As the Nazis rose to power": Ibid., p. 2.

26 She wrote that: BF, "The E.R.A.—Does It Play in Peoria?," *The New York Times Magazine,* November 19, 1978, p. 134.

27 Dorothy W. Douglas: Horowitz, "Rethinking Betty Friedan," p. 9, identifies her as a fellow-traveler.

28 "In Peoria intelligence": BF, "Learning the Score," *We Know the Score,* Highlander, 1941 (BFP-SL).

28 "an honest place": BF, "Highlander Folk School—American Future," Smith College class paper, 1941 (BFC-SL).

28 "second rate," "a step down": Chase, *Feminist Convert,* p. 127.

28 "twisting the substance": *SCAN,* May 9, 1941 (SA-SC); also quoted in ibid., pp. 121–22.

29 "The writer of the editorial was right": Chase, *Feminist Convert,* pp. 122–23.

29 "She has the *bad* taste to spell": Ibid, pp. 132–33.

30 "Operationism in Psychology" was published in *Psychological Review,* May 1944.

30 "Betty has the most": Cohen, *The Sisterhood,* p. 62.

31 "rather strongly in": BF, Smith College class paper (BFC-SL).

31 "I remember the stillness": *FM,* p. 62.

CHAPTER 3: *Meltdown*

35 "angry, cold, mean": BF, personal writings (BFC-SL).

36 The FBI was investigating: Information in this paragraph is from FBI Reports on BF, May 18, June 20, September 4, 1944 (BFC-SL).

36 "I fell in love with a guy that": Paul Wilkes, "Mother Superior to Women's Lib," *The New York Times Magazine,* November 29, 1970, p. 140.

37 "None of these women lived": *FM,* p. 67.

37 "I was determined that": Maria Karagianis, "The Lioness of Feminism," *Boston Globe Magazine,* January 2, 1983.

37 "Our failures only marry": Apocryphal because she spoke in chapel extemporaneously; and because her talks were not recorded, no one is certain whether she said, "Only our failures marry."

37 "Did I think I would be choosing": *FM,* p. 63.

38 "had affairs with married men": BF, "In France, de Beauvoir Had Just Published 'The Second Sex,'" *New York,* December 30, 1974/January 6, 1975. Reprinted in BF, *ICML,* as "The Way We Were—1949," p. 6. Hereinafter cited as "The Way We Were—1949," *ICML.*

39 "They clearly wanted to provoke": BF, "The People Versus Industrial Greed," *Federated Press,* January 22, 1946.

39 "hand over its [entire] wartime": BF, "Big Business Getting Desperate, Promising Postwar Jobs," *Federated Press,* November 19, 1943.

39 "profit-greedy distributors": BF, "Wartime Living," *Federated Press,* November 22, 1943.

41 "sardonic glint in his eyes": BF, *FOA,* p. 272.

42 "a topflight new news editor": BF grievance letter to the Newspaper Guild (BFC-SL).

42 "I wouldn't send you": Author's interview with a staff member; also in grievance letter, ibid.

CHAPTER 4: Love

43 "He brought me an apple": BF, "The Way We Were—1949," *ICML,* p. 7.

50 "We were like our parents": Ibid., p. 13.

52 union had replaced her with a man: Ibid., p. 17.

54 "Women must be treated": United Electrical Workers, "National Conference on the Problems of Working Women," May 1953. UE archive at the University of Pittsburgh. Also SL.

CHAPTER 5: Suburban Housewife

57 "a sado-masochistic free-for-all": Lyn Tornabene, "The Liberation of Betty Friedan," *McCall's,* May 1971, p. 138.

59 "I was making a good salary": BF, "I Went Back to Work," *Charm,* April 1955.

59 "The Most Creative Part I've Ever Played": *McCall's,* December 1956. Reprinted in *Reader's Digest,* April 1957.

59 "The Gal Who Defied Dior": *Town Journal,* October 4, 1955.

60 "Day Camp in the Driveways": *Parents,* May 1957.

60 "We Built a Community for Our Children": *Redbook,* March 1955.

60 "raising their children together": "Happy Families of Hickory Hill," *Redbook,* February 1956.

60 "Only the most neurotic": Cohen, *The Sisterhood,* p. 92. Also in BF, "Up from the Kitchen Floor," *The New York Times Magazine,* March 4, 1973, p. 9.

60 "I felt that I would never": BF, "The Way We Were—1949," *ICML,* p. 14.

61 "Your executive committee": BF, paper reviewing the rent situation, n.d. (BFC-SL).

62 "the fetish is non-conformity": Spectorsky, *The Exurbanites,* p. 67.

62 "In some ways it was": Aimee Lee Ball, "Bye-Bye, Brigadoon," *New York,* March 12, 1990.

64 "I think of my own uneasiness": BF, *SS,* p. 35.

66 "My most vivid memories": Transcript of William J. Goode impromptu speech at BF's seventy-fifth birthday party, February 4, 1996. Transcript is in author's possession.

CHAPTER 6: *Feminine Fulfillment*

70 "so-called brilliant possibilities": Transcript of MC interview with BF, mid-1980s (MCC-SL).

71 "What do you wish": The 1957 Smith College questionnaire is in BFC-SL, as are the answers.

72 "the masculinization of women": Ferdinand Lundberg and Marynia F. Farnham, *Modern Woman, the Lost Sex,* (New York: Harper & Bros., 1947), p. 142 ff., quoted in *FM,* p. 37.

72 "With earlier marriages becoming": *Newsweek,* Special Education Report, quoted in BF, "Are Women Wasting Their Time in College?" (BFC-SL).

72 "I was going to disprove": *FM,* 1984 edition, p. 6.

72 In 1957 she went to a meeting: The SMW was founded in 1948 by Murray Teigh Bloom, Jack Pollack, and Phil Gustafson to provide its members with leverage against poor treatment by magazine editors. It was a disparate group whose members included a former underground organizer for the Communist Party and a former covert agent for the CIA. It later became the American Society of Journalists and Authors.

73 "She was incredibly ambitious": Quoted in Cohen, *The Sisterhood,* p. 93.

74 "During that same time": Transcript of William J. Goode impromptu speech at Betty's seventy-fifth birthday party, February 4, 1996. Transcript is in author's possession.

74 "If the patient doesn't fit": *FM,* p. 114.

75 The response was negative: The rejection letters were dated as follows: *Redbook,* February 28, 1962; *Life,* March 3, 1962; *Esquire,* note to Betty from Marie Rodell, n.d.; *The Reporter,* March 23, 1962 (BFC-SL).

77 "One day," George said: Quoted in Cohen, *The Sisterhood,* p. 96.

77 "If you don't let me speak": Ibid., p. 98.

77 "Girls," Graham asked: *ICML* p. 20.

78 "What next book?": Author interview with an anonymous friend of Betty's. See also Cohen, *The Sisterhood,* p. 96.

78 "With all the troubles we have had": Quoted in Lyn Tornabene, "The Liberation of Betty Friedan," *McCall's,* May 1971, p. 139.

CHAPTER 7: *The Feminine Mystique*

79 "The separation of female sexuality": Eisler, *Private Lives,* p. 283.

80 "In tackling the age and marriage": Davis, *Moving the Mountain,* p. 16.

80 "The problem lay buried": *FM,* p. 11.

81 "have a mission in life": George Leonard, "Abraham Maslow and the New Self," *Esquire,* December 1983.

82 "do not take the ordinary conventions": *FM,* p. 307.

82 In the 1940s: Dr. Jessie Bernard, *American Family Behavior* (New York and London: Harper & Bros., 1942); Ruth Herschberger, *Adam's Rib* (New York: Pellegrini & Cudahy, 1948); Margaret Mead, "What Women Want," *Fortune,* December 1946.

82 "Yet, for all her deference": Diane Ravitch, "Mama in Search of Herself," *The New Leader,* April 15, 1963, p. 29.

82 Beauvoir herself was angry: Deirdre Bair, personal communication.

83 "I read that perhaps ten years before": Transcript of taped BF interview with *Book Digest* editor Martin L. Gross, 1976.

83 "In a certain sense": *ICML,* p. 4.

83 In such an atmosphere: See Horowitz, "Rethinking Betty Friedan," for further discussion.

84 "the usual kinds of boring jobs": "Woman in the News," *The New York Times,* March 23, 1970.

84 "little writing jobs": Judy Michaelson, "Woman in the News," *The Washington Post,* November 26, 1966.

84 In a *New York Post* interview: Joseph Wershba, "Closeup," March 14, 1963.

84 "But when it comes": *McCall's* press release (BFC-SL).

84 "Sweeping generalities": Lucy Freeman, *The New York Times,* April 7, 1963.

84 "Her book is a damning indictment": Marya Mannes, "Don't Sweep Ladies Under the Rug," New York *Herald Tribune,* May 4, 1963.

84 "The feminine mystique is": Alden Hoag, "To Herd Women by a New Dogma," *Boston Herald,* March 11, 1963.

85 "marred...by a pervasive": Ravitch, "Mama in Search of Herself."

85 *McCall's* and *LHJ* were besieged: Letters to the editor (BFC-SL).

86 "*I threatened them*": *ICML,* p. 72.

86 "Some years later": Ibid.

87 "I wasn't very happy": Enid Nemy, "Back Home to Peoria—and a Sequel to 'Feminine Mystique,' " *New York Times,* May 21, 1976.

88 festooned with toilet paper: BF, "The E.R.A.—Does It Play in Peoria?" *The New York Times Magazine,* November 19, 1978, p. 38.

CHAPTER 8: *Death Throes*

89 "Through television, radio, and lectures": Lader, *Abortion II,* p. 38.

91 "Manhattan's aristocracy": Unidentified newspaper clip in author's possession.

92 "It's not simple!": Transcript of MC interview with BF, mid-1980s (MCC-SL).

93 "Carl only struck out at me": Ibid.

93 "My husband began to treat me": Ibid.

95 her four-thousand-word article: "How Mrs. Gandhi Shattered the Feminine Mystique," *Ladies' Home Journal,* May 1966.

95 "For the first time": Indira Gandhi to BF, May 5, 1966 (BFC-SL)

CHAPTER 9: *Founding NOW*

97 "one of the most pervasive": "American Women," Report of the President's Commission on the Status of Women, U.S. Government Printing Office, October 11, 1963.

98 "without a sex amendment": *Moving the Mountain,* Davis, p. 43.

100 "Born a woman, died a person": Author interview with Gene Boyer, August 30, 1994.

100 "Who invited you?": Letter to author from Nancy Knaak, November 6, 1993. See also Cohen, *The Sisterhood,* pp. 134–35.

101 "Betty was talking in her loud whispers": Gene Boyer, oral history, June 12, 1991 (T-COHP-SL).

101 "Friedan's avowed feminist position": Hole and Levine, *Rebirth of Feminism,* p. 84.

103 "It was because Kay": Gene Boyer, oral history, June 12, 1991 (T-COHP-SL).

104 NOW Statement of Purpose: NOW papers in SL.

105 "not battleaxes nor man haters": BF, "The First Year: President's Report to NOW, 1967," *ICML,* p. 124.

107 Starting with their personal: Among the most influential writings were: Pat Mainardi, "The Politics of Housework," in Morgan, ed., *Sisterhood Is Powerful,* p. 447; Dr. Naomi Weisstein, "Kinde, Küche, Kirche as Scientific Law: Psychology Constructs the Female," ibid., p. 205; Anne Koedt, "The Myth of the Vaginal Orgasm," originally published in Shulamith Firestone and Anne Koedt, eds., *Notes from the Second Year* (New York Radical Women, self-published, 1970); also in several anthologies, including eds. Anne Koedt, Ellen Levine, and Anita Rapone, *Radical Feminism* (New York: Quadrangle Books, 1973).

107 Betty called them "pseudo-radicals": Transcript of interview by *Book Digest* editor Martin L. Gross, 1976.

CHAPTER 10: *Divorce*

110 "I used to think, what a phony": Transcript of MC interview with BF, mid-1980s (MCC-SL). Betty also voiced similar sentiments to various journalists.

112 "like being asked to pay": BF, personal writings (BFC-SL).

113 "I would have wanted": BF, unpublished draft of *ICML* ms. (BFC-SL).

113 "I'm going to the Philharmonic": Transcript of MC interview with BF, mid-1980s (MCC-SL).

113 "I went to a bar": Lyn Tornabene, "The Liberation of Betty Friedan," *McCall's,* May 1971, p. 140.

113 "I look back now and realize": Marian Christy, "Betty Friedan Is Still Telling It Like It Is," *The Boston Globe,* January 14, 1990.

CHAPTER 11: *Liberation*

117 "I always felt that Betty": Muriel Fox, oral history, January 1991 (T-COHP-SL).

117 "Ironically, it was I": *ICML,* p. 138.

118 "I am a flower child": Joseph Mancini and Jay Levin, "Andy Warhol Fights for Life," *New York Post,* June 4, 1968.

118 "There are only a few jobs": Heilbrun, *The Education of a Woman,* p. 196.

119 "bring about a complete": Valerie Solanas, "The S.C.U.M. Manifesto," in Morgan, ed., *Sisterhood Is Powerful,* pp. 514–19.

119 "Desist immediately": BF and Muriel Fox telegram to Florynce Kennedy, June 14, 1968 (BFC-SL).

119 "She started to talk": Mary Eastwood, oral history, March 7, 1992 (T-COHP-SL).

120 Ti-Grace, the ungrateful daughter: Ti-Grace formed the October 17th Movement, later renamed The Feminists, an all-woman, antimale group. In April 1970, she was arrested, with Robin Morgan and other women, in an invasion of Grove Press to protest its publication of pornographic books. They were charged with criminal trespass, and the police strip-searched them. Ti-Grace was traumatized. It was a turning point onto a long road of self-destruction. She viewed the state as her enemy and identified with people who hated the police. She formed an affectionate friendship with Joseph Columbo, a Mafia don who organized the Italian-American Anti-Defamation League, an early manifestation of the ethnic pride movement that grew into identity politics. Columbo was shot by rivals in June 1971. Ti-Grace's book, *Amazon Odyssey,* was published in 1975, but she was $45,000 in debt and went on welfare in 1976. Her father, who could have paid the debt easily, refused, saying that he did not like her politics and thought she was antifamily. Eventually, she became a teacher.

120 "So they'll have to": Robin Morgan, "Goodbye to All That," *Rat,* January 1970. Reprinted in Morgan, *Going Too Far: The Personal Chronicle of a Feminist* (New York: Random House, 1977), p. 121.

120 "bras, girdles, curlers": "No More Miss America," Morgan, ed., *Sisterhood Is Powerful,* p. 521.

121 "verve and style": *ICML,* p. 174.

121 "Some people think I'm saying": Jane Howard, "Angry Battler for Her Sex," *Life,* November 1, 1963.

122 "This is the only kind of discrimination": Cohen, *The Sisterhood,* p. 21.

122 "Friedan, the mother of the movement": Susan Brownmiller, "Sisterhood Is Powerful," *The New York Times Magazine,* March 15, 1970, p. 129.

122 "a hurricane": Lader, *Abortion II,* p. 37.

123 "the right of a woman": *ICML,* p. 154.

123 "Now it's time to get": Lader, *Abortion II,* p. 82. Also, Edith Evans Asbury, "Women Break Up Abortion Hearing," *The New York Times,* February 14, 1969,

p. 42; "The Talk of the Town," *The New Yorker,* February 22, 1969, p. 28; Alfred Miele, "Gals Squeal for Repeal," New York *Daily News,* February 14, 1969, p. 5.

124 "As far as I'm concerned": Susan Brownmiller, "Sisterhood Is Powerful," *The New York Times Magazine,* March 15, 1970, p. 129. Also quoted in Heilbrun, *The Education of a Woman,* p. 164.

125 "a hysterical episode": *ICML,* pp. 173–74.

125 Marlene later learned: Marcia Cohen also names Rita Mae, as does Jacqui Ceballos, who recalls that Rita Mae told many people that she had done it.

126 "Do you want to screw around": Author interview with a prospective buyer, May 5, 1994.

CHAPTER 12: *The Lavender Menace*

130 "the lavender menace": BF first used the phrase at a NOW National Board meeting in New Orleans, December 6–7, 1969. Its first public appearance was in Susan Brownmiller's article "Sisterhood Is Powerful," *The New York Times Magazine,* March 15, 1970, p. 140, quoting BF. Susan called it "a lavender *herring.*"

131 "The shallow unreality, immaturity": *FM,* p. 265.

135 "A group of us went out for dessert": Toni Carabillo, oral history, early 1990s (T-COHP-SL)

135 "I have led you into history": *ICML,* p. 178.

135 "that on Wednesday, August 26, 1970": Betty Armistead to BF, February 22, 1970. In another letter, Betty Armistead suggested making plans to elect women to public office in 1972. The idea for the National Women's Political Caucus, which BF cofounded in 1971, may have had its germination here (BFC-SL).

135 "symbolic of the flame": *ICML,* p. 182.

CHAPTER 13: *"Bliss Was It in That Dawn to Be Alive"*

136 "strident, snobbish homewreckers": Christina Kirk, "The Feminine Revolt," New York *Daily News,* August 19, 1970.

137 "the unfinished revolution": Charlotte Curtis, "Women's Liberation Gets into the Long Island Swim," *The New York Times,* August 10, 1970.

138 "looking like a gray-haired": Judy Klemesrud, "Coming Wednesday—A Her-story-Making Event," *The New York Times,* August 23, 1970.

138 "I don't want people to think": "Leading Feminist Puts Hairdo Before Strike" *The New York Times,* August 27, 1970.

138 "That's what I call a male": Barry Cunningham, "Betty: A Day in the Strife," *New York Post,* August 27, 1970.

140 "One hour before her lecture": Lyn Tornabene, "The Liberation of Betty Friedan," *McCall's,* May 1971, p. 84.

141 "Until this year with the publication": "Who's Come a Long Way, Baby?," cover story, *Time*, August 31, 1970, p. 16.

141 "discredited herself as a spokeswoman": "Women's Lib: A Second Look," *Time*, December 14, 1970, p. 50.

141 "Are you a lesbian?": Millett, *Flying*, p. 15. Also in Cohen, *The Sisterhood*, pp. 242–43; Heilbrun, *The Education of a Woman*, p. 164; Stern, *Gloria Steinem*, p. 218.

142 "The line goes, inflexible": Millett, *Flying*, p. 15.

144 "a number of former": Echols, *Daring to Be Bad*, p. 219.

CHAPTER 14: *The Commune*

145 "I was forty-nine": *FOA*, p. 292.

145 "We didn't do it right": Ibid., pp. 292–93.

146 "Betty had some casual invitation": Joan Thorn videotape of twenty-year reunion party, 1990.

146 "We had vicious family": *FOA*, p. 293.

148 "You had to be made of stone": Transcript of MC interview with Betty Rollin, mid-1980s (MCC-SL).

149 "A lawyer friend advised us": Bob Morris, "Road to Good Intentions Is Paved with Paté," *The New York Times*, August 18, 1996.

150 "A dissident group got together": Joan Thorn videotape of twenty-year reunion party, 1990.

150 "What we began was a family": Ibid.

CHAPTER 15: *"The Age Demanded an Image"*

152 "Betty didn't *think* about Gloria then": Transcript of MC interview with Betty Rollin, mid-1980s (MCC-SL).

152 "The minute Gloria came on the scene": Author's interview with Muriel Fox, November 6, 1993. See also Cohen, *The Sisterhood*, p. 311.

152 "Ms. Steinem—sometimes known": Jan Hodenmedan, "Women's Lib Stars Make Up—Sort Of," *New York Post*, February 10, 1972.

152 "I wouldn't say that I started": Paul Wilkes, "Mother Superior to Women's Lib," *The New York Times Magazine*, November 29, 1970, p. 150.

154 "Gloria has all the irritating": "The New Woman," *Newsweek*, cover story, August 16, 1971.

154 "she developed extensive rescue": Heilbrun, *The Education of a Woman*, p. 30. See also Stern, *Gloria Steinem*, p. 28.

155 "I'll do this for two years": Heilbrun, ibid., p. 231. See also Stern, ibid., p. 290.

155 "Gloria had a mattress and box spring": Transcript of MC interview with Lillian Barnes Borton, mid-1980s (MCC-SL). For further discussion see Heilbrun and Stern.

155 "My ultimate protection was this": Steinem, *Outrageous Acts and Everyday Rebellions,* p. 135.

157 "the stereotype of the Eternal": *Newsweek* cover story, August 16, 1971.

157 *McCall's* named her its Woman of the Year: The issue (January 1972) went on sale just before Christmas 1971.

158 "the reluctant superstar": Marilyn Mercer, "Gloria: The Unhidden Persuader," ibid., p. 68.

158 "has never been a part of the organized": "Lib Rip-Off?" *The Washington Post,* February 9, 1972.

159 "the American media created": Germaine Greer, "Women's Glib," *Vanity Fair,* June 1988, p. 32.

159 "ongoing visibility and institutional": Stern, *Gloria Steinem,* p. 284.

160 "I'm still suspicious of the degree": Steinem, *Revolution from Within,* p. 241. See also ibid., p. 387, for discussion.

160 "I am the serious leader": Lyn Tornabene, "The Liberation of Betty Friedan," *McCall's,* May 1971, p. 84.

160 "He got it wrong because": Author interview with Sheila Tobias, October 26, 1994. See also Cohen, *The Sisterhood,* p. 321. Sheila is the author of *Overcoming Math Anxiety* (New York: Norton, 1978) and *Faces of Feminism* (Boulder, Col.: Westview Press, 1997). She was a co-organizer of the first women's studies program, at Cornell in 1968.

161 "I hate that slogan": BF, "To My Daughter," unpublished; written for *Cosmopolitan,* January 1978 (BFP-SL).

CHAPTER 16: *"A Fight for Love and Glory"*

162 "From now on our thrust": Mary Connelly and Anthony Mancini, "Women's Lib Shifts Aim to Congress," *New York Post,* August 27, 1970.

163 "I've helped and freed": Paul Wilkes, "Mother Superior to Women's Lib," *The New York Times Magazine,* November 29, 1970, p. 157.

164 "My election goes beyond": Quoted in Cohen, *The Sisterhood,* p. 314.

164 "Who is this bizarre figure": Quoted in Natalie Gittelson, "Which Ms. Has the Movement? Betty & Gloria & Shirley & Bella," *Harper's Bazaar,* July 1972, p. 80.

165 "From the beginning he did": Bella Abzug, "Martin, What Should I Do Now?" in Brill, ed., *A Rising Public Voice,* pp. 176–77.

165 The Big Four of the caucus: Also present were Jo Anne Gardner (Pittsburgh NOW), Jacqui Ceballos, Barbara Ireton (Washington, D.C., NOW), Brenda Feigen Fasteau (lawyer), Shana Alexander (then editor-in-chief of *McCall's* and one of BF's close friends), Flora Crater (ERA lobbyist), and Jennifer MacLeod (social scientist and first director of the Eagleton Center for the American Woman and Politics at Rutgers, set up to study the status of women in politics and government). Information based on Jennifer MacLeod's notes.

166 "Gloria had a mother-daughter": Quoted in Stern, *Gloria Steinem,* p. 241.

167 "It was a kind of a raucous": *The Hand That Rocks the Ballot Box,* television documentary written and produced by ABC News correspondent Marlene Sanders, which aired on July 26, 1972.

167 "Each of them thought": Cohen, *The Sisterhood,* p. 317. See also Heilbrun, *The Education of a Woman,* pp. 214–15.

167 "You know, it's nice to say": Abzug, *Bella!,* p. 164.

CHAPTER 17: *Political Initiation*

172 "The day before the Democratic": Ephron, "Miami," in *Crazy Salad,* p. 37. (Originally published as "Women," in *Esquire,* November 1972.)

173 "The McGovern...strategists": BF, "What Have Women Really Won?" *McCall's,* November 1972, p. 172.

173 " 'I'm so disgusted with Gloria' ": Ephron, *Crazy Salad,* p. 39.

174 "the mother of us all": Ibid., p. 37.

174 "Gloria's relentless prominence": Germaine Greer, "McGovern, the Big Tease," *Harper's,* October 1972, p. 62.

174 "play[ing] both ends": Ephron, *Crazy Salad,* p. 42.

176 "said sweetly, in effect": *ICML,* p. 225.

176 "Who's going to represent": Lynn Sherr, "Democratic Women," *Saturday Review,* August 5, 1972, p. 7.

177 "I am here now to raise": Sally Quinn, "Women and Politics," *The Washington Post,* August 25, 1972.

178 "The amount of sheer discussion": Ibid.

178 "How did we get the chutzpah": BF, "Up from the Kitchen Floor," *The New York Times Magazine,* March 4, 1973, p. 8.

178 "who sneered": *ICML,* pp. 225–26.

CHAPTER 18: *"Female Chauvinist Boors"*

180 "it has been our practice": Deirdre Carmody, "Feminists Scored by Betty Friedan," *The New York Times,* July 19, 1972.

181n "Most of you": Quoted in Stern, *Gloria Steinem,* p. 258.

181 "Once again Betty Friedan": Ibid.

181 "Having been falsely accused": Ibid.

182 "While prime movers": Lindsy Van Gelder, "Behind the Scenes at Houston: Four Days That Changed the World," *Ms.,* March 1977.

182 "Despite the many early": Steinem, *Outrageous Acts and Everyday Rebellions,* p. 5.

182 "All women have been": An earlier, more elaborate version of her thinking appeared in Barbara Gerkhe and Jeanne Cordova, eds., "Gloria Steinem: 'I'm Tired of Hearing Myself,' " *Lesbian Tide,* January 1974, p. 8.

183 "Betty called at the last": Gloria Steinem, unpublished notes given to author.

183 "Betty, Merry Christmas": All quotes in this paragraph are from ibid.

183 "My mother didn't go": Ibid.

183 Gloria "certainly became": *ICML*, p. xxiv. The Women's Forum was the brain-child of Elinor Guggenheimer, a former New York City consumer affairs director who was active in day care, and who wanted an organization of her peers. The membership fee was $100, an impossible amount for most women. Betty was one of the founders.

184 In her 1991 review: *Allure*, March 1991.

187 "Because I hate her guts": Sally Quinn, "New York Race: Down Mean Streets," *The Washington Post*, September 14, 1976.

187 "As one of my male political": *ICML*, p, 230.

CHAPTER 19: *Treading Water*

189 "I never told anyone": BF, "Up from the Kitchen Floor," *The New York Times Magazine*, March 4, 1973, p. 33.

189 "a solipsist," "a woman-hater"; "her deliberate misrepresentations"; "stunned and outraged"; "As for Mrs. Friedan's": All quotations are from Letters to the Editor, *The New York Times Magazine*, March 25, 1973.

189 Two years later: In the 1975 "Report to the President by the Commission on CIA Activities Within the U.S." (headed by Nelson Rockefeller), the women's liberation movement was listed as one of the targets of "Operation Chaos." The activities of COINTELPRO, the FBI's spy operation, were revealed in Senate testimony and published in 1976 in *Hearings before the Select Committee to Study Governmental Operations with Respect to Intelligence Activities*, vol. 6, November–December 1975, pp. 98–103, 360–66, 540–85.

190 Most of the interview: All quotes in this paragraph are from Myra McPherson, "The Former Mr. Betty Friedan Has Scars to Prove It," *The Washington Post*, February 7, 1971.

192 "I lived with her alone": Wanda Urbanska, "Following in Feminist Footsteps," *Philadelphia News*, October 20, 1981.

193 "intimated that Jonathan": transcript of Jacqueline Van Voris interview with BF, 1973 (CA-SC). Also in BFC-SL.

195 "The students thought": Judy Klemesrud, "Betty Friedan as College Professor: 'Intimidated by the Bright Yalies,'" *The New York Times*, November 11, 1974.

195 During these years: A partial list of Betty's conferences, lectures, etc., in the early 1970s: an in-service program on human sexuality for interns, medical students, nurses, and social workers at the Medical School of the State University of New York, Syracuse, 1968 and 1970; a week-long symposium, "Sex Roles and the Role of Sex," at the University of Hawaii, 1971; an in-service training program on sex discrimination for the American Chamber of Commerce Executives, 1972, and another for vocational and guidance counselors, supervisors, and training directors at the State of Washington School of Social Work in 1973. In 1972 she participated in the Webster College (Missouri) Religious Studies Program "Challenging the Institutions" (for Catholic priests and

nuns) and spoke at the Jewish Community Center in Tampa, Florida, and at Harvard University's Kennedy Institute of Political Science. She also did staff training in race and sex discrimination for the Philadelphia Department of Human Resources. In 1973 she began serving on the board of directors and the Education Committee of the NOW Legal Defense and Education Foundation (LDEF). She was a convenor of the first International Feminist Planning Conference, in Cambridge, Massachusetts, 1973. That same year, the North American Marketing Association invited her to a seminar with Marshall McLuhan for Canadian industrialists, economists, and market researchers on the future implications of the women's movement. She helped organize the First Women's Bank with Madeleine McWhinney, who had been a year ahead of her at Smith. She organized and convened an "Economic Think Tank for Women" in 1974. She developed training programs, conferences, and seminars for corporations, investment bankers, and universities on how to treat women like people and on the economic and personal implications of the sex role revolution. She lectured at the Aspen Broadcasters Conference and at the International Design Conference at Aspen in the summer of 1974. She lectured at Harvard Law School, Smith, Barnard, Mount Holyoke, Notre Dame, Georgetown, Duke, UCLA, Michigan, Chicago, Fordham, Indiana, Princeton, Ohio State, Southern Methodist, Columbia University Business School, the Smithsonian Institution, the University of California–Irvine, the Harvard School of Education, Emmanuel College, Yale Law School, Duquesne University, Mills College, the University of Chicago, Indiana University, Columbia University Law School, George Washington University, Fordham, the University of Virginia, the University of Florida, Vassar, the Woodrow Wilson School at Princeton, the University of Alabama, the University of South Dakota, Ohio State University, and the University of Nebraska. She lived a good part of her life on airplanes. Abroad, she spoke in Italy, Brazil, India, France, Colombia, Iran, the Netherlands, Austria, Spain, Israel, Finland, and Sweden. She attended the International Conference on Women Journalists in Jerusalem in June 1973. She also found time to testify before the House and Senate Committees on the ERA, and at New York State legislative hearings on sex discrimination in employment, education, credit, and public accommodations, as well as on reform of abortion and marriage and divorce laws.

196 "We must begin to give": BF opening statement at the Economic Think Tank, New York, 1974 (BFC-SL).

CHAPTER 20: Global Expansion

199 "Go home, Yankee lady!": *ICML*, p. 258. (Originally published *McCall's*, October 1971.)

200 "I would see the future": BF, unpublished writings on her trip to Israel (BFC-SL).

200 "I never knew the details": Arlynn Nellhaus to author, December 29, 1993. Letter is in author's possession.

200 "I remember how impressed I was": Ibid.

200 In October 1973: BF, "A Visit with Pope Paul," *McCall's*, February 1974, p. 72.

201 Beauvoir looked "prim": BF, "Introduction: a Dialogue with Simone de Beauvoir," *ICML*, p. 388. All other quotations in this paragraph are from BF article "A Dialogue with Simone de Beauvoir," *ICML*, pp. 396 and 398 (originally published in *Saturday Review*, August 1975).

203 "No one in the world": BF, "Coming Out of the Veil," *Ladies' Home Journal*, June 1975.

203 "I am taken aback": Ibid.

203 "there is that same sense": Ibid.

204 "I look at myself, draped": Ibid.

204 "When Betty Friedan arrived": Germaine Greer, "Women's Glib," *Vanity Fair*, June 1988, p. 37.

CHAPTER 21: *Mexico City Thriller*

206 "a ten-year association": Redstockings press release, May 9, 1975. (Copies of the release are available from Redstockings Women's Liberation Archives, P.O. Box 744, Stuyvesant Station, New York, N.Y. 10009-0744.)

207 "I was happy to find": "CIA Subsidized Festival Trips," *The New York Times*, February 21, 1967.

207*n* "She had not been hired": Stern, *Gloria Steinem*, p. 301.

208 "mental masturbation": Marilyn Goldstein, "Next Step Action," *Newsday*, May 20, 1972.

210 "I was very troubled": Mary Reinholz, "Was Gloria Steinem Allied with a CIA Front in the 60s?" New York *Daily News*, June 19, 1975.

210 "a James Bond novel": *ICML*, p. 440.

212 "Who would ransom me?": *ICML*, p. 458.

213 "The amazing thing": Helena Doukidou, taped recollections given to author, 1994.

CHAPTER 22: *It Changed My Life*

215 "The movement today": Mary Nichols, "Ms. Steinem, Are You Now, or Have You Ever...?" *New Dawn*, 1976.

217 "if the parties cannot": Letter of agreement between BF and Random House, September 5, 1974. *Friedan* v. *Random House*, New York State Supreme Court, 1978.

217 "It is disturbing that": Audrey Rowe Colom to Robert Bernstein, September 28, 1976 (BFC-SL).

218 "too marred by factual errors": Twenty-six NWPC members to Robert Bernstein, September 28, 1976 (BFC-SL).

218 "Betty Friedan: Don't Snicker" and "A Few Kind Words for Betty Friedan": newspaper clips, n.d.

218 "It has all the omissions": Jo Ann Levine, "From Betty Friedan: Predictions, Distortions, Truths," *The Christian Science Monitor*, August 3, 1976.

218 "Though Miss Friedan labors": Christopher Lehmann-Haupt, "It May Not Change Yours," *The New York Times*, August 3, 1976.

219 "filled with innuendoes": Stephanie Harrington, *The New York Times Book Review*, July 4, 1976.

219 "resigned from Organized Sisterhood": Shana Alexander, Letter to the Editor, *The New York Times Book Review*, August 15, 1976.

220 "vendetta" against Jim: Affidavit by BF, *Friedan* v. *Random House*, New York State Supreme Court, August 4, 1978, p. 18.

CHAPTER 23: Love Again

221 "It's not complete": Betty Liddick, "Betty Friedan's New Mystique: Middle-of-Road," *Los Angeles Times*, July 25, 1976.

223 "I've come out the other": BF, "Cooking with Betty Friedan...Yes, Betty Friedan," *The New York Times*, January 5, 1977.

225 "When it's really right": Transcript of MC interview with BF, mid-1980's (MCC-SL).

225 "or to be more accurate": BF, personal writings (BFC-SL).

CHAPTER 24: The Last Battle

228 "Is NOW on the Brink of Then?": Judith Coburn, *The Village Voice*, November 17, 1975.

229 "Please make sure": Diamond, *Behind the Times*, p. 179. Leslie Bennetts wrote the ERA series.

229 "I discovered that Betty wanted": Author interview with Gene Boyer, April 14, 1994. See also Gene Boyer oral history (T-COHP-SL).

230 "A thousand for Peoria": BF, "The E.R.A.—Does It Play in Peoria?" *The New York Times Magazine*, November 19, 1978, p. 13.

231 "his black-sheep sister": Ibid., p. 138.

231 "Life moves on": Enid Nemy, "Back Home to Peoria—and a Sequel to 'Feminine Mystique,'" *The New York Times*, May 21, 1976.

232 "I remember one of": Unidentified newspaper clip, March 16, 1981.

233 "an artificial happening": BF, "The Women at Houston, with Thanks to Phyllis Schlafly for Bringing Them All Together," *The New Republic*, December 10, 1977.

233 "She was ubiquitous": Sally Quinn, "The Pedestal Has Crashed," *The Washington Post*, November 23, 1977.

233 "I had made a resolution": Ibid.

234 "I am considered to be": BF, "The Women at Houston, with Thanks to Phyllis Schlafly for Bringing Them All Together," *The New Republic*, p. 19.

235 "I was moved": Alix Kates Shulman to BF, n.d. (BFC-SL).

235 "Gloria Steinem and others": BF, "The Women at Houston, with Thanks to Phyllis Schlafly for Bringing Them All Together," *The New Republic*, p. 16.

236 "The only possible way": Mansbridge, *Why We Lost the ERA*, p. 4.

236 "So diverse have the choices": BF, "Twenty Years After The Feminine Mystique," *The New York Times Magazine*, February 27, 1983.

CHAPTER 25: *Apostasy*

238 "I wrote with the feeling": Mary Walton, "Once More to the Ramparts," *Chicago Tribune Magazine*, October 25, 1981.

239 Betty was given the: BF, "Feminism's Next Step," *The New York Times Magazine*, July 5, 1981.

239 "has come to a dead end": The quotations in this paragraph appear, respectively, on pages 238, 238, 238, 28, and 297 of *SS*.

240 "Such slogans": Ibid., p. 209.

240 "I am not *for abortion*": Ibid., p. 107.

240 "Friedan criticizes the women's": Erica Jong, "A New Feminist Manifesto," *Saturday Review*, October 1981.

240 "In The Feminine Mystique": Mary Cantwell, "What Women Need Now: A New Alliance with Men," *Vogue*, November 1981.

240 "Betty Friedan's The Second Stage": Webster Schott, "Where Do We Go from Here?" *The Washington Post*, November 1, 1981.

241*n* "yanking out the stitches" and "her book is punctuated": Faludi, *Backlash*, pp. 319, 322, 323.

241 "Friedan blames": Angeline Goreau, "Second Thoughts on the Mystique of Feminism," *Newsday*, November 8, 1981.

241 "In fact, they": Ellen Willis, "Betty Friedan's No-Win Feminism," *The Village Voice Literary Supplement*, November 1981.

241 "Oddly, Miss Friedan": John Leonard, *The New York Times*, October 30, 1981.

242 "It was as if people": Maria Karagianis, "The Lioness of Feminism," *Boston Globe Magazine*, January 2, 1983.

242 "I don't think this book": Juana E. Duty, "Friedan: Reaching a Turning Point," *Los Angeles Times*, November 5, 1981.

CHAPTER 26: *Alarms and Excursions*

243 "When my friends threw": *FOA*, p. 13.

245 "I became increasingly": BF, "Twenty Years After," *FM*, 1983 edition, p. xxiv.

245 "One unfinished thing": Mary Walton, "Once More to the Ramparts," *Chicago Tribune Magazine*, October 25, 1981.

246 "some old left types": BF, "A Personal Journey to Nicaragua," unpublished ms. (BFC-SL).

247 "All through this day": BF, "Women in the Firing Line," *The New York Times Magazine,* October 28, 1984.

247 "dead end": BF, "How to Get the Women's Movement Moving Again," *The New York Times Magazine,* November 3, 1985.

248 "I announced to the rabbi": "Jewish Roots: An Interview with Betty Friedan," *Tikkun,* January–February, 1988.

248 "Every inch the high priestess": Sylvia Mehlman, "Woman As Jew: Jew As Woman," *Baltimore Jewish Times,* September 28, 1984.

249 "This is the way women": BF, unpublished ms. on Nairobi (BFC-SL).

250 "You are not a feminist": Mary Battiata, "Under the Tree with Betty," *The Washington Post,* July 13, 1985.

250 "A decade that began": Mary Battiata, "The Conference at Nairobi," *The Washington Post,* July 31, 1985.

252n "assumed an informal": Edwin McDowell, "Women at PEN Caucus Demand a Greater Role," *The New York Times,* January 17, 1986.

CHAPTER 27: *Sag Harbor*

257 "consider some disturbing": Announcement of the Sag Harbor Initiative (BFC-SL).

257 "It was a day for the haves": Carol Agus, "An Addendum to Radical Chic," Long Island *Newsday,* October [exact date unknown], 1987.

258 "people having to step over": *Dan's Papers,* "Countdown to the Sag Harbor Initiative, October 8, 9, 10, 1988," July 22, 1988.

258 "Its failure to attract": Joanne Furio, "Panels Assail Candidates for Silence on Key Issues," *Southampton Press,* October 20, 1988.

259 "great unconscious impetus": Transcript of MC interview with BF, mid-1980s (MCC-SL).

259 "God knows, I had been": *FOA,* p. 367ff.

CHAPTER 28: *California*

261 "Members of homosexual": "Rethinking Feminist Concerns: The Evolution of Feminist Thought," Madeleine R. Stoner, ed., with BF, *American Behaviorial Scientist,* August 1994, p. 1140.

263 As a finale: Ibid. The entire issue is devoted to the think tank.

264 "There was cold, soggy": Marian Burros, "Goal: Living to 150. But Is It Living?" *The New York Times,* July 20, 1994. The last quotation in this paragraph is from author interview with a guest, March 17, 1994.

268 "I hope that you will": Lloyd Grove, "The Senator's Spat with the Feminist," *The Washington Post,* October 16, 1991.

269 "I am going to get": From the complaint filed in U.S. District Court, Eastern District of New York. Also see Bryan Boyhan, "Suspect Arrested for Threatening Feminist Leaders," *The Sag Harbor Express,* January 26, 1995.

269 " 'a bit brusque' ": "FBI, Feminists On Hold," *The East Hampton Star,* May 18, 1995.

271 "I want as many people": Michele Kort, "The Unsinkable Betty Friedan," *Los Angeles Times Magazine,* October 10, 1993.

CHAPTER 29: *The Fountain of Age*

272 "The new studies of aging": *FM,* p. 380, n. 15.

273 "pass on some legacy": *FOA,* p. 612.

273 "With this well-researched": Doris Grumbach, "Onward and Upward," *The Boston Sunday Globe,* September 12, 1993.

274 "will liberate us from": Judy Mann, "Growing Old and Liking It," *The Washington Post,* September 15, 1993.

274 "The fragments of a powerful": Christopher Lehmann-Haupt, "Growing Old with a Can-Do Attitude," *The New York Times,* October 11, 1993.

274 "Betty Friedan's metaphorical": Mary-Lou Weisman, "Golden Daze," *The New Republic,* October 11, 1993.

274 "my friend Mike": *FOA,* p. 27.

275 "Writers are always": Joan Didion, *Slouching Toward Bethlehem* (New York: Delta, 1968), p. xiv.

276 "There seemed to be": *FOA,* p. 474.

277 "a living rebuttal": Joan Smith, "Cry Friedan," *Harper's & Queen,* November 1993.

279 "There came a time": *FOA,* p. 258.

CHAPTER 30: *The Lioness in Winter*

280 "Betty knows how to": Michele Kort, "The Unsinkable Betty Friedan," *Los Angeles Times Magazine,* October 10, 1993.

282 "I have a really good": BF speech at Low Library, Columbia University, October 3, 1996.

282 "If you think politics": *Firing Line,* "Resolved: The Women's Movement Has Been Disastrous," aired on public television in New York City on December 23, 1994.

283 "I was treated like a bomb": BF talk at the Foreign Correspondents Club of Japan, Tokyo; rebroadcast on C-Span, October 8, 1995.

283 "The Beijing police": Maureen Dowd, "Eustace Silly," *The New York Times,* September 3, 1995.

284 "She goes to U.N. meetings": Impromptu speech by Kate Millett at a dinner of the Veteran Feminists of America to honor Bella at the Seventh Regiment

Armory, New York City. December 2, 1994. The VFA was founded and is directed by Jacqui Ceballos. Tapes of the VFA dinners honoring second-wave feminists are in the possession of Jacqui Ceballos, 220 Doucet Road, #225-D, Lafayette, La. 70503.

285 "I feel a sense of failure": Marian Christy, "Betty Friedan Is Still Telling It Like It Is," *The Boston Globe,* January 14, 1990.

286 "To be able to feel": Ibid.

287 "It is a fact that": Message sent by BF to the Veteran Feminists of America dinner honoring Bella (cited above), December 2, 1994.

287 "But now, in my wise maturity": David Sheff, interview with BF, *Playboy,* September 1992.

288 All quotations from Betty's seventy-fifth birthday party, February 4, 1996, are from a transcript of the party, in author's possession.

Selected Bibliography

Abzug, Bella S. *Bella! Ms. Abzug Goes to Washington.* Mel Ziegler, ed. New York: Saturday Review Press, 1972.

Bair, Deirdre. *Simone de Beauvoir: A Biography.* New York: Touchstone, 1990.

Beauvoir, Simone de. *The Second Sex.* H. M. Parshley, trans. and ed. New York: Bantam, 1970.

Bird, Caroline, and the Members and Staff of the National Commission of the Observance of International Women's Year. *What Women Want: From the Official Report to the President, the Congress and the People of the United States.* New York: Simon & Schuster, 1979.

Brill, Alida, ed. *A Rising Public Voice: Women in Politics Worldwide.* New York: The Feminist Press at the City University of New York, 1995.

Brownmiller, Susan. *Against Our Will: Men, Women and Rape.* New York: Simon & Schuster, 1975.

Burnett, Patricia Hill. *True Colors: An Artist's Journey from Beauty Queen to Feminist.* Troy, Mich.: Momentum Books, 1995.

Carabillo, Toni, Judith Meuli, and June Bundy Csida. *Feminist Chronicles, 1953–1993.* Los Angeles: Women's Graphics, 1993.

Chase, Evelyn Hyman. *Feminist Convert: A Portrait of Mary Ellen Chase.* Santa Barbara, Calif.: John Daniel & Company, 1988.

City Directory. Peoria, Ill.: J. W. Frank & Sons, 1898–99.

Cohen, Marcia. *The Sisterhood: The True Story of the Women Who Changed the World.* New York: Simon & Schuster, 1988.

Davis, Flora. *Moving the Mountain: The Women's Movement in America Since 1960.* New York: Touchstone, 1991.

Diamond, Edwin. *Behind the Times: Inside the New New York Times.* Chicago: University of Chicago Press, 1995.

Echols, Alice. *Daring to Be Bad: Radical Feminism in America 1967–1975.* Minneapolis: University of Minnesota Press, 1989.

Eisler, Benita. *Private Lives: Men and Women of the Fifties.* New York: Franklin Watts, 1986.

Ephron, Nora. *Crazy Salad.* New York: Bantam, 1976.

Eustis, Helen. *The Horizontal Man.* New York: Penguin, 1982.

Faludi, Susan. *Backlash: The Undeclared War Against American Women.* New York: Crown, 1991.

Figes, Eva. *Patriarchal Attitudes.* New York: Fawcett World Library, 1971.

Firestone, Shulamith. *The Dialectic of Sex: The Case for Feminist Revolution.* New York: Bantam Books, 1970.

Friedan, Betty. *Beyond Gender: The New Politics of Work and Family.* Washington, DC: The Woodrow Wilson Center Press, 1997.

———. *The Feminine Mystique.* New York: Dell, 1970; Laurel, 1984.

———. *The Fountain of Age.* New York: Simon & Schuster, 1993.

———. *It Changed My Life.* New York: Laurel, 1991.

———. *The Second Stage.* New York: Summit Books, 1981.

Gitlin, Todd. *The Sixties: Years of Hope, Days of Rage.* New York: Bantam Books, 1993.

Gornick, Vivian, and Barbara K. Moran, eds. *Woman in Sexist Society: Studies in Power and Powerlessness.* New York: Signet, 1972.

Greenberg, Joanne (originally published as Hannah Green). *I Never Promised You a Rose Garden.* New York: Holt, Rinehart & Winston, 1964.

Greer, Germaine. *The Female Eunuch.* New York: McGraw-Hill, 1971.

Heilbrun, Carolyn G. *The Education of a Woman: The Life of Gloria Steinem.* New York: Dial Press, 1995.

———. *Writing a Woman's Life.* New York: Ballantine Books, 1989.

Herschberger, Ruth. *Adam's Rib.* New York: Har/Row Books, 1970.

Hole, Judith, and Ellen Levine. *Rebirth of Feminism.* New York: Quadrangle Books, 1971.

Horowitz, Daniel, "Rethinking Betty Friedan and *The Feminine Mystique:* Labor Union Radicalism and Feminism in Cold War America." *American Quarterly,* vol. 48, no. 1, March 1996.

Kelber, Mim, and Caroline Bird. *The Spirit of Houston: An Official Report to the President, the Congress and the People of the United States.* Washington, D.C.: 1978.

Kennedy, Flo. *Color Me Flo: My Hard Life and Good Times.* Englewood Cliffs, N.J.: Prentice-Hall, 1976.

Krich, A. M. *Sweethearts.* New York: Crown, 1983.

Lader, Lawrence. *Abortion II: Making the Revolution.* Boston: Beacon Press, 1973.

Leshnick's City Directory, vols. 34–43. Peoria, Ill.: Leshnick Directory Co., 1916–25.

Mansbridge, Jane J. *Why We Lost the ERA.* Chicago: University of Chicago Press, 1986.

McKeever, Susan, ed. *Fifty Years of Discovery 1942–1992: The Adventures of the Smith College Class of 1942.* New York: Privately printed, 1992.

Mead, Margaret, ed. *American Women: The Report of the President's Commission on the Status of Women and Other Publications of the Commission.* New York: Charles Scribner's Sons, 1965.

Miller, Alice. *The Drama of the Gifted Child: The Search for the True Self.* New York: Basic Books, 1994.

Millett, Kate. *Flying.* New York: Alfred A. Knopf, 1974.

——. *Sexual Politics.* New York: Doubleday, 1970.

Mills, Kay. *This Little Light of Mine: The Life of Fannie Lou Hamer.* New York: Dutton, 1993.

Morgan, Robin, ed. *Sisterhood Is Powerful: An Anthology of Writings from the Women's Liberation Movement.* New York: Vintage Books, 1970.

Nathanson, Bernard N., M.D., with Richard Ostling. *Aborting America.* New York: Doubleday, 1979.

O'Neill, William L. *Feminism in America: A History.* New Brunswick, N.J.: Transaction Publishers, 1994.

Peoria City and County, Illinois: A Record of Settlement, Organization, Progress and Achievement, vol. II. Chicago: S. J. Clarke Publishing Co., 1912.

Pogrebin, Letty Cottin. *Deborah, Golda, and Me.* New York: Crown, 1991.

Redstockings. *Feminist Revolution: An Abridged Edition with Additional Writings.* Kathie Sarachild, ed. New York: Random House, 1978.

Schickel, Richard. *Intimate Strangers: The Culture of Celebrity.* Garden City, New York: Doubleday, 1985.

Spectorsky, A. C. *The Exurbanites.* Philadelphia and New York: J. B. Lippincott, 1955.

Steinem, Gloria. *Outrageous Acts and Everyday Rebellions.* New York: New American Library, 1984.

————. *Revolution from Within: A Book of Self-Esteem.* New York: Little, Brown, 1992.

Stern, Sydney Ladensohn. *Gloria Steinem: Her Passions, Politics, and Mystique.* New York: Birch Lane Press, 1997.

Stoner, Madeleine R., ed., with Betty Friedan. "Rethinking Feminist Concerns: The Evolution of Feminist Thought." *American Behavioral Scientist,* vol. 37, no. 8 (August 1994).

Thom, Mary. *Inside* Ms.: *25 Years of the Magazine and the Feminist Movement.* New York: Henry Holt, 1997.

Tolchin, Martin and Susan. *Clout* (New York: Coward McCann & Geoghegan), 1973.

White, Theodore H. *The Making of the President 1972.* New York: Bantam Books, 1973.

Index

About the Author

JUDITH HENNESSEE is a freelance journalist who writes mostly about women and media. She has written for *The New York Times Book Review, Travel, Arts and Leisure, Ms., Esquire, Mademoiselle, Connoisseur, Vanity Fair, Town and Country, Avenue, Savvy, and Mirabella,* among others. She was a contributing editor to *[MORE]: The Journalism Review* and media columnist for *Manhattan,inc.,* and won the 1986 Front Page Award for her columns. With Dr. Michael Baden, she was co-author of *Unnatural Death,* published by Random House in 1989. She lives in New York City.

About the Type

The text of this book was set in Janson, a misnamed typeface designed in about 1690 by Nicholas Kis, a Hungarian in Amsterdam. In 1919 the matrices became the property of the Stempel Foundry in Frankfurt. It is an old-style book face of excellent clarity and sharpness. Janson serifs are concave and splayed; the contrast between thick and thin strokes is marked.